The Family Interpreted

THE FAMILY INTERPRETED

Feminist Theory in Clinical Practice

Deborah Anna Luepnitz

Basic Books, Inc., Publishers   *New York*

Library of Congress Cataloging-in-Publication Data

Luepnitz, Deborah Anna.
  The family interpreted.

  Bibliography: p. 317.
  Includes index.
  1. Family psychotherapy.   2. Women—Psychology.
3. Feminism.   I. Title.   II. Title: Feminist theory
in clinical practice.   [DNLM: 1. Family Therapy.
2. Women—psychology.   3. Women's Rights.
WM 430.5.F2 L948f]
RC488.5.L82   1988   616.89'156   88–47761
ISBN   0–465–02350–9

For my grandmothers,

Angeline Del Quadri Vicarel

and

Mary Spitler Luepnitz

[The mother] who is unsatisfied by her husband is over-tender and over-anxious in regard to the child, to whom she transfers her need for love, thus awakening in it sexual precocity. The bad relations between the parents then stimulate the emotional life of the child, and cause it to experience intensities of love, hate and jealousy while still in its infancy. . . . The conflict at this age contains all the elements needed to cause lifelong neurosis.

—SIGMUND FREUD
" 'Civilized' Sexual Morality and
Modern Nervous Illness," 1908

To be a good mother, a woman must have sense, and that independence of mind which few women possess who are taught to depend entirely on their husbands. Meek wives are, in general, foolish mothers; wanting their children to love them best and take their part, in secret against the father, who is held up as a scarecrow.

—MARY WOLLSTONECRAFT
A Vindication of the Rights of Woman, 1792

CONTENTS

PART IV

Care and Interpretation: Toward a Feminist Practice of Psychotherapy with Families

ACKNOWLEDGMENTS

IT MAY BE the dream of every writer to work uninterrupted by the demands of a regular job. I was on leave from the Philadelphia Child Guidance Clinic while writing this book, and was therefore able to give it three years of unborrowed time. For allowing me this leave of absence, I thank the clinic's directors, Alberto Serrano and Dennis Piermattei. During those years, I continued to see patients in the clinic's group private practice, and I thank Barbara Edelman and Thera Spiegel for their administrative help.

I am indebted to many people at the PCGC for teaching me both the letter and the spirit of psychotherapy—especially my supervisors, Ann Itzkowitz and John Sargent. I also thank Connell O'Brien and Michael Silver, the directors of the inpatient service, and their extraordinary staff, including: John C. Bracy, Jr., Glenda Bailey, Calvin Gamble, Madlynn Haber, Brenda Pemberton, Myra Bell Bacchus, Sue Oehlberg, and Mary Haake. I am grateful to Rita Griffin, the PCGC receptionist, for taking good care of my patients and me for eight years. David Seaver encouraged me in the early stages of this book, and he taught me something about the costs of living faithful to one's convictions. His death in 1985 was a terrible grief to us, but it doubled my resolve to write a worthy book.

This work draws on several literatures, only some of which I knew well at the outset. Since I do not have formal training as a historian, I relied on outside readers, and particularly on Ruth Schwartz Cowan for her readings of my historical chapter. I benefited greatly from her comments, but the responsibility for the claims made in that chapter (and in the other chapters) rests solely with me. I thank classicist Joel Itzkowitz for helping me translate a passage about the Roman family by Valerius Maximus into English.

I am grateful to John Hartke, and to my classmates at the Philadelphia School for Psychoanalysis for our discussions about Freud and also for their moral support.

A number of therapists and scholars read some or all of the manuscript in preparation, and I thank especially: Deborah Lamb, Scott Budge, Edwin

Harari, Anthony Rostain, Virginia Goldner, Harriet Goldhor Lerner, Michele Bograd, Jay Lappin, Marianne Walters, Betty Carter, Olga Silverstein, Peggy Papp, Grace Strauss, Jorge Rogachevsky, Ginny Christensen, Joan Zilbach, and Rich Simon.

Special thanks go to Joyce Burland for sharing with me her incorrigible genius, and to Teresa Bernardez for her intellectual guidance and for the inspiration of a life brilliantly lived.

Phyllis Chesler helped me, as always, with feminist counsel, and also by her example of tireless political engagement.

I thank Joan Shapiro and my fellow members of the Penn Mid-Atlantic Seminar for the Study of Women in Society for their comments on a draft of chapter 15.

Carol Gilligan generously read five chapters of the manuscript and invited me to present my ideas to her seminar at Harvard.

I thank David Anderson, who believed in the possibility of this project before I did. He is a man of daunting generosity, whose influence on this work is considerable.

I am grateful to Jo Ann Miller, my editor at Basic Books, for applying her redoubtable understanding of psychotherapy and social theory to my work. I thank her for her kindness, for her adroit criticism, and also for respecting my need to do things my own way.

It is a pleasure to thank one of the field's most gifted therapists, Molly Layton, who has had a major influence on the way I think and practice. I am very fortunate that she agreed to read every word of this book and to fight with me and protect me to the end.

I also thank Sherri Grasmuck, who is just the everyday political sociologist, polyglot, mother, author, organizer, saloniste, and expert on "L.A. Law." Her sisterhood has brought me the deepest pleasure.

My family has been supportive to me. I am lucky to have two feminist parents and also a wonderful extended family. I thank my favorite aunt, Mary Orosz, for praying to St. Joseph the Worker for me, and for mailing me fruit from her garden in Cleveland.

My gratitude to my patients, present and past, is leagues deep, and necessarily the hardest to express. I hope that all will find themselves in these pages, and understand how much they have given me.

Thanks, finally, to Judy Wicks and my colleagues at the White Dog Café, for years of good music and good spirits.

PART I

1

Re-membering the Family

VIRGINIA WOOLF once wrote that when a subject is highly controversial—"and any question about sex is that—one cannot hope to tell the truth. One can only show how one came to hold whatever opinion one does hold" (1929, p. 4).

This is a book about psychotherapy with families. The opinion I advance is one held by a growing minority of family therapists: that family therapy as currently conceptualized and practiced is in need of transformation, and that an alliance with feminism could help it immensely.

Challenges to family therapy's theoretical adequacy and political sensibility are not new. Scholars outside the field have depicted family therapy's theory as "revisionist sociology" (Poster 1978) and as "conformist and confused" (Kovel 1976). Other outsiders have accused family therapists of "meddling in peoples' lives" (Szasz 1984) and even of attempting to "restore male dominance" (Herman 1981). What is relatively new, however, is that even respected voices *within* the field have begun to criticize it in some of the same terms: for ignoring ideology (Walters 1985), for failing to consider the social and political context in which families live (Hare-Mustin 1978), and, more generally, for avoiding the problems of extrafamilial systems (Minuchin 1984).

Some critics have recommended a joining together of family therapy and feminism (Hare-Mustin 1978, Walters 1985, Layton 1984, Goldner, 1985), although the type of feminism and the nature of the proposed joining have still to be defined.

The metaphor commonly used in such intellectual syntheses is that of a wedding of two systems of ideas. Nuptials have been announced between feminism and psychoanalysis, psychoanalysis and Marxism, and Marxism and feminism over the past ten years.

I will not propose a marriage between feminist theory and family therapy, however, and not merely because contemporary marriages are often short-lived. Rather, the putative spouses are, to use the jargon of popular sociology, at different "life stages." Feminist theory and practice and family therapy theory and practice were born of different traditions in different historical moments, and have developed according to those differences. Modern feminism, born of Enlightenment ideals of democracy and energized by American Reconstructionist passion, has existed in the United States since the 1850s. Family therapy, in contrast, is only about thirty years old, the brainchild of postwar interpersonal psychiatry and American Pragmatism.

Feminists have simply had an extra century to observe, critique, and propose reform in families. This is not to imply that family therapy has nothing to teach feminists. Feminist therapists, for example, have not developed a unique body of skills for working with families or couples, and they have much to gain from studying family therapy's technical achievements.

Feminist theory can offer family therapy two things. The first is simply a way of formulating a theoretical category of gender. As Virginia Goldner (1985) has pointed out, every theory of the family has employed a means of conceptualizing both generational and gender differences, while family therapy has "hobbled along" on the generational leg alone, making no mention of "male" and "female." Feminist theory of the 1970s, and in particular the work of Nancy Chodorow (1978), can lend family therapists a coherent theory of how gender is constructed within families.

Second, and more broadly, what feminism can offer family therapy is the means of developing a critical and historical knowledge of its subject. Feminist theory can help answer or at least cogently pose questions such as, Why does the family take the form it does at the present time? and, Could families be differently constituted? (cf. James and McIntyre 1983). The conceptualization of these issues could help family therapy rebuild its foundation—to locate itself not in the shifting sands of technique but more stably in an actual theory of the family in society. In part III the discussion will focus on the reasons why cybernetics and general systems theory—the current foundations of family therapy—have made it difficult to address these issues.

4

On Coming to Hold Feminist Opinions

Before joining the field of family therapy, I was a feminist therapist, active in many aspects of the women's movement. Progressive social theory of that time (the 1970s) identified the family as the place where society's mandate about the definition and valuation of the sexes is transmitted most intimately and formatively. The most compelling theoretical works on this subject came from several writers who shared as a starting point the recognition that it is women and not men who take primary responsibility for raising children (Dinnerstein 1976, Rich 1976, Chodorow 1978). Dorothy Dinnerstein, in her intellectually sumptuous *The Mermaid and the Minotaur,* observed that because every human being is first tended by a woman (either the mother or mother substitute), it is woman who is "every infant's first love, first witness and first boss." When infants begin their relationship with mother, they are not even aware that she has an existence separate from their own. Dinnerstein suggests that for this reason, we proceed through life viewing mothers more as objects than as subjects with needs of their own. In that earliest relationship we are completely helpless, completely dependent on this all-powerful woman. It is mother whom we associate with the gratification of our earliest needs and with rage at being ungratified. Our awe of and gratitude for being nurtured, our fear of being abandoned, our pain at having to live in a mortal body—all of these "massive orienting passions" are directed at the female and not the male of the species.

By the time we form a relationship with father, we are much more developed creatures. Our autonomy is more firmly established through increased muscular control, locomotion, and verbal skill. We grow up having very powerful feelings about father as well, of course, but it is never as difficult to separate our identity from his. Our being was never so fused/confused with his.

The projection of infantile feelings onto women goes a long way toward explaining the transcultural phenomenon of *misogyny,* which takes many forms, including contempt for and idealization of the female. It is important to emphasize that both women and men share in this powerful ambivalence toward women. Far from being a "male conspiracy," then, the devaluation of women is actually "woven into the pattern of complementarity between male and female personality that emerges from female-dominated childhood" (Dinnerstein 1976, p. 210).

What is elegant about Dinnerstein's analysis is that it shows misogyny to be the prototype of other forms of social hatred, such as racism. Just as culture defines the male as standard and the female as "other," racism constitutes one racial group as standard and confers the status of "otherness" on those outside it. In fact, the other, the substandard race, is often considered to have "feminine" attributes; blacks are considered by white racists to be more emotional, more sensuous, less intelligent, and more childlike than whites.

Misogyny extends as well to our ambivalence toward "mother earth," which we tend to identify with our image of the earth mother, a bottomless source of riches to be mined and reaped to which you never have to give back. Dinnerstein stakes the claim that the most profound change in human culture would come with the ending of women's exclusive responsibility for child care. She argues that although other types of economic and legal changes are necessary to help women, they will not affect our deepest experience of self and other until men too become the objects of infants' early projections, until women *and* men learn "stably to share the credit and stably to share the blame for spawning mortal flesh" (p. 155).

Understanding the conclusion implied by Dinnerstein and other feminists—that the family is a most important site for social transformation—made me want to know everything about the family: its history and sociology, its cultural and ethnic varieties, its relationship to the state, and its depiction in art. My involvement with family therapy began as an interest in knowing the family in yet another way—by studying at closest range its emotional and political anatomy.

When I began an internship at a family therapy training center, I was surprised not to find the same level of discourse about the family that I had known in feminist circles. There was great clinical mastery to be observed and genuine excitement about creating change, but the subjects of change were "dyads" and "subsystems," not mothers and fathers. Families were discussed in terms of organization and hierarchy, not in terms of intimacy and what feminist therapist Molly Layton has called "the politics of attachment."

At the theoretical level, what was missing is what might be called the "metaclinical" or "metafamilial" issues, those questioning our basic assumptions about what a family is and what it might mean to change it. This lack seemed especially incongruous since systems theorist Gregory Bateson, so venerated throughout the field, had repeatedly encouraged professionals to "examine our presuppositions."

I decided to write this book in order to encourage the inclusion of "metafamilial" issues into family therapy's discourse. Certainly I am not the first to encourage this inclusion. In 1980 the Women's Project in Family Therapy was formed by four of the field's outstanding practitioners: Marianne Walters, Betty Carter, Olga Silverstein, and Peggy Papp. These women have sensitized thousands of family therapists to issues of gender and power through their seminars and presentations in the United States and abroad. Their book is in progress as of this writing.

In addition, since I started research for this book three years ago, a small avalanche of articles on gender has jolted the field, and I shall refer to many of those articles in the course of this text. (Cf. Avis 1985, Bograd 1984, Caust et al. 1981, Brickman 1984, Goldner 1985, Layton 1985, Lerner 1988, MacKinnon and Miller 1987, Weiner and Boss 1985, Wheeler et al. 1985, Lamb 1988, Ault-Riché 1986, Taggart 1985, Bernal and Ysern 1986, and Caplan and Hall-McCorquodale 1985.) Few of these authors, however, share my interest in connecting family therapy with feminist *psychoanalytic* theories. My reasons for insisting on this integration will be introduced later in this chapter and elaborated in chapter 12.

Family therapy's strength has, until this time, been argued and defended on the basis of the pragmatic criterion, Does this method work? and thus traditional family therapists tend to ask feminist therapists how they "do it" differently or better. Clinical results are essential, but the pressure to produce "new moves" that can be demonstrated in workshops and displayed on videotapes carries with it the danger that feminist therapists, too, will be tempted away from developing a viable theory of the family. In this discussion, the cart will not precede the horse: questions of theory, language, and in particular *history* will be granted first place. The case examples offered in the final chapters do not represent a fully formed alternative to mainstream practice. My practice, like that of all feminists in our field, is inchoate: I assume that a feminist family therapy is at least a decade away.

The Importance of History

The emphasis on history in this book will seem inscrutable to some readers. Many family therapists believe that even the history of individual families is irrelevant (a belief I hope to challenge), and therefore the problems of medieval families may appear arcane indeed. Some defense of this reading of the past is perhaps in order.

The first reason for taking history into account has to do with the consequences of not doing so. It has been said that ours is an age of "social amnesia" (Jacoby 1975)—an age in which anxiety about the future leads to a preoccupation with the present, with what is contemporary, novel, youthful. The presumption that what has come before us is necessarily inferior to what we have now has deprived us of the opportunity to ask history who we are.

Women and minorities in the past two decades have endeavored to awaken contemporary consciousness from its collective slumbers. The study of history has been precious to these groups because it is a means of liberating personal identity from the confines of the conventional. For example, although Western culture had maintained for centuries that women are by nature emotional, passive, and irrational, history showed that women had been scientists and revolutionaries, and had run businesses and farms during many of the world's wars. The mass media told us that feminist defiance was brand-new, but women discovered feminist demonstrations led by working women in seventeenth-century England and in eighteenth-century France. (See chapter 10.) The excavation of this treasure, the past, was a source of exhilaration to women. It generated love for our cultural foremothers and deep bonds among us as their daughters. The erasure of women's lives from history became something to monitor closely—and to transform.

Beyond the pleasure of finding roots, the study of history, as these examples show, cannot help but challenge the sovereignty of "common sense," which often leads us to believe that what we have is what we must have. History often exposes common sense to be simply a way of justifying the status quo, or at least of blocking further inquiry.

"Common sense" assumptions about the contemporary family *per se* are a part of everyday life and easily find their way into the discourse of family therapy. We hear and sometimes use the phrase "the new working mother" to describe women who both raise children and hold paying jobs. We also hear and sometimes talk about the novelty of day care, contrasting it with the "age-old" practice of rearing children within the family unit. We lament that although women with careers are performing well in jobs once held only by men, these women are suffering more strokes and heart disease as a result.

Each of these assumptions is incorrect. First, with few exceptions, women have always done work in addition to child care—planting, weaving, as well as working in mills and factories (French 1985). Second, substitute child care has been the norm in every social class for the past twenty centuries; it is the exclusive mother-child bond which is the anomaly (Badinter 1980, Fraser 1984). That is to say, although women and not men have always performed child care, they have usually had some form of help or substitute care from other women (see chapter 10). As for health, women are not suffering more heart attacks and strokes as a result of their increased participation in the work force. On the contrary, women's health has in most ways actually improved relative to men's during the past two decades (Ehrenreich 1983).

I discovered many unexamined assumptions in the process of analyzing the sexual politics of the schools of mainstream family therapy. They result in mistakes ranging from subtle to seismic, a state of affairs that does not help our reputation in the intellectual community. (See chapters 2–9.) Family therapists are interested in change. To change something responsibly, one must know it in context. Because *time* is for human beings the hypostatic context, it is essential to know our subject, the human family, historically.

The Normal Family

If there is anything that history can teach family therapists, it is that the "normal family" has not been a social formation equally protective to all its members. Historian Carl Degler focused his celebrated work about the American family on this very fact, titling his book *At Odds: A History of Women and the Family in America from the Revolution to the Present.* Degler's book researches the many ways in which women's physical health, personal aspirations, and even their coveted moment of privacy have been forfeited for husband and children, in the colonies, on the Iowa farm, in the Victorian parlor, and in the California suburb.

Degler, of course, was not the first to notice the "at odds" phenomenon. The suggestion that marriage as an institution serves the health and stability of men better than women was made in the 1890s by Emil Durkheim, who observed that marriage had a salvaging effect on men. He computed a "coefficient of preservation"—the ratio of the suicide rate of the unmarried to the married—and found it to be higher for men than for women. In 1972 sociologist Jessie Bernard's eye-opening study, *The Future of Marriage,* confirmed and extended Durkheim's hypothesis. Looking at a host of variables, from rates of psychiatric admissions to self-reports of happiness, Bernard found that married men were better off than single men, but that single women were better off than married women. The most radical of her findings was that among married women, those who worked outside the home were healthier than housewives on eleven out of twelve categories of psychopathology, including migraine headaches, insomnia, and nervous breakdowns.

Since Bernard's work was published, scores of studies have examined the social and psychiatric liabilities of marriage for women and of the added risk to those not gainfully employed. The results of these studies have been remarkably univocal (cf. Tennant et al. 1982, Radloff 1980, Kaplan 1983). The findings of gainful employment as a hedge against depression for adults should come as no surprise. It is consistent with all of contemporary developmental theory to view work as the means through which the individual attains mastery, extends the boundaries of the self, and contacts the community. We lay claim to the world on the basis of our social and economic participation in it. It does not seem very startling that women who stay in the house and are financially dependent on their husbands are more likely to develop anxiety disorders, phobias, and depressions.

Nonetheless, these findings about women and marriage, which are practically cliché to feminists, have escaped notice by most family therapists. Citations of these studies rarely appear in the literature, and one finds instead the unargued assertion that the normal family (meaning the family without an identified patient) is benign—and moreover, in the words of Augustus Napier and Carl Whitaker, that "marriage is good for people."

One of the few groups of writers in the field to take on the normal family as a subject is the Timberlawn group, which published their findings in a book entitled *No Single Thread* (Lewis et al. 1976). Curiously, although the Timberlawn group found exactly what Bernard and others have found—that "normal" family life is *not* equally normal for all its members—they obscured this finding in their concluding statements, and their work has not informed therapists, as it might have, about women and the family being "at odds." The Timberlawn work is so often uncritically cited and taught by family therapists* that a detour to discuss this study is warranted here.

The purpose of the Timberlawn research was to define the characteristics of "dysfunctional," "adequate," and "optimal" families. A critique of their research design and methods would be relevant but is beyond our scope here. What is most significant for our purposes is that the authors found that women in the "adequate" (also called "normal") families were "over-

---

*The Timberlawn research is reported at great length in chapter 2 of Gurman and Kniskern's *Handbook of Family Therapy;* it is allotted an entire chapter in Walsh's *Normal Family Processes;* it was discussed uncritically at a major conference at the Philadelphia Child Guidance Clinic in 1983 on "The Healthy Family"; and it is on the syllabus of many introductory courses in family therapy.

10

whelmed with responsibility," "obese," "psychosomatically ill," and "sexually dissatisfied." The men in these same families, however, were "functioning well" and were not sexually dissatisfied. Thus, according to the authors, an adequate family consists of a husband and children who are functioning adequately and a wife who is not. Since the authors postulate (probably correctly) that most middle-class families in the United States fall into the "adequate" category, they were assuming that the majority of American mothers are overwhelmed, obese, psychosomatically ill, and so on. One would expect the authors to see in their data evidence of a grave social problem. They do not. In fact, their concluding statement reads: *"The family is alive and well"* (p. 220, italics theirs). It is simply impossible to reconcile this statement with the statement that most mothers are symptomatic. The subtextual message is patent: mothers are not really members of families.

Some might defend this research by claiming that the authors do mention that their "normal" families did not always insist on male leadership, nor push children toward fixed sex roles. There is no greater devaluation of female leadership, however, nor a more profound training in sex roles than in a family in which mother's needs are sacrificed for the good of the whole. The question of what one decides to term *adequate* or *functional* and what one decides is instead a serious social problem is a question of values or ideology. And indeed the most transformative insight that a feminist perspective can offer family therapists is the realization that ideas do not fall from the sky; they are artifacts constructed by people whose thinking is never ideologically impartial.* The point, thus, is never simply to amass or to categorize information, but to determine the identity of ideas, to ask the question, *Cui bono?*—Whose interests are served if we believe one thing or another about human behavior? To understand that common sense is always *somebody's* common sense is to come to grips with the fact that all questions are at one level political. The alternative, as one scholar has put it, is to proceed as though ideas could "duel gracefully among themselves, all unconscious of whose interests they serve" (Robinson 1978, p. 5).

We might ask, then, whose interests are served if one defines the normal family as the Timberlawn therapists did. It is difficult to ignore the overlap between their work and that of ultraconservatives who believe that women should (1) sacrifice their lives for husband and family, and (2) produce well-behaved and socially compliant children.†

---

*This is an idea that feminism shares with Critical Theory (of Marcuse and others), and it derives from Marx's notion of "ruling ideas."

†The Timberlawn group described the *healthiest* of their "optimal" families as compliant, deferential to authority, and contemptuous of people whom they considered to be "deviants" from their community norms (Lewis et al. 1976, p. 105).

Members of the religious Right in the United States, like family thera-pists, are interested in the welfare of families. Unlike family therapists, however, the Right has been powerful enough to introduce legislation into Congress such as the Family Protection Act of 1973, a bill that proposes to "strengthen the American family" by suspending the civil rights of homosexuals and by banning textbooks that portray the sexes behaving in "non-traditional" roles (cf. Pogrebin 1983). Not all family therapists hold beliefs as sexually conservative as these, but it is of some concern that the field has never made an effort to distinguish its aims from those of the Right, nor even properly criticized the ideology of *No Single Thread.*

A much better attempt at defining *family* comes from Letty Cottin Pogre-bin's insightful book *Family Politics* (1983). Pogrebin suggests that a family consists of "at least one child and one adult who live together, and who make emotional claims on each other." This is a good beginning because it includes not only two-parent families but also single-parent families. It covers both biological and adoptive parents, and homosexual as well as heterosexual adults. The definition does not assume that people's emo-tional needs are met in families, but it acknowledges these claims as being at the heart of modern families.

One could add to this bare-bones definition that the family "socializes" children, because families do indeed make children social. It is equally true, however, that families make children asocial and antisocial by requiring adaptation to a violent culture. What is important, finally, in our attempt to understand the family is that we avoid both the cynical belief that the family is a sinister agent that corrupts the individual—an idea associated with R. D. Laing and David Cooper (1970)—and the opposite position that the nuclear family is a human constant, or the happy ending of a long evolutionary journey—an idea that has perhaps underlain the practice of American family therapy.

Clinical Implications

The ahistorical approach to family therapy and the uncritical acceptance of sexist writing such as that of the Timberlawn group are not matters of ideology alone. Unexamined presuppositions lead to sexist therapy. Al-though, like most newcomers to the field of family therapy, I was at first dazzled by the clinical achievements of the master therapists, I became increasingly uneasy about what was happening in the therapy room.

First, it seemed that it was the mother in the family who, more often than not, was made to feel most responsible for the family's problems. Because mothers seem to be more psychologically resilient than fathers, or more likely to blame themselves, or more invested in the therapeutic process itself, mothers often took the weight of the "unbalancing," while fathers were more gently handled. I heard mothers being cajoled to "stay out," "back off," "clam up," and even "grow up," while fathers were congratulated for their "common sense."

Second, it appeared to me that single mothers were urged by therapists with maddening regularity to improve their appearance and start dating men. Embedded in this advice was undoubtedly the wholesome and non-sexist belief that mothers cannot live totally for their children and need to take care of themselves and pursue their own pleasures. However, many therapists seemed insensitive to the fact that mass culture had overpre-scribed these particular solutions to women, creating as side effects pangs of inadequacy for not being involved with men. Hearing the same message from the therapist that they had read in the fashion magazines ("Happi-ness is a heterosexual romance") did not help these women to deepen or prize their capacity to take care of themselves.

A third problem that struck me on entering the field was that therapists who felt comfortable challenging families in bold terms about many types of issues did not feel they could question the typical division of labor, by which females do all the housework. My colleagues argued with me that if families were happy with such arrangements, then it should be okay with the therapist, too. Therapists, they said, should not impose their "value judgments" on their patient families. It was never clear to me how a therapist knew that a family was happy with its division of labor if he or she had never asked about it, nor why housework sharing involved more "value judgment" than the "lose-weight-and-date-men" prescrip-tion.

It is important to state clearly from the outset that the solution to these problems is not to become sentimental about motherhood, as though women were above reproach and/or should never be therapeutically chal-lenged. Nor is the solution to turn every family session into a discussion of laundry, or to start blaming men instead of women for children's prob-lems. Feminist therapy, to paraphrase Lillian Robinson, cannot be "patriar-chal therapy in drag." The solution is to *problematize* the issues of mother blaming and father coddling—to put them on the table rather than condemn them to the dim corridors of common sense. If family therapy cannot be done well without devaluing women, we should know that. If it can, then we must ask why therapists choose to do otherwise.

Feminism Defined

There are many kinds of feminism. A non-exhaustive list would include liberal, Marxist, Zionist, Christian, radical, and lesbian separatist feminism. What unites them is the desire to reform the social order in ways that would permit the full economic, political, and social participation of women. Feminists believe that gender is socially constituted, not biologically given, and that transformation of those social definitions is possible. Most feminists believe that women and men suffer, although in different ways, from the set of social relationships known as *patriarchy* (defined in the next section). Feminism is not a gender. Not all women are feminists, and some men are. Feminists disagree about issues such as the origins of women's oppression and, of course, tactics of change.

A debate has been ongoing between Marxist feminists, who emphasize the importance of social class (e.g., Barrett 1980), and radical feminists, who believe that the most fundamental source of social tension is sex rather than class (Firestone 1970). The former argue that nonprivileged men as well as women are exploited by capitalist social and economic relations and that they, too, have been erased from history. The latter emphasize that within any given social class, the psychological differences between the sexes overshadow other factors; modern women and men of the industrialized West appear to be "intimate strangers" to each other (to use Lilian Rubin's phrase) almost regardless of class.

In order to emphasize gender issues in this book, I have probably given class issues short shrift; ideally, they should be given equal attention. In fact, what is most illuminating is the understanding of how class and material conditions (crudely speaking, the "outside world") affect psychological and unconscious structures (again crudely, the "inner world"). These issues will be pursued in the full-length cases in chapters 14 and 15.

A second debate internal to feminism, and one perhaps more familiar to family therapists, is that between *cultural-school* (also called relational-school) feminism and what I will call the *sex-role school*. To simplify tremendously, cultural-school feminists emphasize the differences between the sexes, and sex-role feminists emphasize the samenesses. The cultural school is represented by Gilligan (1982), Chodorow (1978), and Dinnerstein (1976), who have shown how historical, cultural, and familial structures affect not only what women and men do but also who we are. They believe that female and male are not simply "roles" that can be shrugged off, but instead that sex differences exist even at the level of unconscious structure. These theorists typically emphasize women's greater psychological tendency to *continuity* and men's greater tendency to *discontinuity* in relationships. These authors have made us reconsider the social contempt for connection, nurturance, dependency, and care—things that have been associated with women and women's work.

Feminists of the sex role school (e g , Bart 1983, Hare-Mustin 1978, Kerber 1986) tend to be very critical of the culturalists. They worry that cultural-school feminists will end up reinscribing the separate-spheres doctrine, according to which men belong to one world and women another (and always lesser) world. They insist that there is no such thing as "different but equal" when it comes to gender. If women become preoccupied with how wonderful it is, after all, to be caring and cooperative, they will never take their place in the public sphere, competing for office, demanding pay equity, becoming astronauts and triathletes. Sex-role feminists often argue the desirability of *androgyny*—an ideal human condition in which gender differences would be submerged in individual differences. They see the culturalists as romantic or even as fuel for the backlash. Culturalists see the sex-role school as valuable in propelling women into full social participation, but believe that their analysis is superficial, that it denies the complexities of the unconscious, that it cannot account for the recalcitrance of gender differences, and that it sometimes overvalues male social and sexual standards (Now girls, too, can grow up to be corporate yahoos?).

The intellectual tension between these two schools is extremely necessary to the growth of feminism. Since, in reality, women and men are alike in as many ways as we are different, most feminists find themselves taking positions based not so much on these labels but on the nature of the issue at hand. When it comes to deciding whether a woman should be permitted to run for president, the issue of nondiscrimination (i.e., the issue of sexual sameness) is obviously paramount. However, if one wants to understand the resistance to and sabotage of female authority, one needs to know how male and female unconscious structures are developmentally shaped (i.e., one needs to focus on sex differences).

Rachel Hare-Mustin (1987) has proposed a useful way of categorizing this set of problems. She refers to "alpha" and "beta" prejudice; the former involves overstating sexual differences, and the latter involves ignoring them. As family therapists, it is important to avoid the alpha error, which would lead one to value only the husband's career goals and ignore the wife's. Conversely, it is important to avoid the beta error, believing that divorce will result in the same economic or psychological problems for the sexes.

I have tended throughout my professional life slightly more toward radical than Marxist feminism, and more toward cultural than sex-role feminism. However, I will draw on all of these traditions throughout this work. (Cf. Thorne and Yalom's (1982) book on the family for a sampling of several types of feminist viewpoints. See also Burland 1986).

A Note on Patriarchy

The word *patriarchy* has been used several times here and requires explication. If it were not such an important word, one might prefer to leave it out, simply because it has been both misused and misunderstood. Mainstream family therapists recoil from it because they hear it less as a critical category and more as an angry epithet. (Some feminists indeed use it as such.) Moreover, a variety of theorists and therapists legitimately object to labeling the modern family *patriarchal* on the historical grounds that the modern family is very different from the father-ruled households of antiquity or of the American colonies. This argument emphasizes the fact that the modern father is notable mostly for his *absence* or exclusion from the family. And certainly it is true that after divorce (involving nearly half of all new marriages), almost 50 percent of fathers terminate contact with their children (Weitzman 1985). Moreover, in American black households, many children grow up with three generations of women but no adult male consistently present (Stack 1976). Furthermore, even in "intact" families, the father is often an outsider. The "peripheral father" is described in many family therapy texts: sometimes he is depicted as the family's "tired nightly visitor," stolid and admittedly marginal; other times he appears as the more voluble Archie Bunker type who, despite his attempts to dominate, can usually be outwitted.

Seriously at issue here is the fact that modern sons and daughters grow up to a great extent in their mothers' care, knowing their fathers sometimes not at all or only through mother. Girls, of course, can formulate their identity by transacting directly with their mothers—by imitating them, refusing to imitate them, and the like; while boys' socialization is necessarily more shadowy. Boys ultimately negotiate an identity based on being simply not-female, or "other than mother." This development, it has been argued, leads to contempt for the mother, and by extension, to all things associated with her. It also leaves fathers without the deeply humanizing experience of really knowing their children.

Modern culture is irrefutably father-absent, but to conclude on this basis that it is no longer patriarchal is premature. The family therapist's implicit motto—"More father and less mother!"—needs to be constrained by an acknowledgment of enduring forms of domination. In the first place, the two depictions of the peripheral father just described, although easily recognized, do not tell the whole story. Many fathers continue to wield tremendous authority in families. It is fathers and not mothers who commit the vast majority of parent-child incest as well as the majority of child murders and kidnappings (Herman 1981, Russell 1986, Chesler 1986). Fathers from ancient times until the early twentieth century have been granted custody of their children on the basis of "father right," and there is growing concern that unfit fathers are using the "new father" hype (in addition to their typically superior financial resources) to fight and win custody battles (Weitzman 1985, Chesler 1986).

Feminist Ann Ferguson has noted that although "father patriarchy" and "husband patriarchy" were characteristic of the first three centuries of American history, the twentieth century is just as surely characterized by what she calls "public patriarchy" (1983). While under earlier forms of patriarchy it was a male *person* who limited the woman's expenditures, freedom to work, and sexual activity, in the case of public patriarchy, it is the state, the welfare agency, and the media that control these things. Whereas husbands or fathers might once have forbidden a woman to terminate a pregnancy, it is the state that now limits access to abortion by abolishing medical coverage for it. The definition of good mothering and of femininity, once delivered by husbands and fathers, is now delivered through therapists and various channels of mass culture.

Public patriarchy is both an advance and a retreat for women, rich and poor, black and white. Since public authority is more diffuse than personal authority, it is easier to cheat on. Being more diffuse, however, it is often harder to identify and to fight. And, ultimately, the patriarchal state is more powerful than any single father. In ancient Rome, to choose the most extreme example, the paterfamilias decided at the time of birth whether his baby would live or die. In the current period, it is a technocracy administered by anonymous fathers that will decide whether an entire generation of children will grow to adulthood.

The conclusion I have drawn from these considerations is that *the modern family of the West is both patriarchal and father-absent.* This apparent contradiction is one that practitioners must face, and it will be a major motif in this book.

This returns us to the matter of what family therapy and feminism have to offer each other. Feminists, it would seem, have taken on the first problem: they have attacked patriarchal barriers through legal and political means. Family therapists have addressed, at least indirectly, the issue of father absence by inventing clinical operations to help bring fathers in. It will be the task of feminists who do psychotherapy with families* to address clinically both patriarchy and father absence.

Remembering the Mother: Steps Toward a Feminist Psychotherapy

There is a folk tale from eastern Europe that is emblematic for this discussion of the family. It is the story of a poor but brilliant craftsman named Manolus, who was elected by the king to build a cathedral. Manolus began his work, but whatever he built during the day fell down during the night. He sought the counsel of a sage who explained to him that he had been cursed and that there was only one way to lift the spell. He was to rise early on the following morning, to go and watch the women gathering at the well, and to kill the first woman who approached him. On the following morning, Manolus looked down at the well and trembled to see his own mother and sisters there, talking and laughing and drawing water with the others. The mother noticed her son and smiled. When Manolus anxiously signaled her to go back, she mistook his gesture for a beckoning and approached. Following the wise man's directive, he slowly led his mother into the foundations of the structure and asked her to stand against a wall, saying that he needed to build a door the size of a woman. Manolus then sealed her body into the foundation so efficiently that no one heard her cry. The curse was lifted, the cathedral stood, and the king boasted of the brilliance of his artisan.

This myth about the sacrifice of the mother for the benefit of culture

*I will use the term "feminist psychotherapy with families" as opposed to "feminist family therapy" in order both to signal a departure from family therapy as it has been practiced and to connote a new emphasis on family psychodynamics, as will be explained shortly.

raises allegorically many questions that will be posed theoretically and clinically here. How exactly do families reproduce the idea that mothers are for sacrificing? Are women complicit in burying their own needs? Just as important, why do the king and Manolus need their tall walls in the first place? Would anything be different if the men, too, could gather in community at the well?

In the following pages, I will summarize attempts by feminist historians, sociologists, and adherents of a branch of psychoanalysis known as object-relations theory to come to grips with these questions. The answers they provide can point us toward new clinical and theoretical objectives. It is important to keep in mind that forgetting the mother or sacrificing her subjectivity diminishes not only the person of the mother, but everyone "of woman born." As a number of contemporary theorists have shown, we human beings *are* our social contexts; we *are* our families. As infants we take in the love and recognition of adults like food. Borrowing some psychoanalytic terms, one might say that if the real mother is silenced or violated, so will the maternal introject, or the unconscious incorporation of the mother—for both male and female children—be silenced and violated. In one version of the Manolus myth, the mother's body is bricked up in a way that leaves her breasts exposed so that her young son can still be brought to nurse (Yourcenar 1985). What can we say about the mother-son relationship portrayed in this image? The boy is being nourished, but now only in a disembodied relationship with his mother. The violence done to *her* ruptures the bond that is so important to them *both.* The maternal introject for the son, a part of himself, is harmed by the harm done to the mother.

The Manolus myth suggests that denial of the mother iş a far-ranging psychological violence. It may, in fact, be *the single thread* (both manifested in the results of the Timberlawn research and then unconsciously denied in the title of their work) that runs through families now and historically. My point here is to emphasize that the hatred of women ultimately corrodes the relational capacities of people attached to women, that is, everyone. As long as human beings are forced to internalize one parent who is socially devalued, they will always devalue the part of the self associated with her. In different ways, women and men will continue to view their longings for nurturance and dependency as harmful, shameful, even monstrous. Hatred of women will always be self-hatred.

Undertaking the intellectual enterprise of remembering the history of motherhood and the family is a first step toward transforming the family (see chapter 10). It is from this base—a critical and historically adequate understanding of the family in society—that issues of clinical methodology must derive. I will try to show that remembering the family in history can inspire the art of "re-membering" families in feminist practice.

What feminist theory of the family can offer the practitioner is, in a word, *telos*, a sense of conscious purpose in our work. Thus the feminist therapist seeks to help the family solve its problems not merely in any way, but in a way that will leave the family less patriarchal and less father-absent. This proposal immediately evokes in some readers denunciation of feminist "indoctrination" and "brainwashing." Indoctrination is, of course, what feminists believe traditional therapists do. Legitimately, however, the question arises, What if the family *likes* to be patriarchal and father-absent? What then?

It is true that all therapy is at one level political, but a psychotherapy hour is a psychotherapy hour: it is not to be confused with a women's studies class. The purpose of therapy is not to lecture about gender, much less to begin some kind of feminist "policing of families." What feminist therapy does is to provide people with more complex choices about how to live as women and men—choices that mainstream therapies do not provide and often even discourage.

The difference between formal political and formal clinical discourse can trouble the novice feminist therapist. The young therapist says: "I understand something about how gender operates in families, and even in the family sitting in front of me. But when I find the courage to explain something like, 'Women in this family don't get heard—just like in the wider culture,' I feel like a clod, and the family, if they like me, politely pretends that it didn't happen."

Interventions that are lobbed like hand grenades will do what hand grenades do—either fizzle or explode. It is true that every problem in every family is gender-related (since people are gendered), but not every problem can be solved by a teach-in. Feminism, in any case, is not a set of techniques or countertechniques; it is a body of theory. The value of any theory to us as practitioners is nil until the theory turns into who we are—into phrase and glance and gesture—until our intellectual powers and our humor settle into it. One cannot, for example, decide to "show respect" to a mother as a clinical intervention. One either respects her, or one does not. Feminism must be to therapists a *sensibility*, or it is nothing useful at all.

The phrase "policing of families" comes from French sociologist Jacques Donzelot (1979), who sees all types of professional intervention as part of a historical trend toward "government through the family." Donzelot emphasizes the state's interest in maintaining strong families, since people without ties to others are harder to regulate. Historian Christopher Lasch (1977), an admirer of Donzelot, is known for his remonstrations against the "rise of experts" and he generally argues that the family should be left alone by therapists and educators. Theorists who agree with Donzelot and Lasch would reject as romantic or wrongheaded the psychotherapy I am proposing here. Questions about what it means for a professional class to make claims on the private lives of citizens—and indeed about whether it is possible for one human being to change another—are not trivial, but I will set them aside in this work, taking as axiomatic the viability and value not only of psychotherapy but also of a certain amount of social regulation of families. See Joffe (1985, 1986) for a feminist critique of the anti-interventionist argument.

In Search of a Method: The Reclaiming of Psychoanalytic Thought

Feminist theory provides *telos,* which is fundamental to psychotherapy, but it is not in itself therapy. Feminist therapy must rest on a developmental psychology and on a clinical language and method, which introduces yet another controversy parlayed among feminists within family therapy. Some feminists argue that a clinical method is exactly as good as the practitioner using it—that is, any therapeutic method under the sun can be adapted to a feminist sensibility. I disagree with this extreme pluralism. Unless one can argue the logical possibility of feminist lobotomies or feminist shock treatments, it is clear that the full range of treatments used by therapists cannot be reconciled to feminism. One is then led to ask whether, even among the more familiar therapies such as structural, strategic, intergenerational, and ordeal therapies, some might not be more compatible with feminism than others.

In my view, the more a method resembles behaviorism, i.e., a method in which therapists talk more about treating symptoms than about treating whole persons, the less plausible is a feminist revision of it. By *whole person* I simply mean the patient as a person embodied with both capacities and incapacities, living within the idioms of gender, culture, race, and class, enhanced and inhibited by unconscious process, making choices in historical time—as she or he relates to the whole person of the therapist.*

A method of therapy that does not consult to the whole person, but only to the symptom, that takes no account of affect, or that trivializes the therapeutic relationship, makes only a faint claim to the label "humanist," let alone feminist. Behavior therapists do not count reflection or insight as curative factors in their treatment. It is sufficient to them that the smoker quits smoking, the bedwetter is dry, the unhappy couple has sexual intercourse.

If all theories generated in patriarchal times and places are to one degree or another patriarchal, where does a feminist turn for a method? Despite the widely known, well-argued errors and excesses of Freudian psychology, many feminists in various disciplines have nonetheless found that psychoanalytic thinking gives our work extraordinary explanatory power and precision (see Mitchell 1974, Miller 1976, Eichenbaum and Orbach 1983, Bernardez 1978, Strouse 1974, Dimen 1986). Rather than reject it, we need to reappropriate the notions of the unconscious, of insight, and of Oedipal and pre-Oedipal politics as well.

On the question of the relationship between psychoanalysis and feminism, Jean Baker Miller has observed in *Toward a New Psychology of Women* (1976) that psychoanalytic theory makes everyone's concern the things that have culturally been the concern of women only: the emotions, sexuality, childhood, relationships, body functions, and the irrational. This is indeed the case, and it has often been observed that all psychotherapy is a feminization process insofar as it aims to build people's abilities to integrate thought and affect and to be in relationships. This explains why some people wonder why a *feminist* family therapy is needed. Just getting women and men to talk frankly and intimately with each other already completes an important feminist requirement. There is truth to this point, of course, but feminism and psychotherapy do not completely superimpose, and so a feminist reconstruction is needed.

The British school of psychoanalysis known as *object-relations theory,* which originated with Melanie Klein and was developed by D. W. Winnicott, W. R. D. Fairbairn, and others, has moved psychoanalytic therapy in a direction that shares more with feminism than do many other therapies. Winnicott's term "the holding environment," which describes the essence of the therapeutic relationship, is a term I will use a good deal. The holding environment refers to the provision of security and trust for the

---

*Whereas most family therapists use the word *client,* I use *patient.* The latter word, I admit, is not perfect, because of its connotation of medicine, but the association of *client* with the world of business makes it so much worse. The word *patient* means literally "one who suffers," and does not have to refer to physical suffering.

patient in a way analogous to the mother-infant relationship. The therapist contains or holds on to the individual's or the family's pain, just as the mother contains the distress of the infant—nondefensively, nonpunitively, reassuringly—thus sending the message that the child's (or family's) feelings and pain are bearable and have meaning. Other theoreticians have characterized the therapeutic relationship in terms of salesperson and client, or of baseball coach and team. The therapist's skills are typically depicted as persuasiveness, ingenuity, and the ability not to be "sucked in." Many of the master family therapists have had little to say about the role of care and empathy in the therapeutic relationship. The fact that object-relations theory not only insists on such care and empathy but also uses the metaphor of mothering—what mothers do—as the essence of healing has clear potential for feminist translation.

It has other potential as well, of course. Not a single one of the originators of object-relations theory was feminist, and thinking in these terms can lead to patriarchal conceptions of motherhood, just as other theories have done. In chapter 12 I will discuss the hazards of object-relations theory. On balance, however, I conclude that there is more to be shared than avoided, from the feminist perspective. Feminists tend to share with object-relations theorists the valuation of insight; that is, both feminist and psychoanalytic theorists tend to believe that problems of transformation/healing are problems of understanding/knowing. Feminists of most schools of therapy hope not merely that women and men will share each other's kitchen and garage chores; they also hope that people will understand themselves and each other better as women and men. Once again, it is important to acknowledge that consciousness raising is different from therapy, but the two can profitably be considered as metaphors for each other. Both derive from a belief in the power of history, of naming our demons, and ultimately in the Delphic exhortation to self-knowledge.*

Feminist therapists work with women and men, individuals, couples, groups, people of all social classes and sexual preferences. Feminist therapists hope to help both women and men appropriate their powers to preserve themselves, to prize interdependence, to be freely for-others, to live fearless and principled lives, to have the capacities for critical thought, political resistance, and sexual ecstasy. Mothers, in the feminist utopia, are

---

*Many feminists interested in psychoanalytic theory have adopted not the British school but that of French analyst Jacques Lacan. (Cf. Gallop 1982, Cixous 1981, Kristeva 1980, Turkle 1978.) The commitment of these writers to call into question all of our ideas about language, gender, and value make their works very important to psychoanalytic theory as a whole. However, because they have applied their efforts more to analyzing literary texts than to patients, they will not be treated in this book except in passing.

not disembodied sources of nourishment but active agents who claim their subjectivity in the tasks of both nurturing and world making. Fathers in this dream world are neither the dreaded evening guest nor the vigilant paterfamilias. The father must be a real member of the family, neither its head nor its foot soldier, neither its backup nor its shadow, but a lover of children, a person capable of both work and friendship. As parents, such women and men, living not necessarily in heterosexual units, would raise children who are at ease with their feminine or masculine bodies, children whose self-concepts neither deny the body nor neurotically confine them to what is conventionally anticipated.

The Psycho-tyranny of "Stuck" and "Unstuck"

Special mention should be made about the issue of language, for language is something that family therapists, even feminist family therapists, have ignored. To write more articles about incest and to blame mothers less will produce little enduring change in family therapy if we continue to talk about families as "functional," "dysfunctional," "positive," "negative," "stuck," and "unstuck." This computer-based and highly imprecise language sounds remarkably like George Orwell's *Newspeak,* and it would be difficult to argue that the results on our thinking could be different. The manufacturers of Newspeak in *Nineteen Eighty-four* reduced the lexicon and emptied it of words with historical and emotional meaning so that unconventional thinking—and even clear thinking—were no longer possible. A change in family therapy that will go deeper than cosmesis will require new words and a rejection of the seductively high-tech sounds of cybernetics. The investigation of language, of course, has always been a primary task of psychoanalytic thinkers. As object-relations theorist D. W. Winnicott (1965) observed, it is true that we use language, but it is also true that "language uses us." In the feminist psychotherapy I will begin to describe here, I will speak not of "dyads," "executives," and "dysfunction," but of mothers and fathers, of history, memory, pain, and desire.

But this is jumping far ahead. Before proposing the beginnings of a new language, it is important to remember the tradition from which we are departing and to which we owe so much. Part II offers a critical review of eight approaches to family therapy, focusing on their ideas about gender and about the family in its social context.

PART II

A Feminist Critique
of Eight Approaches
to Family Therapy

T HE CHAPTERS in this section focus on issues of gender definition and sexual politics as they appear in eight different approaches to family therapy. In reading these critiques, it is important to keep in mind the cultural period in which the field of family therapy emerged, which undoubtedly accounts for much of what will be criticized. The birth of the field is usually set between 1952 and 1961 (cf. Broderick and Schrader 1981), which situates it during one of the most politically conservative periods in American history. This was the decade that saw the end of an era of vast social reforms under Roosevelt and the advent of the cold war, consumerism, and what is sometimes called "the long sleep of the Eisenhower years." Adlai Stevenson perhaps characterized this period best when he labeled 1952 "the year that America passed from the New Dealers to the car dealers" (cf. Hofstadter 1962).

With regard to women in particular, this period fell between two eras of progressive social change—the feminist movement of the turn of the century and the second-wave movement of the 1970s. It cannot be irrelevant that while the early family therapists were writing their first articles and books and seeing their first families, the doctrine of "separate spheres" for the sexes was a dominant cultural motif. American women who had been wage earners during World War II were expected to return home after the war and leave their jobs for the returning men. In the 1950s women had, on average, more children to care for at home—3.8 as opposed to approximately 2 at the present time.

Social scientists of the postwar period described and endorsed the idea of separate spheres. Sociologist Talcott Parsons, for example, ascribed to men the "instrumental" role and to women the "expressive" role in family life. The former referred to working and earning money, and the latter to nurturing children and creating harmony. Traditional American psychiatry endorsed the split between the two spheres and associated family health with the ability to distinguish sex roles clearly. Nathan Ackerman, often called the father of family therapy, adopted this traditional belief. Later family therapists did not insist on dichotomous sex roles, but most of them did not explicitly reject this notion either, even through the 1960s and 1970s. This may be due in part to the fact that those pioneer family therapists fought a fierce and depleting battle in departing from mainstream psychiatry. Explicitly questioning sex roles would have meant further risking their professional legitimacy.

The following eight chapters, with the exception of the one on Ackerman, criticize what seem to me the most influential approaches to family therapy. There is no professional group that trains students in the "Ackerman method," but I have included him nonetheless because he is so important to our history. No effort is made to provide a full analysis of how these eight approaches developed or influenced one another; that would require a text in itself. My objective here is much more modest; it is simply to survey the field's commentary on gender—both the stated commentary and that which exists between the lines.

Some readers may question the focus in the following chapters on the *master* family therapists. Why define strategic therapy or structural therapy only as the originators themselves define and practice it? A survey of attitudes and clinical methods of *all* the practitioners of a given approach would indeed be instructive. However, students of family therapy are trained largely through the use of the "classic" texts, and by imitating what they see on the videotapes of the leading therapists described in this section. It is important for students—and their teachers—to expand their awareness of how these texts and tapes, in ways both direct and subtle, treat issues of gender and define the family in society.

In the following critiques, I point out both what is anachronistic or incorrect about a given author's views of gender, and also what he or she offers that might represent common ground with feminism. The phrase "common ground with feminism" requires elaboration since, as already stated, a feminist family therapy does not yet exist. Feminist approaches to individual and group therapy have themselves varied in principle and technique (Eichenbaum and Orbach 1983, Baker-Miller 1976, Greenspan 1983, Brodsky and Hare-Mustin 1980). Feminist therapies do have in common, however, the following tenets:

1. Psychotherapy is necessarily a weak strategy for creating broad social change. However, as long as a large number of women and men seek therapy, we must offer methods that do not require adap-

tation to the status quo and, where possible, even help people to resist it.

2. Psychotherapy can help individuals not only resolve specific symptoms but also increase the complexity of their ability to think about relationships. Not all feminist therapists use the word *insight* to describe the part of therapy that has to do with awareness, but few would argue its irrelevance to treatment. Since culture has made it difficult for women and men to understand their problems except in overpersonalized and self-blaming ways, many feminists see insight as central to therapy; it can "demystify" experience and create the opportunity to seek new solutions.

3. It is important for therapists to develop methods for treating problems such as wife battering, incest, and eating disorders which, although they occur very frequently among women, therapists have either neglected or treated without an understanding of their social genesis.

4. Therapists hold an inherently powerful position in relation to patients and must treat them with respect and dignity. (The Hippocratic maxim "First do no harm" is often invoked by feminists.)

5. Therapists should undergo their own therapy in order to limit the problem of projecting one's own problems with boundaries, hierarchies, and intimacy onto one's patients.

6. Feminist therapists are concerned with issues outside the therapy room and see organizing for social change as continuous with their work.

Elaborations on these points through the citation of relevant texts and research studies will be made throughout the critiques.

2

Nathan Ackerman:
The Patriarch's Legacy

SOMETIMES CALLED "the father of family therapy," the late Nathan Ackerman made an enormous contribution to the field. He was instrumental in transforming psychoanalytic theory from its singular preoccupation with the individual to a theory, as he himself put it, "of social man." Now lionized within the field, Ackerman was not always appreciated during his lifetime. In fact, according to Phillip Guerin (1976), Ackerman's heterodoxy incited the contempt of his fellow psychoanalysts, and his seminars at Columbia Presbyterian Psychiatric Institute, for example, were typically scheduled to conflict with other seminars that were mandatory for residents. Moreover, his death was not acknowledged in the traditional memorial service held by the prestigious Group for the Advancement of Psychiatry (GAP), of which he was an active member.

Ackerman had an interest in social problems and, for example, wrote compassionately about the effects of unemployment on coal miners and their families in Pennsylvania (Ackerman 1967). With Marie Jahoda, he also wrote an interesting and little-known work on anti-Semitism (1950) in which he criticized certain aspects of modern social life, e.g., competition, "acquisitiveness," and lack of community, as factors promoting racial scapegoating. Ackerman assumed the role of social critic where class and racial bias were concerned, but not where gender bias was concerned; he clearly did not see women as socially disadvantaged.

Nathan Ackerman and contemporary feminists hold in common the premise that gender is a crucial category in understanding human beings and society. The way Ackerman construed gender, however, was far from feminist. In *The Psychodynamics of Family Life* (1958), Ackerman wrote:

> Women in our society are highly confused about their roles as women and as mothers. What has happened to their image of themselves? They are in danger of losing their identity as women. They tend too often to envy the male . . . and to derogate the time-honored function of mothering. They become frigid and are plagued with anxieties about their incompleteness as women. [Pp. 172–74]

Ackerman believed that when women became aggressive, their husbands became passive, and that this "role reversal" was at the heart of most childhood pathology. He wrote:

> In certain families, there is a reversal of sexual roles. The woman dominates and makes the decisions; she "wears the pants." The father is passive and submits to avoid argument. The mother pushes the father towards many of the maternal duties. . . . Such trends as these have had an immeasurable effect in distorting the functions of mothering and in confusing the sexual and emotional development of the child. [Pp. 172–73]

Ackerman did not view gender as a historical construct, something that each society shapes according to its economic and ideological needs. Instead he believed that the differences between the sexes were determined by "nature." He invoked this concept a great deal, arguing that it was "natural" for women to be passive and for men to "wear the pants." The mixed metaphor seems comical, since in nature neither male nor female wears the pants.

Ackerman remained as close to traditional psychoanalysis as any family therapist has, and one would logically expect his views of women to be similar to Freud's view of woman as castrated man. Ackerman wrote: "It is unfortunately true that women who deny their femaleness, who have 'penis envy', build up extensive illusions about their body that warp their self-image and play no small part in maintaining their maladapted role in society" (p. 173). It is interesting that Ackerman should place the words *penis envy* in quotation marks, although he did not do so with other psychoanalytic terms, such as *ego* and *unconscious*. It is as though he wished to use "penis envy" with some reserve or qualification, indicating that he did not quite buy the classical Freudian interpretation. Unfortunately, however, he never elaborated on this usage.

To Ackerman's credit, it must be noted that he did not stake the Freudian claim that woman's superego is inferior to man's. He was instead a "separate but equal" advocate: "Each of the sexes has its special place and merits respect in its own right. . . . Men and women can receive an equal measure of respect for what they give, but they must be differently respected" (p. 173). It is ironic that Ackerman should suggest this concept in the same decade that the Supreme Court ruled in the case of racial difference that "separate but equal" is inherently an unequal proposition. In any case, Ackerman's "separate but equal" was demonstrably specious. On the other hand, he defended mothers, insisting that it was too easy for professionals of all kinds to "ease their own conscience by placing all the guilt at the mother's door" (p. 177). On the other hand, the case examples in his books clearly focus on mothers as "depriving," "overindulging," and "inconsistent." Moreover, Ackerman actually lamented the passing of the age when fathers ruled by physical coercion: "He [the father] has been stripped of all semblance of arbitrary authority in the family. His power to discipline and punish family offenders, *whether wife or child,* has been sharply undercut" (p. 179, italics added).

The word *undercut* here, as opposed to *decreased,* clearly suggests that some injustice has been done to the patriarch. Ackerman seems to have idealized the mid-nineteenth-century father, writing about him that "wife and child deferred to his superior wisdom. He exercised his authority firmly but fairly. His discipline was strict but not abusive. . . . Sometimes he became the tyrant; if so, in the end he suffered for the abuse of his power. Echoes of this older image still persist, but they have grown dim" (p. 179). This portrait is historically inaccurate; to call it a reversal of the facts would not be a gross exaggeration. Wife and child beating were legion in the mid-nineteenth century. The "tyrant" did not regularly suffer for his tyranny, as there were no laws against beating family members and the culture required female obedience in many ways. Moreover, a mother could not legally obtain custody of her children after divorce, regardless of the father's degeneracy, until the late nineteenth and early twentieth centuries (Rich 1976, Chesler 1986). Ackerman does not cite any historical studies; he only appeals to the "common sense" idea that the family was once a glorious institution before being infected by the ills of modernity. Ackerman's romantic fantasy of the virile, involved, and courageous father serves only to indict the modern woman who, by her demands for equality, threatens to cut him down to size.

Ackerman's therapeutic style was consistent with his theoretical views; he was sometimes patently disrespectful to women. In his 1966 book, *Treating the Troubled Family,* he describes a case in which he attempted to soften a dominating mother. He exceeds the boundaries of what most professionals would consider appropriate therapeutic joking by asking the husband if his wife is a "good piece." Ackerman compliments the wife on her charms and then instructs the husband to get her off her "fat ass."

His sexism is apparent in a slightly subtler way in his famous consultation with the Hillcrest family. The father in this family received custody of his children after his divorce because the mother had neglected them. The father had then married a woman with a daughter of her own, and then the couple had a baby together. The family had been seeing a female psychiatrist, and agreed to a consultation with Ackerman which would be videotaped for professional use. The family was later interviewed by Murray Bowen, Don Jackson, and Carl Whitaker.*

In making contact with Mrs. Hillcrest in the first few minutes of the interview, Ackerman seductively dotes on her blue eyes, and asks Mr Hillcrest, "Did she look like an angel to you?" The interview proceeds with the husband doing most of the talking while the wife keeps the children quiet. At the end of the session, Ackerman asks the husband if the wife has "grown up yet." The husband fills the awkward silence that follows by saying, "not completely." This immature angel, Mrs. Hillcrest, is obviously tremendously competent. She has not only raised her own daughter alone, she has also taken on the raising of her husband's two children in addition to their baby. Within two years, this woman has gone from having one daughter to four children. The husband appears well meaning and appreciative of her, but it is clear that, in contrast to her, he feels completely flummoxed about relating to the children. The eleven-year-old son in particular appears depressed and in need of engagement by the father. (We learn only later, in the interview with Whitaker, that the father himself is depressed and possibly suicidal.) When the interview is over, Ackerman comments to the audience about what he would work on if he were continuing to see the family. He states that he would "put pressure on Carol [the wife] to control the older children or they'll take over the marriage." Consistent with his perspective in *The Psychodynamics of Family Life,* he does not recommend helping the father to become equally responsible for his children.

There is another aspect of Ackerman's personal style that is instructive, and to which we will return again in this book; it has to do with *naming.* In the Hillcrest interview, Ackerman attempts to discuss each of the children with the parents, but he fumbles over their names, seeming not to remember them. There is something jarring about a therapist entering a family as a consultant and asking intimate questions without taking the time to address them by name. Thomas Scheff (1966) and other radical

---

*This fascinating set of films called the "Hillcrest Series" can be rented from the Pennsylvania State University library.

sociologists have written about how the use (and nonuse) of names defines power relationships in therapeutic and other social contexts. The situation of a famous therapist (always named) talking to a family in anonymous discourse is one that has persisted in family therapy up to the present time.

As mentioned in the introduction to this section, it is useful to view Ackerman's sexism in the context in which he lived and wrote. When Ackerman was born, in 1908, women were not even permitted to vote. During the course of his adult life, relatively few women joined the professional ranks; for example, only 6 percent of physicians and 4 percent of lawyers were women in 1958 (Udry 1974), when Ackerman wrote his classic text. (Incoming medical and legal classes are now one-third to one-half women.) These data help explain Ackerman's comment on women's mastery: "Woman's aggressiveness and mastery are really a facade. Her facade of self-sufficiency and strength represents an effort at compensation, an effort to console herself for her inability to depend safely on the man" (1958, p. 179). Ackerman might have had a different perspective on women's competence if he had lived to see more women doctors, as well as women astronauts, mayors, scientists, and heads of state.

Finally, Ackerman and the other early family therapists did not have the benefit of sociological research which has since shown that the very notion of women's greater "dependency" is a reversal of empirically shown relationships. It is actually *men,* for example, who are more likely to fall into psychological or physical crisis when forced into "self-sufficiency" by the death of, or separation from, a spouse (Bernard 1972, Bloom 1978, Ehrenreich 1983).

Some feminists would be eager to point out that by 1958 Simone de Beauvoir's brilliant treatise on the status of women, *The Second Sex,* had been available in English translation for five years, and that scholars such as John Stuart Mill and Mary Wollstonecraft had criticized women's social disadvantage over a century before Ackerman lived. Considering the overall cultural and economic climate, however, it is not inappropriate to consider Ackerman a product of a less advanced age. What is more disconcerting than Ackerman's sexist writing of the 1950s and 1960s is the writing of family therapists working two decades later, which continues to lack a thoughtful critique of the family and its sexual politics.

Although few family therapists today would call themselves "Ackerman-style" therapists (as they would "Satir-" or "Bowen-style"), there are nonetheless many family therapists who concern themselves seriously with "the psychodynamics of family life." Ivan Boszormenyi-Nagy and Carl Whitaker both fall into this category, since they use concepts from psychoanalytic theory and its revisions in connection with other concepts to guide their treatment. (See chapters 6 and 8.)

In England, A. C. Robin Skynner is known for his creation of an object-relations approach to family therapy (following the marital therapy of Henry Dicks [1967]). In the United States, a group of family therapists working out of the Washington School of Psychiatry has produced a similar conceptual synthesis, and two of their members, David and Jill Scharff, published *Object Relations Family Therapy* in 1987. I have not devoted an entire chapter to the object-relations school because it is relatively new in the United States and naturally has produced fewer texts and tapes than the other schools. For these reasons, it is less widely known to American audiences and has also had less time to show its full potential with regard to many theoretical issues, including those of concern here. Skynner's (1976) book takes a very conventional view of the sexes, but five years later, when his chapter appeared in the *Handbook of Family Therapy,* that view had become a bit more complex. Likewise the Scharffs, while not producing anything like a critique of gender in canonical object-relations theory, nonetheless assume a more progressive stance than one is likely to find elsewhere in that literature, e.g., on the desirability of fathers' involvement in the lives of young children and on the subject of mothers' work. (See also chapter 12.)

It is simply too early to tell where these contemporary psychoanalytic family therapists will go, if and when they decide to do what Ackerman didn't—that is, thoroughly engage and investigate the subject of gender in theory and practice from a point of view not exclusively male.

3

Murray Bowen: The Politics of Rational Man

MURRAY BOWEN is considered one of the brilliant pioneers of family therapy. He was not only one of the first therapists to consider the family's role in the development of schizophrenia, but he actually hospitalized schizophrenic patients with their entire families in the 1950s, a practice that even today is considered an extremely sophisticated application of systems thinking.

Bowen's name is linked with the origins of the theory of multigenerational transmission of mental illness. The goal of Bowen's therapy is to promote *differentiation* of family members from the "family's undifferentiated ego mass." According to Bowen, poorly differentiated parents raise poorly differentiated children. Adults tend to marry partners at the same level of differentiation as themselves, and thus "pass on" the inability to separate sufficiently from the family of origin. When this process continues for several generations, a family member may eventually become schizophrenic—the ultimate condition of undifferentiatedness.

Bowen contends that the smallest stable relationship is a unit of three people. A two-person relationship under stress will "triangle in" a third person. Very often this means that a couple under stress will involve a child to stabilize their conflict. A child who is already vulnerable in some way is a likely target for this kind of triangulation.

In terms of his method of treatment, Bowen aims to give people a clearer perspective on the family triangles in which they participate and are sometimes caught. Bowen often assigns tasks in which a client must return to his or her family of origin and gather information about a particular relative, or interact in a way that differs from the usual family patterns. During the session itself, Bowen typically directs all conversation through himself, as opposed to asking family members to talk to one another. Better communication is not an end in itself, as it is in some other schools of family therapy. Bowen believes that as people become more differentiated from their family of origin, they will be able to engage more fully in their current relationships and therefore to communicate more effectively. Bowen has also stated that directing all interactions through himself in the therapy room "lowers the level of irrationality." This emphasis on the rational versus the irrational is a topic to which we will return later.

Common Ground with Feminism

Feminist therapist Harriet Goldhor Lerner, who has been trained in both psychodynamic theory and Bowen theory, advises feminists to "take Bowen Family Systems Theory and run with it. Of all the family therapy schools, Bowen theory best fits my feminist values and beliefs" (1986, p. 36). It is certainly true that, like feminist therapy, the goal of Bowen therapy is broader than symptom remission. Bowen is no mere technician of behavior change. He believes strongly in the importance of family members gaining information about their familial history and insight into its significance for their lives. As Goldhor Lerner points out:

> Just as feminists continue to gather facts about "lost women" in history and revise history books to more accurately reflect women's experience, clients in Bowen work are guided through a similar journey with persons on their own family tree. Through both Bowen work and feminism, a woman's sense of isolation about her so-called pathology is replaced by an empathic understanding of the continuity of women's struggles through the generations and the ways in which she is both similar to and different from those who came before her. [1986, p. 37]

Betty Carter, co-author of *The Family Life Cycle,* has also found Bowen theory to be compatible with her feminist worldview. Carter emphasizes the value of Bowen theory in insisting that people continue their dialogue with the family of origin. "Cutoffs" from one's parents, grandparents, and siblings are to be avoided wherever possible. Carter contrasts Bowen theory with a typical outcome of psychoanalysis: "We have all seen people leaving their sixth year of psychoanalysis, feeling "cured" or "free" because they had told off their parents, or written them off. Bowen theory says—if you finish any kind of therapy and cannot hold a conversation with your parents—cannot be in the same room with your own mother—then something is very wrong" (pers. comm. 1986).

Some therapists (e.g., Goldhor Lerner 1986) also argue that the use of the genogram is a hedge against mother-blaming, since the multiplicity of characters and the complex patterns make it less likely that any one person in the family will be singled out as the culprit. Goldhor Lerner writes: "Even for the novice therapist, there are just too many circles and squares in a family diagram to get overfocused on one. Nor is it possible to view mothers in isolation from broader family triangles and patterns" (1986, p. 37). Of this last point, I am not at all convinced, but I would add that Bowen theory and feminism share common ground in their emphasis on therapists working on their own family-of-origin relationships. The maxim "Doctor, heal thyself" is embraced both by Murray Bowen and by most feminist therapists (cf. Eichenbaum and Orbach 1983). Bowen introduced this maxim into the field in 1967 by appearing at a conference and unexpectedly reading a paper about his own family of origin. The substitution of an article referring to the person of the expert himself in place of an abstract theoretical manuscript is the type of behavior that can chip away at the patriarchal dichotomies between the personal and the professional, the private and the public, emotion and intellect. Bowen's 1967 paper, however, emphatically does *not* reflect an interest in eroding those dualities. On the contrary, Bowen in almost every other way promotes patriarchal values, and he is responsible for some of the most politically conservative statements written anywhere in the family therapy literature.

Bowen on Sexual Politics

Bowen's comments on gender are less explicitly sexist than those of Ackerman. Bowen does not write about penis envy, nor does he insist that the husband must "wear the pants." Bowen describes the complementary pattern that develops between an "inadequate" and an "overadequate" spouse and states that men and women can play either role. He avoids the business of trying to understand gender theoretically, arguing that the "ideal situation" is for the wife to function as a woman and the husband as a man, "without having to debate the advantages and disadvantages of biological and social roles" (1978, p. 370).

Although he claims that in his earliest research the most striking pattern seemed to be that of an "aggressive mother" and a "passive father" (echoing Ackerman's analysis), Bowen later concluded: "we could postulate that a fairly normal family is one in which parents can function in either the strong or the weak position, according to the demands of the situation, without threatening either one" (1978, p. 35). The words *strong* and *weak* in this passage, along with the desire to close off the discussion of gender rather than enter it, predicts that Bowen theory will simply repeat the cultural biases about gender that tend to overimplicate mothers in the explanations of children's problems, and indeed this turns out to be the case. A consistent theme in Bowen's work is that mothers "overinvest" in their children because of their inability to separate from their own mothers, who in turn could not separate from their mothers. Feminist theorists such as Dinnerstein (1976) and Rich (1976) have also discussed how difficult it can be for mothers and children to establish adequate boundaries with each other. The difference is that these theorists place the mother-child relationship in social and historical context, whereas Bowen does not. Thus, maternal "overinvestment" retains the connotations of a vexing character problem, too easily translated into maternal blame.

The tendency in Bowen theory to overimplicate the mother and to minimize the father's role is evident in Bowen's description of how pathology develops in a child. He begins his description with the concept of a triangular emotional process "through which two powerful people in the triangle reduce their own anxiety and insecurity by picking a defect in the third person. . . . " The idea starts as one involving *two* powerful people. However, just one paragraph later, the process is suddenly defined as one between mother and child:

> Specifically it begins with an overanxious mother devoted to being the best possible mother and having the most wonderful child. The child becomes anxious in response to the mother's anxiety. Instead of controlling her own anxiety, she anxiously tries to relieve the child's anxiety by more anxious mothering, which makes the child more anxious, which further drives her anxious mothering, etc. She can never slow down to see her own part. Instead, she seeks for causes for the problem in the child and goes to see physicians seeking a positive diagnosis and a new avenue through which to structure and focus the mothering. In periods of calm, she might neglect reality needs of the child. The process continues through the years until the child is functionally impaired. . . . Eventually she seeks the help of a psychiatrist who, in the implementation of sound

principles of medicine, examines the patient, diagnoses his illness, and agrees to treat the illness as a pathology in the patient. . . . By the time this severe process has reached an advanced stage, the patient is so functionally impaired and so programmed to act the part of the pitiful one, that the process is irreversible. [1978, pp. 434–35]

At last we learn of the father's role in this tragedy: "The father plays a passive role in the mother-child relationship, adding his approval to her actions" (p. 435).

Bowen claims to believe in the importance of the father's role, and of course he hospitalized fathers with their schizophrenic sons and daughters. Nonetheless, one reads very little about fathers even in the clinical material contained in Bowen's major volume, *Family Therapy in Clinical Practice* (1978). One of the few cases Bowen describes at length in that book focuses so exclusively on the mother's lack of differentiation that the father vanishes inexplicably from the account. The case begins with the following sentence: "I will start with a mother with two young children, one that grows up with a poor level of differentiation and another with a good level of differentiation. The same mother can have two children that are quite different" (1978, p. 426). The father in this family is alluded to only through the fact of impregnation; thereafter he is invisible in this case, which begins with the child's birth and ends when she is an adult. Bowen writes: "The mother's first child was conceived when her life was unsettled and anxious. Anxiety and marital disharmony decreased during pregnancy. . . . The child, a girl, was tense and fretful and required more than average mothering attention. A second child was born 18 months later" (1978, p. 426). This is the last clue we will hear about father's presence.

The older child at school age developed school phobia, which was resolved through intervention by a competent teacher. The girl became a good student and maintained a very close and compliant relationship with her mother, until age thirteen when she tried to differentiate from this mother who was so "overinvested" in her. Bowen states that in an effort to pull away from this engulfing relationship, the girl joined an antisocial peer group and began shoplifting, having sex, and using drugs. She became addicted and got hepatitis from the injections. She was in two serious car wrecks with the boyfriend who was supplying the drugs. She managed to finish high school, but moved in with the boyfriend, "and they manage to live without working except for part-time jobs in antiestablishment activity." Bowen tells us that the younger child, the son, "led an orderly life." He did well in school and has plans to marry. We know that the father in the family is not dead because Bowen says that this adult son has maintained close relationships with his parents without being affected by their problems with his sister.

The only other adult who is mentioned in this case is a teacher who was involved with the daughter and who was allegedly drawn to the child because she herself had a "poor level of differentiation" since she was "relationship-oriented" in her own life. Bowen clearly links this girl's miserable life with her mother's inability to separate from her child. He writes: "Much of mother's psychic energy, which included worry, concern, "love" and anger, etc. were invested in the girl, and the girl invested an equal amount of herself in the mother. . . . The mother's degree of undif- ferentiation that fuses with the child is determined by her total amount of undifferentiation and by the amount absorbed elsewhere" (p. 429).

So pernicious is this mother's "overinvestment," according to Bowen, that even the possibility that she felt some genuine love for her daughter is denied by him, and he places the word *love* in quotation marks. The son is saved, according to Bowen, because the mother has invested all her "undifferentiation" in the patient. One can only conclude from reading a clinical profile such as this one that *being an expert in genograms does not ensure that one person on the genogram will not be made a villain*. The decontextualization of maternal behavior is one of the main problems with Bowen theory. Another problem concerns his concept of differentiation.

Differentiation

The concept of the "differentiated self" is, according to Bowen, one of the key ideas in his work and, he believes, also one of the most misunderstood. Bowen has repeatedly insisted that the truly differentiated person is not synonymous with the "rugged individual" or the "lone wolf," as some critics have charged. Bowen does *not* equate differentiation with separation or isolation from others; on the contrary, only differentiated people can have mature, loving relationships.

At this level of analysis, there is relatively little controversy. No one would defend "reactivity" (Bowen's antonym for "differentiation") as the goal of therapy or of life; we might all agree that people who only react to others and who cannot make their own choices are not free to work and love well. The problem arises when we leave this very fundamental level of analysis and ask for conceptual elaboration. What are the actual characteristics of the differentiated person? How do we know differentiation when we see it? In order to answer these questions, Bowen developed his "Differentiation of Self Scale" which can be scored from 0 to 100, with the top score denoting the completely differentiated person and zero the condition of total reactivity, or "fusion." Leaving aside the questionable practice of quantifying issues as ontologically complex as these, we see the emergence of a very clear and disturbing value system about "selfhood." On the basis of Bowen's insistence that differentiation does not mean unconnectedness, one would expect that the high point of the scale would be characterized by phrases such as "the ability to integrate thought and feeling," "the ability to tolerate conflict and avoid cutoffs," and "the capacity both to compete and to collaborate." Strangely enough, however, the language Bowen uses to define differentiation is *not* the language of the integration of those capacities. Instead, to describe the differentiated person he uses words such as "autonomous," "goal-directed," "intellectual," and "being-for-self," while the poorly differentiated person is described with the words "seeking love and approval," "relatedness," and "being-for-others." The origin of this dichotomy lies in Bowen's belief in the separation of the rational and the emotional systems within human beings. Bowen writes:

> The most important differences between man and the lower forms is his cerebral cortex and his ability to think and reason. Intellectual functioning is regarded as distinctly different from emotional functioning, which man shares with the lower forms. Emotional functioning includes the automatic forces that govern protoplasmic life. It includes the force that biology defines as instinct, reproduction, the automatic nervous system, and subjective emotional and feeling states, and the forces that govern relationship systems. [1981, p. 305]

Although Bowen goes on to say that there is some "overlap" between the two functions, he concludes with the thought that "it is possible for man to discriminate between the emotions and the intellect and to slowly gain more conscious control of emotional functioning" (p. 305).

It has not escaped the notice of recent critics (e.g., Hare-Mustin 1978, Goldhor Lerner 1986) that what is valued in Bowen's system are the qualities for which men are socialized and what is devalued are those for which women are socialized. Bowen's use of the word *reproduction* in the quotation just cited is very instructive. He associates it with emotional states and with "lower forms," but the fact is that reproduction has been the social and biological function assigned to women throughout history. Bowen does not address the issue of how a woman, given the expectation that she will have primary responsibility for nurturing children, would be able to "be-for-self" as much as a man can, given his different training. Society, it might be said, actually *schools* females into undifferentiation by teaching them always to put others' needs first and by denying them the same degree of discretion as men with regard to their economic and physical fates.

Bowen's separation of the thinking and feeling spheres recalls the Platonic division of the soul into the rational and the feeling (or "vegetative") parts. Plato believed that the rational part was dominant in people of the nobler classes. Feminist philosopher Genevieve Lloyd, in her fascinating book, *The Man of Reason: "Male" and "Female" in Western Philosophy* (1984), has analyzed how all of the major philosophical schools from the Socratics to Hegel have in some way elevated reason as a principle, associating it with men and men's activity, and devalued emotion, associating it with women and women's activity.

This tradition has been carried over into the twentieth century by social scientists, and has made itself evident in the judgments of modern therapists. The most dramatic demonstration of this set of issues was provided by the now classic study by Broverman et al. (1972). In that study, the authors found that therapists defined the healthy male as "rational," "independent," and "aggressive," and the healthy female as "emotional," "passive," and "dependent." Most significantly, these therapists defined the healthy *adult* with the characteristics of the healthy male. Broverman and her colleagues argued that women are offered a double bind by the helping professions: either they possess the character traits of the "adult" but reject their "femininity," or they conform to the "healthy female" qualities but fail to match up to the healthy adult. Bowen's (1978) volume was published six years after the widely discussed Broverman study, but he does not cite it, nor does he comment on the potential problems his scale might pose for women.

A different perspective on these same issues is provided by Harvard psychologist Carol Gilligan. In her celebrated book, *In a Different Voice* (1982), she not only documented another area of social science—moral development research—in which gender differences affect outcome, she also questioned whether certain male-oriented characteristics that are found at the top of the scale should really be considered superior. Because Gilligan's findings are so relevant to Bowen's notion of differentiation, her work will be discussed at length here.

Gilligan began her work with a critique of Lawrence Kohlberg's well-known research on moral development. Although Kohlberg had argued that his scale of the six stages of moral development applied as well to females as to males, females rarely obtained a score above three on this scale! Gilligan proposed to address this disparity by listening closely to the ways in which boys and girls reached their answers to his hypothetical moral dilemmas. One example will suffice. It involves the "Heinz dilemma," which is presented to the respondents essentially as follows: A man named Heinz cannot afford a drug that will save his wife's life, and the druggist will not give it to him. Should Heniz steal the drug? Gilligan found that her eleven-year-old male respondent answered yes, and used a conventional values hierarchy to explain that life is more valuable than money. The eleven-year-old female, however, answered in a way that was not as pat. She began by commenting on the unfairness of a system in which people can die because they cannot afford medicine. She considered the possible consequences of the theft. If the husband were caught and jailed, she asked, who would take care of the wife? Would the husband know how to administer this drug? The girl ultimately answered "no" to the research question, and said that Heinz should instead find ways of raising money for the drug.

It appears on a careful reading of these answers that the two children have approached the problem from different conceptual sets—not that the girl's thinking is less advanced than the boy's. The boy is thinking in terms of rights and logic; the girl in terms of care and responsibility. Gilligan states that throughout her research, she found that males defined morality and responsibility in terms of *rights* and the need to *limit* their behavior from infringing on others. Females, on the other hand, defined morality in terms of *caring* and of *extending* their actions to fulfill others' needs. Kohlberg was not interested in the quality of those differences, and so in the case of the Heinz problem he would simply score the girl a full developmental stage lower than the boy.

Gilligan notes that the error of equating human experience with male experience is also evident in the work of Erik Erikson, whose life-cycle theory is taught in many family therapy seminars. Briefly, Erikson acknowledged that although for males the stage he called "autonomy" precedes the stage of "intimacy," the two stages are always interwoven for females. Despite this astute observation, Erikson nonetheless proceeded to present the "human" life cycle in terms of the male pattern: first autonomy and then intimacy. Women can reach the higher stages only by acting in "nonfeminine" ways, something Erikson certainly does not advocate.

What Gilligan's research forces us to ask, ultimately, is not simply how scientific scales can be made "fair" for women, nor even how we must change society so that women can be oriented more toward "autonomy" or "achievement" or "being-for-self." Her work guides us to ask a more

profound question: Do we really want to constitute those traditional values as our psychological *summum bonum?* Perhaps, she argues, the condition
of society demands that we begin to cultivate different qualities, i.e., those
that have been associated with women's lives and experiences: nurturing,
caring, and being-for-others.*

Jean Baker Miller (1984) has suggested that the metaphor of geographical distance implicit in the notions of "separation" and "differentiation"
may simply be inapt for the description of what actually happens in
human maturational process. Children, even infants, do not really distance
themselves from mother as they grow in competence and skill. Rather,
their relationship to her becomes more *complex.* The caring, the cognition,
the capacity to make sense of the "other" becomes more and more embel-
lished, better informed, more able to contain contradiction. Bowen might
say that he means the same thing by "differentiation" as Miller does by
"the increasing complexity of the self-in-relation." However, if we can
express the same idea with either of those linguistic tropes, why ought we
to choose the terms that refer to distance and difference rather than to
engagement and complex continuation? These questions do not yet allow
final answers, but the question of language must at least be accepted as a
question by Bowen theorists—and by all family therapists—in order to
enlarge our understanding of what separation and distance really mean to
us as social beings.

Bowen on Social Theory

Bowen is one of the few family therapists who has attempted to apply his
ideas about therapy to society at large. His politics, as revealed in his 1978
volume, are far to the right of center. In two essays on "societal regression," Bowen explains that: "In the past 25 years, society appears to have
been slipping into a functionally lower level of differentiation or emotional
regression. . . . These observations are based on the same criteria used to
estimate family functioning, which is the amount of principly determined
'self' in comparison to the 'feeling orientation' which strives for an immediate short-term solution" (p. 438).

Bowen goes so far as to estimate that this regression amounts to "a full

---

*Gilligan's work has not gone uncriticized, of course. See, for example, Kerber (1986),
which includes a response by Gilligan.

10 points on my scale in 25 years." Here Bowen is considering the period from 1949 to 1974, during which his essay (included in his 1978 volume) was written. Since Bowen writes ahistorically, one can only guess at the events to which he refers. Given that in 1949, there were still white-only schools and lunch counters in the United States, and that women were barred from many schools and professions as well, it is difficult to see (although street crime rates were definitely lower) how that time period could be considered generally *more* progressive. Bowen contends that "permissive sexual norms" are an indicator of societal regression, in a passage clearly referring to homosexuality: "Forms of sexuality, previously disapproved and called perverse by society, have now become more accepted" (p. 280). Bowen insists on a link between sexual permissiveness and social deterioration, despite the well-known fact that history's most repressive societies, including Hitler's Germany and Khomeini's Iran, have been extremely harsh about sex, typically decreeing that it belongs exclusively to marriage. If Bowen had intended to refer to sexual behavior that *does* erode the social fabric, he might have cited rape or incest, but they do not appear among his complaints.

In short, Bowen's examples of societal regression always target the behavior of society's least powerful members. For example, he labels "regressed" and "emotional" the behavior of the Americans who demonstrated against the war in Vietnam, but not the behavior of those who perpetrated it. He calls "regressed" the students who demonstrated on campuses, but not the National Guardsmen who shot them.

Bowen's most reactionary position emerges when he attempts to explain why society is regressing. He suggests that humankind has recently become more "anxious" due to overpopulation and other problems, but that "we" can no longer discharge our anxiety by seeking new frontiers. He writes:

> Man has long used physical distance as a way of "getting away from" inner emotional pressures. It was important for him to know there was new land for him, even if he never went to it. The end of World War II was an important nodal point in a process in which the world became functionally smaller at a more rapid rate. . . . After the war, *the colonial powers began to grant independence to their colonies, and it became more difficult for citizens to get away to a colony.* [P. 441, italics added.]

The question is this: If *regression* means for a colonial power to give up its colonies, then to whom does the word *man* refer in the first sentence of the quote? While the tone of the sentence seems to reach for a universal chord, it is clear by the end that *man* and *we* refer only to a tiny, imperial elite.

As for Bowen's opinion of the feminist movement *per se,* Harriet Goldhor Lerner says that "Bowen and his followers view feminism as an emotionally reactive position that can lead clients down the non-productive path of linear thinking (i.e., blaming men) or the relinquishing of self-responsibility" (1986, p. 39).

There is obviously much in Bowen theory that has been and can be of value to feminists, but it will remain important to reformulate concepts such as "differentiation" and to make family systems concepts arise from a different worldview.

4

Virginia Satir: The Limitations
of Humanism I

IN 1970 the Group for the Advancement of Psychiatry (GAP) published a survey about the influence of the leading therapists on members of the field. Participants in that survey cited as most influential to their own work not Murray Bowen or Nathan Ackerman, but Virginia Satir. Satir's books have sold hundreds of thousands of copies, and she has reached millions of people through her workshops and media appearances all over the world.

Satir was in the delicate position of being the only woman—and a social worker—among the founding parents of family therapy, most of whom were male psychiatrists. It is often the case that a lone professional woman in a group will be expected to "mother" the men in the group (Kantor 1977), and I asked Satir about her experience in those early days, during an interview in 1984. Satir stated that during a large part of her career, she consistently found herself on panels with five or six men, and that, indeed, a conflict-mediating role often fell to her. Did Satir experience respect from the men in those early years? She told me that she did: "All of the men learned from me, and they have shown me a great deal of respect over the years. I am on good terms with each of them. But some of the second generation of family therapists have been antagonistic to my work, calling it 'not deep' and 'too female' " (pers. comm. 1984).

The recognition due Satir is inconsistently granted in the family therapy literature. In *Foundations of Family Therapy* (1981), Lynn Hoffman properly acknowledged Satir's "extraordinary and unique contribution" and praised "the power of her presence with families." Many authors, however, fail to realize that Satir was practicing family therapy before most of the revered male therapists. For example, in Carlfred Broderick and Sandra

Schrader's otherwise excellent history of the field, "The History of Professional and Family Therapy" (1981), they state that Satir had "become interested in family work while on the staff of the Chicago Psychiatric Institute, and had heard about Bowen's project in Washington. When she finally met Bowen, he told her she should get to know Jackson and so in 1959 she joined the staff at MRI [Mental Research Institute]" (p. 25). This makes Satir seem like a passenger, and differs from her own account. According to Satir, she saw her first family in therapy in 1951, and started the first training program ever in family therapy in 1955 at the Illinois Psychiatric Institute. This was four years before she joined the staff of the Mental Research Institute with Don Jackson and Gregory Bateson.

It seems odd, moreover, that Satir was not allotted a chapter in Alan Gurman and David Kniskern's *Handbook of Family Therapy* (1981). The editors comment in their preface that, while Satir's influence on the field was "enormous," her work was not represented in their *Handbook* because "no discernible school or therapeutic method has evolved from her contribution" (p. xiv). The editors say that they omitted Lyman Wynne and Theodore Lidz for the same reasons, although it would be difficult to argue that either man's clinical influence on the field has equaled Satir's.

The tendency to overlook or underestimate Satir's contribution is metonymic of a larger tendency in the field to elide from its professional history the formative contribution of *social work.* * The social work movement has been active and powerful in the United States since the nineteenth century and, as Lois Braverman has pointed out in an important article (1986), many of the central tenets family therapists have claimed as bold new forms of social and clinical thinking (e.g., the very idea that families and not individuals should be treated) appeared in the writings of the early social case workers decades ago. Broderick and Schrader (1981) described a social worker named Mary Towle who argued the importance of doing family treatment with troubled children in *1930* at the American Orthopsychiatric Association. From what was recorded of that meeting, we know that her audience listened indifferently to the idea, and spent the rest of the session debating whether notes should be made in front of patients.

Braverman (1986) found the following exegesis of "systems thinking" in a social work lecture presented in 1919:

*Broderick and Schrader's history of family therapy in *The Handbook of Family Therapy* (1981) devotes at least some attention to the importance of social work, but other histories—for example, that of Guerin (1976)—erase it. A two-hour presentation on "The Roots of Family Therapy" at a major conference in 1984, while including dozens of other influences on the field, similarly left out the contribution of social work completely.

> The individual members of a family cannot be treated successfully without treating the family as a whole. . . . No individual is wholly an individual. He is himself plus every other person. . . . The more continuous his associations with any particular group of individuals, the more intimate his relationship to them, the more their daily practices coincide, the less likely it is that he can be understood without understanding them. [P. 17]

It should also be noted that family therapists of the current period (e.g., Minuchin 1984) who advocate the expansion of family systems concepts to systems larger than the family, such as courts, hospitals, and the community, are really speaking about a set of activities that began with nineteenth-century social workers and activists such as Jane Addams and Lilian Wald (cf. Addams 1910, Levine and Levine 1970). Addams had a profound understanding of the impact of social context on human process and problems, which she turned into programs to help families, neighborhoods, battered women, immigrants, and juvenile offenders. In fact Harry Stack Sullivan, who is cited by many contemporary family therapists for the salutory influence of his "interpersonal psychiatry," claimed to be a great admirer of Addams and to have learned enormously from her community-based creation known as Hull House (Greenberg and Mitchell 1983). John Dewey, who also influenced Sullivan's work—and all of American social science for that matter—also claimed Addams as one of his "heroines." Thus Addams has some claim to being the great-grandmother of family therapy. A deeper investigation along the lines of Braverman's (1986) work into the female ancestry of our discipline would be instructive indeed, but is beyond our purpose here. Our focus in this chapter is limited to one important member of the social work profession: Virginia Satir.

The work of Satir is by no means above criticism, but she has succeeded in producing a method of treatment that is as distinctive and teachable as that of anyone in the field. She herself helped formulate the notion that symptoms of individuals in families express family pain. Satir works on the belief that children's symptoms are related to marital difficulties in which they become triangulated. She thinks that the origin of marital conflict lies in unresolved problems with the family of origin, and especially in a "lack of nurturance" in the family of origin.

Many of Satir's key concepts are revealed in her well-known case "A Family of Angels." This case, which was published in 1967 in Haley and Hoffman's *Techniques of Family Therapy*, concerns a family with a seventeen-year-old son who had a psychotic break while the family was traveling in

Europe. During the first interview with the family, Satir moved beyond the symptom (bizarre behavior) and began tracking the family's ability to talk and listen to each other. She elicited their history in order to help them understand how they were attempting to settle ancestral issues through the symptom. The parents in this family, it turns out, were first cousins. The husband had always had a close relationship with his mother, who disapproved of the marriage. The daughter-in-law remained plagued by this rejection from her mother-in-law/aunt. She also felt betrayed by her husband, who favored his mother over her. Satir explained the situation in this way:

> It's a matter of self-esteem again. The mother didn't feel that she counted for anything, and wherever she could, she tried to get some kind of validation of her worth, which is pushed onto Gary (her son). What comes out here is that Gary sees that he can be useful to his parents in two ways: first to make life worthwhile for his mother and give what the father didn't give; second, by his extreme behavior, to give his father clues about how he can live. If he can accomplish these two things, if he can get father to be more interesting to mother, then mother perhaps can use father instead of him. At the end of this tape, there is a problem about who is going to live with the mother-in-law. Again, symbolically, you'll see how Gary will be the rescue agent. [Haley and Hoffman 1967, p. 150]

Satir's thinking is intergenerational, and her interpretations seem sympathetic in a way that is never contrived. She does not exert herself to "positively connote" human behavior. She seems really to view human strivings sympathetically. Reading her *Conjoint Family Therapy* (1967), one can only conclude that Satir's method is as fully formed as that of any of the major family therapists.

As for language, Satir draws on the vernacular and on functionalist and "systems" metaphors, apparently in the effort both to reach a wide audience and to satisfy the professional canon. Satir shares a problem with many family therapists: her concepts lack precision and a sense of the history of ideas. For example, one of her most central concepts, if not *the* central one, is "self-esteem"—which she never really defines. Satir writes: "I do not postulate sex as the basic drive of man. From what I have observed, the sex drive is continually subordinated to and used for the purpose of enhancing self-esteem, and defending against threats to self-esteem" (1967, p. 55). This is a rather standard tenet derived from ego psychology. Satir does not cite the origins of her notion of self-esteem, however, nor does she define what she means by "self." Is a "self" what we call the "ego" and nothing more? Does it include the unconscious? If we posit self-esteem as a universal feature of existence, how can we explain cultures in which it is subordinated to the integrity of the group? More urgently, perhaps, how do we account for behavior that violently drives self-esteem out of existence?

One can, of course, find examples of comparable oversimplification and crude use of language in most family therapy texts. Why, then, are Satir's works singled out as "not deep"? It may be because Satir aims toward accessibility in her written style; she does not believe that truth lies in its concealment, as the "new epistemologists" seem to (see chapter 11). It seems to be the case in our culture that obscurantism rather than clarity is what is scientifically commanding. Academicians seem not to trust a theory they can understand. It is well known that when social science, for example, was attempting to gain respectability within the university world in the 1950s, it chose to adopt the language of the hard sciences. (A professor at Yale has referred to this tendency as "physics envy.") It is no accident that the "avant-garde" in family therapy talk about "recursive loops" and "schismogenesis" and not "empathy" and "love."

Satir's work is not only accessible, it accessibly discusses *nurturance,* a matter so taboo under patriarchy that it must always be disguised as "unconditional positive regard" or "positive countertransference" or "multidirectional partiality." Satir, undaunted by the taboo, writes unapologetically about the uses of care, trust, and even affection in the psychotherapeutic situation. She believes that whatever therapists can offer to patients "to expedite learning and exchange (touching, holding hands, asking the patient to do him a favor, sitting comfortably as peers do) is utilized to help the patient grow within the context of the relationship" (1967, p. 182). And, in fact, anyone who has observed Satir at work knows that she uses all of these techniques and more. She does family sculpting, and she holds and rocks people in her lap, in her effort to nourish the famished infant soul within the pained adult.

I would not argue that such therapeutic particulars are essential to good therapy. The potential for therapeutic camps to divide on the issue of "how far to go" in therapeutic nurturing is well known. (It was in part over the issue of hugging the patient that Freud broke with Ferenczi.) The point here is simply to underline the fact that what is trivialized in Satir's work is what is actually the essence of therapy: compassion and the creation of a healing relationship.

The scorn that some therapists show for work such as Satir's cannot reflect merely a reticence about veering away from traditional talking therapy. Certainly, to ask a patient to scrub the floor in the middle of the night or to throw food in the garbage, as some strategic therapists do, is more outlandish than anything Satir does in therapy. Nonetheless, the issue of nurturing patients seems to raise more anxiety in therapists than any other kind of intervention. Nurturing is too closely bound to our wish/fear of dependency on woman, our first "other," our tie to life, the proof of both our goodness and our vulnerability, as Dinnerstein has so beautifully narrated it (1976). If Satir is seen as the "mother" of family therapy, there can be no doubt that she will be the object of our conflicting maternal passions.

Common Ground with Feminism

Satir's belief that the essence of therapy is the relationship between therapist and patient is quite compatible with feminism. She is concerned with helping people resolve symptoms, but never is that the ultimate goal of her therapy. Satir has not written much about gender, but she does work clinically toward helping people transcend their gender roles in therapy by supporting women to succeed in both the public and the private worlds, and by helping men to experience and express emotion. Satir said in our 1984 interview: "A piece of what I've always done is to help people to integrate their maleness and femaleness. I am my cognitive side and my affective side." Satir also mentioned that she thought women were blamed more than men in family therapy. She commented, "Mothers are expected to give more and they can never give enough, so people get mad at them. Women have either been dumped on or put on a pedestal, and that's the same thing." It is interesting that even in "The Family of Angels," published in 1967, Satir showed the ability to confront both the father and the mother. In fact, in that interview, she confronted the father first. An important way Satir proposes for therapists to deal with their tendency to blame mothers is to go through their own family "reconstruction" to understand the personal "baggage" they bring to the therapy room.

Another aspect of Satir's work that also touches on feminism is the issue of naming. In "The Family of Angels," Satir says good-bye to the family and shakes hands, saying each of their names: Lois, Gary, and so on. Satir does this often, asking people in the family what they like to be called and sometimes lingering over the fine point of what it means, for example, to be called "Suzanne" as opposed to "Sue." She believes that attention to names shows respect and caring, as well as the ability to differentiate among the family members. This is perhaps striking only in contrast with the other founding parents of family therapy. It was mentioned in the discussion of Nathan Ackerman (chapter 2) that he fumbled with the names of the Hillcrest family. There is a videotape of a session with Salvador Minuchin in which he asks the mother her name more than once in the course of a session, without apology.* Carl Whitaker avoids the issue altogether at times, referring to fathers as "Dad," mothers as "Mom," and siblings as "Sis" or "Junior," and so on. I have attended many family therapy conferences in which at least one trusting soul approached the microphone to ask, "Dr. X, did you forget the father's name to make him work harder, or to get him angry with you? Or was it to remind the family that you are just a consultant, not permanently attached to them?" The answer from Dr. X is nearly always, "I am just bad with names."

To be "bad with names" is not the same kind of handicap for a therapist as having poor penmanship or a trick knee. Naming, as Satir knows, is a profoundly important human activity. Naming is a tool of induction (as when we classify the chemical elements), a way of asserting power (as when we label certain acts as criminal), and a way of cherishing (as when we call people by fond diminutives). Naming has historically been a way of locating individuals in their social class, and it still operates in that way. People with advanced degrees are called by their titles; secretaries are called by first names or pet names. In chapter 12 we will discuss the idea that power itself is the power of naming; that is, to construct history, and thus to select what merits the record, is precisely to name some things as deserving the life of memory while expunging others.

I will take this opportunity to state one way that family therapy needs to change. To some, this suggestion may seem utterly obvious; to others, it will be disqualified as "too feminine." It is this: therapists must know their patients' names. Therapists must know how to *pronounce* their patients' names. Therapists must let patients know what they should call them. Even when entering a family for a one-session consultation, the therapist should know everyone's name. Finally, therapists who are "just bad with names" should just practice remembering.

_____

*See "A Family with Whitaker and Minuchin," available through the Philadelphia Child Guidance Clinic.

The Limitations of Satir's Work

Most family therapists are more skilled in clinical practice than at theory making, and Satir is no exception. She does not present a rigorous critique of the theories that preceded family therapy any more than male therapists have done. In terms of being able to situate the family historically, Satir makes only a token effort. She makes reference to the effects of the Industrial Revolution on the family, but these comments are confined to a few pages and do not allow a comprehensive analysis.

Satir's viewpoint is a thoroughly humanistic one, and through examining her work we can see both the necessity and the limitations of humanism. Satir's fallacy is the fallacy of believing that one can change the world by appealing to principles of therapeutic change alone, ignoring the global political changes that must be understood and grappled with. Satir said in our 1984 interview: "If tomorrow morning, every school, every family, every workplace had a transformation in the middle of the night to love and value themselves and treat others likewise, you know we would transform like *that!*" [snapping her fingers]. This is hardly a theory of social renewal. It cannot help us understand the extraordinarily complex problems of development in the Third World nations, nor the dismantling of weapon systems, nor the bitter mystery of AIDS. There are *reasons* that people do not decide in the middle of the night—or by the light of day—to love and work as well as they might. Freud tried to explain those reasons, using terms like *eros, thanatos, repression, neurosis.* Feminist commentators, using the concepts of sex-class, hegemony, and the ubiquitous love/hatred of woman, have also tried to make sense of the fact that we cannot easily change ourselves or our systems. Satir, however, has no theory that will help explain violence or the evil that has broken individuals and entire peoples on the wheel of history. Low self-esteem simply cannot account for the eradication of entire nations.

Moreover, although Satir has participated in and run women's groups, she clearly does not see as part of her project the building of a feminist therapy. Satir emphasizes, "I am for *personhood.* I want to help women find their self-worth and take their place in society. But not at the expense of men." Her extreme caution, although understandable, separates her from social and sexual radicalism.

Virginia Satir courageously lived through the experience of being the only woman among those who launched the field of family therapy. All women can learn from her about how to work within the dominant order without becoming demoralized. She recounted one anecdote that is particularly instructive: "Years ago I was on a panel with Murray Bowen, and at the end of my presentation Murray said in front of a large audience, 'Isn't Virginia wonderful? She gets to all the right places by all the wrong means.' And then he got up to kiss me. I could have used that as a downer. But *I* have something to do with how I respond to that." Satir's equanimity in this encounter with the proponent of "rational man" is forever instructive.

5

Salvador Minuchin: The Matter of Functionalism

THE WORK of Salvador Minuchin is known to family therapists throughout the world. Minuchin is perhaps second to none in creating therapeutic enactments and helping family members redefine their plight in a way that illuminates every member's participation in it. Minuchin's work has been extremely influential; his classic *Families and Family Therapy* (1974) has been translated into eleven languages and has sold over 100,000 copies in the United States alone. Minuchin is known for his interest in the politics of certain extrafamilial systems, which is one feature of his work that overlaps with feminism.

Common Ground with Feminism

Although Minuchin has never written about gender as a category or about sexual politics in the family, neither does he overtly prescribe sex roles for men and women. In one of his later books (1981), moreover, he makes a statement clearly demonstrating respect for nontraditional families, specifically, for families in which the adult couple is not legally married or is not heterosexual: "This [couple's] agreement does not have to be legal to be significant, and our limited clinical experience with homosexual couples with children suggests that family therapy concepts are as valid with them as with heterosexual couples with children" (Minuchin and Fishman 1981, p. 16).

Minuchin's therapy does not reify the symptom as much as strategic therapy does. Whereas the strategic therapist learns enough about the family's relationships to remove the symptom, Minuchin works conversely to use the symptom to instruct him in the transformation of family structure. His goal is to help the family reorganize so that it will be less likely to develop symptoms and also to enhance its sheer potential for growth. Minuchin thus casts his role not as a doctor (as Ackerman did) or a salesman (as Haley seems to) or a "tickler of the unconscious" (as Whitaker might), but as a "distant relative to the family"—an image much more compatible with feminism than the others. It is an image I find particularly helpful because it provides a balance between closeness and separateness between therapist and family. A distant cousin, for example, who sees her extended family only occasionally will behave with the respect that their unfamiliarity requires, but also with the caring and loyalty that their kinship allows. Minuchin correctly notes that the charge against him by Thomas Szasz of "meddling" in families (cf. Simon 1984) is basically specious. All therapists "meddle," whether their style is that of Minuchin, Satir, Haley, or Szasz himself.

Minuchin does not discount insight in the way the strategic therapists do. He hopes that the family will learn to understand something about their "dance of transactional patterns." He has said in seminars at the Philadelphia Child Guidance Clinic that the therapist can help the family toward a more correct epistemology: instead of seeing itself as a group of individuals including one patient, the family can come to see itself as a "multibodied organism." Minuchin is not, however, interested in family history; he does not work toward helping the family see the relationship between their dance and the dance of the family of origin, a step that is important to many feminist therapists (e.g., Goldhor Lerner 1986, Layton 1984).

A final common item between structural family therapy and feminist therapy is the concern with the social and political events outside the family. Minuchin's own commitment to social issues is evident from his personal history (cf. Simon 1984). His first job as a psychiatrist involved working with poor delinquent boys at the Wiltwyck School. In 1967 he published, along with three co-authors, *Families of the Slums,* the only book in the field about poor families. Along with several colleagues, he initiated a program at the Philadelphia Child Guidance Clinic to train black men and women from the community as family therapists.

Minuchin's views overlap with feminist views even to the extent that he criticizes the entire profession of family therapy for having "failed" by limiting itself to the therapy room. In a 1984 interview (cf. Simon 1984),

Minuchin commented that "systems thinking" has really not influenced institutions outside family therapy, such as juvenile courts, mental hospitals, and welfare departments, where such thinking is needed. Minuchin notes in that interview that there are even questions about family therapy on child psychiatry boards—a redoubtable sign of its assimilation by the status quo.

Despite these important areas of overlap, however, there are a number of problems with structural family therapy from the feminist point of view which are evident in both theory and practice. Minuchin's clinical work is well known through his use of live interviews with families and through videotapes. A criticism of one of his most famous consultations, "Taming Monsters," will illuminate some of these problems. Minuchin himself says in the commentary portion of "Taming Monsters" that it represents many of the important aspects of his work; it also illustrates issues for which he has been criticized by feminists, for example, unbalancing through the mother and elevating the father.

Case Example: "Taming Monsters"

The family in this tape consists of a father, a mother, and two daughters, ages four and two. The family has sought therapy because the four-year-old is defiant, bossy, and hard to control. Minuchin sees the family as a consultant to Dr. Fishman, who has seen them for six sessions. I will summarize the interview before commenting on the work itself. (An edited transcript of portions of the videotape appears in Minuchin and Fishman's *Family Therapy Techniques.*)

The consultation has three phases: in the first, Minuchin creates an enactment and coaches the mother to gain control of the little girl. In the second phase, he asks both parents to play puppets with the girl on the floor. In the third, he sends the children outside to the playroom and talks with the parents alone.

Structural family therapy focuses on boundaries and generational hierarchies in families. The problem with generational hierarchy in this particular family becomes immediately clear: the child appears to be in charge and refuses to do what her mother asks. The mother is overly deferential to the daughter; she ends each instruction with a self-defeating question mark, e.g., "Sit down, OK?" The husband states in rather authoritarian tones, "I *make* her do it," and both parents agree that his harsher style gets results with the child. At this point in the tape Minuchin describes the system as follows: "An impossible little girl, an ineffective mother, and maybe an authoritarian father." This initial phase ends when the mother reaches some success in settling the child down.

In the second phase, Minuchin creates a memorable therapeutic moment in which parents and daughter play together. The uncontrollable "monster" becomes a delightful and engaging child as she plays with her parents. The father balks at first at the request to play; he doesn't want to sit on the floor. He puts the puppet on his hand and then quickly takes it off. He does manage to stay with his wife and daughter throughout the sequence, however, and Minuchin praises him effusively for his ability to play.

In the third stage, Minuchin talks with the parents alone, and this "unbalancing" phase becomes the most controversial part of the consultation. In structural family therapy, the therapist often unbalances a rigid family system by putting pressure on, or "attacking," one member, a technique that makes change resonate through the entire system. In the unbalancing stage of "Taming Monsters," it is the mother who is the fulcrum for change.

Minuchin's assessment of this family is that the girl acts up because she has an ally in her mother; the child is "standing on the mother's shoulders." In the discussion at the end of the interview, the mother explains that she is soft and indulgent with the girls in reaction to her husband's impatience and harshness with them; he has a "short fuse." She states that she is afraid of his temper and is concerned that he might hurt the girls. Minuchin tells the father that the problem is that his wife does not understand him. "Some way or other your wife has a strange image of you and your ability to understand and be flexible" (p. 167). When the father, with Minuchin's coaching, tells the mother that the daughter doesn't listen to her because mother is her ally and acts more like a "playmate" to her, Minuchin congratulates the husband and tells him to repeat it to his wife so that she will "understand" it.

Minuchin has succeeded in joining with this stolid, peripheral father. But what of the issue of father's harshness with the children? Minuchin tracks the issue of his temper by asking him, "When was the last time you beat your wife?" (p. 168). When the husband replies that he never has, the wife interjects very much in earnest, "No. I'm really proud of that." In the course of the discussion, it turns out that the husband's father was an extremely violent man who used to "tear the house apart" and that the husband had put his fist and shoe through a wall in their home. The mother says at one point, "I've seen the temper and he's completely out of control when it takes over" (p. 168). Minuchin tells the father: "She's selling you a bag of lies! Please do not buy it" (p. 170). Minuchin stands up and throws his own shoe against the wall, asking the father how hard he threw it, clearly legitimizing the action.

In the final exchange of the consultation, the following dialogue takes place:

MINUCHIN [*to the wife*]: You need to change.

MOTHER: Me?

MINUCHIN: You in relation to him, because it is the way in which you are compensating for what you assume is his authoritarian, rigid parenting. It is the same as if you were saying that you need to be soft because he is too hard.

MOTHER: Yeah, right.

MINUCHIN: So something between you two needs to change. [*To husband*]: Can you change her?

FATHER: I don't know.

MINUCHIN: That's your job. You need to change her.

It is difficult to assess the potential for violence in this family on the basis of one interview. Many people who are not "monsters" are capable of putting their fists and shoes through a wall. Thinking systemically, however, it is important to know not only the current limits of the husband's violence but also what the wife does to keep those limits where they are. Some women *can* keep their partners from violent outbursts, but only by cowering, taking tranquilizers, or accommodating in other ways. There are probably cases in which male violence is only a family myth. However, because protective shelters for women are filled beyond capacity with those who have had an arm or a nose or ribs broken by a male partner,* it is more logical when a woman is afraid of a man's temper to ask *him* to convince *her* that she is safe, rather than for a therapist to press her to stop being fearful.

At least as important as what Minuchin has to say about this family, however, is what he does not say. It is interesting that one of the portions of the videotape that was not chosen for transcription in *Family Therapy Techniques* contains the mother's statement about how tiring it is to take care of two preschoolers full-time. She does, in fact, look overwhelmed

---

*Lenore Walker (1979) estimates that one in two women will be physically abused by a man she loves at some time in her life. See also the research of Dobash and Dobash 1977.

and fatigued as she chases her four-year-old around the therapy room while her husband looks on. Watching this videotape, one is apt to think of the Timberlawn researchers and their description of mothers in the "adequate" American family: obese, overwhelmed with responsibility, and without access to outside sources of activity and esteem which the husbands have.

We are not told whether the mother in the "Taming Monsters" case has any outside interests or supports, but there is mention that she is in almost daily contact with her "controlling" mother, who "emphasizes and supports her incompetence" (p. 170). It is not unlikely that she herself feels like putting her fists and shoes through walls in frustration at her life, but does not do so because of the culture's proscription on women's display of aggression. Perhaps her daughter's defiance is a representation of her own would-be rebellion at the husband for his "short fuse" or at other aspects of her life. A feminist approach to this family would take these issues into account before formulating an intervention. This beleaguered mother needs to be empowered to act with proper maternal authority. One would want to minimize the possibility of her leaving a session feeling even more disappointed in herself and and even more confused about her own anger than she was initially. (The doctor, after all, has said that this woman is afraid of something that does not exist.) Simply put, Minuchin has left the family in "Taming Monsters" less father-absent at the cost of making it no less patriarchal, and arguably *more* so.

I do not mean to imply that therapists should never use the "unbalancing technique" or that mothers should never be the ones who are confronted. Most people have experienced the "slap of the Zen master" as very valuable at some point in their lives. We would not want Zen masters to slap only female monks, however.

Minuchin, of course, does confront fathers at times (particularly in later stages of therapy),* but his tendency to unbalance through the mother is much more pervasive. One can observe it both in tapes such as "Taming Monsters" and in more recent interviews (e.g., *A Family with Whitaker and Minuchin*, 1981†). Furthermore, Minuchin himself has never denied this pattern. In an interview in 1985, he responded to questions about feminist criticism of his therapeutic approach to mothers: "If they're [feminists are] saying 'Viewing mothers as overinvolved and the father as the potential separator is a skewed perspective reinforced by the masculine culture,' they are right. If they are saying, 'Minuchin uses that intervention fre-

---

*In the "Taming Monsters" case, there were no later stages, however, as the family terminated after two additional sessions.

†Available through the Philadelphia Child Guidance Clinic.

quently,' they are also right. But if they're saying I'm a knee-jerk chauvinist who doesn't understand the social context in which families live, they are wrong" (Simon 1984, pp. 66–67). Minuchin, however, does not analyze the "masculine culture" in which families live in any of his books, even in the one published during the height of the women's movement (Minuchin 1974). In the same interview, he claims that unbalancing through the mother is "not a political statement," but it is, of course. It could not be anything else.

Some therapists would argue that although it is sexist to rely more on mothers than fathers for change, it cannot be avoided. It is a social fact that women are more involved with children, know more about them, and are more eager to hear about their mistakes. Fathers, these therapists argue, are socialized to be defensive, not to seek help from therapists, and to define themselves more in relation to work than to children. To push on the family's most peripheral member would be foolhardy, according to this argument. It might result in father's dropping out or even pulling the entire family out of treatment—something that is arguably worse for mothers than unbalancing through them.

There is definitely some validity to this argument, and in some cases going through the mother might be in her best interests. Assuming for a moment that this were the case with the family just described, one would want to learn the thinking process of the therapist. As mentioned in chapter 1, the purpose of criticizing the ways in which family therapy recapitulates the mother-blaming of the larger social order is not to suggest that we should simplemindedly turn the tables. The purpose is to problematize the issue, to make it a consistent part of our discussion of families. The videotape of "Taming Monsters" would be much less sexist as a teaching tool if the therapist had described in his commentary how he came to the decision to side with father instead of mother, and what the pros and cons of such a choice might be.

I think students of structural family therapy should understand that an equally effective consultation could have been done with this family by telling the father instead of the mother, "You need to change," given this father's short temper and peripherality and the fact that the mother seems to need some relief.

Feminist family therapist Molly Layton has argued (1984) that treating fathers in therapy with kid gloves is not only unfair to mothers but condescending to the fathers themselves. Layton believes that it is more respectful to say to a peripheral father, "You need to get more involved here," or, building in intensity, "If you ran your office this way, you'd be fired."

It may be that most of us lean on mothers because we have seen the master therapists working this way and, conversely, have seen few examples of therapists challenging fathers. We imitate our teachers and then have the enormously self-reinforcing experience of seeing the traditional moves "work." Why change a winning solution?

If one believes that solving the family's problem is the only thing that matters, then the question of how one unbalances a system is just a matter of style. But if one sees therapy as inevitably a political matter—one that reflects cultural bias and that "feeds back" to amplify or dampen that bias—then this issue is central indeed.

Some therapists have argued that the theory of structural family therapy is itself "value-neutral," and that it should not be confused with the idiosyncratic clinical style of Minuchin or any of its practitioners. They argue that structural family therapy could be taken over "as is" by feminist practitioners, who would simply attach to it a progressive theory of gender, and who would not pick on mothers. This is not so easy or plausible a task as it might seem to some, largely because of one of the major theoretical underpinnings of structural family therapy (SFT), namely, structural functionalism, discussed in the following section.

The Functionalist Foundations of Structural Family Therapy

Structural family therapy rests on certain principles of structural functionalism, a conceptual system that does not fit neatly with feminism and that, in fact, has frequently been criticized for its political conservatism (e.g., A. Gouldner 1970, Poster 1978, Chodorow 1978). Virginia Goldner (1985) has correctly pointed out that *all* family therapy schools owe many of their key ideas to Talcott Parsons, the prolific sociologist known as the father of American structural functionalism. Parsons's concepts are most salient in structural family therapy simply because they are not blended with Pragmatic, Buberian, or existentialist thought in the way the theories of Haley, Nagy, and Whitaker are (respectively).

Neither Minuchin nor any of the major living family therapists adopted Parsons's particular sexual division of labor, but the basic categories for conceptualizing families—the idea that the family can be said to have a "structure" and that it performs "functions" that involve "contracting" and "role negotiations" and that it must "adapt" to society—all derive from Parsons's work.* Structural functionalism dominated all of American social science during the 1950s and 1960s, the very period that saw the gestation and birth of family therapy. These notions have become so integrated into our ways of thinking that it is sometimes difficult to see the functionalist point of view *as* a point of view. Functionalism has come to seem "natural." Students sometimes ask, in fact: "What is so bad about the words *structure* and *function?* How else could one view the social system except as parts that must adapt to the whole?"

The best way to illustrate the worldview implied by structural functionalism is to contrast it with a worldview that differs drastically from it, e.g., the Marxist one. Whereas functionalist analysis emphasizes how the parts of a society fit together like organs to form an intact organism, Marxist analysis sees society as composed of conflicting socioeconomic classes as well as the ideas associated with those classes. Functionalists can explain how parts of a system fit together, but they are hard-pressed to explain how the parts could be fundamentally at odds with one another. In the functionalist logic, if a social phenomenon occurs, it must have been caused by some social "need." Thus, Parsons might say that after World War II, society "needed" women to return home to provide the expressive role. He would not view this phenomenon above all as one more example of women's private destinies being shrunk to fit the needs of the group. Functionalist explanations can justify almost anything in terms of some putative social need. Functionalist historians have even argued that lynchings and witch hunts serve a social need, i.e., a cathartic or "therapeutic" need. Therapeutic for *whom?* one might well ask. (See Daly [1978] on the subject of the functionalist fallacy.)

Functionalist explanations can be used to evaluate whether given parts are functioning effectively relative to the system, but they have no concepts with which to evaluate the rationality or worth of the whole— something that is the trademark of Marxist and other radical social theories, which tend to ask first and foremost, "For *whom* does this system 'work'? Whom does it sacrifice?" It is interesting in this light to note that Talcott Parsons was dubbed the "anti-Marx" by one radical scholar (Poster 1978) since Parsons viewed society as a giant corporation or factory whose departments performed different jobs, contributing to the smooth func-

*Most family therapists, including Minuchin, do not acknowledge Parsons's work, but this is simply part of the pattern of concentrating on clinical and methodological issues and minimizing issues of theory and intellectual roots. Intellectual legacies can be discerned even when explicit citation is not made, through a tracking of the author's lexicon and conceptual organization. It should also be mentioned that functionalism is not the *only* influence apparent in Minuchin's work. One sees also the legacy of certain humanist writers. See Gerald Erickson (1984) on this subject.

tioning of the whole. Functionalists also use the metaphor of society as an organism, with institutions like the family functioning as organs or organelles. As two critics of functionalism have stated: "If a social institution is as necessary to society as the liver is to the body, it would be dangerous to change or remove it. . . . By implying, without arguing the point, that the fundamental goal of society is the same as that of an individual organism—surviving and maintaining a steady state—the organismic metaphor is politically conservative" (Skolnick and Skolnick 1971, p. 11).

The organismic model of society is implied by many family therapies, but it is nowhere more profoundly endorsed than in structural family therapy as described by Minuchin and Fishman in *Family Therapy Techniques* (1981). The authors introduce their second chapter with this quotation from Lewis Thomas, which represents functionalist ideas *par excellence:* "There is a tendency for living things to join up, establish linkages, live inside each other, return to earlier arrangements, get along whenever possible. This is the way of the world" (p. 11). Minuchin and Fishman comment on this quotation as follows: "In human terms, joining up in order to 'get along' usually means some sort of family group. The family is the natural context for both growth and healing, and it is the context that the family therapist will depend on for the actualization of therapeutic goals" (p. 11).

If the family can be considered the natural context for healing and growth, it must also be considered the natural context for violence and exploitation. Functionalist theorists from Parsons in the 1950s to Minuchin in the 1980s have been able to write books about the American family without referring to the staggering rate of wife beating and father-daughter incest within it, because their theories do not sensitize them as much to conflicts of interest as to "mutual accommodation" and "joining up." Even in Minuchin's most recent book, *Family Kaleidoscope* (1984), the subtitle of which is "Images of Violence and Healing," some of the most vital violence-related issues never even appear. In the section on "violence," Minuchin describes a famous parent murder, a relatively well known child murder, and a day in the British family court system when children are put into residential placements. These chapters are again significant for what they leave out, wife beating in particular.

When confronted about the enormous problem of wife abuse in the American family, Minuchin has again expressed the functionalist bias of valuing the continued functioning of the whole as opposed to emphasizing the conflicting interests of the constituent parts. Minuchin said in an interview in 1984: "The feminist movement has opened the ugly Pandora's box of wife abuse. But the solution it has moved to is saving the victims by dismembering the family. Many women's shelters prohibit entrance not only to the spouse of the victim, but also to male therapists" (Simon 1984, p. 31). In the first place, some research has suggested that using a women's shelter reduces a woman's risk of being beaten again, whether or not she returns to her partner (cf. Giles-Sims 1983). Furthermore, if a violent family is "dismembered," the responsibility for the schism lies with the abuser and not with the shelter. What this passage reflects is the assumption that we already know that families can expect a certain amount of misfortune and violence, of which wife beating lies within some normal range. Wife beating itself, according to this logic, does not dismember families. One can see here the shadow of the rather long thread of the Timberlawn research, which told us a decade before *Kaleidoscope* that "adequate" families have functional fathers and dysfunctional mothers. That's just the way it goes.

Minuchin is, in fact, very clear on the point that "the therapist joins the family not to educate it or socialize it, but rather to repair or modify the family's own functioning so it can better perform these tasks" (1974, p. 14). Minuchin also writes, very much in the Parsonian tradition, "The family will change as society changes. . . . Change always moves from society to the family, never from the smaller unit to the larger" (1974, pp. 49–50). These statements obscure the fact that society changes only as men and women change it. To believe that society "evolves" on its own is again to accept the dubious metaphor of society as a giant organism.

A feminist family therapy cannot rest on functionalist principles; it must begin with a critical and historical understanding of the family. It also requires a nonfunctionalist language. I have argued elsewhere that to speak of families' pain, darkness, and pleasure in terms of "functional effectiveness" and "dysfunction" dehumanizes our work. Minuchin and Fishman (1981) employ this language consistently, referring, for example, to families generating "mutual expectations" that continue on "automatic pilot, as it were—as a matter of mutual accommodation and functional effectiveness" (p. 52). Such language can be used to normalize any reciprocal behavior pattern in a family or group, from the most benign forms of cooperation to the most cynical forms of dominance and submission.

I once attended a family therapy seminar on the West Coast in which an instructor asked (for the purpose of promoting critical thought), "Why is incest bad?" All of the responses about "inverted hierarchies" and "inappropriate coalitions" had the patent (if unintended) effect of making emotional and physical crimes of power sound indistinguishable from the scuffles of everyday family life. Feminists, it seems to me, must always remain fixed on the side of writers such as George Orwell on the issue of

67

repudiating vague and mechanical language which can be used to "defend the indefensible."

Finally, it is doubtful that a feminist therapy could follow the structural-functionalist model, because the latter takes too little account of the family's personal history and treats problems largely as they appear in the present. Many feminists believe that explicit attention to one's personal history is as important to empowerment as attention to social history.

There are many feminists who use elements of structural family therapy in their work, e.g., creating enactments, building intensity, unbalancing, and focusing on generational differences. However, the ahistorical and functionalist aspects of structural family therapy leave many theoretical faults. Minuchin himself has helped make thousands of families less father-absent by bringing peripheral fathers into treatment. The task that remains is to address the issue of patriarchy as well.

6

Ivan Boszormenyi-Nagy: The Limitations of Humanism II

THE WORK of Ivan Boszormenyi-Nagy, like that of Virginia Satir, reflects an attempt to create a family therapy that is fully humanistic. Like Satir, Nagy is not interested merely in removing symptoms but in helping people to build authentic relationships. He relies on the principles of theologian Martin Buber, and thus writes in terms of creating "I and thou" relationships within families and between therapist and family.

In his book with Geraldine Spark, *Invisible Loyalties* (1973), Nagy describes his "contextual therapy" as an integration of humanism with key concepts from psychoanalysis, object-relations theory, general-systems theory, and dialectics. Nagy and Spark choose a powerful set of idioms, but the task of integration is not accomplished, and their text is often difficult to follow.

One of the key concepts of contextual therapy is that of conflicting loyalties. Nagy attempts to discover ways in which loyalties to parents and grandparents keep people "stuck" in patterns that limit their capabilities as parents and spouses. The unresolved obligation to the family of origin is called the "original loyalty." Contextual therapists work with entire families, often including extended family members as well, in order to tally up and resolve the "unpaid emotional debts" that are bequeathed across generations.

Common Ground with Feminism

The work of Nagy, while not explicitly feminist in any way, contains within it a number of concepts that share a common ground with feminism. Nagy's work does not contain overtly disparaging images of women, as Ackerman's work does. Moreover, in contrast to Bowen's emphasis on rationality and objectivity, Nagy elevates an entirely different set of constructs. Nagy asks, in fact, whether the traditionally valued characteristics can really help people deal with life's important dilemmas. In *Invisible Loyalties*, for example, Nagy and Spark ask:

> Can it ever be boiled down to subjective versus objective reality testing whether one continues to be available to an aging sick parent or considers him as economically a non-productive burden? We believe that the essence of the solution of such questions does not lie in the extent of cognitive objectivity or effectiveness of coping, but in the courage and ethical sensitivity of one's responding to a call for integrity, an integrity that lies in the totality of a life-long parent-child relationship, rather than in any one person. [1973, pp. 168–69]

Although it is easy to get lost in the gnarled syntax, it is nonetheless possible to discern that the words *sensitivity, courage,* and *integrity* occur much more frequently in Nagy's work than words such as *authority, individuation,* and *rationality.* The contextual therapist's emphasis on the former over the latter, and on the importance of remembering the past as opposed to ignoring it, overlap with the values of most feminist therapists (e.g., Baker Miller 1976, Eichenbaum and Orbach 1983).

One gauge of the sexual politics of a given therapeutic approach is whether any feminist therapists have adopted it for their own clinical purposes, and feminists *have* been attracted to Nagy's work. An excellent illustration is Denise Gelinas's (1983) article on working with families in which parent-child incest has occurred. In her article, Gelinas criticized other family therapy approaches (e.g., Machotka, Pittman, and Flomenhaft 1967) for blaming the mother, and sometimes the child as well, for the father's sexual abuse. Gelinas integrates a very intelligent "loyalty analysis" with a "power analysis" of incest, which places the responsibility completely with the adult. Gelinas writes that "at times children seek attention and affection in ways that can be construed as sexy; but it is the adult who has the knowledge and the responsibility to differentiate between affection and actual sexual contact" (p. 328).

Gelinas suggests that Nagy's concepts of loyalty, fairness, and the "re-volving slate" are very constructive in doing responsible therapy with incestuous families. She points out that incest victims usually do feel loyalty to the abusing parent, and that this loyalty must be taken into account if one is to make a therapeutic alliance with the patient. Gelinas uses Nagy's concepts to describe a typical profile of the incest victim: "A child will 'allow' herself to be parentified in large part because of her loyalty toward her family, especially her parents. Because of this filial loyalty, children attempt to assist, reassure, and protect their parents, often at astonishingly young ages, and under pronounced parentification a com-plete role reversal can occur, with the child caring for the parents. . . . Eventually the parentified child begins to meet the needs of other family members to the exclusion of her own" (p. 320).

It is clear that such daughters will grow up to be attracted to men with deep needs for a caretaker, men who are often immature, narcissistic, and even psychopathic. These qualities often characterize the male abuser, and so the cycle of father-daughter incest is repeated.

Sexual Politics in Nagy's Work

Despite the fact that there is great potential for the integration of contex-tual therapy with feminism, Nagy himself has not mentioned feminism, nor raised gender as a subject, in any of his written works to date. In his best-known work, *Invisible Loyalties* (1973), Nagy and Spark make only an oblique mention of women's needs, and this in a passage that is confused and misleading. The following is probably the most inscrutable commen-tary on the subject of women in the entire literature of family therapy:

> A sizeable number of *women* are joining in efforts at assertiveness and "libera-tion." For thousands of years, women have deserved and been accorded societal protection and privileges to compensate for their biologically determined vul-nerabilities. From the dawn of civilization it has concerned society that young women can be exploited by involuntary sexual participation through rape or seduction. . . . The physiological processes of menstruation, pregnancy, child-birth, lactation, etc. all tend to make women unilaterally vulnerable. They are entitled to receive compensatory measures from society so that reciprocal fair-ness can prevail. Otherwise, the mothering capacity of many women will be undermined by their feeling of unilateral, sex-limited exploitation. [P. 385]

What is insidious about this kind of writing is that it does not appear to be overtly misogynist, as does some of Ackerman's work. Its mystification lies precisely in its apparent support for "assertiveness" and societal "protection" of women against harm and violation, while at the same time perpetrating its own violence—denying the well-documented story of women's treatment in history (see chapter 10). Far from being concerned with women's needs, social mores and juridical practice have long made wife beating, wife raping, and sexual harassment acceptable.

It is instructive that the passage ends with an endorsement of continued "compensatory measures" for women, but not, apparently, for the benefit of women themselves. Rather, the point is to make sure that their "mothering capacity" is protected. The implication is, furthermore, that if the mothering capacity *is* undermined, it will be because of women's *feeling* that they are exploited, not because they are exploited.

There is no other statement about women or about feminism in *Invisible Loyalties* that might illuminate this passage, or "compensate" for it. Moreover, in 1981, eight years after its publication, Nagy's chapter in *The Handbook of Family Therapy* (Gurman and Kniskern 1981), written with David Ulrich, does not show any new sensitivity to gender or sexual politics. One might therefore predict that Nagy's clinical work, despite its strong humanism, would be characterized by the typical family therapy pattern of blaming or overimplicating mothers. It should be emphasized again that Nagy is not a therapist whom one would ever hear referring to a female patient as "a good piece," as Ackerman did (see chapter 2). On the contrary, his style is gentle and respectful and he has openly criticized therapists of other schools who "attack" or blame one family member in order to achieve a particular therapeutic goal. Nonetheless, there are subtle forms of mother-blaming throughout his work. In a chapter entitled "Family Therapy and Reciprocity Between Grandparents, Parents and Grandchildren," for example, three out of four case examples involve adult patients struggling with loyalties to female relatives only—to mothers, grandmothers, and great-grandmothers.

CASE EXAMPLE

An entire chapter in Nagy and Spark's *Invisible Loyalties* is devoted to the treatment of a family in which both parents were involved in abusing their four-year-old daughter. The child was hospitalized at two-and-a-half and at four years of age for beatings by the parents, who also used to place her in a closet without food when she had a temper tantrum. The other children were aged five, two, and one, and the mother, twenty-five, was pregnant once again. At first, the mother had wanted many children and did not try to prevent pregnancy. Later, however, when she decided on a tubal ligation, her husband refused to sign the necessary medical consent forms. When she became pregnant by him for the sixth time, however, he abandoned the family and went to live with another woman.

The account of this case offered by Nagy and Spark indicts the mother much more severely than the father. The authors describe the mother as "a very deprived, distrustful, paranoid person. She not only had strong unmet dependency needs, but revealed a split in object relations, with her mother being a good object and Leona being the bad one" (p. 293). As for the father, however, his deserting the home, according to the authors, "can be defined as a negative therapeutic reaction. Despite his wife's changed attitudes in the marital and parental relationship and his in-laws' reacceptance, nothing counterbalanced his basic reaction of feeling used and exploited. His 'unfinished business' with his family of origin interfered with the capacity to involve himself in a more constructive way with his children" (p. 293). These two descriptions evince a double standard: mother is mentally ill ("paranoid") and father has "unfinished business." Nagy and Spark did not invent the fact that people expect more from mothers than from fathers, but there is nothing in their work to challenge it.

Needless to say, in this particular case, both mother and father were egregiously troubled individuals. The mother, however, at least remained with the children. The father refused to visit his wife when the new baby was born, and also refused to see the therapist again. He was later jailed for nonsupport. He did, however, eventually sign "the necessary legal papers to have her tubes tied." The irony that this man—an abusive father who deserted six children—could still have the power to decide what this woman could do with her body is completely lost on Nagy and Spark; they do not even comment on it. Contextual therapists understand very well the legacy through which the abused child grows up to be an abusive adult. Because their view is blind to social history, however, they fail to see the link between this woman's inability to preside over her own physical functions and the criminal attacks on the child's body. The difference between the two acts is that the first is sanctioned by law and the second is not. The *link* between them is that both acts are part of a long tradition of socially defining women and children as property of husbands and fathers.

If this mother's integrity as a woman had not been violated through many generations, she would have had a different relationship to her female child. If the female body were not an object of extreme cultural ambivalence, the father too would have a different relationship to the daughter. These contextual issues are simply missing in Nagy's theory.

A Final Word on the Language of Contextual Therapy

The language of Nagy's contextual therapy includes key tropes that under-mine his humanism. His use of the concepts of "ledger" and "accounting" and "double accounting" serve to mix the language of humanist ethics with that of money and business. This use of buying-and-selling meta-phors to describe the human dilemma is antithetical to a feminist sensibil-ity. Nagy might well argue that in using the word *accounting,* he does not mean to promote the commodification of existence, but merely to use a term that corresponds to the way people actually think. There is indeed a large segment of the population that thinks of life in terms of a business and work ethic, but adopting this language as one's clinical idiom gives it unnecessary legitimacy. People who, under the wash of Western material-ism, are prone to think of their friendships as good or poor investments, and their romantic partners as potential career assets, can fit the accounting language comfortably into their relentlessly commercialized worldview. The mixing of money metaphors with theological ones brings to mind the Protestant sect of Calvinism, whose doctrines explicitly vindicate the entitled.

In short, although reading Nagy's work leaves one with no doubts about the humanistic intent and philosophical base of his work, that intent and that base are subtly eroded by the undertow of metaphor.

Nagy's work is instructive particularly because it is "so close and yet so far" from feminist therapy. Nagy's work, along with that of Satir, shows that humanism, as traditionally defined, is simply no guarantee at all against mother-blaming. No matter how benign the therapist, no matter how knowledgeable about legacies, this type of theory can lead one to the kind of treatment described in the child-abuse case cited here—and to see in it no contradiction with humanism.

Because what is human has so long been equated with what is male, humanism that is not explicitly feminist continually, quietly, and often unintentionally reinscribes the myth of Manolus into social history.

7

Strategic Family Therapy: Perfecting the Unexamined Life

STRATEGIC THERAPY is not associated with a single leader, as are structural, symbolic-experiential, and Bowen therapy. I will focus this critique on the *strategic* therapy of Chloé Madanes (1981, 1984) and the *problem-solving* therapy of Jay Haley (1976), alluding to other significant "strategists" in the process (e.g., the *brief therapists* of the Mental Research Institute [MRI] and of the Milwaukee group, and also Peggy Papp, Olga Silverstein, and their colleagues at the Ackerman Institute).

Strategic therapists, notwithstanding practical and theoretical differences among subgroups, believe in solving presenting problems with minimal emphasis on learning the family's history or generating insight. They usually do not insist on working with the entire family present, as other family therapists do. Strategic therapists are also known for their rejection of words such as *healing, growth,* and *transformation,* in favor of cybernetic and combat metaphors: *strategy, ploy, maneuver, sabotage,* and *tactic.* It has been suggested that these combat words reflect the cold-war language of the 1950s, when cybernetic science emerged (cf. Boscolo et al. 1987).

Strategic therapists hail as their mentor the late Milton Erickson, a maverick therapist who used unconventional directives and even hypnotic trances to help patients resolve their behavior problems. Haley (1984) recounts Erickson's treatment of an old man with insomnia by instructing him to rise at 2 A.M. to scrub the kitchen floor. The man, according to Erickson, was not suffering from anxiety or loneliness at night; he simply had "excess energy." Influenced by Erickson, contemporary strategic therapists relabel or "reframe" symptoms to make them seem more normal and less pathological.

Strategic therapists are known for their unusual methods of solving problems. They sometimes explicitly instruct the family *not* to change, for example. This is called the "therapeutic double bind" because if the family does change, then the goal has been reached, and if the family does not change, then its members are cooperating with the therapist, a sign of engagement with the treatment. Strategic therapists also prescribe to clients the very symptoms they brought in to change. For example, a woman who complained of having unsatisfactory relationships with men was told not to try to meet men for a while, and if she absolutely had to go out, she was to make herself less attractive in some way (Fisch, Weakland, and Segal 1983).

Strategic prescriptions may be quite ordinary, e.g., telling a wife not to cater to her depressed husband so that he will have to be more active (Fisch, Weakland, and Segal 1983), or quite outlandish, e.g., telling an abusive husband to fondle his wife's breast whenever he has the urge to hit her (Madanes 1984). The therapist's goal is to figure out how the symptom works in the system and then to determine the particular strategy, tactic, or countermove that might undo it. (Each of the prescriptions just described was reported by the respective authors to have eliminated the symptom.)

Strategic therapists are extremely goal-oriented and symptom-focused. They tend to show even less interest than other family therapists in understanding the family as an institution. Their texts offer no analysis of the contemporary family in context; rather, they plunge into questions of how to "create change" as expeditiously as possible.

Common Ground with Feminism

In the works of the strategic therapists, one finds no references to penis envy and no criticism of women who "wear the pants," as is the case with Ackerman's work. There are no discussions of overanxious or undifferentiated mothers, as in Bowen's work. In this regard, the writing of the strategic therapists is nonsexist.

Strategic therapists share with feminist therapists a manifest concern in being "helpful," in trying to bring relief to the client or family. This is in contrast to therapists such as Carl Whitaker (see chapter 8), who disclaim interest in problem resolution *per se* in favor of "shaking up the system" or "tickling the unconscious" of the family. In addition to Whitaker, there are psychoanalytic family therapists (e.g., Scharff and Scharff 1987) who define their goals almost exclusively in terms other than symptom relief. One might say that while some schools of therapy undervalue the goal of problem solving, strategic therapists grossly overvalue it.

It is noteworthy that strategic therapy can be used and has been used in ways that help women become stronger and more assertive. One example from Madanes (1981) will illustrate this point. A married woman with three children had been bulimic for thirteen years. Her husband was a workaholic and very withholding; he forbade her to spend money, for example, although they were well off. Madanes describes the woman as follows: "She was the subdued, dependent wife in every way, except that she vomited." Madanes concludes that the symptom was a way for the wife to rebel against her husband without appearing to rebel. She states: "If this interpersonal gain could be maintained by some other means, without the symptom, then the symptom would disappear. That is, if the symptom was a way of getting back at her husband and if another way, just as effective or better could be provided, then the wife would stop vomiting" (p. 40).

Madanes reframed the bulimia as "wasting food" and instructed the wife to throw five-dollars' worth of food into the garbage each day. Her husband was to do the shopping during the week to make sure that his wife and children had what they needed, and he was to verify that she had thrown out the stipulated amount of food each day. Other tasks were given within twenty-two sessions spanning twenty-three months. At the end of treatment, the wife had stopped vomiting and was taking courses and was "interested in her own development." The husband had become more responsive to the wife, and they had gone on vacation together.

It is not difficult to understand why this treatment worked. The woman was able to get back at her husband by wasting money, and she was probably getting more close attention from him than she had before, since he was involved in each step of treatment. In this case, strategic methods were used to make a wife less submissive to her husband. However, there is nothing in strategic therapy that would rule out making a wife *more* submissive to her husband if such a change would remove a symptom.

Sexual Politics

In the literature of strategic family therapy, as in the family therapy literature in general, there is no discussion of gender as a category or of problems such as incest, spouse abuse, and women's double shift of housework and outside job. In the strategic literature, references to feminism *per se* are infrequent and dismissive. For example, Arthur Bodin, in his chapter on the Mental Research Institute (MRI) in *The Handbook of Family Therapy* (Gurman and Kniskern 1981), mentions "the feminist movement" only to say that the late Don Jackson beat feminists to the punch. Bodin writes: "Jackson was a man ahead of his time in attacking sex-role stereotypes before the feminist movement had given birth to the concept of 'androgyny' "* (p. 274).

Jackson did write in progressive terms about sex roles in his 1968 book with William Lederer, *The Mirages of Marriage.* Bodin's implication, however—intended or not—is that nothing significant has been added by feminists since Jackson wrote: "Today both sexes can perform most social functions equally well, and the rigid social resistance to role diffusion is becoming a genuine frustration to those who seek self-expression in roles outside the boundaries of their defined sex-roles" (p. 36). Although this is a refreshing change from a comment on the same topic by Ackerman, Jackson's view of gender and women's position in society lacked both depth and accuracy, even for the time.†

In any case, to return to the critique of contemporary strategic therapy, a tendency not to prescribe gender-typed behavior and the occasional use of strategies to help a submissive wife assert herself do not mean that a therapeutic approach is generally nonsexist. For example, the mere fact

---

*It is true that some feminists endorse the idea of androgyny, but other feminists disdain it, preferring to emphasize the differences between the sexes. In any case, it is fallacious to say that the feminist movement "gave birth" to the concept, since Plato used it in his famous dialogue *The Symposium.* In that dialogue, written in the fourth century b.c., Plato mentions that the word *androgyny* has taken on "derogatory" connotations—meaning that 2,000 years ago, the word was already old.

†In the same book, Jackson makes the outrageously misleading statement that "women control and spend more money than do men" (p. 34), and he does not discuss at all the disparity in social opportunity for the sexes. The danger of the "beta error," to use Rachel Hare-Mustin's (1987) terms (i.e., paying too *little* attention to the complexities of gender difference), is shown in Jackson's work, and it is probably his influence that led to the fact that the beta error is more prevalent throughout the field than is the alpha error, so apparent in Ackerman's work.

that strategic therapists do not value the inclusion of all family members in treatment, as do contextual and structural therapists, easily yields the unintended consequence of laying the burden on mothers to attend sessions and to be the one who must change. In our culture, if a therapist does not specifically request the father to attend a session, chances are good that the mother will be the one who brings the child to see the therapist, as she usually does with doctors, dentists, and music teachers. In Steve De Shazer's *Keys to Solution in Brief Therapy* (1985), for example, the majority of families described involve only mother and children.*

Strategic therapists insist that they are not interested in changing family structure and that their work is value-neutral. Faith in the fiction of value neutrality leads therapists more often than some would suspect to the dissemination of conventional prejudices. Examples of conventional misogyny are not hard to find in the literature of strategic therapy. In one case supervised by Madanes (Madanes 1981), a depressed husband is congratulated for getting his wife to have sex with him the way he likes it. The therapist says, "And you put her, it sounds too strong, a little more in her place sexually, by demanding what you have coming to you" (p. 192). Is it really impossible to treat depression in men without "putting women in their place," or at least without inducing a man to believe he has done so?

Several commentators (e.g., Bograd 1985) have criticized strategic therapists for their unabashed, although unclaimed, sexism. Bograd writes: "If I respect the father's wishes to keep the status quo, I help maintain a primary interpersonal context that perpetuates inequality between husbands and wives, if not that of women as a class" (p. 6). Chlóe Madanes responded to this criticism in a 1986 interview. She said: "My job is not to require people to have the kind of marriage I think they should have. I think it is unethical to impose one's political ideology on patients" (quoted in Simon 1986, p. 67).

Madanes claims that her own therapy, in contrast to those that advance a "political ideology," is based strictly on "common sense" (Simon 1986, p. 25). In practice, however, the apparent (to some) dichotomy between ideology and common sense tends to disappear. All therapists have a point of view that has the "feel" of common sense to those who share it and the odor of ideological bias to those who do not. Madanes's own work shows

*No fathers in that book bring a child to treatment explaining that they cannot convince their wives to attend or that their wives are too busy. There are, in contrast, mothers who make such statements about their husbands. The mothers in De Shazer's cases are not attacked, and sometimes they are warmly supported, but nonetheless this therapeutic position does nothing to call into question the fact that the contemporary family usually has an overburdened mother and a distant father.

this. When the bulimic woman described earlier sought treatment, it was to stop vomiting, not to become a less subdued housewife. It was common sense to Madanes to see the symptom as a failed attempt at rebellion and to help the woman gain autonomy as part of the treatment. Any feminist therapist will see the logic in this approach, but such logic would not be persuasive to conservatives who believe that women *should* be subdued housewives. Common sense is always *somebody's* common sense, and each somebody has a worldview inscribed with beliefs about sex, class, race, and other distinctions that are fundamental to social existence.*

The belief that only *certain* therapeutic approaches reflect political judgment, or that one's ideology does not always affect one's therapy, runs through the family therapy literature in general, but particularly among strategic therapists (as well as Milan systemic therapists, described in chapter 9). Such therapists endorse the slogan that "the customer is always right." That is: one should not make judgments about the lives of others; one should give the client what the client requests. The flaw in this argument is perhaps definitively shown in the following example from the work of a psychotherapist and writer named Frantz Fanon.

A French policeman sought help from Fanon for his headaches and insomnia. The location of treatment was Algiers during the French-Algerian War, and the policeman's job was to torture Algerian patriots, "sometimes for 10 hours at a stretch." Fanon wrote: "As he could not see his way to stopping torturing people (that made no sense to him, for in that case he would have to resign) he asked me without beating about the bush to help him go on torturing Algerian patriots without any prickings of conscience, without any behavior problems, and with complete equanimity" (1963, pp. 269–70). There are no simple solutions to Fanon's dilemma. The most univocal error, according to Fanon, however, is to live under the pretext that one can act without or above political and moral choices in the practice of one's profession.

It is relevant here that Jay Haley showed an interest in the issue of therapist power in his *Problem-Solving Therapy,* and inveighed against therapists' acting as agents of "social control" through the practice of psychiatric hospitalization. However, Haley displays a competing tendency in that same text to dismiss the question of politics altogether. Haley writes: "The therapist can define all problems as economic and cultural. But then he

---

*Another clue to Madanes's views on gender is her article "With a Little Help from My Friends" (1983), in which she describes a variety of ways in which her own ideas have been confused with or attributed to her husband, Jay Haley. That she realizes that this is of sufficient importance to bring to public attention is positive. However, it is regrettable that she does not acknowledge that the cultural presence of feminism has helped people see these confusions as noteworthy.

must become a revolutionary to solve each problem. Such an approach does not seem practical. Not only must the therapist have evidence that a revolution would create a society that would solve the problem but furthermore the client must wait in distress while the therapist organizes the revolution" (1976, pp. 4–5).

This theoretical position tends to discourage discussion of the politics of therapy. It can easily be used as an apology for therapeutic indifference to certain facts of social existence. The fact that psychotherapy is a poor means to achieve revolutionary change is no reason to do therapy that is sexist (or racist or homophobic). By extension, as therapists who write about and teach a particular approach to therapy, it is important to make our points of view explicit to one another and to open those views to challenge, rather than claim that they don't exist.

Behavior Change versus Insight: The Dualistic Error of Strategic Therapies

In *The Tactics of Change* (1983), Fisch, Weakland, and Segal describe at length the case of a fifteen-year-old girl who runs away from home and is intractably embattled with her parents. The family is in constant uproar: everything seems to start a fight. When the therapist meets alone with the parents in the first session, the father mentions early on that his daughter has a "forty-inch bust" and that she has "been that way for two years." He believes that this is a source of social discomfort to her. Indeed, as the case is described, it appears that both father and mother are also uncomfortable about their daughter's emergent sexuality—more so, perhaps, than the parents of most daughters. The therapist notes that the parents persistently mention the daughter's "unreasonableness." She defies them regardless of how hard they try to reason with her. The therapist tells them they have tried too hard to reason with her and that they should give her "some of her own medicine." Instead of engaging in a battle when the girl asks if she can buy some clothes, for example, the parents are to say something like, "No, because it's Wednesday." They are given other directives as well, such as, "to spill a glass of milk over her" and then apologize for it, and not to give her the birthday gift she asked for. The daughter reportedly settles down, stops leaving the house, eats dinner with the family, and, much to their delight, takes up sewing. The therapist states that the tactic used here is called "benign sabotage" and involves taking a one-down position to the adolescent in order to gain control. In refusing to "do battle," the parents were showing confidence in their ability to play by their own rules. One might say that it was their fear of her that had made their daughter feel insecure and thus test their limits.

It is not essential in strategic therapy to discuss with the family how they feel about having a daughter grow up, about her being sexually active, about the possibility of her getting pregnant, nor to discuss their own upbringing or setbacks with regard to these issues. Although this family appears happy with the results of treatment, it has not helped them to reflect on the problem in a way that might help them to deal with their other children in adolescence. (Will they spill milk on them, too, or, in any case, assume they must go one-down to be one-up with their children?)

Similar questions arise when one considers the case of the bulimic woman described by Madanes. At the end of treatment the woman was no longer vomiting, but she had not been given the gift the reader receives—that of understanding the symptom as a metaphor for her powerlessness as a woman.

The problem with strategic therapy from the feminist point of view is not that it aims to solve problems but that it depicts this aim as antinomic to insight. Strategic therapists posit what is essentially a *dualism* between reflection and change. Since understanding is not incompatible with behavior change, it is not obvious why strategic therapists insist on this bifurcation, why, in the words of Lynn Hoffman, their motto seems to be "Down with insight!" Why could a therapist helping a woman to stop vomiting not also help the couple name their anger and their shame and identify the problems that have so exasperated them in their life together?

Even when a client attempts on her own to share or explore an understanding of a problem at the end of treatment, the strategic therapist sometimes cuts off the discussion. This occurs in "A Modern Little Hans" (in Haley 1976) when, after the boy's phobia is cured, the mother begins to talk about her loneliness in the marriage. The therapist seems almost to flee from her reflections.

To pose my question in the language of strategic therapy: Why, after deploying tactics for successful change, is there not a mandatory "debriefing" in which family and therapist discuss the symptom as metaphor, and learn from each other about the process of change? Why do at least some strategic therapists seem content to see the members of the family go away scratching their heads?

There are several reasons usually offered for rejecting insight-inclusive interventions, but none of them is satisfying. For example, Haley (1976) makes the point that insight is superfluous because people are already aware of the reasons for their problems and that it is "discourteous" to remind them of the obvious. He writes: "if a wife is 'depressed' and one notes that her depression occurs whenever her husband avoids her sexually, it is naive to assume that she and her husband do not know the depression is related to the marriage" (p. 213). It is this statement that seems naive; people often fail to see connections in their lives that are obvious to others.

The more common argument against insight is that therapy works just as well or better without it. However, as Gurman and Kniskern point out in their survey of outcome research in family therapy (1981), there has been no documentation of such a claim, and in fact, there is some evidence that therapies that work on improving communication are most effective (p. 749). Even if research should some day show that strategic therapies "work" better than other methods, however, the simple criterion of "what works" remains problematic, as the Fanon example shows. What works for one person may not work for another person within the same system.

The depreciation of insight among strategic therapists extends also to their beliefs about training therapists. Strategic therapists do not believe, as do other family therapists (e.g., Bowen, Whitaker, and Satir), that the therapist needs to investigate his or her own life and family in order to be a competent practitioner. Haley writes, for example: "The student will change with *action, not reflection* about himself. Just as the families treated by this approach are not expected to confess all, neither are the student therapists" (1976, p. 176, italics added). Strategic therapists think of their work not as healing but as fixing or even selling. In discussing how to approach different kinds of families in therapy, Fisch, Weakland, and Segal (1983) use the analogy of selling a Rolls Royce to two different kinds of customers. Some strategic therapists "actually send students out to watch how car salesmen persuade customers to buy a product" (Hoffman 1981, p. 277). Just as salesmen are not interested in critiquing capitalism, strategic therapists are not interested in criticizing the institutions of marriage and the family. Through the absence of such critique, strategic therapists sell the important, although unstated, idea that the family as an institution is sound, and with minor repairs will run smoothly.*

*The motif of automobile sales in the family therapy literature seems to go back at least to William Lederer and Don Jackson, who wrote, "Assume for a moment that for a thousand dollars one can buy either a 1935 Chevrolet with a hundred thousand miles on it or a brand-new Cadillac. Why would anybody buy the Chevrolet when he could buy the Cadillac? The same question can be asked about marriage" (1968, p. 20). With regard to family therapy, it would seem that Adlai Stevenson's comment about America passing from the New Dealers to the car dealers could not have been more prescient.

The "brief therapists" add to this tradition the insistence that therapy be done in as few sessions as possible—five being preferable to six. This aspect of strategic therapy opens it to charges of being isomorphic with the worst of Occidental society, seeking the "quick fix" as opposed to long-term solutions. Gregory Bateson, who is continually cited by strategic therapists, himself warned against being lured by quick and discrete change of any kind. Bateson was extremely distrustful of goal-oriented programs and criticized Haley on precisely this set of issues (cf. Mary Catherine Bateson 1984, Malcolm 1978).

I do not share Bateson's pessimism about planned change, whether in families or in other social systems. It is the emphasis on behavior change in opposition to, or without, critical reflection that is antithetical to feminism.

A Note on Pragmatism

It is regrettable that although strategic therapists like to use the words *practical* and *pragmatic* to describe their work, they have not appealed in any notable way to the philosophical school known as Pragmatism, developed by three American scholars: C. S. Peirce, John Dewey, and William James. One of the problems with strategic therapy is not that it is pragmatic, but rather that its originators have failed to explore the meanings of that term and to define their methods accordingly.

Pragmatism, as developed by Peirce and Dewey in particular, was far more sophisticated than any of the cybernetic or systems explanations the strategic therapists have used as their theoretical base. Dewey, in his discussions of social process, went far beyond the facile "the customer is always right" and "the ends justify the means" maxims of contemporary strategic therapists. A brief explanation of the core of Dewey's Pragmatism will shed more light on the limits of strategic therapy.

Pragmatism for Dewey was emphatically not a matter of finding quick solutions to problems, as he explained in his essay "The Development of American Pragmatism." His work was devoted to dissolving the long-standing dualism between rationalism and empiricism, between thought and action. In *Reconstruction in Philosophy* (1920) Dewey wrote that the duality between thought and action had ruined both science and the humanities in the West. It had given the world on the one hand a crude science which was unacquainted with ethics and history, and on the other hand, a philosophy that was perilously removed from the world and politics. It was his goal to unite understanding and action—reflection and observable change—in science, in philosophy, and especially in education. The "reconstruction" referred to in his 1920 title refers to mending the split between science and ethics so that "means" and "ends," far from being used to "justify" each other, would become part of a single process. Equally fascinating, as early as 1920, Dewey had criticized the "organic" view of society, now embraced by systems thinkers as though it were avant-garde!*

In proposing a kind of reconstruction in family therapy, I cast my lot with certain revisions of psychoanalytic theory for a new theoretical language—a position to be elaborated in chapter 12. However, it is probably true that those who prefer the American to the European philosophical tradition could establish an equally credible foundation for family therapy from an adequate knowledge of Pragmatism. Pragmatism could assist in the exploration of what it means to say that a method "works," and would also offer a language that is equipped to deal with power in a way that cybernetics is not.

Without such a base, strategic therapy rests on the shakiest theoretical foundation of any of the schools of family therapy. Its popularity has not suffered because of this, and it may expand in the future for economic reasons, as the nation pulls back further from its responsibility to provide health care and as insurance companies cut back on the number of sessions for which they will compensate a therapist (cf. MacKinnon and Miller 1987 on the economic issue).

A Feminist Strategic Therapy?

Since feminist therapists are interested in helping people solve problems, there is no reason why feminist therapists could not use an occasional strategic technique, such as assigning tasks in the course of a therapy whose goals are broader than symptom remission.

---

*Dewey understood that the cell is *not* a good metaphor for society because it keeps us from seeing the reality of irreconcilable interests in social systems. In one discussion, he mentions management and labor, and even the problem of the sexes, as evidence that the organic metaphor is inapt.

It is also true that there are a few situations in which insight is not a primary goal of treatment. There are, for example, some people whose capacity for insight is truncated, such as the mentally retarded and very young children. I once worked with a family in which both parents were retarded, and my goal was to help them keep their adolescent daughter out of danger on the streets; it was a "behavioral" goal that had nothing to do with helping them understand their families of origin. Another case involved a nine-year-old girl with anorexia nervosa, and, unlike adolescent patients, this girl left treatment with more weight on her bones but with relatively little ability to think about the meanings of her problem. In these types of cases, the work of the feminist will resemble in some ways the work of the strategic therapist.

However, whether strategic therapy overall is compatible with feminist premises, or is less compatible with feminist premises than other approaches to family therapy, remains an open question. The unremittingly inapt metaphors of strategic therapy (the militaristic, the cybernetic, and the sales metaphors), along with the insight/action dualism, lead one to believe that they are irreconcilable.

It is essential to note that not all feminists, of course, agree on this point. Peggy Papp, for example, considers herself both a feminist and a strategic therapist. Indeed, Papp's work overlaps with traditional strategic work (she works to solve the problem, gives prescriptions, and sometimes uses paradox), and yet one senses a difference as well. The treatment described in her 1983 book *The Process of Change* (while not dealing with gender or feminism) seems less austere, more "relational," and not so minimalist as the strategic therapy I have been describing. She sometimes explains things very directly to families in a way that an "insight-therapist" might. It is surely no accident that one reviewer used these very points to criticize her work and question whether Papp was doing "real" strategic therapy (Coyne 1985). The reviewer saw this as a flaw in her work; I see it as a struggle to improve the old method.

The work of Olga Silverstein may represent an even greater departure from the strategic therapy of Haley and Madanes. In her 1986 book with Brad Keeney, Silverstein provides transcripts of four sessions in which she works in close proximity with a family, relating to them in a highly personal manner. She does not give the family a task in any of the sessions, nor does she prescribe a ritual or use paradox in the usual sense. Silverstein has said that she nonetheless calls her work "strategic" because of its planned aspect. As a therapist, she forms a goal for each session; she does not believe that therapy should "flow," in the less structured manner of the more psychodynamic therapies. I would be tempted to find a name more descriptive of her exquisitely relational style, but this, after all, is not my task.

One can hypothesize that feminists who have been trained in strategic methods and continue to use them will end up creating a new hybrid. I am afraid that conventional strategic therapy, however, can be used as just another Occidental attempt to make the unexamined life worth living.

8

Carl Whitaker:
Playing with Patriarchy

THE "symbolic-experiential" therapy of Carl Whitaker could be characterized as the mirror image of the strategic therapies. Whitaker claims to have no interest in the symptom brought in by the family; certainly he does not see it as his task to help resolve it. He typically "turns his back on the scapegoat" and directs his attention to the family, inviting them to develop a caring and probing relationship with him. Whitaker sees all symptoms as mere signals of, or even noisome distractions from, the real existential problems faced by families—birth, growing up, separation, marriage, illness, and death. Whitaker is most interested in sensitizing the family to its own unconscious life. If the family arrives for a session without one of its members, for example, he may tell them that they elected that member to act out their reservations about treatment. It is not uncommon for him to invite the family to return only if everyone can be persuaded to attend.

Whitaker's impact on the field has been considerable. He has brought new language and a certain permission to attend to issues of intimacy as well as authority, and to the therapist's *intuition* as well as to models and theories. Family researcher Pauline Boss has written of Whitaker's influence on her own empirical work, stating that it was Whitaker who "pushed me to notice the symbolic, to note what could not be easily measured or quantified. . . . Whatever discoveries about stressed families I make as a family researcher and therapist, they are indelibly marked by Whitaker's regard for the intuitive and symbolic" (1987, p. 156).

Common Ground with Feminism

As a result of his psychodynamic training, which included the study of Melanie Klein and Carl Jung, Whitaker learned to work with gender as a significant therapeutic category. He speaks and writes of "mothering" and "fathering" and of "maleness" and "femaleness." He does not use the overtly sexist language of conventional psychiatry, as Ackerman did, nor does he critique it. One learns about his ideas regarding gender mainly through observing his clinical work, and in that clinical work one sees at times a deep appreciation for women and for qualities that have been associated with women—nurturance, continuity, expressiveness, vulnerability. Anyone who has attended seminars with Whitaker will be familiar with certain phrases he uses with families: "Men are hopeless squares"; "Women struggle to bring men alive"; and "Most Daddies are jealous that they can't have babies." These comments in context do not smack of the sentimental notion that women are "morally superior" to men. Whitaker's comments, to my ear, seem genuinely appreciative of women rather than fulsome.

Whitaker believes in challenging people about their self-deceptions, and he challenges women forcefully at times. What is unusual about Whitaker is that he also seems to have the ability to confront fathers in therapy. For example, in one family in which the father reported that his blood pressure soared at any show of "human incompetence," Whitaker chided in return, "Anything that challenges your father rule!"* Later, when this man said that he had never accepted his mother's tenderness, Whitaker answered, "I know. That's what makes your wife's job so gruesome." It is interesting that even in 1963, in his interview with the Hillcrest family, Whitaker was more confrontational with the husband than were any of the other therapists who saw the family, and he learned, as none of the others did, of the father's depression and vulnerability.

Although Whitaker makes no reference to feminist theory in his books, there are some hints that he respects the social changes initiated by the women's movement. Here is an example from *The Family Crucible,* written with Augustus Napier:

> Family therapy exists in a society where a great many women are attempting psychological growth, and the changes they are making are exciting. The

*See the videotape *A Family with Whitaker and Minuchin,* available through the Philadelphia Child Guidance Clinic.

women's movement is a powerful force in almost every family we see, and both therapy and therapist must somehow respond to it. . . . When a wife-and-mother tries to make some of the complex changes called liberation without any collaboration with her husband and children, she may succeed in gaining personhood only at the cost of great bitterness and guilt. The most expensive sacrifice may be the marriage. But if the family, especially the couple, can work together through these agonizing transactions, the outcome may be positive. While wife and mother is the pioneer, everyone in the family can achieve both a sense of individual autonomy *and* a sense of closeness and unity. [Napier and Whitaker 1978, p. 234]

This passage reveals the authors' preference for keeping the family together, since it implies that any other outcome would not be "positive." Although one might object to this unexamined bias, the fact remains that this is as elaborate and sympathetic a passage about feminism as one will find anywhere in the family therapy literature. Furthermore, it is important not to overlook the fact that the one case that Napier and Whitaker chose to describe at book length in *The Family Crucible,* the Brices, is a family in which a central therapeutic issue is the woman's need either to transform or to leave the marriage that is crushing her.

The Brice family consists of David, a lawyer, Carolyn, a homemaker, Claudia, a rebellious teenager, and two siblings. The family seeks therapy because Claudia has run away from home and expressed suicidal thoughts. She has become resistant to all authority, especially her mother's. Napier and Whitaker devote the early sessions to probing into the parents' families of origin. Whitaker believes that families of origin send "scapegoats" into the world who meet and marry and spend the rest of their lives "fighting over which family of origin to reproduce." He does not believe that it is sufficient to gain insight into the family and jealously guard it; he hopes that his thoughts and hunches will be used by the family to untangle its painful knots. He tells the parents in one of the early sessions: "You agreed to get Claudia between you as a way of helping you heat up the marriage. Dad could team up with Claudia and Mom would get jealous and very angry. Then Mom and Claudia agreed to heat up their fight as a way of finding out what it was like to really fight things out" (p. 31).

The marriage becomes the next focus of therapy. David has always been married to his business, putting the family second. Carolyn has always resented this, but has never challenged it. Through the process of therapy, she becomes acquainted with the disappointment in her life and with her indignation at having to "plead with her husband to love her." This new awareness on Carolyn's part is extremely disruptive for her husband. Napier and Whitaker understand his fear in terms of his own family of origin: "David was happy that his wife's domesticity replicated for him a relationship that had been very comfortable. He liked having 'mother' Carolyn at home and he, like his father before him, was even fussy about how his wife did her housekeeping" (p. 214).

Thus, as Carolyn begins to think in terms of her own needs, David suddenly comes up with a job option in Boston, which would move the family away from friends, community, and, of course, therapy. Boston also happened to be where David's parents lived. This job possibility creates such a clash of interests in the marriage that the couple considers separation.

The husband goes to the job interview, but he returns in despair, revealing in the next session that his father had been behind the offer, having furtively arranged an interview with a large company for his son. David was enraged and humiliated that his father would see him as so inadequate that he needed rescuing. The expression of this pain became the beginning of David's examining of himself, and led to some individual sessions. Whitaker and Napier's immediate response to the revelations, however, was to invite the extended family to treatment in order to work through the crisis.

In a session with David's parents, David confronts his father for the first time. The therapists suggest that this confrontation had never before occurred because the older man had not had a close alliance with his own father. The discussion of David's father's life leads to exploration of the grandparents' marriage, and the therapists learn that the grandmother feels lonely and abandoned by her workaholic husband, just as Carolyn had felt. Whitaker connects the entire job-in-Boston affair to the grandparents' unconscious wish for help from their son, and a corresponding willingness on the son's part to return to his parents instead of dealing with the needs of his own family. Thus, a therapy that began with the request to control a rebellious adolescent girl ends with a challenge to two fathers to give up their excessive attachment to business and finally join their families.

The result of the therapy is that the grandparents returned to Boston and entered couples' therapy, and David and Carolyn remained where they were and continued to work on their relationship. According to the therapists, Carolyn became active in the women's movement and started taking courses in women's history and literature.

Sexual Politics

Carl Whitaker has been known to say in seminars that he has no theory. This, of course, can be very frustrating to students who are trying to learn what he does and to make it their own. But there are also advantages to his irrepressibly "right-brain" style. In a context in which the only respected theories are patriarchal, *not* to have a theory can be a way—witting or unwitting—of rejecting the dominant professional laws. Whitaker does indeed reject the conventional therapeutic jargon. He speaks to colleagues, to his families, and to his readers about "craziness," not "schizophrenia." He describes families as "cozy," "cuddly," "murderous," and "gruesome," not as "functional" and "dysfunctional." In the entire family therapy literature, perhaps no definition of the "healthy family" is as palatable as Whitaker's:

> The healthy family maintains a separation of the generations. Mother and father are not children and children are not parents. The two generations function in these separate role categories. Members of the same generations have equal rank. However, there is massive freedom of choice in periodic role selection and each role is available to any member. Father can be a 5-year-old, mother can be a 3-year-old, the 3-year-old can be a father, the father can be a mother, depending on the situation, with each family member protected by an implicit "as if" clause. [Whitaker and Keith 1981, p. 190]

Whitaker's example of the "as-if" clause in action is equally pleasing: "For example, the 6-year-old son says to daddy, 'Can I serve the meat tonite?' and daddy says, 'Sure, you sit over on this chair and serve the meat and the potatoes and I'll sit over in your place and complain' " (1981, p. 190).

Whitaker's use of language is not completely jargon-free, but it is distinctly different from that of most other family therapists. The difference makes itself known in both the content and the style of the passage. The content states more clearly than anywhere else in the social science literature on the family that family health should not be defined by generational boundaries or gender differentiation alone, but also by the ability to reject and overturn them. It is not only acceptable to tamper with conventional structures, it is actually the *sine qua non* of Whitaker's approach. Experimentation and fluidity become as important as stability and "role clarity." The playful style of the passage replicates and enhances the content. It is not typical for experts in any field to write serious books about parents making sarcastic remarks to their children, but this passage is emblematic of Whitaker's therapy. He believes in the therapeutic importance of play and of "tickling the family's unconscious."

Whitaker's approach has been described as "take it or leave it," since he does not necessarily expect or encourage a family to return to therapy after the first session. His tickling of the unconscious reaches its fullest expression when he is doing a consultation with a family (as opposed to being the regular therapist). He has been known to sit back and simply report his own "crazy thoughts" to the family, e.g., "I just had a thought that if you were a boy instead of a girl, you could be your mom's father," or, "If you two insist on fighting, you should do it to orgasm." The quirky iconoclasm of Whitaker's work is at once its most unteachable and inscrutable part as well as the source of its appeal. Whitaker does not devote much effort to explaining himself, and the reader is left wondering exactly where his clinical technique came from, or at least where in the literature of social science in general or of psychotherapy in particular we might find a similar hypostatization of caprice.

This question led me to wonder whether the late French psychoanalyst Jacques Lacan might not have been Whitaker's fraternal twin. Despite the almost comical outward differences between them—Lacan, the delicate esthete; Whitaker, the bulky Wisconsin farm boy—the similarities in their work are striking. Lacan perpetrated an extraordinary act of rebellion against classical psychoanalytic theory. Instead of moving farther and farther in the direction of strengthening the ego, leaving unconscious life in the background (as the American ego psychologists did, for example), Lacan went in the opposite direction. Suspicious of the ego, he dealt largely with the unconscious—with desire, sexuality, gender, play, and fantasy—much as Whitaker does.

Seeing Lacan in therapy was allegedly like consulting the oracle; he was capable of making a few provocative comments and ending the session after five minutes. Whitaker also refuses to be bound by conventional therapeutic time. He will cut a session short and walk out, or go well beyond the hour, depending on his gut feeling about the family. Like Whitaker (or, at least, Whitaker at his best), Lacan had no interest in helping patients adapt better to social conventions; he believed instead in the power of analysis to liberate the self from the ego's tyranny.

A key Lacanian concept is that of *jouissance,* which translates roughly as "pleasure" or "free play." (In French it also means "orgasm.") *Jouissance* for Lacan replaces the usual "functional effectiveness" or "social adaptation" as the goal of therapy and of living. Here again we see a parallel to Whitaker's playfulness. Lacan called Western culture "phallocentric," and he believed that it was necessary to disentitle and debunk what is usually elevated in our culture, e.g., the rational, the objective, and the "law of the father" (Lacan 1966).

This similarity between Whitaker and Lacan is of interest, among other reasons, because French feminists have found Lacan's ideas very politically appealing (see Irigary 1977, Cixous 1981, Kristeva 1980).* It seems to me, in fact, that if a Lacanian feminist were to do family treatment, her work would resemble Whitaker's more than it would that of any therapist reviewed here.

The problem with Lacan's therapy is that it was directed to a very sophisticated clientele, and the same sort of problem has shadowed Whitaker's therapy. His work seems to be less successful with families who suffer from poverty in addition to existential problems. Less educated families who do not immediately pick up on Whitaker's approach as avant-garde sometimes (although not always) view his comments as "crazy" or simply disrespectful.

Limitations of Whitaker's Work

Despite some overlap with feminism, it would be incorrect to label Whitaker's work "feminist." He ignores feminist theory just as he ignores mainstream theory. At times he seems to come close to analyzing certain therapeutic traditions that are gender-related, but then he pulls back, as in this example from *The Family Crucible:* "The mother is so central a person in the family that we couldn't afford to have her pulling against us. . . . if mothers lack interest in the process, it will founder. They are truly the key to the family's psychological life and the gate through which any intruder must enter" (Napier and Whitaker 1978, pp. 94–95). The authors at least acknowledge here what is usually not acknowledged—the fact that women *are* the "gate" through which therapists intrude. Their choice of words implies their sensitivity to the fact that most therapy involves a special push on female family members. Not to comment at all, however, on the fact that this therapeutic practice can reproduce the cultural tendency to sacrifice mothers' needs for the benefit of others is a telling oversight.

*A problem with the French feminist writings is their density. See Sherry Turkle's extremely lucid book on Lacan, *Psychoanalytic Politics: Freud's French Revolution* (1978).

At other times, in fact, Whitaker's ability to comment on or satirize the conventional wisdom about the family and about gender disappears completely. For example, in 1983, in a conference on "The Healthy Family" in Philadelphia, none of the speakers, including Whitaker, criticized the family as an institution or raised sex roles or gender identity as an issue. At that conference, there were no echoes of his statements in *The Family Crucible* about the influence of the women's movement, or of the value of "playing" with genderedness in the family (as in "the mother can be the father, the father can be the little girl," etc.). Moreover, since Whitaker is even more disinterested than most family therapists in sociological theory and research on the family, he sometimes makes statements that perpetuate cultural mythology about the family. For example, in *The Family Crucible* he states: "Marriage *is* therapeutic. . . . And marriage helps people to change: to grow more sensitive, more caring, more responsible, more aware of the needs of other people" (1978, p. 115). To the two million women who were battered by their husbands this year, that paragraph would read like a grim parody.

In addition to Whitaker's originality and wisdom, one can see in his work the bowdlerized existentialism that runs rampant in the American "human potential" movement. For example, Whitaker has often claimed that the most important thing a therapist can do for a family is to "help them have an experience." What, one wonders, would constitute *not* having an experience? A favorite Whitaker maxim is that "adults are just children grown inadequate," suggesting the Rousseauian notion that people are born good and are corrupted by culture. Indeed, Whitaker shares the romantic view of madness that is usually associated with the work of British anti-psychiatrist R. D. Laing. For example, in interviewing a man diagnosed as schizophrenic in 1985, Whitaker commented that the patient was "the me I wished had happened." And he says directly to the young man: "I am very admiring of you for having the guts I didn't have" (quoted in Simon 1985b). Of course, people labeled "psychotic" are less a menace to the planet than the "sane" people preparing wars in the Pentagon. But to see schizophrenia as the only or the best alternative to Pentagon-style sanity is to be hopelessly lost. At best, one might call this attitude quixotic; at worst, it is a way of distracting people from other possibilities, such as organizing for social change.

In short, Whitaker, unlike most family therapists, addresses himself (indirectly) both to father absence in families and to certain aspects of patriarchy. However, because he does not do either with consistency or clarity of intent, both these aspects of his work can be overlooked by students as merely idiosyncratic. One can easily imagine symbolic-experiential therapists of the future paying close attention to intergenerational patterns and "tickling the family's unconscious" and *not* noticing, as Whitaker and Napier did with the Brice family, that the mother was doing all the housework.

Feminist therapists may be able to use Whitaker's irony, warmth, and *jouissance* if they can make these part of a therapy that is consistently mindful of social reality.

9

Milan Systemic Therapy: The Myth of Mythlessness

THE MILAN family therapists are often identified with the strategic school of family therapy, and they still acknowledge a large debt to the strategists. However, because they claim to be moving ever farther away from strategic thinking, they are treated separately from the strategists here.

The history of the Milan school begins with Mara Selvini Palazolli, a child analyst known for her work with anorectic patients (see *Self-Starvation,* 1974). Disappointed with the results of individual psychoanalytic treatment for anorexia and interested in the work of Gregory Bateson, she and a group of colleagues turned to family therapy and specifically to the strategic work of the Mental Research Institute (MRI) for a new paradigm. In 1974 Selvini Palazolli, along with Gianfranco Cecchin, Luigi Boscolo, and Giuliana Prata, published *Paradox and Counterparadox* (the Italian edition), which described their new systemic method of treating families with a schizophrenic member. Their method placed a great emphasis on the work of the *team.* One mixed-sex pair of therapists would work with the family, and the other pair would operate as the observing team behind a one-way mirror. Information was gathered from the family by means of "circular questioning," a method that underscored family members' relatedness to one another. Thus, the question would not be, "Why don't you eat?" but rather, "What does mother do when you don't eat? Father? Who is most upset about it? Least upset?" and so on. At the end of the session, the therapists would give a message to the family that involved "positive connotation" of the symptom. The message always described to the family how the symptom was important to each member of the family, and it advised them not to change.

In 1979 the team of four split, and the two women went off to continue developing their method, while the men decided to devote themselves to clinical training, which now includes running a training institute and consulting to Milan-style teams in a variety of locations. Selvini Palazolli states that she wanted to continue to make major changes in her method because she was disappointed with the many failures experienced using paradox and counterparadox. Along with a new team, she developed a very different way of working, much more confrontational and less interested in positive connotation. Selvini Palazolli is now concerned with investigating the family's "dirty games"—the games of deceit and power that families play. She poses what she calls "terrible questions" to these families (which continue to be families with grave, long-standing problems). For example, she might say to the schizophrenic son in a family, "Why did you have to go mad to be with your Momma? Couldn't you do the same as a sane person? Wouldn't she have been moved by you if you had not gone mad?" (quoted in Simon 1987, p. 19).

After a few sessions of gathering information and forming hypotheses with her team, the family is given the "invariant prescription"—a directive instructing the parents to leave the house together without making any explanation to the rest of the family, and usually leaving a note that says something like, "Tonight we are out." If questioned by the children, the parents are to respond with something like, "This matter concerns only us." Selvini Palazolli believes that schizophrenia and other serious disorders in families are caused in part by a child's taking sides with one parent who is locked in conflict with the other. In families where such powerful parent-child coalitions exist, the prescription that the marital couple should go out without informing the children can be an act of unprecedented boundary making. In some cases it is dramatic enough to make headway with families that had not responded to other forms of treatment.

Selvini Palazolli claims a high success rate for her work, but her claims have been challenged by Carol Anderson and others who point out that her conclusions are based on a very small sample of families (in Simon 1987). She is also criticized for the overly simplistic character of her model, which can lead families to blame themselves and their "dirty games" for the presence of a schizophrenic member in their family. Undisputed, however, are her warmth, vitality, and commitment as a researcher and as a clinician.

THE SEXUAL POLITICS OF SELVINI PALAZOLLI'S WORK

Selvini Palazolli does not fetishize the symptom, as many strategic therapists do. Her goal is to treat the family, not just to fix a symptom or a malfunctioning part. Another overlap with feminism has to do with her use of the team. Family therapists of many schools work in teams, of course, but Selvini Palazolli and the other Milan therapists seem to consider it more essential to their method than others. As Selvini Palazolli has said, "To understand without the team is quite impossible" (quoted in Simon 1987, p. 19). This is analogous to the feminist criticism of the ideology of the rugged individual, who can subsist alone without support, feedback, or encouragement from the group. Her statement reminds one of the feminist maxim that there are no individual solutions, only collective solutions.

Selvini Palazolli has not written prescriptive statements about sex roles in families, but neither has she included the insights of any of the feminist theorists into her work. Feminist family therapist Marianne Ault-Riché reports writing to Selvini Palazolli in 1983 with the question, " 'Do you have any thoughts about the special needs/dilemmas/issues regarding women in family therapy?' Her response was a simple 'No' " (1986, p. 11).

In a more recent interview, Selvini Palazolli stated: "In my opinion, it is wrong for therapists to impose their ideas of how families should be" (Simon 1987, p. 31). In the same interview, she mentioned "patriarchal society" in passing, but in response to a probe of that statement, she opted out by commenting on the fact that women get a lot out of "playing the oppressed victim" in families (p. 31). Thus, despite the innovations of Selvini Palazolli's work and her obvious strength as a therapist, she has not advanced the field beyond the untenable position of a "value-free" therapy.

The same error inheres in the work of the other Milan group of therapists, led by Boscolo and Cecchin. These two men, along with Lynn Hoffman and Peggy Penn of the Ackerman Institute, have published a book entitled *Milan Systemic Family Therapy* (1987), which consists of conversations among the co-authors about theory and about several cases that are presented in transcript form. I will focus the remainder of this chapter on their work, because it is more comprehensive than Selvini Palazolli's recent work and so avails itself of a fuller critique.

The Work of Boscolo and Cecchin, As Revealed in Dialogues with Hoffman and Penn

In *Milan Systemic Family Therapy* we learn that Boscolo and Cecchin, like Selvini Palazolli, have rejected much of the language of strategies, maneuvers, ploys, and countermoves that had characterized their early work based on its MRI influence. Boscolo explicitly criticizes the anti-insight bias of the strategic therapists: "Richard Rabkin in *Strategic Psychotherapy* divides therapy into prescriptive and insight therapies. That is a dichotomy we do not accept. We believe behavior and ideas are related. That's why some of our questions are aimed at thoughts and others are aimed at producing information about behavior" (p. 112). Hoffman makes a related point in stating that "ideas, beliefs, myths, values, perceptions, fantasies, and other such internal productions have come out of exile and are once more in fashion" (p. 19). I consider these statements to share a common ground with feminism, because feminists tend to condemn the dualism between action and reflection, thought and feeling.

Boscolo and Cecchin criticize classical psychoanalytic thinking as "linear," and yet one finds in their 1987 book not infrequent reference to the following words and concepts: the family's *dynamics* (especially as reflected in the team's *dynamics*), the *unconscious, resistance,* and even *healing.* These may be leftovers from their early training, or they may reflect a rediscovery of these concepts.

Boscolo and Cecchin are particularly interested in therapy as "constructed reality," and they believe that the therapist becomes part of the therapeutic system, which includes the family, other therapists, and the social context as well. Unfortunately, they have not followed through with this idea by showing how the therapist's political point of view affects the therapy.

THE SEXUAL POLITICS OF BOSCOLO AND CECCHIN'S WORK

Like all other schools of family therapy, Boscolo and Cecchin do not include the insights of feminist theory in their work, nor do they critique the modern family as an institution. Boscolo and Cecchin share Selvini Palazolli's interest in "neutrality," a word they use frequently in their book. Let us stop and explore a bit more fully what is really meant by it.

Neutrality appears to have at least two meanings in the work of Boscolo and Cecchin, the first of which is not controversial. Cecchin says, for example: "Neutrality is to accept the whole system; it's not to be outside or to be cold. It's to feel a sense of compassion, interest, and curiosity about a family's dilemma: How did they get there? How did they organize themselves that way? We try to see the logic even in situations that are repugnant from a moral point of view" (p. 154). Most therapists would not take issue with this definition of neutrality; a therapist must seek to understand everyone's point of view and show compassion all around. However, Boscolo and Cecchin add another aspect to this definition: they believe that therapists should not work out of a political or moral point of view, or should somehow tuck it away so that it does not influence their therapy. In the course of this discussion, Boscolo and Cecchin raise the issue of "social control." It is of utmost importance, they claim, not to influence a family any more than necessary and not to keep them in treatment for too long. Boscolo states that "consumer society" makes people think they need therapists, and that therapists should therefore "decondition a family from having the idea that they need therapy" (p. 116). The behavior modification term *decondition* seems an odd choice for an author who is inveighing against social manipulation.

The authors refer sympathetically to the works of R. D. Laing and the anti-psychiatry movement of the 1970s. Laing, however, at least critiqued the institution of the family as repressive to the individuals within it, while Boscolo and Cecchin take the romantic position that the family is "self-healing" and that "if you let them alone, they improve" (p. 115).

MacKinnon and Miller, in an article addressing the Milan method, show the problem with the laissez-faire posture of these therapists, and they vigorously challenge the concept of neutrality:

> Because the problems and conflicts within the family reflect larger social issues and viewpoints, whatever stance the therapist takes, even the stance of avoiding taking a stance, reflects a political position within the larger system, regardless of the therapist's intentions. Relationships cannot remain neutral, nor therapists apolitical in such a context. [1987, p. 148]

This idea is the one invoked in chapter 7 with the example of Frantz Fanon and the policeman. Although most of our cases present less daunting moral choices than Fanon's, the point remains that therapeutic neutrality is not something that is good or bad; it is something that is impossible. Promoting it only advances what feminist Diana Hume George has called "the myth of mythlessness."

An example from the work of the Milan therapists themselves illustrates this clearly. In two of the four cases presented in their 1987 book, Boscolo and Cecchin pay more attention to the mother's contribution to the problem than to father's. The most compelling example of their lack of neutrality lies in the case called "The Family with a Secret," in which the original therapist, Dr. S., has requested a consultation from the Milan team after three sessions with the family. The older daughter, Lisa, who is not the identified patient, had made a serious suicide attempt. In the family's third session with Dr. S., the mother stated that the husband had made several attempts to have sexual contact with Lisa. Lisa told the mother that the father had been sexually interested in her since she was nine years old. The parents were unable to discuss the issue in front of the daughters, and forbade the therapist to bring it up in front of them. The parents agreed to the Milan consultation on condition that incest not be mentioned.

Therapists from all orientations who have treated incestuous families have encountered the problem of the "family secret." Therapists approach this dilemma in many different ways, e.g., by complying fully with the secret, or complying only initially, or refusing to collude with it at all. What therapists from all schools seem to have in common when it comes to incestuous families, however, is the tendency to make the incest "belong" to the mother instead of the father—to make her the source of the problem.

In "The Family with a Secret," Boscolo and Cecchin direct a lot of questions to the mother about her first marriage, about how her first husband related to each child, and about why her first marriage ended. The therapists' post-interview discussion seems to focus on the mother. Boscolo states, "In reality, the mother wanted the daughter to love the husband because she is afraid he will leave her." And Cecchin states, "It's the mother who gives the confusing messages. She wants the two rivals [father and daughter] to love each other" (p. 158).

When asked why similar questions were not asked of the father, Boscolo responded, "I think it was an omission. Retrospectively, it would seem very good to ask some questions about the background of the father. This would balance the information we got about the mother." Cecchin immediately adds, however, "The danger is that we would connote him negatively: 'Maybe there is some explanation why you are this kind of man' " (p. 159). Cecchin's comment reveals a fear not only of confronting the father directly with the sexual abuse but even of implying that his actions might be the subject of "explanation" in the way the behavior of other family members is subject to explanation. No such worry about connoting the mother negatively is expressed.

In "The Family with a Secret," the therapists' prescription involves the mother and daughter spending more time together. This is a good idea, but the therapists' formulation of it is extremely unsophisticated. Cecchin states, "Instead of commenting on the incest between Lisa and father, the incest should be between Lisa and mother." The allusion to incest between Lisa and mother is repeated. "Suppose now you create incest between mother and daughter" (pp. 170, 172). What the therapists seem to mean is that they would like to see more closeness between mother and Lisa. But to substitute the word *incest* for *closeness* is to obscure or even deny the difference between them. To imply linguistic equivalence between these two words is to take a political position that is grossly insensitive and clinically wrong.

A follow-up one-and-a-half years later revealed that Lisa had gotten married and had a baby. When asked what made the therapists "see progress" or "feel hopeful" about the family at this point, Boscolo responded:

> Well, Lisa being married and out of the house, of course. . . . In the first two sessions, the wife was antagonistic to the husband, now she agreed with him. The whole family agreed with him.
>
> CECCHIN: What was impressive was the way the *father suddenly became the leader* in the situation. He was setting the rules: "Now we do it this way." This man sat dumbfounded in the previous session and here he is saying, "This is my family, *these are my daughters.*"
>
> HOFFMAN: Which could be seen as bad or good, depending on your point of view. [P. 181, italics added.]

It is encouraging to note Hoffman's challenge of Cecchin here, although the issue unfortunately is immediately dropped instead of explored.

Certainly it is difficult to see what this case has to do with neutrality. The ironies here remind one of Simone de Beauvoir's comment in *The Mandarins* that people who profess to be apolitical often end up being reactionary. In this situation, Boscolo and Cecchin insist on taking "no" stand about the politics of family life, while at the same time tacitly taking the conventional stand, one that minimizes the meaning of incest, and/or attributes the problem to the mother's actions.

CONCEPTUALIZING THERAPY: THE THERAPIST AS MIDWIFE OR
GYNECOLOGIST?

Boscolo and Cecchin describe their method as "Socratic" because their time with the family consists largely of posing questions, as Socrates did with his students. Socrates compared himself to a midwife, because he saw his task as not handing out truth, but rather assisting at the birth of understanding by asking questions. Anyone who has read the Socratic dialogues knows that there was a gentleness in Socrates' manner, a genuine respect for his interlocutors, and often a feeling of affection among them.

Is the analogy of Socrates to the Milan method apt? It is at times, such as in a case entitled, "The Anorectic Store," in which one finds a reciprocal discourse between therapists and family. The therapists, after instructing the parents to go out alone together, engage in a discussion with the parents in which the parents are allowed to ask direct questions about how the intervention will help the anorectic to eat, and the therapists give fairly straightforward answers (Boscolo et al. 1987, p. 230). The dialogue in this case is relatively uncontrived. In other cases, however, indeed in most of the Milan systemic cases, the therapists act on the family "from above" (or at a "meta-level," as they say). They sometimes imagine the therapeutic role in quintessentially impersonal terms: "You have to offer yourself as a cybernetic loop so that they can utilize you," says Boscolo (p. 180). In "The Case of the Crying Boy," the therapist appears less like a midwife and more like the stereotype of the male gynecologist, who asks questions of the patient, does not elicit any questions from her, and finishes by handing over a prescription.

In feminist psychotherapy with families, the therapist develops a close connection with the family, and is able both to nurture and to confront all family members. In general, it seems unnecessary (and unpleasant, to some therapists) to treat families at such a great psychological distance as the Milan approach often implies. I do not mean to suggest here that therapy done at this distance is never appropriate or desirable. In some situations, it may be warranted or even essential. I have had some experience with a Milan-style team at the Philadelphia Child Guidance Clinic. The families we saw together had been through years of therapy, both inpatient and outpatient, and their problems seemed robust indeed. In one case, our team's interventions over several months in very few sessions seemed to produce remarkable change. The Milan therapists have not written much about why they think the method works; Hoffman refers to the mystery and excitement that the ritual and the "other" team provides. My own sense is that the psychological distance we created through the absence of personal engagement with the family made our team into powerful parents whom the families chose to trust and obey. In other words, Milan systemic therapy works for the same reason all psychotherapies work—because of characteristics of the therapist-patient relationship, what Freud called "the transference." All family therapists evoke family members' feelings about their own parents. While practitioners such as Satir or Nagy might evoke memories of, and longings for, a nurturant, proximal parent, the Milan therapist appeals to the part of us that longs for an omniscient and formidable parent, whose unexplained directives we can follow without having to think for ourselves. (From a child's perspective, probably *much* of what adults say sounds like Milan-style rituals and prescriptions.) Families who have gone through terrible pain and have tried every technique and read every self-help book sometimes find tremendous relief in a therapy in which the practitioners, through the metamessage of their unapproachability, convey quasi-religious authority and inspire hope for a cure. (It has often been suggested that miracle cures occur at Lourdes because the journey itself and the excitement and drama over the ritual magnify the supplicants' belief in God's power to act on their behalf).

The longing for omniscient help may be part of the character structure of the Milan clientele, or it may be a result of the desperation of these individuals caused by their acquaintance with catastrophe, or both. Whether this type of transference is good or justifiable or preferable under what conditions and with what limitations are questions that should remain open, for both feminists and nonfeminists who employ the Milan method.

PART III

History and Insight:
Toward a Feminist
Theory of Psychotherapy
with Families

10

The Family in History: Gender and Structure in Five Types of Families from Antiquity to the Present

The tradition of all the dead generations weighs like a nightmare on the brain of the living.

—KARL MARX
The Eighteenth Brumaire of Louis Bonaparte, 1852

In an age that has forgotten theory, theory has to begin in remembrance.

—CHRISTOPHER LASCH
Introduction to Russell Jacoby's *Social Amnesia,*
1975

THE DISCIPLINE of family therapy is demonstrably rich in technique and notoriously deficient in theory. The construction of an adequate theory of family therapy rests contingent on understanding the family in its temporal context, which is to say, on understanding the family historically. Historical thinking, as pointed out in part II, is missing from, and to varying degrees incompatible with, structural functionalism, behaviorism, conventional psychodynamic thinking, and prefeminist humanism, which have been pressed into service by various schools of family therapy for theoretical legitimation.

One of the best arguments for the importance of historical perspectives comes from the Batesonian heuristic device known as "double description" (1979), a term Bateson used to teach the benefits of investigating phenomena from more than one information source. To illustrate this concept, Bateson pointed out that the right and left eyes present slightly different pictures to the brain at any given moment. The difference between the two views is information of a different logical type and contributes to our ability to see depth in the visual field.*

We can use this metaphor to understand the importance to family therapists of historical thinking. As therapists we are accustomed to seeing "overinvolved mothers," "peripheral fathers," and "triangulated children." Although we "see" troubled families through clinical eyes, we can choose to view them also through historical eyes. The latter view reveals the way that culture limits social and sexual choices and shapes the structures that clinicians come to think of as inevitable. Inclusion of both perspectives introduces depth into the practitioner's vision, and cannot help but affect the way treatment is conceptualized and carried out.

Another way to explain the importance of historical thinking is to show the problems that result from avoiding such thinking. In part II, we saw that the leading authors in family therapy have either treated the family as ahistorical, or given it an entirely mythical history. As a result, we have seen a number of unsupported assumptions pervade the literature, e.g., that the family follows certain universal laws across times and places, or that the family was once a glorious institution before being corrupted by the ills of modernity, or that the family was once a place hostile to individual freedoms and children's welfare until it evolved to the "benign" structure of the contemporary period.

To construct a theory of family therapy that rests even lightly on any of these notions is to be lost from the start. The analysis that follows, in attempting to derail each of these faulty trains of thought, will make several points:

1. Far from being universal, the closely bonded nuclear family of the contemporary period is not a historical constant, nor is the intense interest in children's needs a constant.

2. While the contemporary family is not universal, neither is it historically unique. In fact, the allegedly "new" working mother, the

---

*"Double description," also called "multiple description" and "multiple specification," is explained by Bateson in *Mind and Nature* (1979). Bateson acknowledges C. S. Peirce's notion of *abduction* as the inspiration for his own term. Peirce (1908/1958) used *abduction* to refer to a kind of reasoning through metaphor that could be added to our categories of thought, along with *deduction* and *induction*.

"new" practice of substitute child care, and the "new" phenomenon of women protesting their conditions are all centuries-old.

3. The contemporary family is in some ways the same as, and in other ways different from, other family forms, and it cannot be said to have "progressed" on a single course from barbarism to the Waltons. As we shall see, the families of Roman antiquity share more in common with modern structures than do families of several intervening centuries. This conclusion, unlike the first two, differs from those of widely read historians such as Phillipe Ariès—a point to be discussed shortly. Understanding that social transformations do not occur in linear or even step-wise fashion is important. It helps us to ruin the myth of progress, a myth that impedes change by providing the intellectual alibi for complacency.

4. Finally, the contemporary family—neither historically unique or universal, nor the happy ending of a long journey toward it—derives its structure from the bourgeois family of eighteenth- and nineteenth-century Europe. It is this family that introduced the pattern I have called *patriarchal but father-absent* (see chapter 1).

There is a wide gap in the text of family therapy in regard to history,* and the lengthy discussion that ensues is meant to compensate in part for that gap. Nevertheless, I attempt here neither a complete nor a definitive history of the family. Family history is a relatively new branch of history, and many of the issues raised remain subjects of scholarly debate.

It is tempting, when reviewing family history, to "begin at the beginning" and to speculate about what the first human families might have been like. Nineteenth-century scholars such as Bachofen (1861) and Engels (1884/1968) wrote on this subject, suggesting that a matriarchal world had preceded the dawn of male dominance and private property. Contemporary feminists (French 1985) claim that although there is no evidence that a matriarchy—a society in which women rule men—ever existed, early societies may have been *matricentric*—organized informally around units of mothers and children (cf. de Beauvoir 1952). Feminist anthropologists have argued against the assumption that patriarchy is inevitable because male dominance is "natural." On the contrary, many species, such as lions and elephants, are matricentric, and male domination of females may exist

*There is one book, *The Mirages of Marriage,* by William Lederer and Don Jackson, that begins with a chapter entitled "The Origins of Marriage and the Family," but the authors cite not a single source and the chapter is replete with errors of fact and interpretation. In addition, Froma Walsh's *Normal Family Processes* (1982) contains a chapter on family history by Tamara Hareven, but the historical perspective does not inform the rest of the book.

more consistently within the human species than in any other (Hrdy 1981). Historian Gerda Lerner (1986) has contended that patriarchy probably began only 6,000 years ago and that it was firmly entrenched by 3000 B.C., as evidenced by extant Sumerian laws.

As fascinating as it is to consider shards of evidence from prehistory and to speculate, for example, about how the discovery of men's role in procreation might have changed social organization, our focus here will be different; only periods for which written documentation exists will be considered. In order to illustrate certain key points about changes in family structure and the social organization of gender, I have selected five family forms for inspection here: (1) the upper-class family of the Roman Republic, (2) the aristocratic family of sixteenth- and seventeenth-century Europe, (3) the peasant family of sixteenth- and seventeenth-century Europe, (4) the bourgeois family of eighteenth- and nineteenth-century Europe and America, and (5) the working-class black family of contemporary America.

The chapter concludes with a discussion of how the information synthesized here can instruct the actual practice of feminist psychotherapy with families.

The Upper-Class Family of the Roman Republic
(509–27 B.C.)

One of the most striking features of historian Sarah Pomeroy's landmark book about women in antiquity, *Goddesses, Whores, Wives and Slaves* (1975), is the difference she shows between women's lives in ancient Greece and in ancient Rome. Whereas in Greece, most wives were sequestered with their children in special "women's quarters" (the *gynaceum*), Roman women held a central place in the household and also appeared in public routinely. The duties of Roman women included weaving cloth, teaching children, and supervising servants. Their work was respected and sometimes eulogized by male writers (Balsdon 1962). The father's centrality and final authority were clear, however. For example, a newborn child would be placed at the father's feet: if he chose to take the baby in his arms, it was accepted into the family; if not, it was taken by a servant and "exposed" on the highway. Some rejected infants were retrieved by passersby and raised as slaves; many simply perished. Girls were more often exposed than boys, since the Roman warrior culture valued sons. The Roman practice of infanticide was less common than it was in Greece in the same period. In addition to more frequent exposures, Greeks, during certain times, allowed mothers who nursed daughters only half the rations of those who nursed sons (Pomeroy 1975, p. 85).

What can be said about the care and development of the Roman infant? Despite the practice of infanticide, sources agree that Romans cared a great deal about the children they raised. We know that Roman women breast-fed their own infants; wet nursing, a custom widely practiced in subsequent centuries, was used, but not commonly. Women of the upper classes had servants to help them with child care, but nursing was considered an important maternal occupation. Roman commentators around the end of the Republic considered it a sign of decadence that women were beginning to entrust too much of the care of their children to servants (Balsdon 1962, Joshel 1986). Babies were given a first name during a ceremony that took place when they were eight days old, and birth certificates were issued (Balsdon 1962). We also know that Roman babies were swaddled, which involved wrapping the baby from foot to head in bands of stiff cloth, usually over a softer tunic, in order to keep the bones straight and to provide warmth. How often the Romans changed the infants' clothes while they were swaddled is not certain.

It is impossible to talk with confidence about the nature of the bonding between mother and infant, since the Romans did not write in our psychological terms and, perhaps more important, because every extant source was written by a male. Because the mother-infant relationship was valued and lyricized, and because the Roman woman was allowed some help but was warned not to employ too much help, it is reasonable to hypothesize that infancy for the upper-class Roman child of 200 b.c. had something in common with infancy for the modern child. Certainly there is more overlap between them than there is between mother-infant relationships of Roman times and of the subsequent ten centuries, as we shall see.

One stands on much firmer ground in discussing the daily life of the young Roman child. Roman children played with toys and games that were different from those of adults and that could be easily recognized by modern people: blocks, dolls, hoops, and stilts. For pets they had dogs, quail, and mice, the last being used to pull little wooden carts (Balsdon 1962). Both boys and girls learned to read and write and were instructed at home by their mothers. Schools existed but were attended mainly by boys, while girls remained at home and learned the household crafts. Many Roman women did become educated and some even became writers and orators, but, as mentioned, none of their work has survived. It was said that the best Latin was spoken by the noble women of the great houses of Rome (Johnston 1903).

During the early republic, fathers took their pre-adolescent sons to the Senate with them in order to acquaint them with public life (Balsdon 1962). Mothers and daughters are described as being closer than fathers and sons. They related to each other as best friends, in fact, until the daughter's wedding day. The custom on that day was for the mother to dress her daughter with a sash tied around the waist, which only the husband could untie. During the ceremony, the groom took the bride away from her mother with a "ritual show of force," again suggesting the degree of closeness between them (Balsdon 1962).

Marriages were arranged by the fathers of the two young people, based on political plans. In fact, during a long stretch of Roman history, a father could divorce a daughter from her husband and marry her to another man, without giving her a reason or any recourse. The woman's husband had considerable power as well. He could divorce or even kill her for adultery, while she could do little about his infidelity. Roman men apparently extremely disliked seeing their women drunk. Early in Roman history, women were not permitted wine at all. One man beat his wife to death for drinking wine and was acquitted of murder by King Romulus (Balsdon 1962). One Roman writer explained that the reason women are kissed by their relatives on greeting is in order to smell their breath for alcohol (Pomeroy 1975). The taboo on drinking was clearly related to the idea that women were very sexual creatures and that, under the influence of alcohol, they would become totally licentious. (The taboo was a brutal one, but the Roman woman was not suppressed in the way Victorian women were—by being taught that they had no sexual desires.)

A change for Roman women came around 200 B.C., in the middle of the republican period, when Rome fought two wars with Carthage. These Punic wars drained men out of Rome, and women were left to run businesses, farms, and families. When the men returned, they expected the women to return to their subordinate position—a phenomenon that has repeated itself throughout history. Some of the Roman women protested, however, and actually demonstrated in the Forum. They demanded, in particular, the repeal of the *lex oppia,* a law forbidding women to carry more than a tiny amount of gold or to wear costly materials. The Senate was forced to debate the issue, and the debate was reportedly fierce. Cato argued that women should be denied this privilege simply because they felt so strongly about it; he insisted that female greed was insatiable (Balsdon 1962). Other senators spoke in favor of the women, however, and the *lex oppia* was in fact repealed. *This puts the first successful (recorded) feminist protest at 195 B.C.!* (Pomeroy 1975, Balsdon 1962.)

In Rome after the Punic wars, as in the United States after World War II, the divorce rate soared. We do not have statistics from Rome, but divorce and remarriage are discussed a great deal in Roman literature and were seen by the Romans themselves as a sign of social decay (Balsdon 1962). Before a marriage failed completely, however, there was a preventive measure available: the ancient Romans of the second century B.C. could participate in something like what we call "marital therapy." This fascinating custom is described—much too briefly!—by Valerius Maximus, who wrote books about Roman history and mores around 20 A.D. (Apparently, by the time of his writing, the custom had already ceased to exist.) Valerius's purpose in describing this practice seems clearly to be one of illustrating that the older generations were more ethical and more devoted to marriage. He wrote:

> Whenever a difference arose between two spouses, they sought the temple of the goddess Viriplaca on the Palatine. There, after hearing each other out, they ended their quarrel and returned home in peace. This goddess, called Viriplaca because she pacifies husbands, is surely most venerable. Perhaps she deserves a unique and special homage since she guards the daily peace of families. Her very name reflects the honor owed by women to the majesty of their husbands in an equal tie of endearment.*

This is the earliest example I know of an attempt by married people to improve their relationship by participating together in a ritual. It is delightful to us because the essence of the ritual apparently was not the receipt of advice nor the prediction of the future but *talking to each other ("invicem loquitis")*. The temple in question, moreover, was located on the Palatine, which happens to be the place where Romulus and Remus were nursed by the she-wolf. It is not clear whether the Romans drew a connection between these two events, but the association of a therapeutic ritual with a place of primordial nurturance is compelling. What is disconcerting, however, and all too familiar, is that a premium is placed on placating the husband so as not to unbalance his majesty; *Viriplaca,* in fact, means the "appeaser of husbands." All roads, it seems, lead to unbalancing through the mother!

---

*Valerius Maximus, *Factorum Dictorumque Memorabilium,* 2, 1, 6. This three-volume work on Roman mores has not been translated into English. The above is my translation from the French edition of 1834, which I verified with classicist Joel Itzkowitz.

A NOTE ON THE WORK OF ARIÈS

What is most significant about this glimpse of Roman social history is that the Roman concepts of childhood and family appear to be closer to the twentieth-century concepts than are those of the intervening centuries. The reader who is familiar with the work of French historian Philippe Ariès will already have noted a substantial difference between the preceding account and the thesis of his classic text, *Centuries of Childhood* (1962). In that book, Ariès posited that the concept of childhood (i.e., the very notion that children are different from adults and require special understanding) did not exist until the thirteenth century and did not flower until the eighteenth. Ariès began his analysis with the Middle Ages and described the lack of distinction between adults' and children's toys and dress, the lack of documentation of children's ages, the widespread practice of sending babies out to wet nurses, and the depiction of children in art as merely miniature adults. It is unfortunate that Ariès did not take antiquity into account when he concluded that the concept of childhood was not discovered until the thirteenth century, for the study of Rome clearly produces many counterexamples to his thesis.* It would probably be more accurate to say that childhood was *rediscovered* between the thirteenth and eighteenth centuries. The danger in knowing only Ariès's work is that one may draw the conclusion that society has moved on a consistent path of progress from one century to the next. (Lloyd De Mause [1974] makes this error explicitly, arguing that society has evolved through a series of stages from brutal to benign with regard to the treatment of children.) We will take up this issue of the ideology of "progress" later in this chapter.

In any case, Ariès was certainly correct about the period of social history he chose to describe. His book is an encyclopedia of information about childhood from the Middle Ages to the modern period, drawing on hundreds of paintings, diaries, letters, and sermons. Barbara Tuchman (1978) concurs with Ariès that the Middle Ages produced almost no books on child care at all, although medieval people did write about how to care for pets, how to make ink and rat poison, how to behave at a banquet, and how to keep a husband happy. Medieval paintings show people in a host of human activities—eating, sleeping, dying, praying, hunting, and playing with pets—but not tending to children (Tuchman 1978).

---

*Even in Roman art and sculpture, one sees that children were portrayed as round, precious, and "childlike," with their own type of clothing and hairstyles—not merely as shorter adults. See, for example, the Roman collections in the Metropolitan Museum of Art in New York, the Cleveland Museum of Art, and the University of Pennsylvania Museum in Philadelphia.

116

The medieval Church, as Ariès points out, tried somewhat in vain to encourage better treatment of children. Some priests scolded that the roads and latrines resounded with the cries of abandoned babies. The Church, however, certainly did not see childhood in the modern way—as a time of innocence preceding the corruptions of socialization. On the contrary, priests quoted St. Augustine who had written, "No, Lord, there is no such thing as childhood innocence. The nature of childhood is completely negative and consists in the absence of true will. . . . Is it not a sin to lust after the breast and wail?" (quoted in Badinter 1980, p. 36).

Even as late as the sixteenth and seventeenth centuries, among both the aristocracy and the peasantry, the child was not considered to be precious and all-important, and indeed the structure of the family was quite different from what it became in the eighteenth and nineteenth centuries.

The Aristocratic Family of Sixteenth- and Seventeenth-Century Europe

Mark Poster, in his brilliant book, *Critical Theory of the Family* (1978), provides an analysis of the aristocratic family that forms an illuminating contrast to the modern family. Poster writes generally of sixteenth- and seventeenth-century Europe, rather than focusing on a single country, because his purpose—like mine—is to describe the history of the family and not the history of, say, France or England. I, too, will speak in general terms about this period (and the following two periods as well), making national distinctions where warranted.

Aristocratic families accounted for a tiny percentage of the populations of European countries in the sixteenth and seventeenth centuries—perhaps 1½ percent of the French population, for example. Poster describes the noble household as containing 40 to 200 people, including parents, children, relatives, and servants. The role of the man was to serve the king, to maintain order in his household, to make political deals, and to make decisions about his children's marriages and his daughters' dowries. The role of his wife was to preside over the social life of the court and to bear sons for her husband. Some women were taught to read and actually became learned, but educational trends varied greatly according to country and time period. British historian Antonia Fraser states in *The Weaker Vessel,* her work on women of sixteenth- and seventeenth-century England, that while Elizabeth I could translate Greek into Latin and advocated female literacy, her successor had a different view. James I, in fact, refused to educate his daughter because he believed that, like "taming foxes," it would only make females more cunning (Fraser 1984, p. 122). A few academies in the Middle Ages had accepted women, but this practice had stopped by the seventeenth century. Fraser, in fact, concludes that the position of women was in some ways *worse* by the year 1700 than it had been in 1600.

Like Roman women, aristocratic women of the sixteenth and seventeenth centuries were thought to enjoy sex just as men did. Both women and men of the aristocracy had affairs, and these were fairly public (Poster 1978). In contrast with the women of antiquity, however, the raising of children was not seen as a major female occupation. Aristocratic babies were not only raised by servants and taught by tutors, they were breast-fed by wet nurses who typically lived in the household. According to French historian Elizabeth Badinter, agencies for recruiting and screening wet nurses date back to the thirteenth century in France. (While the use of wet nurses was common only among the aristocracy until the sixteenth century, it later spread to other classes.)

Wet nursing was common all across Europe. Historian Lawrence Stone, in his monumental *The Family, Sex, and Marriage in England,* states that well into the eighteenth century the work of child care in general and of breast-feeding in particular was "entirely without social prestige" (Stone 1977, p. 270). Stone mentions a variety of reasons why aristocratic women employed wet nurses: illness after childbirth, the fact that nursing interfered with other activities, and also a "psychological hostility" to children. Badinter, in writing about France, concurs that the ideology of pleasure and leisure that surrounded the nobility did make children seem a nuisance. On the subject of indifference to children, the sentiments of philosopher Michel Montaigne are often quoted to characterize the attitudes of upper-class parents. Montaigne wrote: "I have lost two or three children in their infancy, not without regret, but without great sorrow" (quoted in Ariès 1962, p. 39).

What can we surmise, then, about children's early development in the sixteenth- and seventeenth-century aristocracy? Clearly, the first few months of life were not what they became in the modern family, and what they had perhaps been in Rome of antiquity—a time of close bonding with an attentive mother. Other developmental stages were equally different from those of the modern child. Infants of the sixteenth and seventeenth centuries were still being swaddled, for instance, and one can be fairly safe in assuming that the swaddling bands were not replaced as often as diapers are in contemporary nurseries, at the first sign of a wet spot. (Indeed, it would have been impossible to detect the first sign of wetness through the coarse fiber of the bands.)

It has been argued that children of the seventeenth century did not undergo an intense emotional encounter with their parents about the mastery of bladder control. There was no concept of "toilet training" until the modern period, and in fact, adults themselves urinated almost everywhere indoors (Poster 1978). The issue of childhood sexuality, moreover, was not something unfathomable or taboo to people of the seventeenth century. There was a general absence of privacy, since palaces had no corridors and one always had to walk through another person's rooms to get from one place to another. It was not unusual for children to see adults, particularly servants, having intercourse. Childhood masturbation was also not a matter of concern at this time. If we can speak of an "Oedipal stage" in this era, we cannot assume it had the same meaning that it does for the modern child. Poster commented astutely on this subject:

> Aristocratic sons may have had hostile feelings towards their fathers, but without the same intensity, without the same play of love against the body, without the same reliance on the father for support and identification, without the same value to the mother, without her deep concern and tenderness, without therefore needing to internalize the father as deeply. Surely . . . aristocrats had unconscious structures, but only the bourgeois generated an unconscious that was defined in terms of the denial of the body. [P. 177]

Another way of saying this is that aristocratic children grew up forming identifications not with particular adults but with the household itself, and with the family line. Aristocrats, then, would have grown up blaming their misfortunes on a family curse, on the stars, on a political defeat, or on God's wrath. They would not have blamed them on their parents' misreading of their early emotional needs, as modern people do. Of course, aristocratic parents wanted their children to bring honor to the family name, but they did not view children as their main source of emotional fulfillment, nor as proof of their competence.

Aristocratic children might be pitied by modern people for having had such formal relationships with their parents, but it may be that they did not experience the kind of emotional blackmail so common in the more tightly bonded, upwardly striving modern family.

The Peasant Family of Sixteenth- and Seventeenth-Century Europe

The peasant family of the same period was very different from the aristocratic family. Ironically, however, in some ways it shared more in common with the nobility than with the middle-class family of subsequent centuries, as we shall see.

Peasant families were relatively small, a finding that challenges the common misconception that peasant families in early European history had three generations co-residing. British historian Peter Laslett (1972) put this notion to rest in his well-known demographic research. Laslett found that average household size in England has held to approximately 4.75 in England from the sixteenth century to the twentieth. Laslett's data, however, should not be interpreted to mean, as some academicians summarily assumed, that the family has not changed drastically in 400 years. Four or five people can live together in radically different ways. The manner in which they deal with intimacy, the way they show each other respect, the point of view they have of gender and of their relationship to the community can be and has been very different.

In fact, the peasant families of sixteenth- and seventeenth-century Europe were extremely different from modern families of similar size. Authority was vested in the village, not in the conjugal unit; therefore life took place in the context of the entire village, not at the household level. Work, for example, was not a private event done in the isolation of the family's dwelling, much less in the solitude of the modern "office."

Collaboration was of the essence in this world. Laundry was done in great communal tubs, and crops were planted and harvested by villagers working together. The work was terribly hard and always tied to the climate. If it is a mistake to romanticize the past, however, it is also a mistake to think of it only as "the bad old days." The premodern world was one in which the realms that we have come to call the "productive" and the "personal"—the realms of work and home—were integrated rather than split apart (cf. Lasch 1977). In peasant culture, there were no workers making identical widgets for hours in factories whose din prevented conversation and whose rules forbade breaks for water or rest. This is an important set of issues to which we will return.

Turning to peasant mothers for a moment, it is interesting that the sentimental mother-child bond did not characterize their families any more than it did the nobility's. By the sixteenth and seventeenth centuries in some countries, not only the upper classes but also middle-class families (e.g., families of merchants and artisans) were sending their babies out to the countryside to wet nurses. At one point, in fact, the supply of peasant women wet nurses could not meet the demand in France (Badinter 1980, p. 42). Lawrence Stone says that "the use of rural wet nurses was more or less universal among all but the lowest classes in French towns and cities." Stone notes that the practice died out in France "only in the late nineteenth century and in Germany only in the twentieth, to be replaced in many cases by bottle feeding" (p. 273). The use of wet nursing has also been described in middle-class urban families in Italy of the sixteenth century (Ross 1974).

Although most peasant women nursed their own children, peasant babies cannot be said to have had an infancy comparable to the modern type, since those mothers were also nursing other babies for pay. (When breasts ran dry, babies were given a rag soaked in a gruel-like mixture to suck on, according to Badinter.) Furthermore, peasant babies were not only swaddled like babies of the noble class, they were hung by the swaddling clothes from hooks in barns while the women worked. They were not held close to the mother's body as are modern middle-class children, or as babies of native American societies were. Swaddling clothes were sometimes not changed for three weeks at a time, and babies suffered terrible infections from lying in their own excrement (Shorter 1975, Badinter 1980). In France, babies were packed like sardines into carts only a few days after birth to be transported to a wet nurse in the countryside. Five to fifteen percent died from falling out of the carts or from freezing weather, according to extant police records of the late eighteenth century (Badinter 1980). Babies were weaned at eighteen months of age, but only one child in four lived that long. Those who survived returned to their parents at the age of four or five and were sent away again at the age of nine to apprentice at neighboring farms (Badinter 1981). Given that children performed the same work there that they might have at home, this seems a somewhat peculiar practice, and one for which there is apparently no definitive understanding (Tuchman 1978). Perhaps parents believed that children would learn better manners in other households, or that it was easier to teach children who were not one's own. It may also be that they felt they could get more work out of strangers' children or abuse them more readily than their own.

At any rate, it is not surprising that children did not develop deep relationships with their parents. Children's lives were governed not by their parents' do's and don't's, but by religious and community mores. One would expect that their loyalty and affection was directed more diffusely to the community than to their parents. Edward Shorter (1975) describes the youth organizations of this period—groups devoted to a particular saint, for example—as being of greater importance to their members than were their biological families.

The descriptions offered by social historians of daily life in the sixteenth and seventeenth centuries are illustrated in the 1983 film *The Return of Martin Guerre.* * The film portrays the small dwellings inhabited by conjugal units, and it shows the absence of privacy and the salience of community. We see communal work being done, as well as the way in which the village enters the boundaries of the marital couple. On the wedding night of the protagonists, for example, the priest enters the room where they are lying in bed and blesses them. The other villagers enter their room, making bawdy jokes and offering good wishes. The protagonist deserts the village—an unusual event for the times—and, in his travels, meets a man who decides to return to the village and impersonate him. The impostor manages to fool everyone in the village, including, at least temporarily, the man's wife. When suspicions about the impostor are finally raised, the couple is taken in hand by the village and sent off to a tribunal of priests for judgment. The community, not the individual couple, is sovereign. Indeed, the individual counts for so little in this world that one can be mistaken for another!

The sociability of this period appeals to the sensibilities of many an alienated modern scholar. (It is said that people working the fields talked and sang together.) It is important, however, not to romanticize this period. Lives were short and physically exhausting, and women were at the mercy of their reproductive systems—and of their husbands as well. In England, for example, the "Lawes Resolution" of 1632 affirmed that a man was permitted to beat "an outlaw, a traitor, a Pagan or his wife, because by the Law Common, these persons can have no action" (Fraser 1984, p. 466).

This era, moreover, coincides with the most extensive assault on women in all of European history: the witch trials. The extent of the trials and burnings of women in Europe in the fifteenth to seventeenth centuries, and the reasons for them, are subjects still under debate by historians. Because of this controversy, several colleagues advised me not to mention the trials here. It would be indefensible, however, to ignore this subject simply because of the controversy and uncertainty surrounding it. It is impossible to obtain reliable statistics for any subjects or events before the modern era. Even when the question is as straightforward as the population of

---

*The film was made in collaboration with Princeton historian Natalie Zemon Davis. See her book, *The Return of Martin Guerre* (1983).

France, accounts vary by as much as 80 or even 100 percent (Tuchman 1978, p. xvi). This does not keep historians from writing about France. Thus, the fact that estimates vary from one hundred thousand to several million witches burned should not be used as a reason to omit the trials from descriptions of sixteenth-century European life, particularly if one is interested in the family. Can the institutionalized execution of women in a given historical period really be irrelevant to understanding motherhood in that same period?

The Catholic Church burned Joan of Arc at the stake in 1430, but the trials did not peak until the sixteenth century (French 1985). This peak was influenced by the publication of the *Malleus Maleficarum (The Witches' Hammer,* 1486), written by two priests and endorsed by Pope Innocent VIII who wrote an introduction to it. The *Malleus* was used for a century, instructing the clergy in the matters of identifying, trying, and executing witches. The authors, Fathers Sprenger and Kraemer, maintained that the devil chose women instead of men to be witches because women are "feebler in the mind and body than men," are "intellectually like children," and experience "insatiable lust." The witch trials were concentrated at first in Austria and then spread throughout Europe. In Toulouse, records show that 440 women were killed in one day. In Trier in 1585, two villages were left with only one female inhabitant each (French 1985). Children of the condemned women were often flogged in front of their mother while she perished in the flames.

Making sense out of this gynocide (as feminist Mary Daly has called it) is a redoubtable task. Most of the women executed were old and poor, and many of them practiced the old religion (Fraser 1984). The Church, reacting to the Reformation that threatened its doctrinal hold and imperial wealth, wished to rid itself of remaining pagan elements. Fraser comments that a large proportion of the accused women in England were midwives, and the era of the trials coincides with the replacement of female healers by male physicians whose new medical academies excluded women. Finally, there is a suggestion in the *Malleus* that it was better for a husband to accuse his wife of witchcraft than to divorce her, since divorce meant excommunication from the Church and "keeping" her meant enduring "daily strife."

The witch trials were caused and fueled by many factors, but it is reasonable to hypothesize that the heterodoxy, the healing power, and the autonomy of these women were significant threats to the Church. Szasz (1970) made a case for the witch as social scapegoat—someone on whom to place blame for the common misery. People of the premodern period were, of course, more at the mercy of *nature* than are modern people, and, as Dinnerstein (1976) has pointed out, women have always been associated with nature—with both its nurturing, sustaining power and also its cruel indifference. Many cultures split the image of woman into good and evil types which reflect the two faces of nature. In this historical period there was the witch, who was considered evil, hypersexual, and responsible for spreading disease, and there was the Virgin Mary, who was good, asexual, loving, and forgiving.

It seems to me hardly coincidental that this unprecedented assault on the female sex should overlap with the period in Western history when the mother-child relationship was so tenuous. It is remarkable that none of the social histories of the family (e.g., Shorter 1975, Ariès 1962, Poster 1978, Stone 1977, Badinter 1980), all of which make much of the absence of "mother love" during this period, mentions the absence of love *for* mothers. A mutually causal connection between them is suggested by the fact that in the modern period, as the status of women rises, so does the importance of children and child care. It may be that the more a given society prizes children, the better care it will take of its childbearers. Or, perhaps, the more a society values women, the greater importance it will assign to the work associated with women. In addition, to borrow a psychological analogy, it seems that we nurture well when we feel nurtured. The degree to which women are entitled by their society and nurtured by their peers, the greater, perhaps, will be their capacity to do many things well, including loving children.

In any case, the point should not be lost that the erasure from history of the phenomenon of witch killing is itself part of the phenomenon. The executions represent the intent on the part of some patriarchal sectors to eliminate midwives, or bad wives, or the "bad mother," from the social group. Traditional history books sustain the intent by failing even to mention these women. Textual elimination by historians, done in the name of avoiding subjects that cannot be investigated with accuracy, is what makes it easier for nonhistorians—family therapists, for example—to ignore the brutalization of women, past and present. The field of family therapy erases wife battering continually by producing text after text about "troubled families" without mentioning it.

A British marital therapist, whose book on marriage does not mention battering, has gone so far as to assert that "gross wife abuse" was actually "rare" in premodern England, based on the fact that it is not often recorded in parish registers, and on the reasoning that such abuse would have hurt the economically important collaboration between spouses (Hafner 1986, pp. 3–4). Hafner, in his otherwise worthwhile book, does not mention the fact that wife beating was not a crime, or that mutual dependency has never been much of a deterrent against the brutalization of wives. If the witch burnings had been part of the common fund of European historical knowledge taught in schools, it seems unlikely that humanistic authors such as Nagy and Spark could have written or even implied that society has always been concerned with providing women special protection and "privileges" without at least mentioning the most blatant historical exceptions.

The last two sections of this chapter have focused on the social and sexual disenfranchisements of women in the sixteenth and seventeenth centuries, but it is important not to leave this period without mentioning a very different aspect of it. Women were not simply victims or passive observers of social process during these two centuries—far from it. Historian Lawrence Stone reports that this period saw the emergence of "militant feminist ideas" among the English urban artisan population, a social group we have not had time to examine here. In 1642, a group of four hundred women organized to protest their economic conditions. Stone reports that these women "coolly faced a barrage of criticism that they were claiming to 'wear the breeches,' " and that " 'it can never be a good world when women meddle in state's matters' " (1977, pp. 225–27). This was not a one-time demonstration, moreover; the movement continued at least seven years and included the women's petitioning the House of Commons in 1649. Nonetheless, in the face of other politically conservative changes occurring in government and culture, the movement did not survive. One may say that feminist sentiment went underground in England, and did not re-emerge until Mary Wollstonecraft's *A Vindication of the Rights of Woman* in 1792. (See also Fraser on this subject.) In France, feminist uprisings occurred around the time of the revolution at the end of the eighteenth century (cf. French 1985).

The Modern Family: From the Bourgeois Family of the Eighteenth and Nineteenth Centuries to the Present

A bourgeois class emerged with the transition from feudalism to capitalism in different countries at different times (by 1500 in Italy and somewhat later in England and France). We will be focusing specifically on the bourgeois class in Europe from about 1750 on, because it is from this group—an urban group with a greater concentration on intimacy and privacy—that

125

the modern family descends. Our discussion will begin in Europe and take us up to the American family of the present, ignoring topics such as European-American immigration and pioneer families, in order to concentrate on broad ideological changes.* This history will reveal the origins of the categories that have become the staples of family therapy discourse: the "overinvolved mother," the "peripheral father," the "triangulation of the child," and the pervasive problem of separating from the family of origin, or "leaving home," as these occur in white families. (American black families are described in the next section.)

Historian Edward Shorter, in his influential *The Making of the Modern Family* (1975), suggests that three phenomena that began in the eighteenth and nineteenth centuries mark the emergence of the modern family: the sentimental mother-child bond,† the cultivation of home as separate from workplace and community, and romance-based marriage.

MOTHERHOOD

There can be no doubt about the fact that the eighteenth and nineteenth centuries saw a change in the ideology of motherhood from that of the previous period. The importance of the close mother-child bond, which appears to have existed in ancient Rome, again took root in the French Enlightenment, and particularly in the work of Jean-Jacques Rousseau. Rousseau, writing in the late eighteenth century, advanced the notion that people are born free and are corrupted by society. He was fascinated with "primitive" people such as American Indian tribes, and urged that all people learn to live according to nature. Rousseau promulgated the idea that infants be treated with great care, not handed over to strangers. He recommended that mothers breast-feed their babies and stop swaddling them so that they could move their limbs freely. Rousseau believed that

*In fact, this section, as its heading states, focuses only on middle-class families. The history of working-class families during this period—particularly that of men and women in factories—is an important one as well. The structure of working-class families in the nineteenth century was different from that of middle-class families of the same period, but it was the structure of the middle-class family that survived and "spread" to other classes. In the interests of not making this chapter excessively long, I have deleted the working-class family for this precise reason—that it was eventually taken over by the bourgeois forms. See Shorter (1975) and Poster (1978) for a discussion of this issue.

†Shorter, like Ariès, overemphasizes the novelty of the close mother-child bond by comparing the modern period only to adjacent centuries and ignoring antiquity. Moreover, although Shorter's book contains a vast amount of valuable information about the modern family, it suffers from the assumption that the sentiments that characterize modern families were always present in people and were somehow just waiting to be let out. See Poster's (1978) criticism of Shorter on this score.

women were intelligent and should be given support and education for their "natural" role as mothers and wives.

This romantic view of motherhood also had its unromantic side. Badinter claims that motherhood became important in France at this time because the country was interested in increasing its population for political reasons, particularly to colonize the new world. Badinter wages the Marxist contention that every society simply invents the definition of motherhood that it needs to function economically.

Whatever the reasons—and there were many—for the new cult of motherhood, Rousseau's philosophy spread rapidly across Europe and America and found its way into Sunday sermons, doctors' advice to patients, and educators' books on child care. Physicians began to warn that women who did not breast-feed would cause their children epilaxis, diarrhea, and sweating (Badinter 1980, p. 156). Mothers were to devote themselves exclusively to child care, and anything that might go wrong with the child was associated with her incompetence. What emerged, in fact, was a belief that behind every criminal, alcoholic, and madman was a mother who had not done her duty. Maternal guilt was born—or at least given a new lease on life.

The pressure on women to be attentive mothers apparently worked. Bourgeois women of this period did indeed immerse themselves in the care of their children. They began breast-feeding and felt guilty if they could not. It would be logical to hypothesize that the reason mothers became closer to their children at this time was simply that children were beginning to live longer. Surely it would have been very painful to attach oneself to a child who was likely to die in infancy. As logical as this argument sounds, however, the data do not support it. A number of scholars have argued vigorously against this idea, insisting instead that it was the increase in maternal attention to children that lowered the infant mortality rates (Shorter 1975, Degler 1980, Badinter 1980). And, indeed, it seems significant that in countries such as Austria and Germany, where Rousseau's message did not take an early hold, the mother-infant relationship did not change significantly, and infant mortality actually increased during this same period (Shorter 1975, pp. 202–3).

Most of Europe saw a revolution in the definition of adequate child care as a result of Enlightenment ideals. Never before, it seems, had women's lives been so exclusively equated with mothering. One hundred years after Rousseau, philosophers were still writing statements such as, "The maternal instinct dominates everything else . . . for, from the cradle onward, woman is mother, mad with motherhood" (Jules Michelet, quoted in Badinter 1980, p. 215). (The metaphor of madness in association with exclusive mothering is indeed interesting, in light of the fact that another major "occupation" for the bourgeois woman became that of psychiatric patient.)

It is easy to see that this new emphasis on the preciousness of motherhood and the sacred duty of attentive child care had a major effect on how children were treated and how personality was shaped within the family. Without doubt, the new emphasis on childhood had many salubrious consequences for children: infanticide and abandonment were now considered social abominations; children were no longer sent out to wet nurses, or apprenticed out to neighboring households and farms. In the old regime, not only were children sent away for major portions of their lives, but often mothers were not even informed about their welfare or development. Now mothers witnessed their children's first steps, taught them their first words, and invested their self-esteem into the growth and perfection of their little ones.

This new attentiveness also contained a large measure of repression, however, particularly with regard to sexuality. Before this time, there had been little social concern with children's sexuality; children would often see animals and even adults having intercourse, and there was little fuss over childhood masturbation. The Victorian world, as is well known, had a horror of "self-abuse," and child-rearing manuals of the period instructed mothers in devising cardboard tubes to slip over babies' elbows to prevent them from reaching their genitals (Poster 1978). Physicians warned that masturbation caused every problem from acne to insanity, and toilet training was done in a harsh, disciplinary way (cf. Miller 1983b).

The adult dominion over children and their bodies was nothing new, of course; children had always been beaten and abused. What was new was that the physical controls and punishments were being administered in the name of improving the child's personality and, even more important, in the context of an intensely personal parent-child relationship. Poster (1978), in contrasting the peasant family with the nineteenth-century bourgeois family, stated that the bourgeois child, unlike the peasant child, had to pit bodily pleasure against parental approval—exchanging physical gratification for maternal love. Repression in the bourgeois family thus made it the breeding ground for the kind of neurosis that Freud was to describe.

Although mothers' involvement with children clearly increased at this time, fathers' involvement probably decreased. (It is interesting that in all of Rousseau's writings about child rearing, the father's role is not mentioned.) The nineteenth-century bourgeois father did some physical disciplining and some moralizing, but he was no longer the omnipresent figure of the old regime who had worked the fields with his sons for some years and taught them his skills. (The peasant boy, who was apprenticed to another household, would have had *another* father as his boss for that period of time.) The bourgeois son, however, might grow up in the nearly exclusive company of his mother, since father was out of the home, at work. Social conditions were thus ideal for the creation of what is now called the "overinvolved mother" and the "peripheral father."

THE CULT OF DOMESTICITY

The rise of capitalism in the eighteenth and nineteenth centuries meant that the family, once a unit of production, became instead of unit of consumption. Whereas families had once baked their own bread and made their own clothing, soap, and furniture, these items were now manufactured and could be purchased in stores with wages earned. Home and workplace, which had previously been one and the same place, were now split into two distinct spheres. Ariès (1962) describes this process taking place among professional men like lawyers, not only among merchants and craftsmen. Mark Poster states: "Men had to leave their homes and establish separate, functionally differentiated places of business. The home was no longer a place of production, but one of leisure, of time outside the work world" (p. 170).

For the rising middle class, this created a sharp division of the world according to gender. Of course, a distinction had always existed between women's work and men's work, but in agrarian society the two sexes nonetheless had worked in the same physical space, often side by side in the fields. Family members could talk to each other, and men and women basically knew what the other was doing. The new regime brought men out of the home; they belonged to a new sphere—one of business, white collars, and sometimes travel. Women, conversely, belonged to the family; they were no longer "workers" but domestic "angels." Whether the new doctrine of the "separate spheres" was a step forward or backward for women has been the subject of some controversy (cf. Smith-Rosenberg 1986). Some commentators view the bifurcation of the bourgeois world according to gender as a step backward for women precisely because it made their work invisible. (No one would have asked a peasant mother whether she worked; nearly everyone has asked contemporary mothers that question.)

Bourgeois wives, moreover, were forced to embody a stifling ideal of femininity: unambitious, morally superior, asexual, and physically delicate. Their clothing surely kept them from "running around" in any sense of the term; their corsets applied as much as twenty-one pounds of pressure to their internal organs (Ehrenreich and English 1979). Moreover, women in this era lost a very important social task that had long been theirs: healing. The medical profession had been trying since the Renaissance to replace female midwives with male doctors, and by the nineteenth century doctors had almost won the battle in England and America. Women, who had always been in the care of each other, particularly during childbirth, were increasingly in the hands of male professionals. Turning specifically to the United States for a moment, it is a little-known fact of our history that the American Medical Association managed to criminalize abortion during the nineteenth century. *Abortion had been legal in the United States for the previous 100 years.* The AMA fought a sedulous campaign against abortion, arguing that only female self-indulgence could motivate women to reject pregnancy, and that the choice to abort was leading women to "irresponsible," nondomestic lives (Smith-Rosenberg 1986, pp. 236–37). Women, who could not yet vote, were clearly in no position relative to male physicians to influence the legislators who sealed their fate.

In *For Her Own Good: 150 Years of the Experts' Advice to Women* (1979), Barbara Ehrenreich and Deirdre English describe how women of the eighteenth and nineteenth centuries were made to trade their role as healers for one as patients. Many women, undoubtedly suffering from their unproductive and understimulating lives, were treated for years with psychoanalysis, psychosurgery, and "rest cures." Charlotte Perkins Gilman's powerful novella *The Yellow Wallpaper* (1899) describes an intelligent and creative woman who is given doctor's orders to do nothing but rest, not even to write, and who is actually driven insane by her treatment.

There is another side to this controversy about the effects of the "separate spheres" ideology. Some scholars have argued that this change was actually the beginning of modern women's emancipation. It did, after all, remove the father from the home, thus beginning to unravel some of the earlier ties of patriarchal control. The bourgeois woman had her own domain. She actually had privacy from her husband for at least part of the day, and had a good deal of responsibility for running the household in his absence. She knew, for example, what was going on with the children and the servants, and had the power to give or withhold information from the husband who had not been present. Some women (usually unmarried) also managed to get an education. Indeed, the first group of educated women in the United States managed to get their degrees during this very period. Because they were considered to be angels of good will, women were permitted to do some charitable work outside the home, and some women even lectured about abolitionism and women's rights. It was this era, after all, that produced Susan B. Anthony, Elizabeth Cady Stanton, Lucy Stone, Sojourner Truth, and Jane Addams.*

Both sides of the controversy about the result of separate spheres for women have partial validity. In fact, one might say that the host of social contradictions contemporary women face—our mixture of educational opportunities with our continued financial inequality and overdependence on male professionals—derives from the contradictions of this historical period.

ROMANTIC LOVE/SEXUALITY

In the premodern era, marriages had been arranged by the older generation for the younger. Among the aristocracy, the matches were made on the basis of dynastic/political requirements, and for the peasantry, on the basis of economic considerations. There was, accordingly, less expectation that marriage would bring the kind of personal satisfaction and "growth" that is part of the modern view. People have always had romantic feelings, of course, and fallen in love, but these feelings were not typically associated with marriage until the eighteenth and nineteenth centuries. Couples in the old regime had hoped for health, freedom from want, and compatibility with each other; couples in the new era expected romance, excitement, and happiness.

The new type of marriage had obvious advantages: people were now free from the yoke of the family of origin and had the chance to take their own destinies in hand. Certain other aspects of the newly modern world, however, made the dream of the perfect marriage hard to realize. The first had to do with sexuality. It was surely difficult to reach conjugal bliss if one of the partners was considered to be free of sexual desire—to feel, in fact, dread and shame over it. The bourgeoisie and, in particular, the Victorian world, had difficulty conceiving of mothers as sexual. Just as women had for centuries been considered overly sexual by nature, they were now considered asexual by nature. Women were made to think of their sexual feelings as pathological, and were subjected to treatments that were nothing short of sadistic. Ehrenreich and English write:

*It should be noted that nineteenth-century feminists themselves disagreed about separate spheres. Some, such as Anthony, emphasized the importance of women's attaining the same legal and social rights as men, while others emphasized the importance of elevating the status of what most women did: care for children. Rather than fighting the new abortion laws, some early feminists fought instead for women's right to say no to their husbands' demands for sexual intercourse, quite a radical plea for the time. See Ellen Du Bois (1978) and Linda Gordon (1977) for a history of early feminists and reproductive issues.

The most common form of surgical intervention in the female personality was ovariotomy, removal of the ovaries—or "female castration." In 1906, a leading gynecological surgeon estimated that there were 150,000 women in the United States who had lost their ovaries under the knife. Some doctors boasted that they had removed from fifteen hundred to two thousand ovaries apiece. According to historian G. J. Barker-Benfield: "Among the indications were troublesomeness, eating like a ploughman, masturbation, attempted suicide, erotic tendencies, persecution mania and simple 'cussedness.' Most apparent in the enormous variety of symptoms doctors took to indicate castration was a strong current of sexual appetitiveness on the part of women." [1983, pp. 123–24]

This maltreatment was not limited to women of the United States. Jeffrey Masson (1984) describes the case of Emma Eckstein, who endured a series of nasal surgeries intended to cure her desire to masturbate. (The nose was thought to be related to sexual feelings.) Although Freud is blamed (correctly) for his pathologizing of the Victorian woman, he at least recognized that women had sexual desires and that it was the repression and not the expression of desire that would prove debilitating.

Male sexuality of the nineteenth century was addled by its own repressions and contradictions. In that world of business, money making, and social climbing, young men were taught not to "squander" their energies on love too early. They were socialized to see in sexuality everything that was unbusinesslike: lack of control, emotional expressiveness, and, quite literally, "spending," as Mark Poster has described it. Poster concluded: "A gospel of thrift was applied to semen as well as to money" (1978, p. 169). Thus, bourgeois men were themselves forced to deny their sexual desires toward the women they loved until they had amassed certain amounts of capital—and in the meantime to seek the company of prostitutes. Venereal disease reached epidemic rates in the nineteenth century and ruined many a marriage and career (Marcus 1964, Janik and Toulmin 1973).

In addition to sexual repression, another aspect of the new social order affected the quality of marital relationships: the alienating quality of men's work itself. Of course, in some ways, the emergence of the urban, industrialized, professional world made life much easier for men. Working indoors in offices made them less subject to the physical hardships of agrarian toil and less vulnerable to the vagaries of season and climate.

This transformation from a largely rural to a largely urban economy, however, had its disadvantages as well. Peasants had a different relationship to each other and to their labor itself than did the rising urban populace. In the technical Marxist sense, labor is "alienated" when workers do not own their means of production. Also, a peasant baking bread or carving chairs has the more direct, "sensuous" relationship with the goods produced than does the factory worker producing the same widgets hour after hour. Many social scientists have come to use the word *alienated* to refer broadly to the sense of estrangement modern people have vis-à-vis their work. Not only factory work but also the work of the bourgeois businessman caught up in bureaucratic minutiae can be considered alienated. Unlike the work done in the village, the work of the businessman can be done "at arm's length" from other human beings, as Mark Poster has observed. In fact, in the contemporary period, prestige and power in corporations, for example, correspond to the amount of space between the executive and both employees and clientele. Ranking businessmen have a secretary (or two) between themselves and any potential interlocutor. And the distancing forms of communication, such as the business memorandum, the form letter, and the answering machine, needless to say, did not exist in the old regime.

Peasant life, of course, had its own problems; lack of privacy can be oppressive, and relating continuously to co-workers means constantly subordinating one's own preferences to the interests of the group. It is, of course, impossible to know how people of the past "felt" about their lives. However, it is obvious that life in the premodern world made different psychological demands on people than does modern life. The seventeenth-century farmer was a farmer at any hour of the day. He did not have to don a mask, a professional persona, for the workplace. He did not "wear two hats" each day, or have, as a local television ad states it, "Two banks: one for the businessman in me, one for the *human being.*"

The literature of the industrial world reflects this newly enforced split between the public and the personal realms, at times depicting literal madness as a result of the division. The quintessential example of this is Herman Melville's *Bartleby the Scrivener,* whose protagonist is a clerk in a nineteenth-century Wall Street office. Bartleby refuses to acquiesce to the demands of the bureaucracy in which he is supposed to function, and his dispassionate, "I would prefer not to," in response to requests from his boss, has come to symbolize the individual's impotence in the face of the dehumanized workplace. The mad Bartleby eventually moves into his office, in a poignant attempt, perhaps, to heal the split within himself and, symbolically, the split between home and workplace, personal and public, in the brave new industrial world. (See also Joel Kovel's discussion of Bartleby in *The Age of Desire,* 1981.)

Almost from the beginning of the industrial period, there was some recognition that men's work was difficult, depleting, and even "inhuman." The role of women, thus, was to provide the "haven in a heartless world"

133

for those men (Lasch 1977). The new companionate marriage was supposed to be the antidote to the dehumanized work world. However, these men—who were trained to split off their feelings from their thoughts, who spent their days with other repressed men and away from the more sensuous world of the home and children, who were out of touch with their own desires because that was what was adaptive in business—were not in the best psychological condition to be intimate companions to their wives. Indeed, many women found their husbands detached, taciturn, and sometimes violent. Where could these women turn for conversation, company, and support?

Women had each other, of course, but their contact and interdependence were not the same as they had been in village life. Bourgeois women, whose husbands inhabited a different world from their own, may well have found their *children* to be more emotionally available, more lively, and better sources of support than their husbands. Indeed, in this family structure in which women and children (the less powerful members of society) were set off together from men (the more powerful members of society), it was almost inevitable that *triangulation*—the coalition of one child and one parent against the other parent—would be the order of the day. As mentioned earlier, mothers now knew what children had been up to during the day and were in the position of either telling the father and recommending punishment or withholding the information. The "let's-not-tell-Daddy-you-did-this" syndrome, which is familiar to contemporary therapists, was perhaps extremely common in the bourgeois home of this period.

In general, the advantage for children of the bourgeois family was the protection, the solicitude, the attention to detail about their lives that was now encouraged. The disadvantage to this closeness emerged when the time came to separate from the family. Children of other eras had had a lot of experience being apart from their families before maturity. Indeed, they separated from them as infants, returned, left again to apprentice on other farms, and returned again. In the nineteenth century, there were middle-class children who did not leave home until they were young adults. In addition to being emotionally close to the family and perhaps being the most important companion to the mother, this made it more difficult for children to separate from the family of origin than it had been before.

Another aspect of the issue of leaving home has to do with a very different factor: the social mobility of this class. Modern bourgeois parents wanted their children not only to be happy but to "get ahead," to rise in social status. This excitement about children being financially ascendant is historically unique, since social classes in premodern societies were relatively fixed. We modern people are so accustomed to thinking that striving for a better (meaning more affluent) life is a reason for being that we forget it is not a timeless value. A life devoted to ameliorating one's circumstances and imitating more affluent members of society is peculiar to the bourgeoisie.

This peculiarity, in addition to its obvious economic benefits, also generated a unique psychological dilemma—one that still plagues the contemporary family. It seems to me that the bourgeois family became the only family form in history whose very essence required disloyalty. Children in all families, of course, had to differentiate from them, but for the bourgeois child of the early modern period, differentiation was a most complex and contradictory affair. The bourgeois child was necessarily caught between wanting to move beyond the social class and customs of the family of origin and wanting to remain in the same boat with them. To the extent that the child succeeded in the world (i.e., was loyal), she or he was accepting a set of customs, a geographical location, and even an ethical system that was different from those of the family of origin. But to remain close to the family, of course, meant being disloyal, because the child was then rejecting the parental sacrifice that had been made in order for the younger generation to "get ahead." Thus inherent in the modern family were the seeds of ambivalence, if not an actual double bind. Its message was, "Show us your loyalty by rejecting everything we stand for." The problem that family therapists face each day, which we call one of "leaving home," thus has something to do with the economic and social transformations involved in the rise of capital and urbanization. Because of these changes, young adults had the chance to leave home farther behind than their counterparts ever had before. They actually had the option of leaving behind their social class for a "better life," a choice that would always be fraught with doubt, fear, and sadness for both generations.

It is not surprising that Freud's cases reflect the familial tension I am describing here (although he did not use historical terms himself). One example involves a man who developed a neurosis when faced with choosing between his own desires and the wishes of his family of origin for him to marry "up." Freud wrote in the case of the "Ratman":

This family plan stirred up in him a conflict as to whether he should remain faithful to the lady he loved in spite of her poverty, or whether he should follow in his father's footsteps and marry the lovely, rich and well-connected girl assigned to him. And he resolved this conflict, which was in fact one between his love and the persisting influence of his father's wishes, by falling ill, or to put it more correctly, by falling ill he avoided the task of resolving it in real life. . . . The proof that this view is correct lies in the fact that the chief result of his illness was an obstinate incapacity for work which allowed him to postpone the completion of his education for years. [1909/1963, p. 56]

Similar family dynamics present themselves to family therapists all the time. In a family I saw several years ago, a seventeen-year-old girl developed agoraphobia just as she was about to begin college. Her fear was not of physically leaving home, since she planned to live with her parents for the first year, nor was she worried about performance. The problem had something to do with being the first in the family to go to college. She felt particularly disloyal to her mother, whom, she said, "had never been anywhere." Going to college was exciting to the girl and she wanted her parents to be proud of her. It also meant rejecting the role of sequestered housewife, which had been the only role for women in several generations of her family.

Symptoms cannot be explained in terms of historical and class conditions alone, of course. Not all bourgeois men developed psychoneuroses to avoid marrying up, and not all middle-class girls become agoraphobic when allowed to move beyond the world of their mothers. However, without those historical and social class factors, the symptoms would not be "possible." Peasant boys did not marry aristocratic girls, and girls of the old regime did not have mothers who were isolated indoors, away from the community.

The trend toward the isolation of urban middle-class women in the home began with industrialization and may have peaked in the 1950s in the United States, when women who had held jobs during World War II were expected to vacate them and return to housewife status. Unlike bourgeois women of the nineteenth century, these housewives were not in the company of servants who assisted them with every task from laundry and cooking to entertaining and child care. Unlike the work of peasant wives of the seventeenth century, the laundering and food preparation that the modern housewife did were performed privately, each woman aspiring to her own washing machine, gas range, and other appliances. The image of the 1950s housewife ironing alone in the living room in front of the television set is an image of privatized daily labor that is hard to match in other periods and cultures. Even the women of the Greek *gynaceum* were in the company of their fellow captives.

The ability to do their work in privacy, and to have less backbreaking work to do in the first place, can be seen as positive, of course, but the

stay-at-home modern housewife has never been known for her content-
ment, or even for feeling in control of certain important tasks. On the
contrary, what we know of women of the postwar period is that many felt
demoralized and depressed (Bernard 1972), partly because the work they
did was reported to be so trivial: new, "labor-saving" devices were said to
have eliminated real work. There is truth to the fact that it is easier to wash
clothes in an automatic washer than in a tub, but the mere fact of techno-
logical progress does not tell the whole story. As historian Ruth Schwartz
Cowan demonstrated in her book *More Work for Mother* (1983), modern
housework does indeed involve less drudgery, but it does not take less time
to do. As laundry appliances became more sophisticated, standards of
cleanliness increased. Whereas people once wore clothes and used linens
until they were really soiled, modern family members became accustomed
to dropping everything in the wash after a wearing or two. In addition, the
postwar period would see mothers chauffering children to school, music
lessons, sports, babysitters, and friends' houses—a job that consumes
enormous amounts of time. Studies show that modern housewives do
roughly fifty hours of work per week (including housework plus child
care). Women who have paid jobs do roughly thirty-five hours of work at
home in addition to their forty-hour week (Cowan 1983, p. 200). What is
particularly interesting is that these numbers are not significantly different
from those in studies done in 1912 and 1935! (Cf. Cowan, p. 199).

Moreover, contrary to common wishful thinking, contemporary men are
not doing significantly more housework than before, and this includes men
whose wives have outside, full-time employment. Thus, women who have
paid jobs end up with a seventy-five-hour work week—something even
sweatshops can't match. As Cowan points out: "With all her appliances
and amenities, the status of being a working mother in the United States
today is . . . virtually a guarantee of being overworked and perpetually
exhausted" (p. 213). The exhaustion is not attenuated by the fact that the
work done at home is not only uncompensated but extremely devalued
socially. It is not counted in the gross national product, despite its obvious
importance in reproducing the labor supply and maintaining the national
health. It is instructive to note that the child care done by a governess and
the housework done by a cleaning woman *are* counted in the GNP, but if
the governess or the cleaning woman marries her boss, the same work is
no longer counted; it simply disappears from the social record (Ahern and
Bliss 1976; see also Strasser 1982).

The trivialization of household labor in the industrialized postwar era
and the relative isolation of women from the workplace and from each
other undoubtedly contributed to the fact that married women of the

1950s and 1960s, as described so well by Betty Friedan in *The Feminine Mystique,* suffered depression in great numbers and depended to varying degrees on alcohol and tranquilizers. In the contemporary period, psychiatric disorders and inpatient admissions continue to be dramatically higher for women with children who remain home than for those who engage in paid labor outside the home, despite the "exhaustion factor" of the latter (cf. Hafner 1986).

Since Friedan's book was published in 1963, the work force has become increasingly female. It is somewhat astonishing to realize that in 1980, half of children under the age of six had mothers who worked full-time outside the home (Statistical Abstracts of the U.S. 1981, p. 388). What does it mean for so many women who would have been isolates a few decades ago to have joined the paid labor force? On the one hand, developmental psychology tells us that adults find in work a tremendous opportunity to achieve identity and a sense of mastery. Polls show that the vast majority of working mothers (84 percent in one poll) say they would work even if they didn't need the money (*Newsweek,* March 31, 1986, p. 51). Inclusion in the workplace has enhanced millions of women in their efforts at "soul-making and world-making" (cf. Burland 1987). In my study of women and men after divorce, mothers who became gainfully employed only after the divorce spoke of the new ability to buy clothes and food without asking a husband for money as an utter epiphany, like making the transition from child to adult status at last (Luepnitz 1982).

On the other hand, we know that women's entry into the workplace has not been accompanied by an equalization of male and female earning power. American women still earn about 65 cents on the male dollar, and a female college graduate earns roughly as much as a male high school dropout (Carmen, Russo, and Miller 1981). A man once complained to me in therapy that wives obviously belonged at home: they earned so little in the workplace compared to men that it wasn't worth their effort! And, although working mothers provide good role models to their daughters and sons with regard to women's abilities, they nonetheless have to deal with the cultural vestiges of Rousseau—maternal guilt. It has been said that "mothers feel guilty if they hold jobs, and also guilty if they don't. In addition, they feel guilty for feeling guilty, as well as guilty for not feeling guilty!" (Goldhor Lerner, pers. comm. 1987).

Even when both spouses work outside the home, there appears to be a tendency for husbands and wives to relate mostly to each other and to be relatively cut off from the community (particularly compared to married couples in other epochs). Contemporary spouses make contact with, rely on, talk to, and socialize with each other to a far greater extent than did couples in earlier ages. This isolation of the couple, of course, affects (and is affected by) the different expectations modern people have of marriage. A feminist analysis of contemporary marriage is beyond our scope; Barbara Ehrenreich (1983) and Lilian Rubin (1983) both have written insightfully on the subject. What we can say in brief is that the burden on husbands and wives to be "everything" to each other is very great in the contemporary industrialized West. Since the advent of romantic love in marriage and the end of arranged marriages, the expectation that people will find happiness, fulfillment, and almost a therapeutic experience has made modern hearts heavy with expectation—and disappointment. Both the expectation and the disappointment are reflected in the divorce rates, which climb to 50 percent in some regions, and the remarriage rates of 70 to 80 percent (Weitzman 1985). Approximately one-third of children born in this decade will spend part of their lives in a single-parent home.

The women's movement has been blamed for undermining marriage and the family, and it is certainly true that feminism has tried to undermine certain expectations and behaviors that have been considered acceptable in normal families. Although the divorce rate is extremely high and divorces cause at least temporary upheaval in the lives of all concerned, it is a mistake to oversimplify divorce as "a modern tragedy." As Linda Gordon has suggested, "perhaps families held together by domination, fear, violence, squelched talents, and resignation should not survive" (1977, p. 51).

Family therapists know that even in the "intact" family, the onerous and sometimes contradictory demands made on modern parents often lead to psychological troubles. Parents who cannot relate well to each other sometimes relate better to one of their children. In other families, the couple is able to communicate together, but only about problems with their kids. The contemporary family, for these and more benign reasons, is patently child-centered. One occasionally hears a historian or sociologist remark that the nuclear family has replaced the village in the modern world. I believe it might be more accurate to say that *the child has replaced the village in the modern world.* Whereas the community once provided people with emotional sustenance, a reason to endure hardship, a means of measuring one's worth, and a way of detouring conjugal conflicts, the child seems to provide these things to the family now. Family therapists often see families in which the generations are flipped, and it seems that the children are parenting the parents. One of the common and most useful questions family therapists can ask a symptomatic child is, "Do you worry about your parents?" It is interesting that a recent book by Erica Jong for children about divorce is dedicated "To the children of divorce and the adults they take care of." This means a lot of children taking care of a lot of parents.

It is a truism in family therapy that parents rely on children because they can't rely on each other. What I have attempted to do here is simply to show that historical and cultural factors have made this problem very hard to escape. Several of the dilemmas of the contemporary family that we have discussed here are presented with particular resonance in Arthur Miller's *Death of a Salesman*. Willy Loman is the unsuccessful salesman whose family members try to protect him from his mounting failures at a job that has always been meaningless to him. His sons love him but pity him, and they seem to be much closer and more honest with their mother. Linda Loman and her sons collude to keep certain things from Willy that might offend his pride; Linda herself has no outside commitments and seems to live through her sons. The older son, who had always been an academic star, ruins a chance for a major scholarship out of loyalty to his mother, when he learns Willy is cheating on her. At the end of the play, Willy Loman, like Bartleby, goes mad, and is found in front of his house, raving and *planting a garden*. Willy Loman in his madness turns back the historical clock and returns the world from an industrial to an agrarian place where he would not have had to be tall, debonair, and slick to be liked. His sense of competence as a worker would have ridden on much more than "a shoeshine and a smile," as one character says after his death.

We have seen that the social structural changes of the eighteenth and nineteenth centuries produced a family form ideally suited to the cultivation of the peripheral, shadowy father, the overinvolved, overanxious mother, and the triangulated, overburdened child. As therapists, we have the habit of considering these under the rubric of the personal or even the psychopathological. It is instructive to see them also as historically primed.

The American Black Family of the Contemporary Period

Much of what has been described here with regard to middle-class white families applies as well to middle-class black families of the contemporary period. There are significant differences between them as well, of course, due to the fact that their origins are quite different. The black family has been misrepresented by mainstream sociologists and historians, and it warrants special attention here.

Probably the best-known document written about the black family is Daniel Patrick Moynihan's report *The Negro Family—The Case for National Action* (1965). Moynihan did not deny the devastating effects of poverty and of the legacy of slavery for contemporary black Americans, but he did write about the black family in a depreciative and mother-blaming way. He labeled the black female-headed household "matriarchal" and attached to it the term "pathological." Moynihan contrasted the black family to the white family, which was presumably "healthy" because it presupposed male dominance. He wrote: "Ours is a society which presumes male leadership in private and public affairs. . . . A subculture such as that of the Negro American . . . is placed at a distinct disadvantage" (p. 29). Moynihan did not even bother to explicate what he meant by the latter point. He proceeded to blame black underachievement and unemployment on the fact that black women worked outside the home, and also stated that racism was more destructive to men than to women: "Segregation and the submissiveness it extracts is surely more destructive to the male than to the female personality" (p. 16).

Of all Moynihan's critics, black women scholars and activists were among the most vocal. Angela Davis, for example, viewed it as the gravest insult to black Americans to describe only the weaknesses of the black family and effectively to blame the strong black women who had struggled to keep their children alive. Several feminist voices also questioned the indiscriminate use of the word *matriarchy* by Moynihan and others, since its connotations of power and sovereignty conflict bitterly with the actual conditions of black women.

Poverty is without doubt the number-one problem of the black family. A black child has one chance in two of being born poor (McAdoo 1981). Poverty affects families and marriages in obvious ways, such as causing worry and stress that ensure high levels of interpersonal conflict. Poverty also affects marriages in ways that are not as obvious. For example, it is well known that marriages are severely strained by the death of a child in the family and by the presence of a sick or handicapped child. Black children are twice as likely as white children to die in the first year of life, and more likely to be sick because of poorer nutrition and medical care. This is one factor that accounts for the fact that the divorce rate for blacks is higher than for whites (Glick 1981).

The higher divorce rate is related to another sociological fact. Marriages in any racial group in which the husband earns a great deal more than the wife tend to be more stable than those in which wages are closer in value.

141

The fact that black husbands and wives earn salaries closer in value than white husbands and wives contributes to making black marriages less stable. (This is due to the fact that black males earn less than white males.)

One reason for the large number of single-mother black families is the strength and independence of black women; they may simply be less tolerant of bad relationships and less afraid of being without a man. It was the black feminist attorney Flo Kennedy who coined the now-famous quip: "A woman without a man is like a fish without a bicycle." It is logical that, on the basis of having worked outside the home more than white women, black women came to see themselves as equal to men.

The American black family has an extremely complex history and structure, and slavery is an inescapably large part of its history. The fact that slave families were forcibly broken up by the sale of their members is legendary. One scholar estimates that the average American slave witnessed the sale of eleven family members during her or his life. Slave masters justified these sales by saying that only whites were civilized enough to believe in family bonds or legal marriage. Slaves, they claimed, married only when the masters insisted upon it.

Herbert Gutman's (1976) work on the slave family produced the data that put that apology to its final rest. Gutman found records of slave marriages lasting twenty and thirty years on plantations such as one in South Carolina where the master did not sell slaves. In addition, after emancipation, there was an enormous surge in marriages of former slaves, obviously not attributable to the dictates of the slaveowners. As Carl Degler (1980) has pointed out, it is eloquent testimony to Afro-American culture that black women and men were able to maintain their kinship ties as well as they did in the face of the disruptive forces of slavery.

A notable attempt at identifying the important conflicting themes in the black family of the contemporary period was made by Elaine Pinderhughes in her chapter in *Ethnicity and Family Therapy* (1982). Pinderhughes suggests that Afro-American identity is influenced by three sources: (1) residual cultural patterns from Africa, (2) mainstream American values, and (3) responses to the "victim" system that is created by a cultural context characterized by poverty and racism. Each of these sources has a distinct set of values. The African values emphasize collectivity, kinship, spirituality, conviviality, and respect for the elderly. As Paulette Hines and Nancy Boyd-Franklin have stated: "If western values can be summed up in the Cartesian epithet, 'I think therefore I am,' the African cosmology might be expressed as, 'We are, therefore I am' " (1982, p. 87). The African tradition's emphasis on collectivity resembles the premodern family structure of the West.

The second set of themes is what Pinderhughes calls "American values," which involve individualism, autonomy, accumulation of goods, achievement, efficiency, competition, and privacy. These values were clearly reinforced with the growth of capital in the postindustrial period.

The third set of themes is the "victim system," which includes acquiescence to authority, not planning for the future since it is beyond one's control, disinterest in social change, and escape into whatever drugs or amusement the dominant classes make available.

These three sets of themes combine and conflict in many different ways in black families. In some, the overburdened adults are indeed unable, even with the help of extended kin, to protect their children from the strong influence of the street culture which leads to the court system. (See Minuchin et al., *Families of the Slums,* for descriptions of such families.)

There are other Afro-American families, however, in which family life and especially the structuring of child care approaches what some modern theorists have come to consider the ideal: children are loved and nurtured by more than one adult, and children of both sexes are expected to be involved in helping mothers with children. Several studies, in fact, have shown that black children have less stereotypical ideas of sex roles than do white children (Gold and St. Ange 1974, Johnson 1977). Moreover, because black women tend to come from generations of mothers who have worked outside the home, they are more able than their white counterparts to pass on a belief in women's assertiveness and strength. This appreciation for women's capacities along with the practice of sharing child care and a lower degree of isolation from extended family and from the community are the very qualities that many progressive thinkers have argued are missing from American mainstream family life (e.g., Rich 1976, Chodorow 1978, Poster 1978). There is probably a great deal that white families could learn from black families about raising children, although male scholars such as Moynihan have had a difficult time seeing this.

It would be foolish, of course, to make the error opposite to Moynihan's and romanticize the black family, or indeed to trivialize father absence. (Fifty percent of black families with children are single-mother families [Glick 1981]). Many black men want and need to be more permanently involved with their families. This is true of white men as well, however. (Twenty percent of white families are headed by single mothers [Glick 1981]). My intention is not to minimize the problems of the black family, but simply to emphasize that they should not be contrasted with those of some putative, "healthy" white family. Despite their different strengths and weaknesses, contemporary American families, black and white, share a common feature: they are both patriarchal and father-absent. I am, of course, using the word *patriarchal* as Ann Ferguson uses it, to refer not only to father and husband patriarchy but also to *public* patriarchy. As described in chapter 1, public patriarchy refers to the situation in which fathers and husbands are replaced by male experts—psychiatrists, probation officers, and the welfare system—who continue to regulate women's expenditures, sexuality, and definitions of femininity.

It is true that there are more white fathers than black fathers present in American homes, but studies show that white fathers spend only minutes per day interacting with their children (cf. Osherson 1986, p. 24). The fact that sons must formulate their notions about masculinity on being simply "not female" or "other than mother" is a problem faced by modern black and white families alike. How the fact of fathers' absence or shadowy presence is acted out or resolved in families depends on the resources— economic, social, and personal—available to the individual child.

Afro-American families need to be understood in their complexity and appreciated for their strengths. The inability of contemporary culture to define masculinity and fatherhood in a positive way should not be labeled a black problem.

Conclusions: History as Double Description

Using the terms of family systems theory, therapists view the "overin-volvement" of the mother and the "peripherality" of the father as "dys-functional patterns" which can result in the "triangulation" of children, making it difficult for children to "differentiate" or "leave home." Through the lens of social history, we see these phenomena as neither universally present nor idiosyncratic. Instead they belong to a set of structural and economic changes that occurred during the eighteenth and nineteenth centuries with the transformation from an agrarian to an urban economy, which led to the rise of capital and a middle class. Men in this emergent world were removed from the home, while women were required to devote themselves to child care and "housework"—a category of labor that be-came socially invisible. I have used the term "patriarchal but father-absent" to describe the family form that emerged in this period and that became the modal structure of the contemporary urban family of the industrialized West. In essence, while the person of the father was removed emotionally or physically, the abstract "law of the father" endured.

The father's removal from the home and the family's increasing isolation from the community had, by the contemporary period, almost guaranteed that the child would become the main focus of family life—sometimes the emotional supplier of the parents, sometimes the scapegoat, and sometimes the ally of one parent against the other. Despite the attempt by post-Enlightenment philosophy to portray men's and women's spheres as separate but equally important, the economic and social power differences between men and women endured and continued to affect how children formed alliances with parents. I believe that as long as men have more legitimate authority in the world than do women and children, we can expect women and children to form alliances together. The mother-child allegiances in families, which seem to exclude or preclude fathers, are in some sense the historically prompted survival tactics of an underclass. Understanding this could, perhaps, render a bit less vigorous the knee-jerk contempt some therapists show for "controlling" or "enmeshing" mothers. Historically, this alliance has represented the power of protection from the father's considerable (and sometimes unlimited) authority. This does not make those mother-child alliances salubrious, of course, but without understanding them we cannot fully explain why "leaving home" has come to feel so risky to children, and to mothers and fathers as well.

Whereas family scholars have sometimes said that the nuclear family replaced the village in modern life, I have said that the child has replaced the village in modern life and that this excessive burden helps explain why children feel that they must take care of their parents emotionally, and often develop symptoms in response to stress. I have also suggested that children's attempt to nourish their parents and stay *in* the family conflicts with another modern pressure, i.e., to get ahead socially and financially, and necessarily to *leave* the family. For this reason, one may say that the modern middle-class family appears to *require* disloyalty. In view of the tremendous psychological burden on the modern child, it seems naive to insist that society has become increasingly loving toward its younger members. It is true that infanticide and gross abuse of children are no longer legal, but gross abuse of children nonetheless still exists.

In short, adding the historical picture to the clinical one is like combining the views of the right and left eyes. Through the clinical eye, one sees the behavior of parents in terms of "pathology," "error," "dysfunction," or even what has been called the "dumb cruelty" of families. Through the historical eye, one sees people acting on a stage designed by political and economic process. Therapists who are blind to the latter may come to blame history's victims for choosing incorrectly, when in fact their choices were illusory. To paraphrase Marx, therapists must acknowledge that although families do create their own problems, they do not create them "just as they please."

The depth that historical seeing creates should be a *sine qua non* of the development of a theory of family therapy. Clearly, I have not offered here anything like an actual theory of the family, but I hope to have sketched some broad outlines and made a case for the importance of defining the family not only in the clinical moment but also in social time.

The hard-core proponent of family systems theory may remain skeptical, however, even after the commentary and suasion of this chapter. "Will a knowledge of history help me to practice better, to solve problems more humanely, more efficiently, more artfully?" Perhaps this must be answered by each individual practitioner. The answer for me is affirmative.

THE FRUITS OF HISTORICAL DESCRIPTION: COMPASSION AND TELOS

While I was in the process of writing an early draft of this chapter, a new patient of mine, a single mother named Charlotte, said to me:

> Today while I was in the bathroom potty-training the little one [age 2], the older one [age 9] tried to pull something off the bookcase and nearly pulled the whole thing on top of him. I am a wreck. Today I had this horrible thought that I would run away, and I just hated myself. For thousands of years, women have raised eight or nine children and cooked, and baked, and chopped wood, without any help. I have only two children and I don't work, and I am a wreck.

What does a therapist say to this mother?

Some would argue that her lament is most important as a clue to some legacy from her family of origin, making her feel incompetent as a mother, or for its description of a stressful life and a communication to the therapist for support. It is all of these, of course, but it is also a lucid statement of Charlotte's belief about the world—quite a conventional one, in fact, despite its distortions. Not only is Charlotte's life as a single, unemployed mother tedious and hard, but on top of it, she feels like a historical freak, someone who stands out in the lines of time as a travesty of motherhood. She believes that her life is in all ways easier than the lives of women throughout history. She does not know that the intense mother-child bond is not instinctive. Certainly, she does not know of 1,000 years of apprenticing children out at young ages, and wet nursing; she does not even seem to realize that she works. Consequently, she cannot suspect that her statement contains an actual reversal of social reality. That is, "for thousands of years" women have had *more* help than she has in raising children and have been expected to do much *less* for their children!

Particularly because I was in the midst of writing this chapter, my heart clenched as this woman spoke. I wondered whether this might finally be the moment to use Salvador Minuchin's famous line: "You have been sold a bag of lies! A bag of myths, and please do not buy it!" (See chapter 5.)

Perhaps the words of explanation are not as important as the response invoked in the therapist by such acute self-betrayal on the part of the patient. It bears repeating that feminism need not be the *theme* of therapy; it must simply be its sensibility, its spoken or unspoken center. Just as therapists who learn a patient's individual history come to feel more compassion toward her or him from understanding the choices that the patient simply did not have, so the feminist therapist feels an added dimension of compassion through knowledge of the social history of women and men in families.

Another thing that reading family history can foster is a renewed curiosity and respect for the alternatives that individuals have devised to create families. I hope we will teach our students, for example, not to see lesbian and gay couples who raise children as simply more or less adequate substitutes for the "real thing," but as real families who are, in fact, contributing to the social fund of information on what children and adults need to grow together and flourish. Although alternative life-style families can hardly be said to elude the culture of patriarchy, they nonetheless speak for human power to do more than acquiesce, actually to say "no" to the most sanctioned social and sexual arrangements, and to resist the policing of their own desires.

A related issue is the conventional prejudice we hold against the woman who chooses to be single or to remain "childless." The "childless" woman, as Adrienne Rich has pointed out, has been viewed as a "failed woman," as incomplete, selfish, even contemptible. Rich sees these women as "a great threat to hegemony" in refusing to obey the law of "heterosexual pairing and bearing." Many women without children, precisely because they are free of the quotidian responsibilities of child care and service to the household, have had time and privacy enough to reflect, to understand, and to write. Without women such as George Eliot, Emily Dickinson, Susan B. Anthony, Virginia Woolf, and Simone de Beauvoir, "we would all today be suffering from spiritual malnutrition as women" (Rich 1976, pp. 255–56). How important it is, then, for us as therapists to stop evaluating the "outcomes" of our female patients in terms of their reproductive status! How important that we learn to see what women in patriarchal society gain by remaining childless, in addition to what they give up.

The historical perspective thus offers the therapist a sharpened sense of *telos,* or purpose. The therapist alert to historical process and the larger system can begin at wider levels of analysis and work toward a center. A remembering of the family can lead to its transformation, to a re-membering. Instead of constructing our symptom-solving interventions in *any* way, thereby facilitating the "reproduction of families," we can think differently about our methods. At moments the questions pose themselves as follows: "If I do not endorse the patriarchal, father-absent family, isolated from the community, how can I go about helping this family through its crisis without helping to reproduce its patriarchy, father absence, and isolation? Is there anything I can do (or not do) that will introduce new possibilities for this particular family?" This does not mean that one thinks only in general political or societal terms and ignores the minute particulars of individual women and men. One thinks at the level of both social history/economics *and* personal history and the unconscious. This kind of conceptualizing makes me think of the motto of the international peace movement: "Think globally; act locally." Anything else is an unnecessary partitioning of our existence, one might say a dismemberment.

I have devoted more space here to the discussion of patriarchy and father absence than to the issue of the family's isolation from the community, but the latter is an equally important issue and not unrelated to the former. Father absence becomes more acutely felt by modern mothers and children because they do not have as many community networks to depend on as they did in other times. American black families have been relatively more adept at creating social and familial networks, but even these are being challenged now by economic problems. The black grandmother and greataunt who once cooked, baby-sat, and offered a supportive presence to their employed granddaughters and nieces are themselves now forced to seek employment to help make ends meet (McAdoo, pers. comm. 1987).

Therapists who think in terms corrective to this isolation try to help the family open its boundaries to new members. Estranged relatives, neighbors, nannies, and community groups can come closer to the frontiers of the family and in some cases enter its actual circle. Ordinary family therapy (i.e., one family in treatment at a time) is sufficient to accomplish these ends, but it should also be mentioned that *multiple* family therapy groups exist and can serve such connecting purposes extremely well. I have run several such groups, with five to seven families meeting weekly with two therapists. The families learned tremendously from each other's problems and solutions, and it was not unusual for them to continue to meet when the group ended. (See also Speck and Attneave 1973.)

My final point is that historical analysis instructs the clinician in the urgency of attending to extraclinical change. The material in this chapter challenges the notion that society is like an organism evolving to more complex states, providing ever better and fairer treatment to children, women, and minorities. Historical change is so discontinuous that one cannot always conclude that the lot of any disadvantaged social group is better from one century to the next. The concept of childhood, for example, was better developed in ancient Rome than in the Middle Ages, and women in England were in some respects worse off in 1700 than they had been in 1600. In the United States, women from colonial days until the 1880s could opt for abortion, until the procedure was criminalized for the first time. In 1973, the U.S. Supreme Court decided in *Roe* v. *Wade* that the Constitution protected women's as well as men's rights to privacy with regard to their reproductive lives. To remove this protection has been a goal of the Reagan administration. Thus is "social evolution" a dangerous invention; only deliberate and historically educated action enables social change.

Our focus here, however, is not primarily on social change but on clinical change, and history does not generate clinical methodology. With notable exceptions, family therapists have relied on the language and principles of general systems theory and cybernetics to derive their therapeutic means of acting. By and large they have avoided, or even inveighed against, psychoanalysis as a cache of ideas from which to develop methods for family treatment. The next two chapters propose a reversal of this trend. In chapter 11, I will offer a critique of the "cybernetic epistemology" of Gregory Bateson, showing that its failure to consider gender and to sustain an idiom of persons as opposed to machines makes it unsuitable for a feminist family therapy. In chapter 12, I will argue that a branch of psychoanalytic thinking called "object-relations theory," in its already "feminized" versions, can serve as a sturdier groundwork for feminist family therapy in practice.

11

A Critique of the Cybernetic Epistemology of Gregory Bateson

In the beginning was Gregory Bateson.

—BRODERICK and SCHRADER,
recounting the history of the Mental Research
Institute in the *Handbook of Family Therapy*, 1981

IN MY "index survey" of fifty family therapy texts, I found no name cited more often than that of Gregory Bateson. An anthropologist by training, Bateson became forever a part of the history of family therapy through his participation with Don Jackson and others in research on schizophrenia in the 1950s. Bateson was fascinated with the thinking of Norbert Wiener and Ludwig von Bertalanffy, known as the fathers of cybernetics and general systems theory, respectively. Both of the "fathers" had set out to study phenomena, from mechanisms to biological entities, as systems—that is, as organizations of interdependent parts. They were particularly interested in the capacities of systems to exchange information with the environment and to exhibit self-governing characteristics.

Bateson's amalgam of cybernetics and general systems theory, alloyed with a measure of Russellian logic and post-Kantian constructivism, became the hard currency of family systems discourse. Every school of family therapy, from structural to strategic to intergenerational to existential and even object-relations family therapy, makes use of the cybernetic coin.

Because Bateson used language with a flinty intelligence, and because he saved the field from potential oblivion by giving it theoretical credibility, he is granted almost religious recognition within the field. There is a tendency among family therapists to overstate the originality of Bateson's work and to attribute to him insights more accurately credited to antecedent thinkers. As one Australian colleague, Edwin Harari, commented, "American family therapists believe that the history of the world began in 1955 with Gregory Bateson."

Certainly it is unusual for the intellectual mentor of a discipline to be the target of so little criticism. In the decade since Bateson's death, family therapists have not endeavored to challenge his cybernetic or general systems thinking (he did, in fact, use the two terms interchangeably) but instead have simply elaborated on his views.

The ideas of Bateson, and those of several other "systems thinkers" such as Heinz von Foerster (1973a, 1973b), Francisco Varela (1976, 1979), Paul Watzlawick (1976, 1984), and Humberto Maturana (1980), have been applied to family therapy's theory and practice under the rubric of "the new epistemology" (cf. Keeney 1983, Dell 1982).

Much of the theoretical writing that has filled the journals in recent years has centered on whether family therapy as *practiced* really follows "the new epistemology" or actually reflects more primitive cybernetic ideas, or even the "linear" ideas of cause and effect. Certain notions have thus become suspect in the field as of late, among them the idea that the therapist should deliberately set out to change a system, and that symptoms can be said to serve a purpose within the family. The family therapists who are generally considered to be most systemically "pure" are the Milan systemic therapists. The Milan therapists emphasize constructivist principles in their writings, stating continually that reality is not "out there" but rather is formed actively by the observer who cannot escape being part of the system (e.g., Boscolo et al. 1987, Tomm 1984). The fact that the "new epistemologists" in general, and the "purists" in particular, emphasize that the *person of the therapist* influences the therapy in very profound ways led some critics to hope that they would produce a radical critique of family therapy—raising issues of gender and class, thereby introducing the concept of hegemony into the field at last (MacKinnon and Miller 1987). This, however, has not occurred. As Laurie MacKinnon and

Dusty Miller have pointed out, the Milan systemic therapists, despite their adherence to the new epistemology, are as likely as anyone else to reinscribe conventional social and sexual arrangements. (See chapter 9.)

The article by MacKinnon and Miller is one of several attempts by feminists to show that family systems therapists have ignored what one would expect experts in our field to understand superbly well, i.e., the power of the larger system to shape the smaller (family and therapeutic) systems. Harriet Goldhor Lerner has argued that family therapists seem to have fallen into the trap that individual therapists usually fall into: the latter often try to understand the individual pulled out of the family context; family therapists are trying, just as naively, to understand families pulled out of the social (i.e., patriarchal) context (Lerner 1987; see also Taggart 1985).

Lerner calls for an improvement of cybernetic and systems thinking—by opening it up to the "wider context"—but other critics have suggested the need for an even deeper change. Feminists such as Kerrie James and Deborah McIntyre repudiate the very choice of Bateson's work for our theoretical foundation, pointing out that although cybernetics and systems theory "can provide a useful view of the interrelationships between elements of a system, it can make no comment on the nature of the system itself. . . . It is not that systems theory sets aside a series of questions for the sake of therapeutic intervention. Rather, it makes it impossible to pose them" (1983, pp. 126–27).

Whether or not cybernetics or the new epistemology can be salvaged to make them inclusive of gender and accountable to social and political concerns should probably remain open to question. My impression at this point is that what is brilliant and indispensable about the new epistemology is already old, and what is missing from it is so massive that we probably should spend our efforts in search of a more substantial intellectual scaffolding.

In any case, no feminist has yet read Bateson's work from the point of view of the history of ideas, a task that is requisite to a thorough critique. In this chapter, I will begin this process by discussing some of the origins of Bateson's ideas, particularly as presented in his two most frequently cited works, *Steps to an Ecology of Mind* (1972) and *Mind and Nature* (1980), commenting particularly on his notions about gender and power which reveal the limitations of cybernetic thinking from the feminist standpoint.

152

Bateson and Gender

After a lecture he gave in 1979, I asked Gregory Bateson a question about how one of his ideas might apply to relationships between women and men. He answered very respectfully, "Cathy [his daughter] is interested in that." Bateson himself clearly was not. He discussed in his books topics as diverse as Balinese art, schizophrenia, dolphin talk, and the Treaty of Versailles, but nowhere did he wrestle with the male-female dialectic of Western culture. The closest he came to writing about gender was probably his early paper with Jackson, Haley, and Weakland (1956) on the double-bind theory of schizophrenia. Gender is by no means a focus of this paper, but it is present insofar as the paper turns on an essential tension between a particular "her" and "him." Bateson and his colleagues hypothesized that the schizophrenic's family had three elements:

1) A child whose mother becomes anxious and withdraws if the child responds to her as a loving mother . . .
2) A mother to whom feelings of anxiety and hostility toward the child are not acceptable, and whose way of denying them is to express overt loving behavior to persuade the child to respond to her as a loving mother and to withdraw from him if he does not . . .
3) The absence of anyone in the family, such as a strong and insightful father, who can intervene in the relationships between the mother and child and support the child in the face of the contradictions involved. [1956, pp. 212–13]

The world evoked in the double-bind paper is one in which "she" (the double-binding mother), unrestrained by "him" (her weak and ineffectual husband), drives another "him" (the doubly bound son) crazy. The reasons why this "she" should be so cold and annihilating or should feel "anxious" toward her child are not a part of the theory. Only the son's experience appears to count; only his point of view is represented.

Bateson did not base the remainder of his life's work on the double-bind theory, and in fairness, it was not he but psychoanalyst Frieda Fromm-Reichman who coined the actual phrase "schizophrenogenic mother." However, since the double-bind paper was so influential in launching the field, one might say that the institution of family therapy, like the institution of the family itself, has built deep into its foundations a forceful denial of maternal subjectivity.

After the double-bind theory, gender ceased to exist in Bateson's work, and the tension between "him" and "her" was never again an identifiable subject. In his well-known essay on alcoholism, Bateson identifies the alcoholic as "he," but the tension is located between "him" and "John Barleycorn"—not between the sexes.* In a section entitled "The case of the two sexes" in his final book, *Mind and Nature,* the discussion is limited to the sexual life of bacteria!

Since Bateson's work has been so influential to family therapy, one might well assume that if Bateson had taken more interest in gender, it would not have been allowed to disappear from family therapy as easily and completely as it has. Why—it is irresistible to ask—did Bateson seem so eager to stop writing about women and men and to turn instead to nonhuman systems, and often enough to mathematical abstractions?

Any reader of Bateson knows that one of his favorite aphorisms was "Epistemology is always and inevitably personal" (cf. *Mind and Nature,* p. 98). As a result of Mary Catherine Bateson's (1984) candid and sympathetic biography of her parents, Gregory Bateson and Margaret Mead, family therapists now have the chance to understand better the man behind the double-bind theory and its de-gendered aftermath.

In the biography, entitled *With a Daughter's Eye,* Mary Catherine Bateson draws a portrait of her father as intellectually inspiring, sweetly eccentric, and soulfully devoted to nature. At the same time, however, the daughter sees him as someone personally caught in "male roles," as exemplified by his problems in maintaining connections with other people. She contrasts her two parents as follows: Margaret Mead

> sustained a network of relationships around herself, at once the shelter in which I rested and the matrix of her work and thought. Not so my father, for the most complex actual worlds I knew him to set out to build have been aquaria and conferences, temporary constellations of people who learn to think in counterpoint to each other." [P. 16]

*In more recent work on alcoholism, feminist therapists Claudia Bepko and Jo Ann Krestan have shown how important gender is to understanding the problem. In the first place, it is important to acknowledge the fact that there are millions of women alcoholics. Second, Bepko and Krestan argue that alcoholism itself may be a way of escaping the bonds of one's gender role—an escape into dependency for men and into aggressiveness for women. By extension, the encouragement of "androgynous personalities" is part of the cure (and prevention) of alcoholism in the model of Bepko and Krestan (1985).

With regard to the double-bind theory *per se,* she wrote:

> The same decade that began with his [Bateson's] rebellion against Margaret, a rebellion shot through with resentment against his family and especially against his mother, ended with an analysis of patterns of communication in the families of schizophrenics, above all, of the role of the mother. [P. 160]

The father-daughter "metalogues" in *Steps to an Ecology of Mind* forever assume a poignant overtone in light of Bateson's disregard of his real daughter's intellectual pursuits:

> He used to try to draw me away from other kinds of involvement and seemed almost to forget my existence when I was not with him. Suspecting most of what I did of being a waste of time, he used occasionally to propose the possibility that . . . I might come and live nearby, so that he and I could work together on the development of abstract understanding.* [P. 113]

Because epistemology is personal, we are safe in speculating that the disappearance of gender and the increasingly abstract character of Bateson's work are related to and illumined by his personal inability to negotiate what his daughter called his "darkly complicated feelings about women." It is a credit to Bateson that he did not spend his entire life intellectually hunting down the bad mother, but the cost of giving up that project was the abandonment of gender altogether and a turn to the protection of "mother earth" via his ecological work.

How might Bateson's remark that "epistemology is always personal" apply to the sexes? Some feminists have argued that because *persons* are gendered, *epistemology* is always gendered as well. Carol Gilligan concluded something of this nature with regard to moral development, and Mary Field Belenky and her colleagues, in *Women's Ways of Knowing,* have more recently made the claim for cognitive process itself. Belenky et al. (1986) believe that women and men for a variety of (nonbiological) reasons behave differently as "knowers." Women and men, they say, organize information, draw conclusions, and invest confidence in their conclusions dif-

*Mary Catherine Bateson did collaborate with her father on *Angels Fear,* a book that was published in 1987, after his death. The subject of the book is Bateson's search for "the pattern which connects," and it might be described as a sequel to *Mind and Nature.* Again, there is no acknowledgment of feminist insights or sexual politics, except that Bateson says in passing that he hopes the sexes will always envy and admire each other (p. 170). Mary Catherine writes her own metalogues here, in which the daughter, at last, gets to have some of the "good lines," as she calls them (p. 204).

ferently. The authors refer to "connected knowing," as the type of knowing that does not separate itself from the personal or the political.*

Biologist Evelyn Fox Keller (1985) has argued convincingly that the scientific method itself has been expressed in a highly gendered metaphor. From the writings of Francis Bacon well into the twentieth century, scientists have employed the following paradigm. There is an experimenter who is defined as the "active" subject (nearly always a "he") acting upon nature, who is the passive object of study (referred to often as "she"). Keller found a less conquesting and more connected idiom in the writings of Nobel Prize–winning biologist Barbara McClintock, whose discoveries about genetics had been ignored for decades. Keller hypothesizes that a greater influx of women into the sciences, particularly at higher echelons, would result in different types of scientific language and thought. Bateson, in the meantime, deserves recognition for not using a conquesting language with regard to scientific problems, but he did not go far enough in altering the traditional forms of inquiry, as will be demonstrated in the remainder of this chapter.

One cannot help but wonder, in the face of these gender/knowledge/ authority discussions, how contemporary family therapists would be speaking and practicing today if Margaret Mead instead of Gregory Bateson had become the field's guru! Mead wrote more (volumes more) about families than Bateson did. Certainly we would be speaking about gender more than we do, since gender was a lifelong interest of Mead's. I suspect that we would also be talking about "mothers," "daughters," "fathers," and "sons," instead of "circuits," "dyads," and "feedback loops." There is no way of testing my hypothesis, of course, and in any case, gender is not the only problem in Bateson's work—the ahistorical quality of it is problematic as well. We turn now to the problem of history.

The Avoidance of History in Bateson's Work

Bateson held what might be described as an ambivalent relationship to historical explanation. On the one hand, he wrote a powerful and widely quoted essay entitled "From Versailles to Cybernetics," in which he ad-

*The work of Belenky et al. is interesting, but the danger of what Hare-Mustin calls "alpha error"—overstating sexual differences—is enormous. It would be unfortunate (and not surprising) if people were to misconstrue this work as meaning that women were incapable of thinking as clearly as men do.

vocated—in a distinctly apocalyptic voice—the importance of knowing the past, of being able to situate modern social madness in its historical context. He began this essay by asserting that all of us, young and old, live together in an "insane" world, whose "hate, distrust and hypocrisy" relate back to two pivotal events in the history of the early twentieth century: Woodrow Wilson's drawing up of the "Fourteen Points" and the subsequent signing of the Treaty of Versailles.* Although old and young inhabited the same "insane" present, the difference, according to Bateson, was that the older generation could *remember* how we got here while the younger generation could not. Addressing these younger readers, Bateson stated:

> But from your point of view, we are absolutely crazy, and you don't know what sort of historic event led to this craziness. "The fathers have eaten bitter fruit and the children's teeth are set on edge." It's all very well for the fathers, they know what they ate. The children don't know what was eaten. [P. 473]

Bateson devoted a good portion of this essay to describing the history of the Fourteen Points and the Treaty of Versailles, comparing ignorance of the past to the situation of a man who has been given LSD without knowing it. Despite this clear exhortation to know ourselves through knowing the past, however, and to breaking through the mystifications that keep us from creating social change, the majority of Bateson's work is *not* written from the historical point of view. In discussing schizophrenia, as we saw, he did not inquire into the historical or social context of the double-binding mother, nor did he pose historical questions in discussing the ecological crisis (1970) or alcoholism (1971). If Bateson had been alert to certain features of social history, he might have reacted allergically to the formulation of the double-binding mother. Because he was sensitive to the discovery and construction of *pattern* and *repetition,* he might have seen it as feminists do, that is, as intolerably isomorphic to other forms of sexual scapegoating.

Bateson's work ultimately suffers from what might be called an epistemological reductionism. He sees "pathology of epistemology" (or "dualistic thinking") as the universal corruptor of social process. Dualistic thinking is certainly something to take seriously; perhaps it even makes sense to call it "pathological." This language nonetheless begs the larger question of which political and psychological systems make dualistic

---

*Bateson claimed that the Treaty of Versailles was pivotal because it was the first time ever that a "message about war was used as part *of* the war." This is certainly open to question, if one considers, for example, the way the U.S. government used treaties with native American nations in the eighteenth century, and the way the Greeks ended their war with Troy.

thinking necessary, or make other kinds of thinking impossible or dangerous.

Another and perhaps related problem with Bateson's work is that he did not devote sufficient attention to recounting the history of his *own* ideas. He preferred to emphasize what was "new" about cybernetics and general systems theory, and not what was continuous with a long tradition (Bateson 1966).

Far from being the first to emphasize the ideas of system, organization, structure, and nondualism, Bateson descends from several lines of European philosophers, stretching back to Vico, Kant, Nietzsche, and Freud and ending with the postmodernists.* Bateson does mention some of these thinkers, and others as well, but always in cursory fashion. From the viewpoint of the history of ideas, it seems odd that Bateson would endeavor to write about new ways of describing "mind" without thoroughly discussing the ideas of Freud! The ingenious notion that there is no way of expressing "no" in the unconscious is often credited to Bateson, although Freud formulated this idea explicitly in one of his case reports (Freud 1905/1963).

Perhaps the outstanding example of Bateson's unstated legacy concerns the concept of dialectics. Although Bateson was clearly striving to describe dialectical relationships between body/mind, self/other, person/environment, and so on, the word *dialectic* is absent from *Steps to an Ecology of Mind.* It appears only in the last three pages of his final book, *Mind and Nature,* and is presented with the flourish of discovery. What appear to us as "poles of contrast," he wrote, are actually "dialectical necessities of the living world. . . . How, recognizing the dialectical relations between those poles of contrast, shall we proceed?" (1979, p. 246)† There are many varieties of dialectics with as many political implications (Platonic, Hegelian, Marxist), and we will never know which dialectics Bateson had in mind, nor what he considered to be the limitations of the earlier formulations.

Also unexplored are the striking parallels between Bateson's work on epistemology and that of German philosopher Friedrich Nietzsche, who criticized the Western definition of causality and the "false dichotomy" between person and environment nearly a century before Bateson. In a

---

*Gerald Erickson (1984, 1986) has recently made a similar point about the field's failure to acknowledge intellectual roots. Erickson emphasizes the influence of Ferdinand de Saussure's structural linguistics on all our thinking—especially his notion of system, the synchronic and the diachronic (de Saussure 1907/1974). I agree with Erickson about de Saussure's influence on family therapy, and most particularly on the "new epistemologists," but I have chosen to focus here on some even earlier influences.

†The context of this statement is a memorandum presented to the University of California Board of Regents, reprinted in the appendix of *Mind and Nature.*

section entitled "The Epistemological Starting Point," Nietzsche wrote: "Against all positivism which halts at phenomena: 'There are only facts,' I would say, 'No.' Facts is precisely what there is not—only interpretations" (1967, p. 267). In this same essay, Nietzsche urged us to carefully investigate the *"presuppositions"* by which we "create reality," using some of the same key words that have become the hallmark of Bateson and his students. The correspondence between these two thinkers is hard to overlook. Another example comes from *Steps,* where Bateson states that when a Western person cuts down a tree, he says:

> *"I* cut down the tree," and he even believes that there is a delimited "purposive" action upon a delimited object. [1972, p. 318]

Here is Nietzsche on the same point:

> "Subject," "object," "attribute"—these distinctions are fabricated and are now imposed as a schematism upon all the apparent facts. The fundamental false observation is that I believe it is *I* who do something, suffer something, have something. [1967, p. 294]

The problem, however, is not only what Bateson borrowed from earlier traditions but what he left out: Bateson did not go far enough in his writing about reality as construction. What Bateson's precursors had demonstrated was that what we see, think, and believe is not only mediated or distorted by an epistemological lens but also that that lens is cut according to highly specific sociopolitical requirements. Marx is probably best known for this notion, i.e., that the ideas of the ruling classes of a society are its ruling ideas (1848/1974). Nietzsche, however, added an especially relevant dimension to this notion when he wrote, "It is the powerful who made the names of things into law, and among the powerful, it is the greatest artists in abstraction who created the categories" (1967, p. 277). The next step in this line of thought was the one that feminists announced—that *gender* is a determining factor in the construction of "ruling ideas." That is, the rational, the abstract, and the transcendant command higher status than the emotional, the imminent, and the earthbound because the former are associated with what men do and the latter with what women do (de Beauvoir 1952).

It must be emphasized here that the problem with Bateson's work is not that his ideas have a history. On the contrary: appropriating the ideas of antecedent thinkers is necessary and wholesome. One sees farther when standing on the shoulders of giants, as Newton pointed out. It is essential, however, to keep alive the memory of those intellectual and cultural giants. Failure to do so creates two problems. The first has to do with the resonance or depth that ideas lose outside their historical context. If Bateson had compared his own ideas about epistemology with those of Nietzsche, or his ideas about systems with those of Marx, he would have provided an extra dimension to our understanding of these concepts—a "double description," to use his own term.

The second problem with Bateson's ahistorical style is more serious. Ahistoricism tends to deepen the cultural condition that has been aptly labeled "social amnesia" by radical historian Russell Jacoby (1975). Modern social scientists, according to Jacoby, have developed a tendency to ignore the past, declaring it "honorable but feeble" and then reinventing the wheel in ways that are sometimes inferior to the old. This neglect of the past cannot be explained as personal indolence, a failure to do one's homework; rather, it is rooted in the political and economic structures of late capitalism. An economic system that is predicated on high levels of consumption requires that people develop avid preferences for what is current, new, and youthful. Modern people tend to believe that everything exists for immediate gratification, and that absolutely everything—from plastics to marriages to theories—is disposable. This shortsightedness, ironically, leads to some of the very dilemmas (e.g., the ecological ones) about which Bateson anguished throughout his life, and that equally concern many of his followers.

Thus, while Bateson's writing appears to be bold and radical, at one level it is actually homeostatic with the "disposable past bias" of modern culture. Where certain forms of social amnesia are concerned, Bateson's thinking sadly "goes with the flow."

Systems, Cybernetics, and Power

In chapter 7, the discussion of structural family therapy led to a critique of the metaphor of society as a giant organism or an ecology of organisms. Bateson certainly contributed to the fact that most family therapists subscribe to this model and that they would agree that "the family has to fit with its environment, just as the individual has to fit within the family, or the separate organs have to fit together in a system that is the biological self. And all have to fit together in the ecology of the whole" (Hoffman

1981, p. 348). As discussed in chapter 5, a person who fits comfortably into the "whole"—a person for whom the system works fairly well—may not see any great gaps in this model. However, those who are disadvantaged by the system have difficulty locating themselves in a depiction of the world as harmonious, being more likely to see it as composed of conflicting interests.

The problem becomes even clearer when mechanistic metaphors instead of biological ones are used. Bateson was fond of using the heuristic model of the home thermostat to describe self-correcting systems. The thermostat works on a "feedback" principle; it is set at a number called the "bias" and makes changes according to feedback from the room. When the room cools off, the system works harder; when it overheats, the system slows down. This mechanism has been applied to family process as well: if one person (the patient) gets better, someone else may get worse until the "bias" (the family rule) is changed.

Altering the bias, however, sometimes called "second-order change," cannot easily be explained by general systems theory or cybernetics. There is no construct within the cybernetic canon to account for the fact that persons in the same house typically have different levels of access to the bias. If we shift the example slightly to one where a landlord controls the thermostat for an entire building, the access issue becomes clearer. The system may work beautifully from the point of view of the landlord, but terribly from the point of view of freezing tenants.

Thus, what is missing in the schemas of both cybernetics and general systems theory is ultimately what was missing from structural functionalism: a concept of power. Bateson eschewed the notion of power, insisting that unilateral power did not even exist. To illustrate this claim he chose the example of Goebbels, Hitler's chief intelligence officer, and his relationship to the German masses. Bateson argued that while Goebbels might have appeared to be the "man in power," he nonetheless was dependent on the people for feedback on how better to indoctrinate them. Thus, in systems terms, while Goebbels controlled the people, they also controlled him.

It is significant that many feminists take a moral position on power similar to that of Bateson. That is, many of us would prefer that human beings think much more in terms of dialogue, collaboration, and reciprocity than in terms of achieving control over others. Feminist scholar Marilyn French (1985) emphasized these "systemic" values in her critique of patriarchal cultures, *Beyond Power.* The hope that a transformation in social values will come about, however, must not prevent us from recognizing that it emphatically has not happened yet, and that we ignore the reality of power at our peril. Returning to the case of Goebbels for an example, it is true that an individual among the German masses might express an opinion that could end up influencing Goebbels. But the difference *made* by that difference of opinion depends not on individual "X" but on Goebbels. Individual X can be bribed or eliminated; conversely, no single person can have an equal impact on Goebbels. The masses may rise up against the man in power, but the fact that collective action is required further reveals the power difference.

To clarify these points, it might be helpful to state that some things that exist in dialectical relationship do not involve a power difference (e.g., thermostat and room temperature; Tweedledum and Tweedledee), but not all things dialectically related can be said to have equal or equivalent power (e.g., master and slave, parent and child, employer and employee). It is true that the less powerful can almost always *influence* the more powerful, but the difference between influence and legitimate power is not trivial. Although, for example, some slaves in the American South were allowed to do extra work in exchange for better conditions, it was not in their power to define extra work or, for that matter, to define better conditions. In a more familiar example, children influence parents by trying out new behaviors, but it is not in a child's power ultimately to define his or her actions as "good" or "rebellious" or "sick"; parents and professionals will do that. In seeking a more precise definition of *power,* we might call it the ability to categorize or define things, or, as the vernacular has it, "to call the shots." Or, as Nietzsche said, it is the power to *name* things.

Family therapists, following Bateson, have tried to do without a concept of power and so have maintained the idea that a complementary system should never be described in terms of the relative power of its constituents. This has led to some nefarious ideas that men who beat their wives are in a "complementary dance" with them. The complementary dance theory is said to afford therapeutic leverage, but as a theory it misses the point that the social institutions of naming (e.g., psychiatry and the law) privilege the male partner. From the Sumerian laws of 3000 B.C., which decreed that a disrespectful wife should have her teeth broken with a hot brick (Lerner 1986), to Anglo-American law of the nineteenth century, it has been within the law for men to assault their wives physically (but not the reverse). It would appear, moreover, that many husbands and judges are still not sure whether a marriage license is a license for abuse. (In most states in the United States, it is still legal for a man to rape his wife.)

The concept of power is important to understanding families and marriages. Many therapists continue to resist it because it implies to them that women are innocent victims of men, or that the female self is free from the violence of desire. Women, of course, are not morally superior to men, and feminist therapists have always sought to show women how they collude in their own powerlessness. Economic factors play a large role here, however. A woman who might want to leave an abusive man must enter a work force in which men with an eighth-grade education earn more than women with college degrees (Carmen, Russo, and Miller 1981). A "nonlinear" statement of this power problem might be expressed as follows: *Women do participate in their own abuse, but not as equals.*

It is argued, of course, that even in those situations in which money is not a problem, some women nonetheless remain with abusive men. This is much too complex a question to be reduced to the concept of "complementarity," however, no matter how well complementarity works to describe simple problems such as the "he-watches-football; she-nags" type of problem. The question of why a woman "needs" an abusive relationship with a man is more fruitfully posed, "Why do women need to be in relationships with men so much that they will stay even if abused, and even if financially able to go?" And conversely, "Why are so many men willing to take the risk of losing their intimate relationships with women?" Starting from these questions, it would then be necessary to ask how the culture constitutes those messages and how they are conceived and reproduced in families.

But when the questions are posed in this way, it is clear that general systems theory is no longer helpful; its map is not big enough for the territory. And, in fact, family therapy has not produced nearly as many books and tapes on family violence as it has on problems such as anorexia nervosa, although many more deaths are caused by the former than by the latter. Instead of throwing away the small map of cybernetics, family therapy has instead redefined the territory in terms of problems that its map can locate.

The problem with cybernetic explanation is that it lacks complexity. It is capable of telling us how the family is like a home heating system—how human beings act like self-governing machines—but not how it is different. Furthermore, neither Bateson's formulation of cybernetics nor any of the latest editions contain a theory of human development, or a way of understanding how parents and children form identifications with each other, or how those relationships influence the possibilities of future intimacy. The cybernetic vocabulary does not lend itself to discussions of sexuality, intention, shame, or desire. Contemporary theorists, following the lines of Bateson's work, have not really moved beyond the realm of mechanization in their theory building. Keeney and Ross (1985), for example, have this to say about the "clinical application" of their cybernetic model: "A troubled system comes to therapy, in most cases, with a request to alter the way it changes in order to stabilize itself. This 'change of change' requires a source of meaningful noise into which new structure and pattern can be punctuated" (p. 50). As in the case of Bateson's writing, one senses here something like a fear of too-direct discourse about human passions.

A number of epistemology-conscious therapists have tried to add to Bateson's insights by introducing the work of authors such as Francisco Varela (1979), Magoroh Maruyama (1968), and Humberto Maturana, and none of them has improved on Bateson in the areas critiqued here. Maturana, a Chilean biologist, is known within neurophysiology circles for his research on vision in frogs. Maturana discovered that frogs are structurally limited to seeing only certain kinds of movement; they do not simply scan whatever crosses their visual path. This research led him to write about the "structure determinism" of *social* systems as well, which has impressed family systems theorist Paul Dell enough to state: "Maturana's breakthrough in understanding living systems . . . is comparable in magnitude to Einstein's theory of relativity" (in Simon 1985, p. 34).

Maturana has restated the constructivist argument (i.e., there is no objective world out there, only subjective knowing) in ways so familiar that it has been difficult for some therapists to determine what is new about his work. After considerable effort, one interviewer managed to conclude that Maturana's constructivism is unique in that its support comes from biological evidence and not deduction alone (cf. Simon 1985). In addition, Maturana emphasizes that circular causality as well as linear causality is a myth. While other systems thinkers have admitted that each member of the family has a different view of its reality, Maturana insists that the view of each family member is equally valid, because there is no objective way that the family *is*. Given these notions, it is not surprising to learn that Maturana has nothing to say about feminism and that he has gone so far as to state that "power is caused by submission" (quoted in MacKinnon and Miller 1987, p. 144). In a 1985 interview, he proclaimed the sameness of all ideologies, saying that his work "makes people realize that different ideologies are just different verses" and that we are "co-drifting" in a "multiverse" (in Simon 1985, p. 43).

Perhaps only this depoliticized philosophy whose key concepts are nonresistance and "co-drifting" could have survived under the current military rule in Chile. While writers such as Dell find Maturana's work valuable, others have renounced it as supporting an "ideology of conformity." Colapinto (1985) suggests that if we take Maturana's concept of "structure determinism" seriously,

A Critique of the Cybernetic Epistemology of Gregory Bateson

> We can focus on being ourselves, look inward for coherent meanings, shed our passion to change others, live in the serene equanimity of our own customized bubbles. We can take flight from external chaos into inner stability, Walkmanize our existence and still feel epistemologically justified. [P. 30]

Finally, it is certain that "social amnesia" gained an extra year's sleep from Maturana's statement in his 1985 interview that:

> The other thing that is completely new is that I take both the observer and language at the same time as instrument and as problem. To my knowledge you don't find anywhere, either in philosophy or in biology, a theory that says that we are already in language when we human beings attempt as observers to explain language as a biological phenomenon. [P. 37]

Actually, we find these ideas so persistently in the writings of the French structuralists and poststructuralists—say, from de Saussure to Derrida—that we can grow weary of reading them. Even Maturana's heuristic device of placing words such as *truth* in parentheses to convey their epistemological shakiness is something previewed in the work of the French deconstructionist Jacques Derrida. In *Of Grammatology* (1976), Derrida placed an X through words such as truth (which is read "truth under erasure") to denote a deconstruction or ironizing of language not unrelated to Maturana's. Unlike Maturana, Derrida acknowledges the influence of Heidegger, who put an X through the word *being* in his classic *The Question of Being*.

I have addressed Maturana's work here in order to make the point that it is not Bateson's work alone that is intellectually weak or politically problematic. In fact, the potential for abdicating responsibility for purposive change that is latent in Bateson appears in full force in Maturana's work.

Explanations that begin with cybernetic presuppositions concentrate on how parts of structures affect one another in a particular moment. They all emphasize in various ways that power is a myth and that the study of history is not of utmost importance. Bateson's well-known skepticism about consciously changing social systems, including the family, simply finds a redoubled expression in Maturana's call to political acquiescence.

Conclusions

"The fathers have eaten bitter fruit and the children's teeth are set on edge." Bateson ate the fruit of his intellectual fathers—the cyberneticians, the logicians, and other ahistorical and nonfeminist thinkers—and we, the "offspring," have been left with the ill effects. Bateson, perhaps, knew something about the bitter fruit he ate and why he ate it, but we who know too little of the history of ideas before 1955 are left with some thoughts that do not really nourish and with others that are truly bitter.

This is not to deny Bateson's obvious contribution to family therapy. He did give the field credibility; he did bring us valuable concepts. Perhaps as Alfred North Whitehead said of ancient philosophy, some of Bateson's insights will remain precious to us although his system of thought as a whole will no longer seem sufficient.

It may be that Bateson's extreme emphasis on the role of the environment in creating "mind" was necessary to counter the avoidance of the environment by many traditional psychiatrists. A second and related point is that Bateson's continual use of *ecological* metaphors *per se* made us aware that it is essential not only to think about context in the familial and social sense but also to think about the ozone layer, about DDT and pollution. It is *not* typical of the "masters of abstraction" to concern themselves with the integrity of the biosphere. There is currently a group of family therapists who devote some effort to "preserving the planet" by educating colleagues and families about the probable ecological sequelae of nuclear war. That some family therapists would perceive an easy connection between helping families with psychological problems and saving the physical environment cannot be unrelated to Bateson's persistent and articulate teachings about "the ecology of mind."

Bateson was without doubt a masterful popularizer, an interpreter of some of the most important ideas of the eighteenth to twentieth centuries. His work has all the importance and all the liabilities of popularizations. He brought concepts to readers who would not have known them otherwise, and he phrased them accessibly. Therapists who would not read Kant or Nietzsche will read Bateson and learn about the highly important notion of constructed reality. Very few readers would slog through the unpopular prose of William James or Charles Saunders Peirce, who influenced Bateson a good deal. (The wonderful concept of double description [see page 110] comes to us from Peirce, and it was William James who coined the phrase about seeking "the difference that makes a difference," of which Bateson was so fond.*)

Bateson's turns of phrase, both borrowed and original, and his imaginative heuristics will be of continued value to family therapists. (His biblical citation about "bitter fruit" has been helpful in organizing this chapter.) Bateson's use of double description is one heuristic device that can be particularly helpful to feminists, since it can be used to explain the necessity of looking at the family through the eyes of both its male and its female members. To see the views of both genders gives *depth* to our social vision. When a student therapist "sees" a child in the clutches of an "overinvolved" mother, one might ask the student to provide a second description from the point of view of the mother, considering the history of mothers-in-society. We can use double description to ask, in the words of feminist Pauline Bart, "What is Portnoy's *mother's* complaint?"

Can a feminist family therapy be supported by cybernetics or the new epistemology alone? Some feminists may argue that this is possible; I am very doubtful. But if we should stray from cybernetics, where exactly do we turn to discuss the way that family members live together? How do we describe their "groupness"—the ways they seem to influence each other so predictably, the ways they dream the same dreams, reproduce generation upon generation of lived experience, and, too often, offer each other up to sacrifice?

In the next chapter, I join a growing minority of family therapists in the belief that certain revisions of psychoanalytic theory can best be appropriated and expanded to understand family systems. There are a number of reasons for my choice of psychoanalytic thinking (and, in particular, object-relations thinking). One is that while the male-female dialectic has been described in patriarchal ways, the category of gender at least has legitimacy in that language, and does not need to be argued into existence. Second, although social history and power have not been given enough consideration by analysts, *personal* history and *personal* power are so fundamental to psychoanalytic theory that other uses of history and power can be, and indeed have been, introduced. Finally, psychoanalytic thinking is a good choice because so many feminist authors have already gone to work at revising the theory—and with great success. There is not, and I doubt that there will be, a feminist cybernetics.

---

*Peirce's discussion of "abduction," which became Bateson's "double description," is found in Peirce 1908/1958, p. 368. James's comment is in James 1906/1963, p. 25.

12

Psychoanalytic Theory as a Conceptual Source for Feminist Psychotherapy with Families

A rejection of psychoanalysis and of Freud's works is fatal for feminism. However it may have been used, psychoanalysis is not a recommendation *for* a patriarchal society, but an analysis *of* one. If we are interested in understanding and challenging the oppression of women, we cannot afford to neglect it.
—JULIET MITCHELL
Psychoanalysis and Feminism, 1974

This fear [of dependence] will sometimes take the form of a fear of woman, or fear of a woman, and at other times will take less easily recognized forms, always including the fear of domination. Unfortunately, the fear of domination does not lead groups of people to avoid being dominated; on the contrary, it draws them towards a specific or chosen domination. . . . Traced to its root in the history of each individual, this fear of *women* turns out to be a fear of recognizing the fact of dependence.
—D. W. WINNICOTT
"The Mother's Contribution to Society,"
1957/1986

Children could be dependent from the outset on people of both genders and establish an individuated sense of self in relation to both. . . . This would reduce men's needs to guard their masculinity . . . and would help women to develop the auton-

omy which too much embeddedness in relationship
has often taken from them.

—Nancy Chodorow
The Reproduction of Mothering, 1978

IF ONE ACCEPTS the premise that general systems theory and cybernetics do not constitute an adequate conceptual foundation for a feminist therapy, then one is forced to look to other traditions for alternatives. I will argue in this chapter that the psychoanalytic tradition (defined broadly for the moment) provides a stronger and more suitable scaffolding than GST/cybernetics for a feminist psychotherapy with families. I do this at least somewhat apprised of the risks involved. One colleague warned that it was not feminist politics that would make my book controversial in the field of family therapy, but rather my insistence on the "psychoanalytic stuff." I think this colleague was correct, and I suspect that the obverse problem (psychoanalytic readers rejecting the work for being feminist) will also come to haunt. Nonetheless, I have found that psychoanalytic theory, for all its errors and anachronisms, continues to be a most subtle and powerful means of understanding patriarchy. Conversely, as a student of psychoanalytic thought, I have found that feminism is necessary to bring psychoanalysis to its full radical potential.

The wariness and, in some instances, the contempt between feminists and psychoanalytic thinkers has been occasioned, in part, by misreadings of feminism, bad translations of psychoanalysis, and the inevitable popularizations of both. The more one reads and comprehends both traditions, the more necessary and desirable seems friendship between them, and the more appealing is their application to the treatment of families.

Historical Perspective

A recurrent contention in this book has been that ideas, like families, have histories, and must be understood in their historical contexts. It would be inconsistent with this historical emphasis to rush toward a discussion of feminist revisions of psychoanalysis, and their application to family therapy, without mentioning the origins of these ideas. The originator of all psychoanalytic ideas was, of course, Sigmund Freud, a man whom many family therapists and many feminists love to hate. Freud himself once noted that the gods of the old religion become the demons of the new (1930/1961). While Freud's name was once virtually synonymous with psychology, it is now possible to earn advanced degrees as a therapist without reading a page of Freud. In the literature of family therapy, most authors plunge into "here and now" discussions of family therapy without pausing to differentiate their work from its psychoanalytic origins, and making no conscious acknowledgment of Freud's contribution.

It is understandable, of course, that the pioneer family therapists would have tried to emphasize what was different and new about their work instead of what was derivative from or continuous with psychoanalysis. However, it appears that in an eagerness to present a new form of treatment, they simply dismissed Freud's work as though it had never existed. Even Nathan Ackerman, who wrote perhaps the most about Freud (two chapters in *The Psychodynamics of Family Life* [1958], entitled "Freud and the Psychoanalytic View of the Family" and "Freud and Changing Conceptions of Personality—A Personal Synthesis"), limited his discussion to secondary sources, and managed not to cite a single work of Freud's! Haley's (1963, 1976) references to psychoanalysis reflect a very superficial understanding of it.

Despite these omissions, it remains true that many of family therapy's most cherished concepts are psychoanalytic concepts. Not to acknowledge our origins in Freud's work is to deprive ourselves of the richness of his thought, to risk repeating his errors, and to accelerate the process of social amnesia, which leads us to overvalue the contemporary and to treat everything else as quaint and disposable.

CONTINUITIES BETWEEN PSYCHOANALYTIC THEORY AND FAMILY THERAPY

The task of tracing the conceptual, practical, and political similarities and differences between Freud's ideas and those of family therapists would require a book in itself, and a long book at that. We will have occasion here to touch on only a few items relevant to that history.

Although Freud never saw a family in treatment, he obviously understood a great deal about family interactions. It is clear that he believed in a continuity of emotional life in the family from one generation to the next (Freud 1908/1959). In *Totem and Taboo* (1913) he introduced explicitly the notion of a *family psyche* whose psychological processes were roughly isomorphic to those of the individual psyche. Moreover, anyone who has read Freud's cases can see the importance he placed on knowing the details of the patient's interactions with family members. As Fred Sander (1978) pointed out, there is a decided "family systems ring" to many passages in Freud, such as the following comment on system maintenance from *An Outline of Psychoanalysis:*

> No one who has any experience of the rifts which so often divide a family will, if he is an analyst, be surprised to find that the patient's relatives sometimes betray less interest in his recovery than in his remaining as he is. When, as so often, neurosis is related to conflicts between members of a family, the healthy party will not hesitate long in choosing between his own interest and the sick party's recovery. [1940/1964, pp. 172–73]

Most family therapists assume not only that "we" were the first to pay attention to the psychological life of families but also that we deserve credit for the very notion of illness as "useful." A confusion about the origins of the idea that individuals' symptoms can be considered meaningful and even "necessary" to families at a given moment is suggested in the following passage by Lynn Hoffman in *Foundations of Family Therapy:*

> This puzzling idea—why would a family "need" a symptom?—baffled therapists in the days before it was realized what a beautiful, serviceable, well-constructed artifact a symptom is—thoughtfully provided by nature to help families that were terrified (probably for good reasons) by the threat of change. [1981, p. 323]

Freud had raised the question of the role or meaning of symptoms long before family therapy existed. For example, in the "Case of an Obsessional Neurosis" (mentioned in chapter 10), Freud interpreted a young man's paralysis in terms of his problem in choosing between his own beloved and the woman selected for him by his family. Freud suggested that the man's symptom served him by necessarily postponing the choice.

Freud, of course, did *not* go on to discuss how the symptom in question might have also served the needs of the fiancée, or of the patient's father or mother. Freud's patient was the individual, and did not include the people meaningfully connected to the individual. It was the family therapy movement that made the potentially radical shift of naming the entire family as the subject of treatment. Family therapy can be said to have surpassed psychoanalysis in this respect, and in other ways as well—for example, by making therapy accessible to a larger spectrum of people and by excluding some of Freud's most blatant sexism.

However, family therapy also gave up a great deal in rejecting our psychoanalytic origins. We lost a language that spoke of mothers, fathers, pain, and loss, trading it for a language of "dyads" and "dysfunction." We got rid of Freud's excessive biologism, but we also lost the rich descriptive idiom he had used to depict human dilemmas and their prototypes in myth and history. We got rid of the (to some) untenable pessimism of the "death instinct," but we ended up instead with a naive acceptance of social adaptation as a goal of therapy.

One reason many family therapists felt the need to jettison psychoanalysis has to do with misunderstandings of Freud's work, due partly to poor translations from German to English in the *Standard Edition*. For example, some contemporary therapists disdain Freud's use of terms such as "mental apparatus" and "psychic energy," which sound pseudoscientific and "energy-obsessed." But Freud's work has a poetic/humanistic character that was lost in translation. Bruno Bettelheim has pointed out in a fascinating book, *Freud and Man's Soul*, that Freud used the German word *Seele* ("soul") throughout his work, but that it was translated into English as *mind* which became "mental apparatus." (There is an exact equivalent to *mind* in German, which Freud would have used if he had wanted it.) In addition, Freud used the colloquial, unpretentious words *I* and *it*, whereas the translator chose the Latin words *ego* and *id*. It is in *this* Freud, the Freud in pursuit of the soul, in pursuit of a language to describe and heal it, that we as feminists see our work foreshadowed.

Despite what would seem to be implied by family therapy's forfeiture of psychoanalysis—that we could manage without its concepts—this does not appear to be the case. Words such as *unconscious, repression,* and *projection* slip shyly into an extraordinary number of family therapy discussions because there are ultimately no satisfactory substitutes for them. Some family therapists, of course, would urge us to work harder to get psychoanalytic concepts out of our discourse. However, without a complex understanding of unconscious process, there simply is no way of understanding how violence as well as styles of expressing conflict, sexual taboos, and many human capacities and incapacities are transmitted across the generations. In the words of feminist Juliet Mitchell, "the particular task of psychoanalysis is to decipher how we acquire our heritage of the ideas and laws of human society within the unconscious mind or, to put it another way, the unconscious mind *is* the way in which we acquire these laws" (1974, p. xiv).

There are some feminists in family therapy who have said, "I do use words such as *unconscious* and *projection*, but that doesn't make me interested in psychoanalysis. These words are now part of everyday speech." This is precisely true, but they exist in everyday speech in a highly simplified form. Is colloquial, common-sense usage of words adequate, as long as it implies the common sense of feminists? I think not. I will take the position that since family therapists cannot seem to do without notions of the unconscious, of projection and denial, of transference and countertransference, and of illness as metaphor, then it is to our great advantage to know what has already been written about these concepts, to investigate them in our clinical practice, and to transform them for our purposes. We do this by elaborating notions of the *family's* unconscious, the family's projective system, and the family's transference to the therapist. As feminists we must do so in ways that do not re-inscribe patriarchal relationships.

There are, of course, some writers who have attempted for decades to understand the family psychoanalytically, and they have done creative and important work (Flugel 1921, Dicks 1967, Framo 1981, Skynner 1976, Stierlin 1977, Slipp 1984, Scharff and Scharff 1987, Kirschner and Kirschner 1986, Wachtel and Wachtel 1986). Unfortunately, none of these integrative works, even the most recent ones, mentions feminism at all. Thus, the inexorable next step in this discussion is to address directly the possibilities of orchestrating feminist and psychoanalytic discourses. If this orchestration cannot be imagined, it is of no use to connect psychoanalytic thought with a feminist treatment of families.*

THE INTEGRATION OF PSYCHOANALYTIC THOUGHT AND FEMINISM

Freud's phallocentrism, his view that women envy the penis and have babies as substitutes, is mocked justifiably by feminists and other progressive social theorists. The fact that Freud was one of the few great writers on the subject to admit his own ignorance about women is very partial comfort.

Criticism of Freud's phallocentrism by women analysts is almost as old as psychoanalysis itself. Karen Horney, as early as 1922, challenged the concept of penis envy, saying that Freud's attempts to find a penis in woman was largely an attempt to deny women's own genitality. Horney

---

*An objection has been raised by some feminists to my calling my therapy "psychoanalytic," because I do not use free association, do not keep people in treatment for ten years, and do engage in active dialogue with patients. This characterization evokes "Aaron Green"—the classical analyst depicted by Janet Malcolm in *The Impossible Profession*—but it does not do justice to the range of psychotherapies in existence that justifiably call themselves "psychoanalytic." It is useful to remember that Freud's treatment lasted only six months to a year, that he defined *psychoanalysis* as any treatment that deals centrally with transference and resistance, and that analysts vary tremendously in their level of engagement in sessions—the existential and "modern" analysts being more active and nurturing than the "classical" types.

recommended that analysts turn their attention to *Angst für Frau*—the dread of woman—and suggested that its roots lay in the little boy's fear that his penis is too small for the mother's vagina.

Horney believed that the pan-cultural degradation of women is in part a reaction formation. (The male, in effect, says: "It is not *I* who am inadequate, it is really *she* who is bad, devouring, dangerous.") Horney renounced Freud's patriarchal blindness, but used psychoanalysis to make sense of that blindness and to envision better solutions. Many contemporary feminist therapists have chosen the same path, discarding Freud's view of feminine psychology as a reflection of his Victorian context and personal neurosis, and continuing explicitly to use psychoanalytic thinking for their scholarly and therapeutic work. I think that *not* to make room for a psychoanalytic view of misogyny such as Horney's (or Dorothy Dinnerstein's) is ultimately to capitulate to a purely materialist view of women's oppression, and often to a theory of misogyny as a male conspiracy against women.

Many feminists have become interested particularly in Freud's "early work," the period before he gave up his seduction theory, according to which neurosis is caused by actual sexual abuse in childhood. Freud abandoned this theory, which emphasized the impact of real events in the child's family and social context, and adopted the Oedipal theory, which emphasized *intrapsychic* process. Freud declared that all children have sexual desire for their parents, and thus that patients' accounts of sexual seduction may be imagined rather than remembered. The best book on this subject is Marianne Krüll's *Freud and His Father* (1986). Krüll points out that Freud never completely gave up the seduction theory, and that he continued all his life to deal with actual events in patients' lives. Freud's change of emphasis was not trivial, of course, and may have increased the cultural trend toward underestimating the frequency of sexual abuse of daughters. Krüll's point of view is helpful in that she neither apologizes for the damage done by this change of theory nor attempts to destroy Freud because of it. Instead, she offers a psychoanalytic interpretation of the theoretical change—one that centers on Freud's relationship with his father. (Freud's granddaughter, Sophie Freud, herself a feminist and a therapist, wrote a very positive review of Krüll's book.*)

---

*The reader may be more familiar with another book on this subject: Jeffrey Masson's *The Assault on Truth.* This book is not as carefully reasoned as Krüll's, and for some reason it does not mention Krüll's book, although Masson knew of it. (See also Janet Malcolm's fascinating work on this subject, *In the Freud Archives.*) A most unfortunate result of this controversy about the seduction theory is the debate over which is more important—real events in childhood, or children's fantasies about events. This dichotomy is not meaningful to feminist theorists, and, in fact, many modern analysts have shown a

Psychoanalytic Theory as Conceptual Source for Feminist Psychotherapy

Feminists such as Pauline Bart (1983), who reject as toxic any form of psychoanalytic thinking, have difficulty explaining why many other feminists find such psychoanalytic ideas indispensable. One cannot easily argue that psychoanalysis has been a "safe" choice for feminists, since it has been disparaged in American academic circles for decades. Indeed, many academic feminists who work with psychoanalytic ideas often find they have to fight *two* battles for legitimacy. These feminists have chosen the psychoanalytic tradition not for reasons of expediency but because its tenets are deeply resonant with feminist tenets. In fact, radical feminist Shulamith Firestone (1970), while vehemently criticizing Freud's errors about women, dubbed Freudianism "the misguided feminism" because of the strong correspondence between the two. Most feminists would agree with Freud, I think, that the sexual repression that was (and, in some ways, still is) integral to women's upbringing negatively affects women's intellectual success and achievement. It is interesting to note, then, that in addition to the sexism in Freud's writing, he also wrote this about women:

> Their upbringing forbids their concerning themselves intellectually with sexual problems though they nevertheless feel extremely curious about them, and frightens them by condemning such curiosity as unwomanly and a sign of sinful disposition. In this way they are scared away from any form of thinking, and knowledge loses its value for them. The prohibition of thought extends beyond the sexual field. I think that the undoubted intellectual inferiority of so many women can be traced back to the inhibition of thought necessitated by sexual suppression. [1908/1959, pp. 198–99]

Based on my readings of feminism and psychoanalysis, I find the following correspondences between them.

1. Freud assaulted Victorian patriarchy by ruining the myth of "rational man." The bourgeois gentleman was asked to accept the fact that he was not really "master of his own house" because his mind was beset with urges to which he had no conscious access. Freud showed that there was psychopathology in everyday life and that dualisms between normal and abnormal, proper and perverse, rational and irrational were more apparent than real. Like feminists, Freud showed little respect for what was socially considered "normal,"

___
commitment to combining the insights of the early and later Freud by placing equal valence on real events and fantasy. See, for example, the outstanding works of Alice K. Miller, beginning with *The Drama of the Gifted Child* (1983a). See also Edgar Levenson's brilliant discussion of fantasy and reality in psychoanalytic treatment in *The Ambiguity of Change* (1983).

since it was by definition tainted with repression. (Freud's use of the word *normal* contrasts sharply with family therapists' naive use of the word, as in "normal families" to mean healthy and flourishing families.)

2. Freud's theories privilege the categories of childhood, affect, sexuality, expressiveness, intimacy, body functions, and the irrational—things that have too often been associated exclusively with women, and hence socially disparaged. Women, in fact, have been made to be the "carriers" of these things for society. As Jean Baker Miller (1976) has pointed out, psychoanalysis redefined these as concerns for everyone. Not only mothers and nannies had to be interested in children's theories about reproduction, about their genitals, and about excrement—rather, these concerns had to become the business of all serious men and women if they wanted to understand themselves and the human psyche.

3. Freud's model, like Marx's, is a conflict model. It does not view the individual as fitting harmoniously into society like the parts of a cell, as in general systems thinking. On the contrary, Freud saw society as fundamentally repressive to the individual. One of the most untenable repressions, Freud thought, was the taboo on homosexuality. In several prominent places in his work, he defended homosexuality. He also wrote a letter in reply to a mother who was distressed over her son's sexual preference—a letter that might be written by any feminist therapist to any such worried mother. In it he wrote:

Homosexuality is assuredly no advantage, but it is nothing to be ashamed of, no vice, no degradation; it cannot be classified as an illness; we consider it to be a variation of the sexual function. . . . It is a great injustice to persecute homosexuality as a crime—and a cruelty too. [1935/1961, pp. 419–20]

4. Psychoanalytic theory has always been deeply concerned with the uses of language. Feminists have also made language a central focus, because of the way it shapes our experience as the nondominant sex.

5. Psychoanalytic theory is concerned with the person's history. It emphasizes the curative aspects of remembering, investigating, and gaining insight. This emphasis is analogous to (not identical with) the feminist rubrics of "consciousness raising" and "demystification," which have to do with helping people understand how social and political conditions construct our experience of self. Psychoanalysis as a treatment method does not set out to raise consciousness

about social oppression, but in many instances it does raise consciousness about other repressions, other kinds of domination and disempowerment that are perpetrated by those in authority (parents) toward those who are not (children). This aspect of psychoanalysis is associated primarily with Freud's early work, but it has become an important feature of much of modern psychoanalytic thinking.

6. Freud's notion of the essence of the therapeutic process had much to do with the relationship between therapist and patient. Bettelheim mentions that Freud wrote in a letter to Jung that psychoanalysis was, in essence, "a cure through love." Feminists, too, put an emphasis on the attentive and caring aspects of the therapeutic relationship.

Since Freud's death, a number of schools of psychoanalysis have developed in Europe and the United States. Of these, I find the work that developed in Great Britain, the "object-relations" school, most compatible with feminism.* The origins of object-relations theory are associated with Melanie Klein, W. R. D. Fairbairn, Wilfred Bion, and D. W. Winnicott. Object-relations theory is distinguished from classical Freudian theory by its emphasis on understanding the early years of life—the so-called pre-Oedipal period—which meant a new interest in mother-child interactions. Freud had been so focused on the Oedipus complex and the role of the powerful father in shaping psychic structure that he neglected the role of the mother. In Freud's cases, we find much more attention paid to children's attractions to and fear of the father, than to feelings toward the mother.

This situation changed when Melanie Klein began working with young children. Klein came to believe that the development of the personality begins at birth, and that the early experience with the mother, including her power to hold, to bond with, and empathically to reflect the child, is of fundamental importance. It is the pre-Oedipal phase (0 to 2 years) that sets the groundwork for our capacities to relate to others fully, empathically, and pleasurably. Object-relations therapists, whether working with individuals or families, aim to create what Winnicott called the "holding" or "facilitating" environment, in which those early experiences and wounds can be remembered, understood, and healed.

Object-relations theory is attractive to many newcomers to psychoanalysis because it has a greater interpersonal emphasis than classical

*I mean this from the point of view of a psychotherapist. See the footnote on page 23 about the feminist followers of Lacan.

Freudian theory. Object-relations theorists believe that the basic human drive is not impulse gratification but the need to be in relationships. At the same time, object-relations therapists continue to insist on the importance of the internal representations made of external events. They talk of the maternal and paternal introjects, and of the child internalizing aspects of the parents' relationship, for example, which becomes influential in the individual's future intimate relationships.

Many therapists who become interested in object-relations theory flinch at the use of the term *"object* relations" to refer to the interpersonal. Greenberg and Mitchell in *Object Relations in Psychoanalytic Theory* (1983) explain how the term *object relations* originated in Freud's work on drives, and how it was developed by Klein, Winnicott, and others. We may want to continue to talk about "object relations" because this usage reflects the fact that—like it or not—we do not always form attachments to whole persons, but sometimes only to parts. As infants, for example, we are aware of adults only as they exist for us; we cannot yet suspect the fact of their subjectivity. Furthermore, when infants "take in" the adult, they distort, reshape, divide and split this person in their internal representation. The word *object* reminds us that the internal mother is not the same as the mother herself, since the introject has been subjected to the perceiver's unconscious operations.

But what if this language ends up ratifying—not just reflecting—our tendency to objectify mothers (and others)? Carol Gilligan has suggested that we drop all object language and talk instead of the individual's "maternal story" or "internal mother" (Gilligan, pers. comm. 1988). A thoroughly feminist psychotherapy will, no doubt, require a reinvention of psychoanalytic language. In this book, I will continue to use some of the conventional terms, however, in order to communicate with mainstream readers, and because agreement has not been reached on any alternative usage.

An obvious problem with object-relations theory is that none of its originators was feminist. Indeed, the new emphasis on the importance of the pre-Oedipal period probably has resulted in more blaming of mothers for disturbances of children. Winnicott had hoped, however, that his work would help mothers, and that it would make people more appreciative of mothering, more respectful of the needs we all have for dependency and nurturance. Winnicott believed, as many feminists do, that much male bellicosity is reaction formation against the fear of (and wish for) dependence on women. What Winnicott failed to take into account, however, was that all mothering takes place in the context of patriarchy, and thus all discussions of mothering must include a discussion of patriarchy.

Fortunately, in the past decade there have been some excellent reformulations of object-relations theory by feminist writers. The most widely read feminist text on object-relations theory is Nancy Chodorow's *The Reproduction of Mothering* (1978), an outstanding example of a successful synthesis of psychoanalytic and feminist thought. Chodorow was not writing as a therapist, but her work should be helpful to family therapists because it offers something that does not exist within the family therapy literature at the present time: a theory of gender development. Chodorow's work gives us a theory of gender differences that does not disadvantage women, that does not imply that gender differences are unchangeable, and that locates both the origins of gender identity and the seeds of change within the institution of the family.

As an object-relations theorist, Chodorow posits that there are *psychological* differences (not just biological and cultural differences) between the sexes, and that this has to do with the fact that both sexes are parented primarily by women. This phenomenon of "female-dominated child care" means that infant boys are raised primarily by an opposite-sex person and girls by a same-sex person. Thus, even in the pre-Oedipal stage, boys and girls have a significantly different experience; they begin their lives with different degrees of sameness to the person they first know. The sameness relation results in an extended pre-Oedipal phase for girls, and they are not pushed quite as quickly into the Oedipal stage as boys are. This is not meant to imply that mothers love their daughters more than their sons. Chodorow is not talking primarily about love or acceptance, but about boundaries; indeed, she is describing the origins of all interpersonal boundaries. In the Oedipal stage, the boy is asked to give up his identification with the mother, and to become masculine through identification with his actual father or with a male image that mother and society invoke for him. The girl, in contrast, will not be asked to make this kind of switch. The girl's identity, thus, is founded on a sense of *continuity* with her original relationship, while the boy's is founded on *discontinuity* from his. The girl will separate from her mother as she becomes more involved with other family members, but she will never be expected to disconnect her very identity from mother's, as the boy will. There is, thus, a psychological renunciation, a cutoff (from mother) in the early experience of the male that does not occur, or does not occur to the same degree, for the female.*

Chodorow argues that these differences predispose men and women to experience intimacy differently. They incline women to be less afraid of commitments than men, and men less afraid of discontinuity. There is risk

*See also Irene Fast's (1984) work on gender identity and the mutual envy of the sexes in childhood, which forms a powerful complement to Chodorow's work.

for both sexes in this state of affairs—for women, that they will become too embedded in relationships and lose their autonomy; for men, that they will never learn to connect intimately with others. The most important implication of this, according to Chodorow, is that the differences in relational capacity predispose girls to perform the behaviors that are necessary for mothering itself: continuity, care, and the ability to tolerate a lack of separateness. Thus, the modern family continues to reproduce girls who grow up to do primary child care and boys who do not.

Chodorow in no way denies the cultural and economic factors in the construction of gender differences. She points out that girls are socialized to cultivate attractiveness to males, whereas boys are socialized to view women as objects of consumption and to view themselves as less in need of close relationships.* Furthermore, women's economic position solidifies the psychological inducements to attach themselves to men.

Chodorow believes, however, that social conditioning theories and economic factors alone cannot explain gender differences. I agree that her psychoanalytic account is necessary because it explains what happens "between" the biological level and the cultural level. Other theories imply too little activity on the part of the child being "conditioned" to its "gender role." After all, culture is not transmitted to the individual as water is transmitted from faucet to cup. It is filtered, rearranged, refused, and taken in through processes that psychoanalytic thinkers have described with words like repression, splitting, denial, and introjection.

What the psychoanalytic account does, in a sense, is to push "role training" explanations back to the point where the training is largely nonverbal, unconscious, and fantasy-based. What is learned at later stages in life is somewhat reversible, but what is learned in infancy is relatively intractable. It is not always easy to shrug off professional roles and political identifications, but it is nearly impossible to change the ways one experiences and pursues intimacy—much to the chagrin of contemporary couples and their therapists!

What is unique about psychoanalytic theory, then, is that it helps account for the intransigence, for the unyielding qualities, of gender. It tells us that gender is neither so permanent and monolithic as a biological explanation would have it, nor so amenable to change as social learning theorists—including many overly optimistic feminists—would have it. Neither rewriting sexist textbooks nor abolishing economic discrimination can be expected to change the fact that many men and women feel like

---

*I will not summarize the research documenting sex-role conditioning in children, because this research tends to be much better known than the psychoanalytic accounts of gender formation. See Basow (1986) for a review of the literature.

"intimate strangers" to each other. These differences will not be radically altered until change is made in the way earliest parent-child experience is structured.

Unlike many psychoanalytic thinkers, Chodorow makes recommendations for social change. She recommends that the practice of female-dominated child care be transformed so that males and females do not continue to develop disparate relational capacities. Her book concludes with an exhortation that both men and women be primary caretakers of children.

Chodorow's work shows how mutually enhancing the psychoanalytic/feminist synthesis can be. Without feminism, psychoanalytic theories of gender end up with a "deficit" model of femininity, i.e., woman as castrated man. Without psychoanalytic theory, social learning theories of gender are behavioristic and superficial, and imply an empty organism, passively conditioned without the capacity to rearrange, refuse, repress, and filter stimuli. Without either feminism or psychoanalytic theory, family therapy is rendered "asexual." It stands without a suitably complex means of talking about the hypostatic reality of gender.

I have not had the luxury here of summarizing the work of Chodorow comprehensively, nor of attempting to extend her developmental theory to the psychology of latency and adolescence. Because this book is addressed mainly to practitioners, innumerable metapsychological issues will not be raised in favor of proceding to matters of clinical application.

The Clinical Relevance of Feminist Object-Relations Theory

The object-relations theory of Nancy Chodorow and other feminists speaks to the importance of involving fathers in children's lives and, by extension, in family treatment. This, of course, is not a brand-new concept; many traditional family therapists believe in "bringing father in," but its importance is rarely argued in other than pragmatic terms. Fathers are included in family therapy because they are considered "part of the system"; if they were left out, the systemic intervention might not work. The father's role is often framed as that of "expert" on some issue that will help the family solve its problem (cf. "A Modern Little Hans" in Haley 1976). According to one text, fathers should be included in family therapy because they "give it an authority it would otherwise lack" (Scharff and Scharff 1987, p. 151). One hears few if any family therapists talking about bringing fathers into treatment as a way of reshaping the social and sexual order of things. Feminists know that it is subversive to patriarchy to bring fathers closer to the heart of child care and to bring children into the paternal heart.

Psychologist Sam Osherson, clearly informed by the literatures of both feminism and object-relations theory, has written an eloquent book entitled *Finding Our Fathers* (1986). Osherson discusses Freud's Oedipus complex and notices, as Karen Horney and others did before him, that Freud "forgot" an important part of the myth. In Sophocles's version, the first act of violence is committed by Laius, the father, against Oedipus, his son. Laius gives the infant Oedipus to a shepherd to abandon on the hillside when Laius interpreted literally an oracle saying that his son would kill him and marry his wife. Laius even ran a rod through Oedipus's feet so that he would not be able to crawl to safety. (The name "Oedipus" means "swollen feet.") Osherson uses the term "Laius Complex" to refer to the perpetual wounding of sons by their fathers through neglect, avoidance, envy, and violence. Osherson believes that fathers do fear and resent a son's closeness with his mother, partly because she becomes less available to her husband and partly because the father's role is so ill-defined in the developed West.

In some cases the father's resentment and his own feelings of abandonment by his wife are acted out against the children (and/or the wife). In other situations the father simply retreats from the family, devoting himself to work or other diversions, and becomes a shadowy figure to the children, known to them mainly through the mother. This can be particularly hard for boys. Girls at least have their mothers to imitate, refuse to imitate, and so on. But boys, who have been instructed that they are not to be like the female parent but instead like the male, can indeed end up feeling like the abandoned Oedipus on the hillside.

This abandonment by father can be felt whether or not the father remains physically with the family. It is, in fact, quite probable that fathers' *emotional* absence may be more difficult to contend with than their physical absence, since, like all ambiguous losses, it cannot be easily acknowledged and grieved (Boss 1977). In this, as in many other situations, human beings cannot come to grips with absence that masquerades as presence. Consequently, therapists often find that men whose fathers were physically present can have a hard time gaining access to their longing for closeness with the father and with their anger toward him. They are mystified by the myth of his presence. When questioned about possible resentment toward the father, they may say, "My dad? He was there. He never left us. He didn't beat us." It may take time for men (and women) to feel entitled to their sadness over the fact of father's having been "there but not there." Sometimes only after therapy can an adult son or daughter express the longing and the hatred for this person, whose cruelty or absence or need to be taken care of had been so much an accepted part of "the way things are." Many men without loving fathers grow up expecting women to give them all the warmth and limit setting they were denied—and then hating women for not succeeding in what is, after all, an impossible task.

In short, what feminist object-relations theory has to teach therapists who treat families is the overarching importance of creating a new father, a man who will not be the tired nightly visitor, who will be more than a therapist-appointed expert, more than a coach to his irresolute wife, more than her backup, more than the separator of mothers and children, but an authentic presence, a tender and engaged parent, a knower of children in the way that mothers have been knowers of children.

The obverse is true for our work with mothers. If we must help fathers take better care of children, we must help mothers to care for themselves and to be cared for by others. For the family therapist, it can be a radical act simply to accept the task of nurturing and supporting a mother in a family, helping her to define her needs and wishes and to confirm their validity, while also pointing out what happens when women's needs for nurturance are denied. The point is not to turn mothers into honorary members of the "me generation" but to undo the history of silencing maternal desire for the sake of the family's smooth functioning, represented in the myths of Manolus and the Timberlawn families (see chapter 1).

To help mother reclaim the self does not help only mother. According to object-relations theory we all, as children, form internal versions ("introjects") of our mothers, fathers, and other people important to us. If the real mother is injured or silenced, so will the internal mother be injured and silenced. Children whose mothers have been battered or degraded grow up with a part of themselves—the part they associate with mother—also degraded. This often creates a recalcitrant cycle of devaluing their own needs (and capacities) for the "maternal" activities of loving and nurturing others, and also of devaluing these capacities in others. In short, degradation of the mother is ultimately a self-degradation—for both males and females. Conversely, the reconstitution of motherhood in culture will mean a reconstitution of the self, for everyone "of woman born."

The same is true of fathers. Bringing fathers closer to the family is helpful not only to fathers who, as a result, feel more connected, more important, and less isolated. It also means that the paternal introject for each child becomes less ghostly, less indifferent, less cruel, or less idealized. Children would thus identify the part of themselves associated with fathers with less intimidation, less resentment, less mystification. Because of our robust inclination to reproduce the psychological past in the present, the result of having truly present fathers in childhood would be an inclination in adulthood to seek out male friends, colleagues, mentors, and lovers who are strong and caring individuals.

The emphasis on bringing father closer to children in therapy is not meant to imply the far too common "kick-Mom-out-of-the-driver's-seat" approach. I do not mean that women should not know their children as well, or that therapists should set out to loosen mothers' bonds to children. Neither am I suggesting that families with no father in the house cannot flourish; such a statement would be an indictment of the many such black families, and single-parent families of all types, in the world. I *am* saying, however, that children benefit from having more than one adult active in their lives. Where father is present in the home, he ought to be a real parent and not a consultant. Where he is not present for reasons of death or separation, children should be given as full a picture of him as possible.

This discussion does not attempt to close the controversy on parental involvement with children, nor to answer all our questions about the terms in which to conceptualize families and parenting. On the contrary, countless thorny questions remain. Diane Ehrensaft, in a perceptive article entitled "When Women and Men Mother" (1983), and Susan Rae Peterson, in "Against 'Parenting'" (1983), discuss the issues involved in trying to name the activity of caring for children and to name the people who perform these activities. Is it better to think of one behavior called "parenting," which both women and men do—a gender-free label? Or should we talk instead of women and men "mothering," since "fathering" simply doesn't carry the connotations of attentive and consistent care? Would it be preferable to continue to talk of "mothering" and "fathering" and to apply all our efforts so that those terms do not simply re-inscribe the old distinctions, according to which "to father" means to sire and "to mother" means to do everything for a child? I leave this linguistic puzzle for the reader to ponder.

Earlier I referred to the family of the urban contemporary West as patriarchal and father-absent, and I tried to describe the evidence for my claim with the data of social history. In this chapter, I have tried to show in more clinical terms what it means to call the family patriarchal and father-absent. Feminist activists want to change the patriarchal/father-absent family because of its injustice, its social unfairness. The feminist who is also a therapist, however, must investigate as well the ways in which patriarchy is *psychologically* noxious. I have tried to call attention to the fact that the patriarchal/father-absent family results in the personal privations and clinical crises already familiar to us, and that it reproduces itself within families in the way Chodorow and others have described.

Having attempted to make the case that psychoanalytic thinking is compatible with feminist thinking, and that feminist object-relations theory is relevant to family therapy concerns, I must outline the clinical idiom for a therapy based on these traditions. Of course, any psychoanalytically oriented therapy will privilege the investigation of patients' history and the interpretation of unconscious material, and will make use of the transference and countertransference relationships. In applying these psychoanalytic activities to work with families, we can rely on some of the works of the mainstream object-relations theorists, such as A. C. Robin Skynner and David and Jill Scharff. However, the differences between their work and the work proposed here are significant, since the former take no account of feminism, do not view therapy as inherently a political process, and sometimes make Victorian pronouncements about the family and gender issues.

The suggestion that we view therapy as an inherently political process and therefore take up a feminist revision of psychoanalytic thought is what I imagine will be most objectionable to mainstream object-relations therapists. The purists lament that all branches of psychoanalysis have been forced into interdisciplinary couplings with the conscious aim of enriching psychoanalysis, but with the unconscious aim of destroying its most important insights. American therapists have a particularly bad reputation when it comes to bowdlerizing Freud. According to some critics, Americans started off by embracing Freud with less apparent resistance than anyone else, and then promptly began revising Freud to make his theory more palatable and less pessimistic and his therapy more practical, less painful, and less radical. I believe that there is some validity to this criticism, but also a fair amount of Tartuffery, and both the validity and the Tartuffery are relevant to this discussion of how to transpose psychoanalytic ideas into a feminist version for the treatment of families.

It is true that American psychiatry dismantled much of what was essential to psychoanalysis. The clearest example is the decision by American analysts to permit only medical doctors to practice psychoanalysis, despite Freud's insistence in *The Question of Lay Analysis* that medical training is the *worst possible* training for an analyst. Second, as I mentioned earlier, the American analysts began to place enormous emphasis on helping people to *adapt* and to become what we would now call "good Yuppies," instead of emphasizing the life-searching, soul-making objectives of psychoanalysis as Freud had intended. But equally obvious is the Tartuffery—the piousness—of those who would criticize any and all emendations of psychoanalysis, including a feminist revision of it. Those who disdain the notion of letting *feminist assumptions* about the world influence the sacred concepts of psychoanalysis must ask themselves why they tolerate Freud's (and Klein's and Winnicott's) *patriarchal assumptions* about the world. It is not as though one could write without assumptions, perched somehow above all possible standpoints.

Freud warned explicitly about the temptation of therapists to force their own point of view on others, and thus "create men in our own image," but he violated this maxim perpetually and he was certainly not the stereotype of the value-neutral, abstaining analyst. From reading his case histories and his biographies, we consistently see Freud advancing a worldview, and we also see his capacity to be humanly present with patients—to be warm, comforting, wry, and provocative, not just a blank screen. Freud invited several patients to his home to talk, and his arguing with Dora is legendary. He went to a ball to see the recovered Elisabeth whirl by him in a waltz, and he lent money to the Wolfman. One of his patients, a man still living, said that Freud would sometimes tell him at the end of the hour, "This was good work today."

What I am saying is simply that there is no such thing as "plain old unadulterated psychoanalysis." There are only the various shades of patriarchal and feminist psychoanalysis. One must know the shades in order to make an authentic choice for oneself, and yet so many contemporary analysts have not read a page of feminist theory. It is noteworthy, in this regard, that Freud once said to the patient just quoted, "You shouldn't resist psychoanalysis so much. You should try to learn it."

I would say the same thing to my psychoanalytic colleagues about feminist theory.

DEFINING SOME TERMS FOR A FEMINIST OBJECT-RELATIONS PSYCHOTHERAPY WITH FAMILIES

The defining characteristic of a feminist object-relations psychotherapy is that it is not based on traditional dualisms between the realms of the rational and the emotional, between the principles of action and reflection, between knowledge and purpose. In treating families, I hope to avoid the excesses of both the strategic therapists who disparage insight, and the abstaining psychoanalytic therapists who disparage planful change. The clinical method I propose is one in which the therapist is both directive and reflective.

The Holding Environment Of foremost importance in a feminist object-relations therapy is the provision of what D. W. Winnicott called the holding environment or the facilitating environment. These terms refer to the atmosphere of safety and trust that the parent provides for the child and, analogously, the therapist provides for the patient (Winnicott 1965). Minimally, this means providing the family with a room where they meet regularly with the therapist, a room that is protected from outside interruptions as much as possible and that is equipped to be comfortable. Maintenance of confidentiality is an abstract extension of this physical holding. More profoundly important, of course, is the emotional holding that the therapist provides by listening attentively to each member of the family, by being empathic, respectful, and expert. In fact, every kind of therapy has some version of the concept of the holding environment.

If a patient or a patient family does not feel sufficiently held or contained by the therapeutic environment, they will not be free to make changes. Psychoanalytic theory, and specifically object-relations theory, simply makes this concept more central than other therapies do, pointing out its important ontogenetic roots in the dependency of the human infant. Most newborn animals can, on the day of birth, do most of the things the adult can do. The human newborn, in contrast, is utterly at the mercy of the adults in charge. Thus, human beings are simply destined to tolerate much more displeasure and anxiety than other species. Melanie Klein believed that babies "split off" some of their internal feelings of discomfort and "badness" and project them onto the environment in order to preserve their own sense of goodness. For the human infant in the contemporary West, the mother usually *is* the environment for a period of time. Thus, the infant splits off feelings of displeasure, projecting them onto the mother (or onto the breast, if the child is too young to have a concept of mother). The mother's (in some cases, the father's) response is to contain the baby's fear by her (or his) physical act of holding and soothing, and by the message that is thereby sent that the baby's needs are not destructive or unbearable. This can be an extremely difficult task for the parent. The baby inevitably will make the parent feel angry, overwhelmed, and inadequate at times, and yet the task is still to contain the feelings and comfort the infant.

The family therapist working with object-relations assumptions must do the same as the attentive parent. The family projects all sorts of feelings, needs, and fantasies onto the therapist. The therapist, as a result, feels drained, idealized, persecuted, and confused at times. However, she or he must learn to *empathically nurture* the family, to hold on to the split-off feelings without becoming defensive, without attacking back. In the case of the developing infant, the provision of holding and empathic mirroring leads to what Winnicott called the growth of the "true self," the self that is capable of experiencing its own feelings. The loved child has the chance to become an adult able to identify his or her own physical and emotional needs as distinct from the feelings and needs of others.

If, however, the baby is not loved, the true self will not develop. If, for example, the parent in daily contact with the child is depressed, the child may learn to accommodate more to the parent's mood than the reverse. The child, in a sense, becomes the caretaker of the parent, and will not be prepared to distinguish its own desires from those of the other. In Winnicott's terms, the true self goes into hiding, and a false self—a "caretaker self"—emerges. The false self may be able to function adequately in the world, but is nonetheless characterized by grave problems in relating to others. For example, people with eating disorders often do not know when they are hungry or full; they rely on external cues for how to satisfy themselves, and, typically, their desires for love and sex are equally "false." Many such patients were caretakers of their parents, and they are at a loss as to how to define their own needs and wants. The good therapist (or the good enough therapist, to paraphrase Winnicott) contacts the caretaking self respectfully, and through the holding and containing experience, makes it safe for the true self to develop.

Object-relations therapists, like most therapists, tend to formulate their theories independent of the perspective of social history. To keep the discussion of true and false self from total rarefaction, it is thus important to add that the relationships that children have with their parents vary according to culture, class, and time. I discussed in chapter 10 the fact that in late capitalism, erosion of community has led to a state of affairs in which the child replaces the village. The contemporary child is often the parent's confidant, measure of self-worth, and reason for being. A situation in which the child is expected to be the emotional caretaker of the parent because no one else fulfills that function cannot be divorced from the issue of the false self.

Moreover, the problem of the child as emotional caretaker obviously can apply to both genders, but it has special relevance to girls, since girls are more often defined by their nurturing activities. This issue of true and false self for women is a major feature of Luise Eichenbaum and Susie Orbach's book *Understanding Women: A Feminist Psychoanalytic View* (1983). The authors specify that in childhood, the needy little girl is made to go into hiding because of the social value placed on women's being the givers and not the receivers of nurturance. The treatment for many women has to do with making it possible for the true, needing self to come out of storage and receive sustenance, first from the therapy and soon from the world.

Critics have reacted to Winnicott's concept of the holding environment because he uses the metaphor of *mothering* to describe the concept of therapeutic *holding*. This would be a problematic metaphor only if Winnicott believed that for some biological or moral reasons *only* women could do the mothering, or if one thought that mothering was the only thing, or the most important or satisfying thing, a woman could do. Winnicott did not state any of these ideas, nor do any of his feminist readers. When one thinks of other metaphors used for therapeutic activity, moreover—e.g., fixing, maneuvering, restructuring, paradoxing, and the many other military, cybernetic, and business metaphors in use—then the terms *holding* and *mothering* seem like a commendable improvement. In fact, it is striking that so *little* interest is given in other theories of therapy to activities that have to do with empathy and care. Many conventional family therapists even disparage such notions ("That's touchy-feely social work stuff"). Most feminists would agree, in contrast, that problems of healing are problems of understanding, and that, in essence, the cure *is* "through love" (cf. Gilligan 1987).

Transference and Countertransference Contemporary object-relations therapists place great emphasis on the quality of the patient-therapist relationship in their discussions of transference and countertransference. The countertransference, they believe, is not simply unanalyzed material that should be gotten out of the way, but is an inevitable part of being a person in therapeutic contact with another person. The feelings one has as a therapist for a patient can be used as information about what might be going on in the family. If the therapist consistently feels intimidated by or angry with a family, this affect becomes information for a hypothesis about the family's process. After sifting through countertransferential thoughts and feelings, the therapist formulates interpretations that will be helpful to the family. Object-relations therapists do not jealously guard insights about the family's process, nor do they hope to toss interpretations around like firecrackers in order to "shake up the system." The point is to offer interpretations in ways that enable people to claim them and to make sense of their life together. One interprets with care, and shows care through adroit interpretation. If all goes well, the family will leave therapy with the ability to provide a better containing environment for each other, and to take a more reflective, self-observing position toward themselves.

On this matter of holding and of forming interpretations, Scharff and Scharff (1987) have introduced a very helpful construct called "negative capability." The term derives from the poet Keats's description of Shakespeare's own negative capability, by which Keats meant the capacity for "being in uncertainties, mysteries, doubts, without any irritable reaching after fact and reason" (Keats 1817/1974, p. 704, and quoted in Scharff and Scharff 1987, p. 210). "Negative capability" is helpful in emphasizing that the therapist must have not only the "positive" capacity of understanding and interpreting but also the opposite capacity, that of sitting without knowing, without understanding, and without forcing oneself to know before one knows. This concept of negative capability has provided me with a way of naming a part of my everyday life as a therapist that had not been named, and that thus caused more anxiety then than now. One might say that a good enough *theory* is needed for therapists to feel contained and safe. Without it, the therapist will feel anxious and unable to relate authentically and generously to patients.

Projective Systems   Projective systems, as articulated by A. K. Robin Skynner, are our beliefs about the world, and particularly about intimate relationships that are formed in early life, which tend to remain unconscious but which nevertheless powerfully predict and direct our intimate lives as adults. In Skynner's words, a patient may assume, on the basis of her or his projective systems, constructed in childhood, that "mother, and so the world, will always gratify (or will never gratify) and that father (and so the world) will always punish (or will always be outwitted and defeated)" (Skynner 1981, p. 52). When therapists feel themselves being put in the role of all-gratifying mother, for example, they can understand this fact as part of the projective system of the patient, and interpretations about these systems can be very compelling to patients. (See chapters 14 and 15 for examples.)

The therapist forms hypotheses and makes interpretations based not only on family members' projections onto the therapist but also on their projections onto each other. The process through which one family member is "chosen" to contain the projections of another member is called *projective identification.* Melanie Klein first used this term to refer to a process occurring in the mother-infant twosome, but it is now used by object-relations therapists to refer to many varieties of relationships (cf. Box et al. 1981). Through projective identification, one family member can become the carrier of the family's anger, anxiety, or sexual desire. Conversely, the problems of one individual member can become writ large on the entire family, which "agrees" unconsciously to contain it. The therapist's dealing with these issues begins the process of the family's reclaiming the split-off or projected feelings. Instead of storing all their anger in an acting-out teenager, for example, the parents begin to "own" their own anger and thus undo the projective identification. The teenager is thereby freed of the obligation to contain the family's affect.

Many traditional family therapists of the object-relations school have worked deftly with these concepts, but again the feminist perspective adds understanding that is absent from their accounts. If a teenage son is acting out mother's rage against father, for example, it is important not only to realize that the son is containing her anger but also to remember and to respond therapeutically to the fact that women have historically paid a high price for the direct expression of anger—from being labeled "hysterical" to being killed as witches. In working with the family, feminist therapists may or may not want to mention the social taboo on women's anger, but they would definitely have it in mind in helping the mother to claim her fury.

Object-relations family therapists also need to know a great deal about the families of origin on both sides, because very often the projective identifications involve people in earlier generations. For example, it is not unusual in cases of anorexia nervosa for a high-achieving, perfectionistic daughter actually to contain the father's longing for his mother whom he idolized.

Transgenerational Repetition   The notion of *transgenerational repetition* of problems is extremely important to object-relations family therapy. It derives in part from Freud's notion of the "repetition compulsion" in *Beyond the Pleasure Principle* (1920/1959). Contemporary psychoanalytic thinkers, most notably Alice Miller, have expanded Freud's notion to describe the ways in which we unconsciously reproduce in adulthood relationships we had with our parents—and those our parents had with each other (Miller 1983a, 1983b, 1984).

The therapist who works with couples will find this set of ideas very useful in understanding the ways that each partner reenacts the rules, transgressions, and conflicts about intimate behavior found in the preceding generation. The therapist works to show how each partner came to choose the other—often for the precise purpose of recreating the parents' marriage. We tend to repeat the emotional lives of our forebears for two main reasons. The first is that what we experience is simply what we know best and what we assume to be universal. A man with a depressed mother unconsciously learns to associate femininity with depression. Similarly, women who are abused by men in childhood often grow up thinking that they deserve abuse. Such people are not doomed to reproduce the past forever, but without help of some type, they have an excellent chance of doing so.

The second reason that we repeat is the effort to master experiences of childhood. The man with the depressed mother may have been engaged as her comforter as a child, but of course could not cure her depression. He may, however, believe that he can cure his fiancée of hers. The woman with the abusive father may feel about her abusive boyfriend, "If only I can get this dangerous man to love me!" thereby mastering the situation in childhood when she could not protect herself from father. One woman in therapy who had had alcoholic parents and chose partners who drank explained to me, "There is this lasting hope to be kissed by someone with alcohol on their breath."

Object-relations therapists, like all psychoanalytic therapists, believe that the more unaware people are of what the past held, the more likely they are to repeat it—that is, only if unconscious conflicts are made conscious can they be transformed. Another way of depicting this tendency to repeat the past is Gregory Bateson's favorite passage from the book of *Ezekiel:* "The fathers have eaten bitter fruit, and the children's teeth are set on edge." Bateson pointed out that it is not so bad for the parents; they know what they ate. But the children who invariably suffer the effects of the bitter food do *not* know, and they will continue to take in what is sickening, believing that there is nothing else.

The feminist object-relations therapist does more than merely make interpretations about material that is being repeated or played out. She or he also works directively to make change more plausible in the real relationships of the present. At least some adults, if they choose and struggle, can move beyond repetition of the past, and treat their loved partners as more than stand-ins for mother and father. Feminist therapists need their cognitive capacities and a genius for care to heal wounds left by unsympathetic parents, and to validate needs that family and culture have disallowed.

It is important to emphasize that despite the common ground between traditional object-relations theory and feminist principles, the differences between them are large. Scharff and Scharff, who have written the most comprehensive book on the subject, *Object Relations Family Therapy,* take a very nondirective posture with families, sticking mainly to interpretation. In 1987 I observed a case presentation they did on a family with a school-phobic child. For eleven months, the therapist empathically interpreted the family's process, never making any sort of plan to help the child go to school. The child did not go to school, and the family moved across the country very abruptly, leaving treatment. This therapy is a clear counterexample of proper treatment from the feminist perspective. Our work is to interpret *and* to help plan, not simply to interpret.

192

Since I am usually in the position of defending insight to family therapists who hold it in contempt, it is odd to be in the opposite (but equally
important) role of describing the fatal error of an approach that devalues
planful change. Thomas Mann best expressed this problem of overanalyz-
ing in *The Magic Mountain:*

> Analysis as an instrument of enlightenment and civilization is good, insofar as
> it shatters absurd convictions, acts as a solvent upon natural prejudices, and
> undermines authority; good, in other words, in that it sets free, refines, human-
> izes, makes slaves ripe for freedom. But it is bad, very bad, insofar as it stands
> in the way of action, cannot shape the vital forces, maims life at its roots.
> [P. 222]

The feminist therapist with an object-relations orientation does not stop
at analyzing the family, but leads the patient to action, making suggestions, stirring up debate, and sometimes giving advice. The feminist therapist is definitely concerned with helping the family achieve symptom-
relief, not in just any possible way, but in ways that allow the family to
be less patriarchal, less father-absent, and more connected to the community than before. Needless to say, these changes are more plausible with
some families than others, and therapists must, of course, acquire sensitivity for the kinds and degrees of transformation that can be hoped for. Such
limits are part of any therapeutic orientation, no more or less relevant to
feminist than to conventional therapy.

The difference I have pointed out between the Scharffs' work and my
own leads, perhaps, to the question of the *limits* of nurturance, care, and
advice that can properly come from the therapist. The question of "how
far to go" is an old one, dating back at least to the break between Freud
and Ferenczi, when the latter proposed hugging patients as part of treatment. There are family therapists who believe in showing physical affection to patients. Virginia Satir, for example, has been known to hold hands
with a patient or rock someone in her lap. Other therapists attend the
weddings and graduations of patients and buy them gifts. There are therapists whose emphasis on *reparenting,* i.e., compensating for the deprivations
of withholding parents, leads them to take patients out to lunch or shopping for clothes.

I do not normally touch patients except to shake hands, which I often
do before each session. At the end of a *termination* session, some families
will reach out for a hug to say good-bye, and I always respond. I do not
attend patients' weddings and personal parties, nor buy them gifts. The
curative love both psychoanalysts and feminist therapists have written

about can and must be communicated largely through words. It seems to me that a therapist who thinks that she or he must buy a gift for a patient in order to compensate for a withholding parent is expressing doubt in her or his own ability to give as a therapist gives. The heuristic phrase that I would use to help students think about this issue of limits is the one used by Anna O. to Breuer in the 1890s: the "talking cure." You do not hold hands with patients or take them shopping, because psychotherapy is a talking cure.

I have criticized the work of the Scharffs at several points, but their book is very valuable and summarizes many of the ideas of Klein, Bion, Dicks, Skynner, Box, and others who have influenced the thinking of many feminist therapists, including myself. Unfortunately, the Scharffs ignore the work of object-relations theorists whose political point of view differs from theirs. The most notable omission in this regard is their failure to cite the work of Nancy Chodorow, although her discussion of gender is more sophisticated than theirs and her book preceded theirs by nine years. Nonetheless, their theory is not so blatantly patriarchal as one might expect of authors who do not cite a single feminist work. Unlike some other family therapists, they explicitly assume the existence of women who work outside the home, and they mention day-care centers without calling them "second best" to the stay-at-home mother. They also acknowledge that "in modern marriages" some fathers have become primary caretakers of children, and they cite a good deal of research on the father-infant relationship. Indeed, this is the direction in which object-relations theory needs to develop—going beyond the mother-child unit. When Winnicott said "there is no such thing as an infant," he meant that a baby has to be in a sustaining relationship or he or she simply cannot exist. He therefore proposed that we talk of "nursing couples" instead of "infants." Family systems thinkers, in effect, pointed out that the "nursing couple" itself has a context that is *sine qua non;* mothers do not nurse infants in a social vacuum. The relevant others, therefore, had to be considered both in theories of development and in treatment. Fathers, and also siblings and extended family, were added to the picture.

Feminist theorists have looked beyond both object-relations theorists and systems theorists in their definition of *context,* making it include class, race, and the culture of patriarchy. Literally *nothing* that a mother does is comprehensible outside the sometimes supportive, sometimes predatory, always impinging context of her other intimate relationships and of her place in the social system.

Care and Interpretation

A feminist object-relations family therapy, then, begins with the provision of a *holding* or *caring environment* for the family so that family members feel safe enough to make themselves known to the therapist. The therapist uses the elements of their history, as well as data from the *transference and counter-transference relationships,* to decipher the presenting symptoms and other *projective systems* in the family with certain clear aims in mind. The aims are to help relieve the symptom in ways that leave the family members better able to understand one another, and to provide a holding environment for one another. The therapist opens up choices to the family that allow them to be *less patriarchal, less father-absent,* and *less isolated from their context* than before. Remembering their early experiences and the emotional lives of their own families leads to a change in the present, to a re-membering.

This is only a bare outline of a therapy, of course. To proceed further, it is necessary to show these ideas in practice. The final chapters of this book illustrate the beginnings of a feminist psychoanalytic therapy with families.

PART IV

Care and Interpretation: Toward a Feminist Practice of Psychotherapy with Families

Psychoanalysis is in essence a cure through love.
—FREUD,
in a letter to Jung

In the first legend of the Grail, it is said that the Grail . . . belongs to the first comer who asks the guardian of the vessel, a king three-quarters paralyzed by the most painful wound, "What are you going through?"
—SIMONE WEIL
Waiting for God, 1951

T HE CASES presented in the following three chapters should not be viewed as examples of fully formed feminist family therapy, but rather as steps toward it. The treatment described in the first case is particularly inchoate, since it involves a family I saw while still a trainee, trying to learn traditional family therapy techniques. I include this case because it illustrates particularly well some content areas that the feminist literature has illuminated far better than the mainstream family therapy literature has. Although treatment was rendered by a beginner, the clinical dilemmas raised nonetheless illustrate some limitations of traditional theory and practice.

I also wish to point out before proceeding that the style of presentation in the following three cases is different from what the reader may be accustomed to. In the majority of family therapy books, authors offer thirty or forty pages of verbatim transcript of cases, usually with an editorial commentary running alongside it. The purpose of verbatim transcription, I assume, is to show the case in its most "objective" form in order to give the reader a most accurate understanding of what happened during the session. I find such presentation not only tedious but unhelpful to an understanding of the case. The problem with the verbatim approach is that all of the metacommunication—the gestures, tones, glances that family therapists insist are the *essence* of communication—is removed, leaving only the *content*, which can dangerously mislead.

Authors sometimes add descriptive comments to the speakers' statements, such as "pulling his chair close to hers" or "starting to cry," but one nonetheless loses anything like a living, chromatic sense of how the family members were in the moment. I have chosen a different style of presentation from the usual "cinéma vérité" variety. I have tried to describe family members and our process together with the narrative detail that will make them comprehensible as persons, introducing dialogue where appropriate.

This manner of presentation, of course, creates a new problem—that of imposing a single organization on material that could be arranged differently, in *Rashomon* fashion, by each person who had been present. Having to choose between the two types of errors—being either too objective or too interpretive, too absent or too present as a reporter of the process—I have chosen the latter set of problems. I believe that although the bias of my own conceptual framework distorts the report, such bias always exists, even in deciding *which* portions of verbatim transcript should be excerpted for a book and which should be left out. My bias is at least more public, and it is the awareness of bias that is paramount, since it can never be eliminated. A theoretical style that implies false notions of "objectivity" does a far greater disservice to the reader by advancing the "myth of mythlessness." I have chosen this style also for aesthetic reasons, following in the tradition of psychoanalytic authors from Freud to Kovel, who obviously believe in reconstructing patients' stories, and not simply recording their words like a court stenographer. Keeping the narrating "I" prominent in the text is also something valued within the feminist literary tradition (cf. Woolf 1929, Daly 1978).

The material presented in the next three chapters is based on families whom I actually treated. Identifying details were changed in the interest of guarding confidentiality.

Each of the three cases to be described was initially an inpatient case. Some family therapists question the validity of hospitalizing one family member, since such isolation of the patient is "anti-systemic." I find hospitalization an acceptable form of treatment, particularly when the family presents a life-threatening symptom such as attempted suicide or severe psychosomatic illness. Such short-term hospitalization can avert disasters such as death or long-term institutionalization. The systemic use of the hospital has been cogently explained by Combrinck-Graham et al. (1982) and Brendler (1987).

13

The DeWitts: The Case of a Therapist in Transition

JILL DeWITT was a high-achieving, well-liked fifteen-year-old, referred to our inpatient program by her pediatrician for anorexia nervosa. Jill was five feet five inches tall and had dropped from 135 to 85 pounds in one year. She had not menstruated in six months, and her abnormal serum electrolytes and vital signs put her in medical danger. Our intake office had gathered the following information from the referring physician. Jill was an only child living with her mother, who was a medical technician. The parents had divorced when Jill was eleven, and Jill had visited her father on weekends until recent years when she began insisting on more time with her friends. Mr. DeWitt held an executive position in a computer company and lived fifty miles away from mother and daughter. Jill had started a diet when she was fourteen, intending to lose twenty pounds. She told the doctor that when she reached her goal, her father teased her about still having "stocky thighs." According to Jill, she decided at that moment to lose more weight, and in fact dropped an additional thirty pounds.

Mrs. DeWitt reportedly battled regularly with Jill about her daily intake, which was becoming smaller and more fastidious. Mrs. DeWitt had taken Jill to three outpatient therapists in their hometown, but was dissatisfied with all of them. One therapist wanted to see Jill individually three times per week; another recommended antidepressant medication. The third therapist set up a kind of behavior modification program with a reward system for each pound gained. Jill said that this therapist was "weird," and refused to return to her after the third session. She was continuing to lose weight, however, and in desperation, Mrs. DeWitt called her ex-husband and asked for his help. The parents met together with the pediatrician, who recommended that they apply for short-term hospitalization at our facility. The parents agreed to apply for admission, although they lived 2½ hours away by car. The pediatrician suggested that if they were admitted to our program, we might help them locate a suitable outpatient therapist located nearer to them.

The Evaluation Session

In the evaluation session, Jill sat quietly between her parents with the hood of her jacket pulled over her eyes. Her parents seemed to be kind and caring people, weary with concern. I explained that the purpose of the meeting was to evaluate the family's need for our short-term hospital program, and I posed an open-ended question about what was happening in their family. Mrs. DeWitt, a slight woman who resembled her daughter, answered softly, "Well, Jill, as you know, is anorectic, and Dr. White suggested that this was the best program for her." Mrs. DeWitt continued for a few minutes, stating that Jill had started out "chubby" and had "done a good job" of losing weight, but had gone off the deep end since August. Jill was now afraid that anything but lettuce and diet soda would make her fat. Only since she had been barred from all school sports had she agreed to eat one meal per day. However, she insisted on eating it in a health-food restaurant that listed the caloric value of each item. Her mother found herself making the thirty-minute drive to this restaurant whenever Jill would agree to eat. Mrs. DeWitt had also caught Jill vomiting after one of these meals, and although Jill claimed it had not been self-induced, her mother was worried that she might become bulimic.

I stopped Mrs. DeWitt at this point and at several other points to engage Jill, but she would not respond. When I commented to Mrs. DeWitt that she had been putting herself out quite a lot for Jill lately, she said, "I wondered if I should be giving her so much attention for this, but the pediatrician said, 'Well, maybe she needs some extra attention from you now.' "

Mr. DeWitt, a slightly overweight man with a kind face and a thick Texas accent, waited for his wife to finish before he spoke. When I asked for his view, he said, "I've never been so confused in all my life, ma'am. The doctor says to give Jill more attention. I'm no expert in anorexia, but this driving around to low-calorie restaurants sounds crazy to me." Mr. DeWitt said sincerely that he believed his ex-wife was a good mother, but that Jill had a tendency to be headstrong and spoiled and could get Mom to march to her tune. I asked about the amount of contact he had had with Jill over the years. He said their visits had been regular until she became a teenager. He said he resented not seeing her for months at a time, but felt he could do nothing about that. Mrs. DeWitt interjected, "You can't force a teenager to visit a parent."

It was clear that the parents viewed Jill's anorexia in different ways, and when I asked them to talk with each other about what needed to happen, Mrs. DeWitt stated, "I do want your input, Jim, but the bottom line is you don't know much about nutrition." Mr. DeWitt answered, "Is the point here to become an expert in carbohydrates, or to get Jill to eat?"

My team members, who were seated behind the one-way mirror, rang me with the advice to punctuate the father's comment—to congratulate him, in fact.* The point was indeed to get Jill to eat; she was starving herself. The team suggested I raise the intensity by stating further that the mother was letting her daughter starve by allowing her to call the shots. I hung up the phone and delivered these ideas, slightly paraphrased, to the family. As I did this act of unbalancing, of joining the father against the mother-daughter alliance, something seemed to happen. Mr. DeWitt moved his chair closer to the circle, and Mrs. DeWitt told Jill angrily to take her jacket off. Jill, looking surprised, removed the hood. I asked Jill if it were true that her mother spoiled her.

JILL: In some ways.
DL: Such as?
JILL: Well, people say that "only" children get anything they want because they don't have to share with anybody.

Jill allowed herself to be engaged in a sort of philosophical discussion about the pros and cons of being an only child. She brightened when I complimented her on her intelligence and verbal skill. In the course of the discussion, she also revealed that she knew she was too thin, something that is prognostically good for anorectic patients.

DL: Ask your mother why she spoils you—gives in to your childishness.
JILL: Mom, you know you do.

*For the reader unfamiliar with this procedure, most schools of family therapy place a team behind the mirror, especially for training students. The team can ring the therapist on a phone inside the room and either offer a suggestion or ask the therapist to come behind the mirror and talk.

MRS. DEWITT: This child does more housework than I do! She is extremely independent and grown up!

DL: I believe you. I believe that she is either like thirty-five or like five. You have to start treating her like she's fifteen, or she'll never grow up.

By the end of the session, my team and I had reached the conclusion that the family could definitely benefit from our program, but it was up to them to decide. It would mean a big commitment of time and energy on their part. Both parents said they were in favor of participating, but Mrs. DeWitt said that Jill had reservations because of the amount of school she would miss. She said Jill also wondered whether she could have visitors, home passes, and so on. Mr. DeWitt commented that Jill should ask those questions herself. I asked Mrs. DeWitt's permission to call in one of the day counselors to explain all the details of the program to Jill. She agreed, and the counselor emerged from behind the mirror and joined comfortably with Jill.

While they talked, I continued my conversation with the parents about their own concerns, thus creating within the room a separation between the generations and their respective interests. This segment ended with the counselor shaking hands with Jill and saying, "Jill has just said she would like to give the program a try." There was a brief pause and Mrs. DeWitt turned to me and asked, "Isn't it dangerous to gain weight too fast?" The buzzer sounded and my team said, "Tell Mom it might be dangerous or scary for *her* if Jill acted fifteen, but that it is not dangerous for Jill. Ask Mom what she herself needs not to be so afraid."

I put these points to Mrs. DeWitt, who cried and said, "I need some support." I pointed to Mr. DeWitt.

DL: You can no longer support each other as husband and wife, but you must support each other as parents of Jill. You can't do this alone, Mrs. DeWitt. [*to Mr. DeWitt:*] Why doesn't Mrs. DeWitt believe you will help her? Is there some reason?

MR. DEWITT [*after a brief pause*]: "No, she's just a little mule-headed like Jill. Marilyn, Jill is not the only problem-child in this room. I can benefit from this therapy and so can you.

Mrs. DeWitt nodded but continued to cry. Throughout the interview I struggled with misgivings about the things that had been said to Mrs. DeWitt. She had come to us already beleaguered, already drained, and had been zapped by me, by her ex-spouse, by her fifteen-year-old daughter, and by an entire faceless team of experts from behind the mirror. Nonetheless, my misgivings were submerged beneath alternating layers of concern and relief. The interventions my team had recommended were clearly working: the family was moving from the position, "Jill is an anorectic," to the position, "We all need to change."

A therapeutic contract was made explicit, written down, and signed by each member of the family. It listed items such as mother being firmer with Jill, mother accepting father's ideas and support, father being supportive to mother, Jill eating enough to reach a discharge weight to be set by the parents, and Jill working on speaking up and acting fifteen. The family agreed to attend a minimum of three sessions per week for four weeks. We would help them locate a family therapist in their hometown who would see them after discharge.

DISCUSSION OF THE EVALUATION SESSION

I met with my team and supervisor later that day. The consensus in the group was that the DeWitts were nice people with a classic case of an overinvolved mother and an underinvolved father. One colleague said that "Mom" probably didn't want Jill to grow up because then she would be left all alone. My supervisor agreed that it would be important to find out whether Mrs. DeWitt had been dating. Another colleague followed up this thought, saying that Mrs. DeWitt had probably subtly cued Jill not to visit her father, knowing that he would have lain down the law about her eating, and then Mom would have lost her buddy. Another hypothesis was that both parents were feeling lonely and were using the anorexia as a way of making contact with each other again and perhaps reconciling. It would be important to track this possibility carefully and to define Marilyn and Jim as parents of Jill who were collaborating in a crisis, and not as spouses.

Whatever the function of the anorexia in the family, my colleagues clearly viewed the task of change in terms of instituting clearer hierarchy. Authority was the overarching theme in the discussion of this case, as in many anorectic cases. Many of the questions I had about the patient's body image, sexuality, and dependency needs were considered "mere content." Anorexia, in the judgment of many of my colleagues, was essentially another way of saying "dysfunction." Its particular character, its history, its potential for signifying the meaning of femininity or female power in the family were not considered relevant to treatment *or even to our own clinical discourse.* When pressed, my colleagues did not argue that Jill had no problems with autonomy, sexuality, dependency, and so on. However, they assumed that if the parents became better "executives" and did not stand in Jill's way, then other developmental issues would simply fall into place.

CONTACT WITH THE REFERRING DOCTOR

When I phoned the pediatrician to inform him that Jill had been admitted, he said he wanted to read me something from an old chart from a previous family doctor. It said that when Jill was between the ages of eight and nine, Mr. DeWitt had engaged her in mutual genital fondling to the point of orgasm, approximately once a week. The note said further that the parents had split up when Jill was eleven, and that only after Mr. DeWitt was out of the house had she told her mother what had happened. According to the doctor's notes, Mrs. DeWitt confronted her ex-husband immediately, and Mr. DeWitt admitted to it right away. Mrs. DeWitt then phoned their family doctor, who advised that Mr. DeWitt speak to Jill about it and tell her it was not her fault and that she had done the right thing by telling her mother. The family had never mentioned this to Dr. White, the current pediatrician. He had come across the information while searching for some medical data about Jill.

After this phone call, I went directly to my supervisor, who was extremely supportive and helpful. He recommended that we do the next session as previously planned, focusing on the food protocol, since Jill was in fact in physical jeopardy. We would introduce the issue of sexual abuse in a later session. He assumed, as I did, that it was impossible for this history of father-daughter incest to be irrelevant to the family's current crisis. We assumed that Jill's developing sexuality had reawakened anxiety on the part of each of them, which had to be dealt with in some way or any weight gained in the program would simply be lost again after discharge.

I asked my supervisor to recommend the best videotapes on working with incestuous families. I had watched dozens of examples of therapists working with anorectic girls of every age of onset, degree of severity, and ethnic background, and these had been tremendously helpful. My supervisor told me he knew of not a single videotape on incestuous families—nor even of a book about incest and family therapy.

What surprised me even more was that not all the therapists who learned of the case in our ongoing seminar agreed with us on the course of treatment. One senior therapist seriously questioned the relevance of including the issue of incest in the therapy at all. After all, he argued, the family had come in asking for help with anorexia. They had not asked us for help with their feelings about "past familial traumas." He said sympathetically that I had perhaps fallen into a trap common for neophytes—that of being distracted by the "hot issues" from the past and failing to deal with the dysfunction in the present. A more junior colleague added that dealing with incest ran the danger of making father into the villain and thus doing a "linear" kind of treatment. If I dealt with the incest, he said, I should be sure to make the mother "co-responsible."

These arguments, although well intended, were not at all persuasive. It was true that the family had not asked for help with the problem of incest, but they had also not asked for help in getting their daughter to speak up or in improving their "executive functioning." Nonetheless, we had seen fit to convince them that these things were causally related to Jill's problem. Second, it was hard to see incest as a "distraction." How could a parent who had mistreated his eight-year-old daughter's body lecture her at fifteen for mistreating her body? A girl abused at such a young age by someone she loves might well resist looking sexual at fifteen, might sacrifice her health before having to deal with the issue of sexuality again.

The third objection, that dealing with incest would be unfair to the father, was of no account. Framing the mother as the co-abuser of the daughter in order to retain systemic purity struck me, even as a new therapist, as clinical nonsense. Dealing frankly with this issue, of course, would not mean being unsympathetic or disrespectful to the father; that would not be good psychotherapy. The point was simply not to extend the mother-blaming bias of the outside world to the world of the therapy.*

The Second Family Session

The second session was a lunch session in which all of us ate together, and the parents were asked to take charge of how much and how fast Jill ate. Jill had eaten nothing on her first day in the hospital, saying that the food did not appeal to her. Her mother had brought in some lunch for all of us, but Jill continued to complain about certain aspects of it. With a great deal of support and challenging from me, the parents were able to work together to get Jill to eat most of her lunch. This was framed as a success, and at the end of the session they were asked to choose a discharge weight within a safety range suggested by their pediatrician. They were then asked to set a target weight which Jill would have to reach after discharge. Finally, they were told the details of our typical weight-gain program: the

---

*Readers who are shocked that a family therapist would place such high value on protecting the incestuous father are referred to the case of Boscolo et al. (1987), discussed in chapter 9 of this book.

patient is required to gain a certain amount of weight per day, e.g., half a pound. If she succeeds, she participates fully in the activities of the inpatient classroom. She can do schoolwork, crafts, or sports or socialize. If she fails to gain weight, she remains in bed all day without company or the privilege of reading and writing. She is allowed nothing but bedrest in order to conserve calories. She may request as much food as she wants, and a bedpan is provided and emptied as needed. Dr. White had already described the program to the family, and I was simply filling in the details.*

On the day of the lunch session, both parents had decided to spend the entire day on the unit getting to know the staff and becoming versed in the program. I arranged to see them alone in the evening to bring up the subject of sexual abuse. I sat with the two of them and told them exactly what Dr. White had relayed to me over the phone. There was a very long silence. The most important question, of course, was whether or not the abuse was ongoing, and thus whether it was safe for Jill to be visiting her father at all. Mr. DeWitt responded immediately that it was not ongoing, and that it had occurred "no more than six times" over the course of a year during which he had been doing a lot of drinking. He said that it started when Mrs. DeWitt began a typing course that met once a week, in preparation for returning to work. On those nights, he was left to put Jill to bed.

I asked Mrs. DeWitt if she were afraid to leave Jill alone with her father. She said "only in the very beginning. But by the time I found out about it, he had already stopped drinking for two years, and he really did seem different. Our family doctor had spoken with him and told me he thought it was okay. I didn't want to say, 'Okay, now, you can never see your father again.' "

The discussion continued in a fairly intellectual way until I asked which one of them had more nightmares about it. Mrs. DeWitt broke down and said that it was probably she, because she felt so guilty about it. She said she had read all the magazine articles stating that where "it" [incest] happens, you nearly always find a working mother, or a mother who is ill, sexually frigid, or neglectful of her children. She concluded that since she had been "none of the first three," then she must obviously have neglected Jill. She felt horribly guilty that Jill had not felt able to tell her about it until after the divorce, and worried that it was still hard for Jill to confide in her.

*This protocol so resembles the nineteenth-century "rest cures" for hysteria—another female "illness" related to sexuality and power—that many feminist therapists will consider it anathema. When a symptom is life-threatening, a therapist sometimes sees no alternative, and this plan is less objectionable than force-feeding or intravenous feeding which are also used to cure anorexia. See Barbara Ehrenreich and Deirdre English's *For Her Own Good* for descriptions of the rest cure first used by Dr. S. Weir Mitchell in Philadelphia in the nineteenth century.

She stated that she had wondered whether the anorexia were somehow related to the sexual abuse, but did not know how to broach the subject with Jill. Mr. DeWitt told his ex-wife that it was not her fault. I asked if they would be willing to discuss the abuse in a session with Jill. Again, there was a long pause before they agreed. Mr. DeWitt, to my surprise, said, "one of my reasons for wanting Jill admitted was so that we could finally clear the air."

An Individual Session with Jill

Since a child's experience of sexual contact with a parent is nearly always one of being violated or overwhelmed, it seemed important not to repeat this experience by forcing Jill to talk with her parents about the incest without any preparation and without her consent. I thus decided to raise the issue with Jill alone first. (Again, other therapist colleagues thought this a questionable intervention, since the *family* and not the therapist must be the center of change.)

When I first raised the abuse issue with Jill, she was terribly angry and said it was none of my business. She cried for a while and then talked for a long time. Her first concern was her father: she devoted several minutes to telling me that he was not a bad person. She said she had even wondered about the wisdom of telling her mother, because "it got her all upset" and, in addition, "it probably helped cause the divorce."

I had already discussed the chronology of the events with the parents, and so I could inform Jill that she had remembered the events incorrectly; her parents had split up before she told her mother about it. I stated that there had to be other reasons that they split up, but she said she doubted it, because they never fought.

In response to my query, Jill stated that she was no longer afraid that her father might "do anything" [sexual] to her, but she said there were some things he did that made her stop visiting him. One was that he was a "perfectionist" and nagged her about getting good grades, never praising her for her good performance. His criticism bothered her a great deal and sometimes took the form of "gross humor," as she put it. She gave this example: "Like once my friend Angie was over swimming at my dad's and she said my chest was too big for my bikini, and my dad said, 'Naw, you could wipe those things out with Clearasil.'"

Jill said it was easier just to avoid her dad than to tell him her feelings. She said she would appreciate it if I would tell him these things for her. I suggested that her mother could give her support in talking these things out with Dad, and she seemed amenable. We scheduled a mother-daughter session.

Mother and Jill

There was a great deal of therapeutic work to be done between mother and daughter and very little time during the inpatient stay to do it. In the session with Jill and her mother, we talked about certain "misunderstandings" and, with Jill's permission, I related to Mrs. DeWitt her confusion about the reason for the divorce. Mrs. DeWitt assured Jill that she was completely wrong, and explained quite well what the reasons for the divorce had been. She stated that they had married young, that she had been a subservient wife, and that when she had talked of returning to work, Mr. DeWitt had been very upset. When she did find the courage to go back to work, she found that she herself changed a lot and could not get along with him at all.

There were a tremendous number of affective issues that could only be superficially touched on in this session. For example, I assumed that Jill's belief that her reporting of the incest had caused the divorce was in part a wish that her mother had become so angry and protective of her that she had divorced Mr. DeWitt in protest. Her mistake probably also reflected some guilt about having "taken mother's place" with father.

What was accomplished in this session was that Mrs. DeWitt told Jill that she was on her side and wanted to know about anything that hurt or bothered her about Dad or anyone else. Mother said she would definitely support Jill in the next family session. Jill said she was nervous about it, but thought everyone would feel better afterward.

The Third Family Session

The tension in the room at the start of the third family session was extraordinarily high. Jill had lost half a pound the previous day, and her parents were ready to jump into a discussion of calories. When I redirected our focus, Mr. DeWitt was the first to speak, saying that he was "nervous as hell" about the session and hadn't slept at all. Nonetheless, he said he was glad that we would discuss "the past" because he feared it had ruined the relationship between Jill and himself, making her avoid visiting.

> MR. DEWITT: Jill and I have not been close at all these past two years, and it hurts. You used to make me feel special, Jill, and you don't any more. Only two weeks ago, when the doctor said you might need a hospital, did you put your arms around me and say, "Daddy, I'm scared"?

Jill's eyes were glued to the floor.

> MR. DEWITT: I want you to tell me that I'm okay, Jill. I am so sorry for what I did back then. God knows I'm sorry. [*his voice breaking*] All I want is for you to tell me I'm still a good person.

I was not expecting this plea for love from Mr. DeWitt. Noticing the expression on Mrs. DeWitt's face, I moved to sit next to her and asked what she was feeling. She said, "Sick. And upset." Mrs. DeWitt began shaking her head as though her feelings were too big for her words. She fumed:

> MRS. DEWITT: How could you *dare?* Jim, God damn you. You could actually sit there . . . ? Jill is not the person to tell you you're okay! And in the first place *you are not okay!* I don't blame her for not visiting! You put her down and put her down the way you used to do to me! And then you tell her she's still too fat or too thin or—[*crying*] I can't even talk straight.

Mr. DeWitt appeared shaken and he didn't look at her at all. He said later he had never seen his wife so out of control. Mrs. DeWitt told him, "I want you to treat Jill with respect!"

The room felt heavy with tension. After a long pause, Mr. DeWitt said "I just feel like a monster. Like the worst creature on earth." He paused a long time, as everyone looked at the floor. Then he asked me, "Am I monster? I guess I am."

His tone was not flippant, but earnest. I felt relieved that he had been candid, since some incestuous fathers, I had heard, either deny their behavior or refuse to discuss it. Nonetheless, I felt tremendous indignation that this man who had had sex with his own eight-year-old daughter could calmly complain that she did not make him feel "special" enough. Throughout this session I struggled with the necessity of being supportive to Jill and Mrs. DeWitt and being appropriately confrontational to Mr. DeWitt, but not too hard on him. The voices of my colleagues were still in my ears, whether I agreed with them or not. And, indeed, there were at that time no other "voices" to choose from; I had never seen a feminist therapist working with an incestuous family. My supervisor suggested that I remember how psychologically fragile Mr. DeWitt must have been to react so excessively to his wife's plans to get a job. He was a man with a $100,000 job and important responsibilities, but emotionally he was a child.

In response to Mr. DeWitt's question, I simply said: "Doing something terrible doesn't make a person into a monster. But Mrs. DeWitt is right. Jill needs to count on *you* for support and not the reverse."

This segment ended with Mr. DeWitt saying that he did want to be supportive to Jill, and that he was ready to hear whatever she had to say.

JILL: I love you, Dad, and I would like to be perfect for you. But I can't. I work hard to get 95s, and what I get from you is usually, "Why not 98?" I need some praise sometimes.

Her point seemed valid, but her affect was very flat. She stared at the floor and sheepishly, slowly, said she had one more thing to ask.

JILL: If you could just not, you know, kiss me right on the mouth when we say hello . . .
MRS. DEWITT: Don't ever kiss Jill on the mouth . . .
MR. DEWITT: Now wait a minute here [*turning to me*]—that's not offensive, that's just the way I show affection.
DL: Jill just made herself very clear!
MR. DEWITT [*defeated*]: I guess she did. Jill, really, I was just trying to show my love.
DL: You need to show love in ways that don't violate.

Jill was crying softly.

MR. DEWITT: You have my word, Jill. And please tell me when I do something that bothers you. I might not be aware of it.

MRS. DEWITT [*to Jill*]: And you have to tell me, Jill, when something like that is bothering you.

JILL: I know. I was embarrassed.

Mr. DeWitt spoke very respectfully to both of them, and he praised Jill for speaking her mind in the session.

It had been an exhausting session. I complimented each member of the family for taking risks and caring enough about each other to go through this long and painful discussion. I excused Jill and spent some time alone with the parents.

Mrs. DeWitt said she still felt anger but was basically glad that Jill had spoken up so well, and that maybe Mr. DeWitt was "beginning to get the picture." Mr. DeWitt said he felt "very pained" but that there was a huge weight lifted just to have the matter "out of the closet," since he had never said a word about it to anyone. "Not even your best friend?" I asked, naively. He said he had never had a best friend. He had buddies at work and a lot of women he dated, but no one he could really talk to. Mrs. DeWitt, in contrast, had told two close women friends about the incident over the years.

I was aware, even at that time, of literature describing the difference between the friendships women have with one another and those that men have. In retrospect, I think I asked about a best friend out of my own anxiety about having to be Mr. DeWitt's only confidante. I *wanted* him to have a best friend so I would not be his only one.

I had excused Jill to demonstrate the fact that she should no longer be the caretaker or confidante to him, but this role was also no longer appropriate for his ex-wife. After twenty minutes of talking with them both, I suggested that Mrs. DeWitt join Jill, and I spent an additional hour with Mr. DeWitt. My assumption, which is certainly arguable, was that while Mrs. DeWitt and Jill would know how to get the support they needed from other patients and staff on the unit, Mr. DeWitt would not know how to do this, and that it was he who needed the most attention at the moment. I asked him to talk to me about his life. Again, this was not something I was trained to do within the structural model, but it felt right to me.

He spoke of growing up in a family in which no one had ever given him a word of praise. He described himself currently as a workaholic who never felt that anything he did was of value. He said that Mrs. DeWitt had been very sweet and docile, "like a puppy dog," in the early years of their marriage, but that she had changed and become a completely different person. I empathized with his feeling of inadequacy and aloneness. I offered to help him find a therapist in his hometown just for himself, because he deserved to have some help with the tremendous pain he had been carrying around. He was not enthusiastic about the idea, but agreed to consider it.

The Remaining Work

Jill had gone upstairs that evening, eaten her dinner, and asked for a snack. In the previous four days of hospitalization, she had gained only one pound. After the "heavy session," as she later called it, her weight gain proceeded smoothly, with only a few slips. For example, one day as she was nearing her discharge weight, her mother caught her throwing out her whole lunch. With renewed strength, Mrs. DeWitt simply ordered more food and did not engage in a power struggle.

I met with Jill alone a few times; she was eager to get home and "get on with life." She said her dad had been less critical of her in the past few days, and she was feeling closer to her mom. I held two sessions with Mrs. DeWitt alone to talk about her own life. She had several close women friends who gave her a lot of emotional support, but they were married and were not usually available to spend time with. She also mentioned that there wasn't much money for socializing, much less vacations. It was in this context that she told me with some shame that she had indeed worried at first about Jill's visiting her father, but felt that if she forbade visitation, he might cut off child support, which she needed badly. "He is still one of the few men I know who pays child support with no argument, on time, no court battles. When we split up I was earning six thousand dollars, and she was in private school. What else could I do?"

I could see it had been a bitter decision for her and I added my thought that, "This is a choice you never should have had to make. It put you in a position that no mother should ever be in, but which a lot of mothers unfortunately are." I offered her my sincere support and encouraged her to think about work options in the present that would be more financially rewarding. I also recommended some therapy sessions for herself with the new outpatient therapist, and this appealed to her a great deal.

214

A number of sessions were held to discuss the plans for Jill's eating after discharge. We discussed how fast she had to gain the rest of the weight, how much choice of food she should have, whether she could exercise, which privileges would be denied if she stopped eating, under what conditions she should be readmitted, when she should visit her father, when she should do things with friends, and so on. In these sessions we worked on the parents' negotiating openly and constructively together and on including Jill's opinion to the extent that she acted her age.

After twenty-nine days Jill had reached her discharge weight, and the family terminated treatment with us. They were very pleased with the program and thanked every staff member who had worked with Jill. I had located a family therapist in the town where mother and Jill lived and thoroughly discussed the family's treatment with her. She described her approach as "eclectic," using techniques from structural, strategic, and family-of-origin approaches. She agreed to remain in periodic contact with us about the family's progress.

Follow-up Reports on the Family

The outpatient therapist (OPT) saw the family for a year. For the first six months she saw mother and daughter on a weekly basis, with father attending when he was able. Some of these sessions were spent with Jill only. For the second six months she saw the family every other week, and then once a month.

One Month After Discharge: According to the OPT, Jill had gained four more pounds and had made her way back into school with little problem. She had visited her father once and they had gone to see his parents together. Mrs. DeWitt seemed at ease and was talking about a career change. Mr. DeWitt told the OPT that I had been a "tremendous help" to him.

Three Months After Discharge: Jill had gained another six pounds, which put her at the target weight set by her parents. A male teacher at school had told her in jest that she was "practically huge," and she had become alarmed about her weight gain and started a diet. With the support of the OPT, Mrs. DeWitt forbade Jill to play sports until she began eating normally. She contacted Mr. DeWitt who supported the idea.

One Year After Discharge: Jill's grades were excellent and her weight was stable. Her father had become involved with a woman and was considering marriage. Mother's father had died, and she was dealing with this loss in therapy. She had not yet made any career change.

Two Years After Discharge: At Christmastime I received a letter from the family with mixed news. Mr. DeWitt had remarried and moved back to Texas. Jill had a steady boyfriend and they had decided to apply to the same colleges since they were interested in the same field. Mr. DeWitt argued against this idea, saying that it reflected "the wrong priorities." He suggested that she move in with his wife and him in Texas so she could attend the excellent university near his home. They had a major fight and she told her father he could not "plan her life" and that she didn't need him. Mr. DeWitt stated that she could not treat him as "just the banker," and refused to pay her tuition. Mrs. DeWitt was furious with him, and implored him to change his mind. The OPT made a long-distance call to Mr. DeWitt, suggesting that he pay one semester's tuition and then stop if Jill's grades were not satisfactory. He refused, saying that his was the only common-sense plan, and that it was completely illogical for her to make college plans on the basis of her relationship with her boyfriend.

The result was that Jill went to a small liberal arts college which gave her a partial scholarship and allowed her to work part-time. She was angry and disappointed in her father, but happy about school.

Final Contact: Jill received excellent grades during her first year at college. She had gained ten pounds during the first semester, however, and had taken up bingeing and weekly vomiting in order to control her weight. She described this as "epidemic" behavior in her dorm, and said that while she herself felt ashamed of it, other girls spoke openly and casually about their "barf buddies."

Commentary

I wish to make it clear that I do not believe that this case demonstrates the total failure of traditional family therapy. In the first place, it could not; the treatment was given by a novice therapist in a situation that allowed only four weeks of treatment. In the second place, some of the most hallowed principles of family therapy did prove constructive with this family, whereas previous efforts that had not involved the family had failed. The idea of getting the parents to work together was quite important; had they continued pulling Jill in separate directions, she might not have survived.

On the other hand, it is not unusual to see a family in which the traditional issues of "executive functioning" and "generational hierarchy" are treated alone, and although the anorectic patient may gain weight, there is a relapse, and sometimes multiple hospitalizations, after the treatment ends.

In contrast to some of my colleagues who learned about this case, I believe that the discussion of the incest was extremely relevant to Jill's progress. It was immediately after the "heavy session" in which the incest was discussed that Jill began to eat. At that point, although all the feelings and thoughts about the father-daughter and mother-daughter relationships had not yet been addressed or even raised, Jill was relieved enough to begin her journey back to physical health. She returned to her room and ordered extra food for the first time, as if to say, "The adults are going to make it safe for me to grow up." What seems remarkable about this now is that it was almost by accident that I learned of the incest; the family did not volunteer the information, and the previous therapists had not discovered it. It may have emerged anyway in the course of treatment, especially since Mr. DeWitt mentioned that he had hoped hospitalization would help to "clear the air" on this subject, but one cannot be sure about this. It is possible that if I had had a different supervisor, I might have been guided to put all my energies into the traditional structural goals of using the father to separate the mother-daughter "enmeshment." Jill might (or might not) have gained weight, but she would have been violated once again by our misperception.

We could speculate endlessly about whether or not the traditional methods failed the family. In any case, the methods indubitably failed me as a therapist. Using the mainstream literature alone, I had no means of answering or even posing the questions that now seem most important:

1. What choices do family therapists have in working with incestuous families? When does one move toward cutting off an incestuous parent from a child, and when does one seek to repair the relationship?
2. If the language of "poor boundaries" is too vague and euphemistic to describe sexual relations between parent and child, then what words and what set of ideas *could* adequately explain how an intelligent man like Mr. DeWitt, who at times seemed sensitive and sincere, could use his eight-year-old girl for sex and then complain years later that she no longer made him feel "special"? How could

one explain his withholding of college funds that he could easily afford, requiring his daughter to struggle financially for years simply because she had found a boyfriend?

3. What language and what set of concepts could one use to talk about the *mother's* reality in an incestuous family, without making her seem either totally adjacent to the father-daughter relationship or an actual accomplice to the father?

4. Was the DeWitt family anomalous, or is father-daughter incest present in some real or metaphorical form in many families with eating disorders? Indeed, exactly how prevalent *is* incest?

The approaches to family therapy that include family-of-origin work would have provided answers to some of these questions. The model I was trained in took little stock in family history, and so what I knew about the DeWitts was simply what had emerged spontaneously (e.g., Mr. DeWitt had mentioned that his parents were critical of him and had not given him support and confidence). Based on her year of work with the family, the OPT had added that Mr. DeWitt's father had been a volatile drinker who beat his wife and children, and Mr. DeWitt had always felt deep shame that he could not protect his mother, whom he saw as "small and helpless" in contrast to his bullying father. He had always believed himself to be more like her—gentle and soft-spoken—than like his father, who was callous and carping.

Psychoanalytic thinkers who have written about families have assisted us in understanding how parents such as Mr. DeWitt grow up to repeat the past, in this case by abusing his paternal power, just as his father had (see Skynner 1976, Scharff and Scharff 1987, Miller 1983b). Such psychoanalytic thinking leads us to hypothesize that Mr. DeWitt's parents had been *absent* in some significant ways as well, given his strong reaction to his wife's plan to get a job, and later to Jill's going off to college with a boyfriend.

Mrs. DeWitt's mother had died when she was nine years old. She had not been abused, but she had been given a lot of responsibility at a young age for raising four younger siblings. This means that Mrs. DeWitt lost her mother at around the same age that Jill was abused. Mrs. DeWitt's mother "separated" from her daughter through death at the same age that Mrs. DeWitt separated from Jill to go out to work. It is possible that Mrs. DeWitt was reexperiencing the loss of her mother at this time and that without sufficient support from Mr. DeWitt, or others to talk to about her feelings, she became simply less "tuned in" emotionally to her family and missed signs of Jill's distress she would not otherwise have missed.

The DeWitts: The Case of a Therapist in Transition

Working in a psychoanalytically informed family therapy would lead us to test these hypotheses by taking a careful history of the family, and also by attending closely to the relevant transference issues. As constructive as these psychoanalytically derived ideas are, even they do not answer the questions about this family as fully as some of the feminist literature has been able to do. Judith Herman's *Father-Daughter Incest* (1981) has been extremely helpful to therapists working with incestuous families. On the basis of the extant research that Herman summarizes and critiques, we learn that approximately 20 to 30 percent of all female children have a sexual encounter with an adult male before puberty; for 4 to 12 percent of them, that encounter is with a male *relative.* * In every known study the abusers have been men, except in a single study in which 94 percent were men and 6 percent were women. (See Russell 1986 for a discussion of the sexually abusive mother.) The abuse typically occurs between the ages of nine and twelve, and the secret is kept for an average of 3.1 years.

Jill was a bit younger than average when her father began having sexual contact with her, but in other ways she is typical. Nearly half of all victims are the only or the oldest daughter, and their mothers usually do not work outside the home. (Jill's mother had not taken a job until Jill was ten years old.) Incest typically continues for three years (in Jill's case only one year). Usually it does not include penile penetration, and it is perpetrated by a father who appears as a "neat, clean professional man" publicly, but is "domineering" with his children. Half of incestuous fathers beat their wives.

In developing her ideas about incest, Herman reviewed the major anthropological, moral, and philosophical works on it. She points out that theories of the incest taboo explain everything except the striking fact that it is almost always the male who abuses the female. Whether incest is viewed as a biological law that prevents inbreeding, or a social law that creates exogamy, or a psychological law that promotes viable interpersonal boundaries, or all of these, the taboo should, theoretically, apply equally to both sexes. Herman points out that only by understanding the incest taboo in the context of patriarchy can one understand the asymmetrical application of the taboo to the sexes.

Herman reports the astonishing fact that in the Bible, Leviticus 18 explicitly forbids over a dozen types of incest, but does not mention father-

---

*Diana Russell's excellent book *The Secret Trauma* (1986) reports an even higher incidence. She studied a demographically representative sample of 980 women, using first a mail interview and then a person-to-person interview. Sixteen percent of the sample had had a sexual experience with a relative (including step-relatives) before the age of fourteen. Exhibitionism and verbal stimulation or propositions did not count.

daughter incest at all! How might this be understood? Herman contends that under patriarchy, if a man abuses his sister, he offends his father. If he abuses his sister-in-law, he offends his brother. But if he takes his own daughter, *no other man is offended.*

Herman believes not that men are more innately exploitive than women, but that men are psychologically prepared and socially permitted to behave in ways that make this kind of violation more plausible to them. Her explanation echoes the work of Nancy Chodorow. Herman writes:

> The common product of this normal, female-dominated developmental process is an adult male whose capacity to nurture is severely impaired, whose ability to form affectionate relationships is restricted, and whose masculine identity, since it rests upon a repudiation of his identification of the first person who cared for him, is forever in doubt. Sexual contact with a woman of inferior status affords this psychically rather fragile and constricted person the only permissible outlet for expression of a wide range of emotional needs: the need for intimacy, comfort, etc. [1981, p. 56]

This portrait of a psychologically fragile person fits Mr. DeWitt well.

What becomes of incest victims in their adult lives? Herman studied sixty women in therapy, forty of whom had been incest victims and twenty of whom had not. She found that only a few of the incest victims led debilitated lives. The majority did *not* act out, become antisocial, or abuse their own children. The effects of the incest appear most frequently to cause only inner turmoil and despair about their own value and integrity. Herman's concluding statement on the legacy of the daughter is this:

> Thus did the victims of incest grow up to become archetypically feminine women: sexy without enjoying sex, repeatedly victimized, yet repeatedly seeking to lose themselves in the love of an over-powering man, contemptuous of themselves and of other women, hard-working, giving and self-sacrificing. Consumed with inner rage, they nevertheless rarely caused trouble to anyone but themselves. In their own flesh, they bore repeated punishment for the crimes committed against them in childhood. [P. 108]

Herman suggests that what is paramount in incest cases is to restore the mother-daughter relationship. She feels that the girl must be able to talk with her mother about the incest, and to obtain support and be forgiven by a parent who must be her mother and not her father. (Almost all girls, she says, feel guilty about being sexually abused.) The person who must show the strength to understand, to take control, and to nurture is her mother, her role model. It is the mother, after all, who will have the job of protecting her and her sisters from further abuse. Herman believes that perpetrators should be brought to court more often and that women, so rarely the offenders and so often the victims of sexual crimes, ought to serve as their judges.

Herman's emphasis on healing the mother-daughter relationship is a welcome change from the more common professional attitude of blaming the mother, and thereby upholding male sexual right. Indeed, in some families, incestuous fathers have no interest in change, and see unilateral control as their prerogative. The treatment modality of choice for these fathers is prison. Other fathers who have committed incest do want help. It is best to work with the entire family, to attend to both the mother-daughter *and* the father-daughter relationships where possible. I base this on the psychoanalytically derived assumption that a daughter whose father acknowledges his abuse and seeks help is less likely to go out in search of an overpowering man as a husband or lover. Her internal representation of the father will be more benign than that of the daughter whose incestuous father is simply written off as a beast. Such scorn for the father, while understandable, does not ensure that the girl will not seek beasts for partners. It seems inescapably true, as analysts such as Alice Miller have compellingly described, that we seek to relive in adulthood what we experienced of our parents in childhood.

A significant issue in understanding families where incest has occurred has to do with when it gets reported, and when it surfaces or resurfaces as a problem in the family. In this family, it is probable that Jill's reaching adolescence reawakened anxieties about the incestuous relationship for both Jill and her father. Mr. DeWitt's joke about wiping out her breasts can be read as a wish. Removing Jill's breasts would serve the dual purpose of keeping her childlike and innocuous in the way that had pleased him, while also removing the danger that some other male would find her sexually attractive and take her away. In any case, Jill's thinness also served a purpose from her own point of view. Her dieting brought her closer and closer to the "perfection" she felt her father wanted, and also made her less sexually identifiable to other males who might also use her.

Mrs. DeWitt's reactions to the incest also "fed" Jill's anorexia, because her guilt made it difficult for her to set limits on Jill's behavior. She indulged Jill's whims about food, and did not simply put a stop to the excessive dieting as she might have with another child. She herself was probably made anxious by Jill's emergent sexuality in adolescence, and may have subtly encouraged the weight loss as a defense against her own shame and fear. How does a mother teach a daughter to demand respect from males, to be cautious about sex, and to follow the mother's advice, after mother has been "the last to know" about certain sexual things?

None of the members of the DeWitt family had been able to talk about the experience of living in their family. Jill acted out her experience, and talked with her body by way of the anorexia. Each member of the family had borne a private pain, and their fantasies, rages, and fears of reprisal had not been named. One of the healing tasks of therapy is to direct a discourse through which this naming occurs so that it does not need to be acted out by the patient (or by the next generation). The process with the DeWitts was only a beginning, but it brought a measure of relief.

The process I am trying to describe is probably best illustrated by a myth that warrants retelling. It is the myth of the miller's daughter who is asked to spin straw into gold. She is saved by an ugly dwarf who performs the spinning in exchange for a promise to surrender her firstborn child to him. The daughter agrees, hoping he will forget about this horrible pact, but years later when she has a child, the little man returns. He tells her that the only way she can save herself is to tell him his correct name. The daughter is close to despair, for she has no idea of the man's identity. With the help of friends and aides who investigate his whereabouts, she is able to learn his name; when she shows her knowledge of it ("Rumpelstiltskin"), her life begins to belong to her.

The fundamental idea of this myth—that the ability to name our demons is an inescapable part of freeing and healing the self—is a familiar idea to all insight-oriented therapists who work with individuals. It can apply equally well in the treatment of families.

HISTORICAL PERSPECTIVE ON THE DEWITTS

The relationship between the DeWitts's dilemmas and the material discussed in chapter 10, on the family in history, is perhaps obvious. The DeWitts are a good example of the family pattern I have called patriarchal but father-absent. As for father absence, Jill had lived in her mother's company since the age of ten, and seen her father, who had moved fifty miles away, only on weekends. Even when the family was "intact," in the first ten years of Jill's life, Jill had still been in the primary care of her mother, as most children are. It was Mrs. DeWitt who had helped Jill with homework, cooked and done laundry, taken her to doctors and music lessons, bought clothes and arranged birthday parties, settled arguments with peers, sewed costumes for school plays, and driven her to low-calorie restaurants. All of this "father absence" and "mother presence," however, obviously did not mean the family was not patriarchal. Not only did the father exploit the typical age and gender hierarchies that exist in nearly all families, but he did so at the precise moment when his wife began to move in the direction of increased autonomy.

We can say that during the process of therapy, for at least a few moments, the family became less patriarchal as Jill witnessed her mother hold her father accountable for his mockery of parental power. ("Jill is not the person to tell you you're okay!") And the therapist had supported mother ("Mrs. DeWitt is right"), which allowed Jill to express her own anger at her father for the first time. The father-absent character of the family was amended, if only slightly, as Mr. DeWitt participated in the therapy sessions, collaborating with his ex-wife and listening to Jill speak her mind.

The outcome of the treatment was certainly not what one would have hoped. Jill eluded her father's demand that she live with his new wife and him in Texas, but he could not relinquish enough control over her to let her have a close boyfriend. I assume that everyone in the DeWitt family (and in all families, for that matter) had resentments and revenge wishes, but father had the option to act out his resentment by withholding the material means she needed to become competent and autonomous.

In addition to being patriarchal and father-absent, this family also follows the pattern of the contemporary urban family in its relative isolation from the community. The father in particular had no close friends—a fact that was not helped by the reality that his company could relocate him at any time. Mrs. DeWitt had women friends, but she and her husband did not have people whom they counted on together. The extended families did not live in the area, and the family belonged to no church or social organizations. The fact that this father and to some extent the mother were so focused on Jill is continuous with the historical trend since industrialization of the removal of community and kin networks from the family and the consequent overloading of the child. Even in the premodern world, of course, child abuse was rampant. However, if a father injured a child in earlier epochs, it is highly improbable that he would look to her for support, forgiveness, and validation of his worth as a man. Not even a spouse had that role. A man who felt as unhappy as Mr. DeWitt would have turned to his extended kin, to the church, to the guild, and to God to unload his burden of wrong and begin anew.

As a twentieth-century middle-class child, Jill had to play all those parts. As incest victim, she was forced not only to take a wife's role to her father, but she also assumed the role of the entire community to him. Her body became the ground where he could plant his longing for love, acceptance, and "specialness." Unlike a wife who would expect reciprocity, Jill, as a child, gave without demanding, without criticizing, without threatening her father. I am not blaming the lack of community for incest itself, since incest occurred long before the historical blows to community. I am simply adding that the father's seemingly inscrutable wish that the daughter absolve him and console him reflects the culture of modernity, in which children are expected to be psychologically as well as physically responsive to parents, to be their confidants and the final vindicators of their lives.

FEMINIST INTERPRETATIONS OF ANOREXIA

Anorexia has become a glamorous disease in the developed urban world; being underweight is a condition that elevates one's social status. It has been remarked that the American diet industry earns profits that are greater than the gross national products of some developing nations. Pictures of very thin women ("winners") are used by advertisers to sell cigarettes, cars, and soap, turning the female body into "live bait," as Sheila Mac Leod has said (1982). The manufacture of the desire to be slender is simply big business, and this fact should be included in any attempt to understand "anorexia in context."

Profit alone cannot explain the Western dieting mania, however. Profits would be greater still if the industry could "hook" men as well as women on the value of changing their body size. Our clinical experience tells us, however, that men do not define themselves in terms of their appearance nearly so much as women do, and, in fact, relatively few anorectics are male. The asymmetry can again be explained in economic terms. As long as women are financially dependent on men, they will need to work harder to attract and keep men, and thus to *use themselves as live bait.*

There is another level of explanation, however, for the fact that both women and men are obsessed with women's physical size and form. To understand it, we must turn to the work of feminist scholars such as Dorothy Dinnerstein and Nancy Chodorow, who emphasize the massively ambivalent feelings human beings have toward their first caretaker. Kim Chernin, in her feminist works on anorexia, *The Obsession* and *The Hungry Self,* asks us to remember how the female body must have looked to us as infants. In comparison to ourselves, mother's body must have seemed "a veritable mountain of flesh," and in our adult contempt for female softness and girth, we are trying "to expunge the memory of the primordial mother who ruled over our childhood with her inscrutable power over life and death" (p. 143).

Not every culture demands that women's figures be slender, but all the major cultures have sought to shape or twist or mutilate women's bodies in certain ways in order to make them more appealing to men. Corseting in the Victorian era, genital mutilation (still practiced in twenty-six African nations), and foot binding in the Orient are examples of this need for male control of the female form. One might argue that the circumcision of males is also a form of mutilation, but it has never been done under the pretext of making men more attractive to women or more submissive to them. Men's bodies are also mutilated in battle, but this is not considered *erotic*.

Consider, in contrast, the practice of foot binding, which existed for 1,000 years in China and Japan in every family that could afford it. Girls' feet were bound at birth in order to produce in adulthood the tiny (three-inch-long) stubs that men found so sensually pleasing, and that inspired a good deal of erotic poetry. Chinese mothers detested binding their baby girls' feet, but knew that the girls would not be marriageable without their little "lotus hooks." A Chinese proverb advised that a mother who loves her daughter must not love her feet. (See Daly 1978 for an account of foot binding.) The same feelings distress many modern mothers as they watch their preadolescent daughters begin to diet and to cast increasingly critical gazes at their healthy young bodies in the mirror. Can a mother who loves her daughter honestly tell her that being ultra-thin is not good or important? It can be very helpful to anorectic patients and their mothers alike to read books such as Chernin's (1981), Mac Leod's (1982), and Orbach's (1978), which discuss and demystify many of these conflicts that patients believe are entirely idiosyncratic.

The importance of bringing up the "psychopolitics" of anorexia is to point out that anorexia is indeed culturally homologous to incest, and that this realization can be clinically useful. In both eating disorders and incest, we find the reduction of the whole girl or woman to her parts. The female subject becomes feminine object, from the point of view of others and eventually of herself. The anorectic feels that she is nothing but her thighs and buttocks; the sexual abuser also sees the girl as little more than that. Both anorexia and incest are supported by a social context that makes use of female fragmentation in many ways, with the result, as the Lacanian feminists might say, of reducing the "whole" to a "hole"—vagina or mouth. Both eating disorders and incest are expressions of female powerlessness, and their "cure" is female choice and authority.

Judith Herman sees these power issues as relevant to all families. She states that "overt incest represents only the furthest point on a continuum—an exaggeration of patriarchal family norms, but not a departure from them" (p. 110). Denise Gelinas (1983) has recommended that family history-taking always include the question, "Has anyone in your family been sexually abused?" pointing out that most families will not bring it up themselves, but almost all will admit it when asked. I think that when a family presents with an eating disorder, this question is all the more important, for the reasons described above.

If female autonomy is the "cure" for families with anorectic or abused daughters, how does the therapist proceed? While she or he, of course, devotes some sessions to the daughter alone, helping her to gain independence from the family while still remaining connected, the therapist must support the mother in the same way. If not, the daughter is put in a terrible bind: "Shall I be autonomous in the way my therapist encourages me to be, or subservient like my role model is, or has usually been?"

Therapists endorse female autonomy in a number of ways, most pervasively by listening more, and silencing less, than we have normally been taught to do. In all cases, the therapist must be educated about the relationships among female depression, powerlessness, and the denial of anger. Women like Mrs. DeWitt have typically gone through years of self-loathing, lethargy, and feelings of hopelessness and boredom. The therapist helps these women turn some of their aggression outward instead of in, against the self. Feminist psychiatrist Teresa Bernardez has written that "women's problems with the expression of anger, rebellion and protest are central to the understanding of women's difficulties in creative and active pursuits" (1978, p. 215). Many therapists feel intolerant and even contemptuous when a woman is angry, especially if she expresses her anger in a way that is shrill, blaming, or petulant. The traditional therapist often cuts off this affect in an effort to help the woman "gain control." Bernardez, however, makes this important observation:

> The loss of connection, happening when negative feelings are openly expressed, is so feared by many women that frequently the expression of anger is accompanied by tears, expressions of guilt and sorrow in a cluster of responses that contaminate the expression of anger or nullify it altogether. In this complex response the woman appears to be expressing her anger, her conflict and fear about it, her sorrow at the loss of a relationship, the sadness at her own self-betrayal and her impotence in making herself clear, all at the same time. This response is so often encountered that it appears to be a kind of anthropologic finding, culture-bound and sex-specific. [P. 216]

Women's first expressions of anger will not necessarily break the silence like the thundering voice of Sojourner Truth. Much more often, this new angry voice will sound like Mrs. DeWitt's: "Jim, God damn you. You could actually sit there . . . ?"

Why is it so hard for people, therapists included, to respond properly to women's anger? The expression "angry woman"—often applied to feminists—is an epithet so damning that it is usually not considered to require elaboration. Bernardez believes that we cringe at female rage more than at male rage because of an exaggerated terror of maternal destructiveness, based on infantile fears of the mother's unlimited powers. We must learn to understand and cherish women's first steps toward what Winnicott called "the true self," the self that knows its own desires and is not fraudulently for-others. I agree with Bernardez that the therapist's containment of and respect for women's anger can lead over time to the most direct, well-timed, and powerful uses of it.

The issue of women's anger and female autonomy are closely related to the issue of nurturance. Women in our culture are socialized to nurture others, not themselves. In some families this is made very overt, as the women do the food preparation but serve themselves last. In striving to lead other-directed, service-oriented lives, women often fail to realize their own need to be taken care of, and despise those needs when they do feel them. In relationships, men are socialized to expect that women will take care of their emotional needs, but women are not socialized to expect the same of men. It seems that one of the common ways women do allow themselves to be nurtured is through eating—sometimes in the company of others and sometimes furtively. It is interesting in this light to recall that one of the litany of adjectives used to describe the mothers in the Timberlawn study's "adequate families" was *obese* (see chapter 1). How might we understand this common finding? It has been suggested that if a person were to design a job that was fattening, one would make sure this job included a lot of cooking, tedious chores performed alone, much contact with small children and little with other adults, low prestige, and no compensation. In addition, one would want the job to be so mindless that "munching would be fascinating in comparison" (Streitfeld 1987). This is a fairly accurate job description for the stay-at-home mother.

Overeating to compensate for the lack of other kinds of satisfaction obviously creates a conflict with social standards for female attractiveness. Women begin to diet, and a self-defeating cycle sets in, in which deprivation leads to even more eating. The obesity of the Timberlawn mothers may be the result of this dieting-and-feasting cycle, which begins with the urge to feed "the hungry self," in Kim Chernin's words.

What happens to the daughters of the Timberlawn mothers if they should grow up to want better lives? Some of these daughters will share the fate of Jill DeWitt's classmates, and begin a career of bulimia. Molly Layton has suggested that many college and professional women feel conflicting emotions about their own competence and high ideals. Many are the first women of their families to be entering "power professions" and competing in formerly all-male preserves. To these women, that world is exciting, desirable, and necessary, but it is also dangerous and different from the world of their mothers. It is quite expectable that women would be ambivalent about choosing lives of adventure, discovery, and risk over lives of service and domesticity. The to-and-fro quality of the decision—to be like mother, or to break into professions that would not have accepted mother, and may not fully accept her either—is reenacted in the binge-purge cycle, in which the candy bar, or the "power lunch," is taken in and then expelled.

In a feminist therapy, patients come to have compassion for their own dilemmas, to see their desires for nurturance as wholesome and self-preserving, and to learn to meet their needs with open requests.

This discussion has so far concentrated on the role of mother and daughter, but what about the father in families such as the DeWitts? One feminist reader of this case criticized me for "getting rid of" the family, and of Mr. DeWitt in particular, by offering too soon to find another therapist who lived closer to them. I had made this suggestion with the conscious intention of being helpful, but I now agree that it was a clinical error. Unlike Mrs. DeWitt, Mr. DeWitt had never opened up to anyone before me, and my first response was to send him to someone else! The more correct intervention would have been to invite him to remain in treatment with me. It would have then been up to him to say, "No, it's too far away; can you find me someone in my hometown?" In retrospect, I think that my escorting him away, like my desire that he have a best friend, was an example of a countertransference acting out. Had I been thinking in terms of psychoanalytic theory at the time of treating this family, I would have discussed (rather than sheepishly concealed) my feelings about this family in far greater detail with my supervisor, and I might have avoided this error.

Some of the issues I would raise in therapy with this father if I were treating him now would have to do with his abandonment fears, his problems with intimacy, and his feelings about his father, who clearly did not provide a model of viable masculinity for him. I would probably see myself as trying to be the good parent to him, especially by setting limits.

Some therapists are now treating incestuous fathers in all-male groups, which are offered in connection with individual or family treatment. Such therapy can help correct the error in the cultural sphere of leading men to expect that women can or should or will meet all their emotional needs, and that other men can never do so. It is useful, where possible, for men to learn from each other that their dependency needs are acceptable and that abusing their power as parents is heinous.

The DeWitts: The Case of a Therapist in Transition

Here I am simply restating Gelinas's (1983) suggestion that in order to understand the incestuous family, one needs both a "power analysis" and a "loyalty analysis." Without the former we are left with theoretically flimsy notions about fathers exhibiting "poor boundaries" with their daughters, and we ignore the reality of childhood rape. Without the latter, we have only a sociological analysis which does not take into account the contradictions of human motives, conscious and unconscious. As feminists, we may *wish* that a child who has been abused would not want to protect that parent, and would put her needs above his, but this does not seem to be the case. If I had not respected Jill's devotion to her father the first time she rushed in to tell me he was not a bad person, I might never have been able to proceed as her therapist.

In cases where the father's competence is marginal, but total cutoff from the child is not warranted, the therapist can recommend through the courts that visitation take place only under supervised conditions, such as in the home of grandparents or other relatives who are reliable and accountable. The therapist can also recommend that visitation with the child be permitted only on condition that the father remain in family and/or individual treatment. If I were seeing the DeWitt family now, I would have made unequivocal use of these options.

There are, of course, an enormous number of issues about incest that have not been addressed here: how to deal with the legal system, what to do when the abusive parent does not admit to the offense, how to treat brother-sister incest, and how to treat the male incest victim or the (rare) problem of the female perpetrator, for example. With limited space, I have chosen to focus on only one of the most common incestuous family constellations. If family therapists *as a group* could become expert in dealing with even this one type of family violence, we would give our culture a gift it has not yet seen.

14

The McGinns: "Irrational" Mom and a Method to Madness

IN THE CASE of the DeWitt family, discussed in the previous chapter, treatment was initially conceived along traditional structural/strategic family therapy lines. In the cases presented in this and the next chapter, some techniques from structural and strategic therapies appear, but only as they fit into what I will call a *feminist psychoanalytic family therapy.* The therapy is feminist insofar as gender issues receive special attention and the therapeutic *telos* (conscious purpose) is to help the family in ways that leave them both less patriarchal and less father-absent than before. The clinical categories of this therapy are psychoanalytic (deriving specifically from object-relations theory), and include: (1) the therapist's creation of a holding environment, (2) the interpretation of events and projective systems within the family, and (3) close attention to transference and countertransference issues (see chapter 12).

In the DeWitt family, the importance of gender issues was relatively obvious. It is essential to realize, however, that gender issues are important in every family—not just those in which the identified patient is female or the symptom is gender-linked, like anorexia nervosa. In the McGinn family, the patient was a male teenager whose presenting symptom was out-of-control asthma. There were no issues of physical or sexual abuse, homosexuality, or single parenting. Nonetheless, if one treated the McGinn family without considering gender, one would miss what appear to me as the family's key issues.

It might be useful to comment in advance about what makes feminist psychoanalytic family therapy different from traditional family therapies. Like many feminist therapists (and all psychoanalytically oriented therapists), I believe that an investigative capacity and the insight that results from it can be both empowering and healing. Thus, one of the achievements of the therapy was the family's greater capacity for self-reflection. Second, the father became more authentically present in the family, not just the backup or support to his wife but someone who could relate fully to his children and discuss them knowledgeably. Another change involved helping everyone in the family to understand and value mother in a different way and to stop devaluing those things they associated with her (e.g., affect, and the "irrational"). Another change was making the family less isolated from the community, and less dependent on their son to satisfy their emotional needs.

I caution the reader once again not to read this case in search of "feminist techniques." Feminism is not a set of therapeutic techniques but a sensibility, a political and aesthetic center that informs a work pervasively. One does not merely make clinical interventions in the family as a feminist; one also greets the family and sets the fee as a feminist.* The words spoken during a session that catch one's attention or that slip by, the things that make one feel warm toward the family, and the things that offend are all determined in part by this sensibility. Given this fact, I have tried to integrate my observations and interpretations of the McGinns and the Johnsons throughout the text of the case, as opposed to offering a "feminist analysis" of them at the end.

*   *   *

Kip McGinn was admitted to our adolescent inpatient service on a Sunday night in December. The therapist on emergency call left this note:

15-year-old white male with history of out-of-control asthma and numerous food allergies. Admitted after serious asthma attack in middle of the night. Blood levels showed zero medication, and patient has admitted that he had not been taking his medications, because he was "sick of them." There is suicidality here, since patient clearly knows the risk involved in not taking meds, and has also been withdrawn and unhappy lately. He told older brother (age 19) that he was "sick of his life" and wanted to "escape." Precipitating cause unknown. Mother is overinvolved—talks for patient. Father is a sales manager in a department store. There is one sister, age 14. The family was told that the assigned therapist would phone on Monday morning.

*When families are seen through agencies, as were the families described in chapters 13–15, the fee is usually collected by the agency, not by the therapist. Among therapists who maintain a private practice, I find that feminists are more likely than others to set aside certain hours for single mothers and other low-income patients who are, in a sense, "subsidized" by those affluent enough to pay the full fee.

After reading the note, I went to meet Kip, who was by that time in the classroom with the rest of his inpatient group. Through the one-way mirror I spotted a pale, redheaded boy with the rounded face typical of children who take steroid medications. He appeared sullen, sitting alone at a chessboard. I introduced myself and explained my role as his clinician. He spoke without making much eye contact, stating that he had simply "forgotten" to take his medications. In response to questions about his family, he said that they were "close" but that they thought he was "weird" and that I would understand when I met them. We talked a little bit about chess, and he continued to move the pieces around the board, though not inviting me to play. At one point he got up, saying that it was time for him to take his medicine. I told him that I would inform him of the time of our family session as soon as I reached his family by phone.

MRS. MCGINN

There was no answer when I phoned the family after meeting Kip. Ten minutes later, however, the receptionist called me out of a meeting to tell me that Mrs. McGinn had shown up in the reception area, angrily requesting to see her new therapist in order to "get some answers." I had not planned to see the family until evening, and at first I felt overwhelmed at Mrs. McGinn's having arrived early and apparently angry. My day was already heavily scheduled, and I was aware of a feeling of wishing to "escape" and go back to my meeting. I wondered if Kip had felt a similar burden of having to overperform for the family in some way which had led to his recent crisis.

In any case, it seemed probable that there was something wrong with the family's "holding capacity"—its ability to provide a feeling of comfort and containment for its members. If this were not the case, then Mrs. McGinn would be sitting with another member of the family at this moment instead of sitting in the waiting room. This led me to think that Mrs. McGinn herself might be overburdened and exploited in the family, and that it might actually be good that she was reaching out for help independently. Since it is something of a historical novelty for mothers' needs and protests to be considered important, I allowed myself to feel comfortable and even pleased to take the opportunity to offer her some extra support. With those thoughts in mind, I greeted Mrs. McGinn in the waiting room without further regrets about leaving my other work behind.

I owed the self-referential process that I was using at that moment, and that I had not used enough with the DeWitts, to having learned more about object-relations theory in the interim between the two families. However, the final outcome of this set of reflections—the decision to go out and meet Mrs. McGinn early—was a feminist outcome. Object-relations theory transformed the first thought, "I would like to escape this additional demand for service today," to something like, "The family is trying to tell me how overwhelmed they feel." But it was this notion refracted through a feminist sensibility that led me to extend myself unambivalently to Mrs. McGinn. It was myself as feminist who produced the second thought, "Here is a mother openly expressing anger and requesting some help for herself. Rewarding this effort is historically rare and completely consonant with my professional *telos.*"

My point here is not to make this decision sound heroic, nor to suggest that every special request made by a mother should be met in this way. I am merely pointing out that even our smallest professional decisions—especially the ones made early in the course of treatment—are informed not simply by our clinical training but also by our private understandings and misunderstandings about the family as a social formation and by our beliefs about the world. Therapists whose worldviews are well considered, complex, and articulable have the opportunity of checking their clinical choices against their beliefs. This level of integration of self, theory, and practice is very sustaining.

But let us return for the moment to the McGinn family, and to the mother in the waiting room. I introduced myself to Margo McGinn, a short, plump woman in her forties with dark, worried eyes. She was French Canadian by birth, and spoke English perfectly well but with a trace of an accent. She took my hand anxiously, saying that she had come down to bring Kip some clothes he had asked for, and felt she shouldn't have to wait until this evening to meet his therapist. I nodded warmly and invited her back to my office. She softened immediately and said she would not take more than five minutes of my time. I said we could take more if we needed it.

Mrs. McGinn posed a lot of questions about the hospital program—what types of patients we had, how long Kip's stay would be, and so on. She was afraid that encouraging him to sign in on Sunday had been "cruel." In the course of our discussion she revealed that she herself had once been psychiatrically hospitalized, and her own treatment had indeed been cruel. The story was as follows: Very shortly after the birth of Kip, she had become pregnant again and was physically ill and depressed throughout the pregnancy. When this child, a daughter, was born, she took care of her as best she could, but had a "breakdown" two years later. Her husband had not known what to do and had followed the advice of the doctors to have her psychiatrically hospitalized. Several relatives helped take care of Cindy and the boys, aged three and six.

While hospitalized, Mrs. McGinn had apparently been completely abandoned. The doctors advised her husband not to visit, claiming that it would only make her "more agitated" and that she needed "complete rest." Her parents lived two thousand miles away, and had not even provided support by phone. Mrs. McGinn added that her family had always preferred her older brother to her. She stated that only the need to take care of her children, and Mrs. Soren, a social worker in the hospital who had been kind, had allowed her to survive that time. *The experience had never been discussed in their family.* Her husband had been simply relieved that she had survived, and that she was ready to care for the children. He had had a "habit of going out late at night," which he stopped when she came home from the hospital. Everyone in the family made an effort to carry on as though nothing had happened. Mrs. McGinn remarked that Cindy seemed to have turned out fine, but Kip eventually became the problem child. This was because, she said, Kip had the same moody personality she had. She blamed this recent crisis on her having picked on Kip recently to be more responsible and to do more work around the house. She had stopped nagging him about his medication, since he resented it, and she felt guilty about this too. In short, she felt she was the cause of his problems and was horrified that he had now been psychiatrically hospitalized, just as she had been.

My early wondering about the holding capacity of the family appeared to be justified. Mrs. McGinn had felt overwhelmed by anguish and guilt during the past twenty-four hours, and this was certainly not the first time. Thirteen years previously, with three young children to take care of, she had fallen subject to her own depression, and in lieu of real help and support, she was turned over to the world of traditional psychiatry. With the aid of Mrs. Soren, she was able to gain the strength to return home. She had continued to see her in treatment for a year, until Mrs. Soren moved out of state for a new job. I wondered if Mrs. McGinn's rush down to see me had something to do with wanting to use all the time we had, in case I, too, would leave the family. She confirmed my thought by asking anxiously whether I would do the outpatient therapy as well, or whether they would have to start over with another therapist. I said I would be available for the outpatient therapy and added that I had no plans to move to another city, at which point she smiled for the first time. I told her that I had seen many families with similar problems make excellent use of the program, and that my goal was to discharge Kip as soon as it was safe to do so.

I asked whether she thought her husband understood that she still had a lot of feelings about what had happened thirteen years ago, and she said she didn't know.

DL: Will you be willing at some point in our sessions to bring it up?
MRS. MCGINN: I don't know. He hates to talk about the past.
DL: And you?
MRS. MCGINN: I will.

She added, however, that her first concern for the moment was Kip, and getting him out of the hospital. I agreed with her and answered more questions about the hospital. We set up a time for a family session that evening, and she phoned her husband and two other children—Howard, age nineteen, and Cindy, fourteen—to tell them to join us. We shook hands, and I went on to finish my morning's work, feeling good about our interaction.

The First Family Session

Gus McGinn was a warm and engaging man with curly red hair that was turning gray. He arrived on time for the session, but alone. The session consisted only of Kip and his parents, because Howard and Cindy, according to Mr. McGinn, had called him in the late afternoon to say that they couldn't leave their jobs to attend the session. I wondered if Mr. McGinn had somehow given them a message that the session was not important, and my countertransferential feeling was that he was "holding out" on me by not bringing them along. This was probably induced to some extent by my having spent part of the morning with Mrs. McGinn, and heard about how he had been insensitive to her in the past.

Mrs. McGinn began the session by thanking me for "saving the day" and allowing her time that morning. She was developing some idealizing feelings toward me. Mr. McGinn also thanked me for taking time for his wife, saying that "Margo does act a bit hasty or irrational, but she means well." Mrs. McGinn did not react to being called "irrational." She apparently thought of herself in that way and did not hear it as an insult. She simply mentioned to Mr. McGinn that she had shared some feelings with me that we would return to later, but that her first concern was Kip. Her husband concurred.

As a feminist, I had a strong visceral reaction to Mr. McGinn's use of the word *irrational* to describe his wife. To my ear, it carried not only his personal frustration with his wife but also a long cultural history of bifurcating the rational and the irrational, uncritically valuing the former and devaluing the latter. The fact that women are often associated with these devalued traits—emotionality, lability, feeling—does not mean that women are always permitted to give them up; on the contrary, families often demand that the mother (and, at times, the patient) express the affect for the entire group. The therapist then must work toward a more equitable distribution of the family's affect—that is, the therapist helps the "rational" family members claim their own emotions.

My goal in this first session, however, was not to begin exploring such issues but rather to make contact with Kip and with Mr. McGinn, and to form an agreement about working together. The debate over the rational and the irrational was sure to return.

Mr. McGinn responded to my questions by explaining that he had worked for twenty-one years in department stores, which he described as "boring" work that he had never liked. When I sympathized with him, he said he shouldn't complain; it was not so bad.

My attempts to engage Kip in the session failed; he barely answered my questions. I asked Mr. McGinn if this were typical of Kip. He answered that Kip had always been "sort of different" and that he would talk when he was in the right mood, particularly with his brother, Howard. When I asked Mr. McGinn to describe Kip before the crisis, he stated that Kip had been a sickly child all his life, with allergies and asthma that kept him out of gym at school. Mr. McGinn said that Kip was considered to have a superior IQ, but barely passed every grade. Several times each year, he would be rushed to the hospital due to an asthma attack, and during one attack (at age seven), the doctors had feared a complete cardiac arrest.

It was clear from this account that Mr. McGinn knew more about his son than some fathers do, but that he was not as knowledgeable about him as Mrs. McGinn was. At several points, he had needed to turn to his wife for details. Mr. McGinn concluded by saying he had no idea why Kip had stopped taking his medication, and added that Kip was "a bit of a mystery."

DL: You say that a bit wistfully, Mr. McGinn.

MR. MCGINN: I'm just so busy. I'd like to do more things with Kip.

Mr. McGinn watched me nodding supportively to him, and then began to talk directly to Kip. He spoke, however, as though Kip were hard of hearing.

236

The McGinns: "Irrational" Mom and a Method to Madness

MR. MCGINN: I wish you'd talk, son. I know I'm busy with work.

MRS. MCGINN: He's angry at us for putting him here.

MR. MCGINN: Kip, I don't know if you're angry or what, but I wish you'd talk. [to me:] He really is a good kid. He's no trouble, really.

I felt frustrated and angry with both parents, as they placed him in the bind of having to speak even as they choked him off.

The mainstream structural family therapist at this moment might have framed Kip's behavior as "immaturity," or "stubbornness" instead of illness or depression, and challenged Mrs. McGinn about how she kept her son so childish. Such a therapist might ask Kip how his mother knew he was angry (Could she see inside his mind?). This therapist might then ask Mr. McGinn if his wife could read *his* feelings, too. If not, then why did he allow her to do this to his son? The traditional therapist might end up asking Mr. McGinn to tell his wife to back off Kip, thus using father to separate mother and child. Most of our cultural expectations—and even the admission note written by my own colleague—had prepared me to see the family in this way. (The note had mentioned mother's overinvolvement, but said about father only that he worked in a store.) It is certainly true that Mrs. McGinn's behavior toward Kip was intrusive and infantilizing, but so was Mr. McGinn's. (My fantasy as I heard father speak so loudly was that he was talking to someone deaf or retarded.) Mr. McGinn, who was less involved than his wife with the children, could have been "brought in" to treatment by the therapist's making him an expert and "elevating his status." While this would counter the family's homeostasis, it would be homeostatic with the culture's devaluation of women, and also condescending to the father. (What message do we give to men in conferring false status on them?) For these reasons, the traditional intervention is not an option for the feminist therapist.

I simply said to Kip, "I wonder if you can get a word in edgewise in your family."

Kip looked up at me, as though he might speak, but he didn't. His parents looked defeated. I explored the issue of suicide with them, asking if they thought Kip wanted to die, what reason he might have for hurting himself, and how his previous asthma attacks differed from this one. The parents said they had no idea why Kip would want to commit suicide, and that no one in the family had ever made such an attempt. They had to admit, however, that this attack differed from earlier ones in that he had apparently stopped taking his medication this time, something he had never done before. They mentioned that he had seemed withdrawn for two weeks previously, but that they had attributed it to his "moods." Mr.

McGinn said, "We are puzzled, honestly. Can you tell us anything, Doctor, about why Kip might be acting this way?"

His tone was earnest, and in fact, this simple question raised another complex set of ideological issues. Parents often ask questions of this nature to therapists, and some therapists are apparently trained to deflect them. Although such questions are sometimes requests for magic, or attempts to distract the therapist, they are equally often well-meaning and answerable questions that should be addressed as straightforwardly as possible. Respecting the family's right to ask questions about the services they will receive is an explicit feature of most types of feminist therapy. Feminists are especially aware of the importance of this respect because of the long history of blatant abuse of female patients (Ehrenreich and English 1978). I make an effort to explain my thinking to the family, my reasons for doing certain things, and my sense of how long treatment will take. This, of course, does not mean that the therapist should tell the family "everything" that she or he is thinking about them; that would not be helpful. To edit is not to be disingenuous, however, for we never say "everything" about a case to anyone. We always select and screen, according to the resources of the listener and our purposes as the speaker. What I am most eager to call into question here is the knee-jerk tendency on the part of some family therapists to abdicate responsibility in such situations, by saying to a husband, for example, "Ask your wife what the diagnosis is." Equally offensive is saying something heavily contrived such as, "Kip is your deaf-mute son. For some strange reason, he thinks you need him to be a deaf-mute. Talk to each other about why he became your deaf-mute son."

I answered Mr. McGinn by saying that Kip's problems with asthma, and his talk of "escape," struck me as an expression of anger, sadness, and confusion. I added that I had seen hints of those things in all three of them, and that this sort of crisis is sometimes the only way a family works things out.

DL: That's why I am interested not just in Kip, but in all of you. You are all my patient.

MR. MCGINN: But aren't we feeling sad and so on *because* Kip is having his trouble?

DL: Yes! And also—and this is what I really want you to see—Kip may be the most sensitive person in the family, or the most transparent. I think his problems may be a symbol for the problems of the whole family.

There was a silence that felt like a "connected" silence.

MR. MCGINN [*nodding*]: I think I get it.

MRS. MCGINN: Like the fire happens over here, but the bad wiring is all around. And it's dangerous.

DL: And it's dangerous.

What I was introducing to the family was the concept of projective identification—the process through which affects and conflicts that "belong" to the family are relocated in one family member. In projective identification, it is as though the family "stores" its anger (or anxiety, or depression, or sexuality) in one (or more) of its members, who contain(s) it, without consciously understanding the process. This storing of the "bad," split-off feelings allows the rest of the family to maintain its internal sense of goodness and to carry on smoothly, on a superficial level. Most schools of family therapy make some use of this psychoanalytic concept, referring to the family's use of a "scapegoat," or "delegate," or "spokesperson." Object-relations family therapists see their task as one of determining exactly what the family is storing in the patient. The therapist then "contains" these split-off feelings *herself* (or himself), until they can be returned to the family in safer forms. It is better for everyone in the family to be aware of her or his *own* sadness (or anger or fear) than to dump the affect onto one member.

My intention in offering this explanation at this point in the therapy with the McGinns was not only to teach them this construct in particular but to begin establishing the expectation that therapist and family would be thinking together about the family's life, and decoding its mysteries. I wanted to inscribe the "we" of the therapeutic discourse, which is common to the best psychoanalytic and feminist therapies.

MR. MCGINN: Well, we might have faulty wiring, but why should this happen now?

DL: That's a good question. We need to figure out exactly this together. Do you have any ideas about this? About something else happening in the family that is important?

I asked briefly about changes happening in the family—deaths or illnesses, or someone leaving home for the first time. They said nothing major came to mind.

DL: This is what we will investigate together. This is the way I work with families. But it's very hard work, and we have to be together. Do you know what I'm saying?

Kip was leaning into the circle, and both parents looked drawn in to my invitation to "investigate" together. They both said they would do anything to help. The last thing I said to them was to make sure that Howard and Cindy attended our next meeting, and Mrs. McGinn assured me they would. As I left, I felt disappointed that Kip still hadn't talked, but I liked the family and felt we would be able to develop a language together. I was eager to meet Cindy and Howard.

The Second Family Session

Cindy did not appear for the second session, claiming (through Mrs. McGinn) that she could not miss a midterm review session after school. Howard did attend, however, and was an impressive young man, attractive and articulate. He began by apologizing for having missed "what apparently was an important meeting." His parents had told him that I said Kip might be expressing feelings for all of them, and he said, "That is absolutely correct." I asked him to elaborate, and he said that everyone in the family kept their feelings secret, including himself. He went on to say that he was not blaming his parents. He sympathized with how hard they worked and was surprised, frankly, that there had not been a major crisis sooner.

As he spoke, both parents smiled with pride at his competence. It seemed to me that Mrs. McGinn in particular gazed at him as though he were ethereal. Indeed, as the session continued, there appeared to be more excitement between mother and Howard than between the parents. This impression of Howard as supplying the libido for the family was heightened by his animated and almost flirtatious style of talking with me. His father was much more diffident with me in comparison.

I asked Howard about any ideas or fantasies he might have about what happened.

HOWARD: Kip has had a rough year in school, and he gets teased for not doing sports. He was saying stuff to my mom lately about how he was going to start playing football, and my mother said "no," because of his asthma. She told him about when he was little and he almost died of an attack. Kip is real sensitive, and I bet that freaked him out.

240

The McGinns: "Irrational" Mom and a Method to Madness

I asked to hear from everyone about Howard's thought.

MRS. MCGINN: I had that conversation with Kip. And I was trying to tell him why it would be dangerous if he played football—the grass and all the exertion.

I asked Mr. McGinn what he thought, and he said he was just all puzzled.

HOWARD [to Kip]: Hey, kid. Is that what freaked you out? Like you could never be normal at all, or it would really kill you?

KIP: You wouldn't freak out?

HOWARD: Well, man, why didn't you say something to me, except "I'm taking off; I can't stand my life." Don't we always talk?

The two brothers argued back and forth, and Kip really did seem very competent. Kip said he didn't want to "take off" and he didn't want to hurt himself. He just wanted to go home.

DL: It's great to hear you say that! Kip, why do you talk to Howard, but no one else?

Kip shrugged in response.

HOWARD: They talk to him weird. They always have. And he's bright and normal.

DL: Kip, why do your parents talk to you like you're not bright and normal?

KIP: You tell me!

DL: No, you have to tell me. If you're not weird, as Howard says, why don't you assert yourself?

KIP: They make it impossible to assert yourself.

DL: How?

KIP: Because everyone gets upset, that's how.

Both parents were pleased to hear this exchange, and I asked what it all meant to them.

MRS. MCGINN: It's true we baby him, and overdo it for him. We were told he was special. He is allergic to literally hundreds of things. When he was little, the doctors said his room should be kept free of dust. How do you keep a child's room free of dust? And you have to cook him all kinds of special foods.

There are good reasons for being protective of a sick child. The family had been persuaded by experts to maximize this protection, however, and they felt very confused and guilty about it. We spent some time discussing their experiences with allergists, nutritionists, guidance counselors, and teachers—almost all of which had been taken care of by Mrs. McGinn.

MR. MCGINN: I used to tell her she was in his hair too much.
MRS. MCGINN: I have to admit it. He did tell me that.
DL: Well, which one of you was keeping his room dust-free?
MR. MCGINN: Like I say, Margo did most of it.
MRS. MCGINN: He was working.

I was thinking about the possible relationships between Kip's symptoms and his parent's marriage, but did not yet have a clear formulation. Instead of challenging Mrs. McGinn's overvaluation of her husband's work—or the undervaluation of her own, revealed in their last statements—I simply decided to share with her my feelings of admiration for her.

DL: I think you did a heroic job in the face of all that advice. Some people would have thrown in the towel.

Mrs. McGinn began smiling like a person who had never heard a compliment. I told her so.

MR. MCGINN: To me, compliments are unnecessary. A person knows if they're doing a good job or not.

There was a brief pause, and Margo turned to Kip and asked if he had taken his medicine that day. This interaction provided a clear window on an important aspect of the family's life. My thoughts were as follows. The McGinns had a sick child; there was no denying that. Margo as mother was expected to take care of him, as well as doing all the other forms of caretaking in the house, which demanded many hours of work with no financial rewards, benefits, paid vacations, social prestige, or compliments from her husband. Instead of expressing her anger about all this *directly,* instead of finding a way to get from her husband the support and nurturance she needed, she, acting both as a woman in patriarchal society and

242

as an individual whose parents had taught her to expect little help from the world, had turned instead to her sons. In this instance in the session, she had ignored her husband's absurd comment about compliments, and instead became absorbed with Kip and his asthma.

I made some comments to them along these lines. The family sat quietly, looking at me, as though waiting for me to continue. Mr. McGinn drew his chair closer to the circle as we talked for several minutes about how Kip's asthma might be in part a distraction from the family's other problems, and how it might become much less problematic if the family dealt with those other problems.

Near the end of the session, Kip broke in by asking a question outright in a session for the first time, without being asked.

KIP: When can I get a pass home?
DL: Are you ready for a pass?
KIP: My group said I'd be ready for a pass when I could talk up to my family. And I just talked up.

I chose to take Kip on, in order to see how much he would engage me. I teased him by saying that the minute he got home he would go back into the woodwork, not take his medicine, and be back on our doorstep next week. He bantered with me in a competent way. He was still having medical tests done, and the doctors wanted to change his medication while he was still in the hospital in order to monitor potential allergic reactions. He had been doing very well on his unit, and had talked with a more sophisticated asthmatic patient about how the latter handled his medicine and his activity level, as well as the snide comments from peers.

I decided to give the family a task for the evening, to see if Kip could continue to act assertive with them. I suggested that they spend the evening on the inpatient unit, cutting up his food at dinner, buttoning his sweater if they thought he was cold, and speaking loudly to him in case he was hard of hearing. Only in this way could he practice telling them that he was a capable fifteen-year-old. I asked Kip to think of a "comeback" for them when they tried to stifle him. He chose "I'm fifteen, you know!" and "Stop that crap!"

The family appeared to like the idea. They were smiling when they left, and Howard said, "I have a feeling this therapy is going to be the best thing that ever happened to our family." I said something complimentary about Howard, and his parents beamed. Given the hypothesis I developed earlier in the book that the child has replaced the community in the twentieth century, I was astonished to hear Mrs. McGinn say, "Howard is our mother, father, son, friend, and brother." Mr. McGinn nodded warmly, "It's true."

The Third Family Session

The third family session was held two nights later. Mrs. McGinn started the session by suggesting that I call them by their first names, and I suggested they do the same with me. Margo reported that Cindy had sincerely intended to show up that night, but now had a virus which had kept her home from school. I was again curious about Cindy's absence and how the family experienced it. Kip said that Cindy was spoiled, and never had to do anything. Margo said, "She really has had the flu, and I was not going to rush her into coming." Howard's comment was jovial, saying she would probably monopolize the whole session anyway, and Gus continued this theme: "When you hear her back talk, Deborah, you may say, 'I liked it better without her.' "

There were suggestions in these comments that Cindy might have something bad to say, some "back talk," or else *too much* to say, and that somehow we should not "rush" toward hearing what it was. Gus changed the subject by saying that the task had gone very well, and that they were surprised at how "lively" Kip had been. Kip remained active in the session as well, asking if they could go off the unit for dinner that night. I asked him during this session to talk about his asthma, and what it had been like to be protected all his life. He spoke a good deal, and it was obvious that he had obtained an important perspective on himself from comparing his life with those of other patients on the unit. He said that at times it had been good to be sick because you "got out of things," like chores, and you "got to skip school." Actually, Kip had missed so much school one year that he had been held back and now, in his teens, he was being teased for having flunked and for being the only boy who had to stay back with the girls when the boys did some physical activity. His grades had been very poor this year, and a teacher had said in passing that he seemed to be "asking to be held back." Apparently this made him feel very hopeless. He had not told anyone, not even Howard, about his teacher's remark. Nor had he shared with anyone his feelings about the side effects of the steroids.

244

KIP: It's gross to be like this, always sick. Kids calling you "moonface" and "potato Kip." I just thought I wouldn't take my medicine for, you know, a little while, and nothing would happen. And how come Damien [another boy in his unit] has asthma and plays every sport? Why can't I?

The answer was that he could. Thousands of children who have asthma participate in sports as long as they know how to recognize signs of being overtaxed and are willing to stop when necessary and take their medications properly. The family had been living in a very small town when Kip first got sick, and the advice they had been given all along had been the most conservative. I scheduled a consultation with Kip and the rest of the family to meet with our doctors to discuss precisely these issues. Howard said he felt he should tell the truth and admit that he and Kip had played basketball and Frisbee a few times "on the sneak," and that Kip *did* know how to stop when he felt tired. Gus and Margo groaned about this for a few minutes, but I suggested that it was actually a good thing and pointed out that Kip's attacks had never been prompted by one of these events.
Kip was ecstatic over the possibilities of living a new life.

KIP: Now I can play ball with my own friends after Howard leaves.
MRS. MCGINN: If you do what they tell you to do, Kip.
DL: Excuse me, did you say "when Howard leaves?"

It turned out that Howard was leaving for an out-of-state college in the fall, and had been given early notification because of a scholarship. I remember this as the most shocking moment of the entire therapy with this family, and I told a colleague that it took my breath away.

MRS. MCGINN: I guess we forgot to mention it. You asked if Howard had recently left home, and we said no, because he had taken his own apartment a year ago already.
KIP: But he's always at our house.
HOWARD: I'm not. But I usually check in every day.
DL: So this is really a major change. This will really be the first time that you won't be seeing your family every day.
MR. MCGINN: It's true. But is that really such a big deal?

Clearly it was such a big deal that the family had not been able to share the information with me. I felt how deeply sad and even frightening it must be for them to be losing their "mother, father, son, friend, and brother."

> DL: I'm wondering if this could have something to do with Kip's acting depressed, and winding up in the emergency room.
> MR. MCGINN: How so?
> MRS. MCGINN: Actually, that crossed my mind. [*pause*] They've been so close. I was thinking that Kipper was going to miss his buddy a lot, and maybe that's why he's been acting so strange and feeling down.

I asked to hear from everyone about their feelings about Howard leaving. The first responses were, "We're proud of him," and, "It's time for him to go." Eventually they began talking about their sadness, about how they would miss him and how odd it would seem not to have him around. I had several thoughts as they talked. One was that Kip was acting out the family's depression over Howard's impending abandonment of the family. A related thought was that this crisis was a way of bringing Howard closer to the family—perhaps warning him not to go. (At one level this notion was validated by the simple fact that Howard, after all, was sitting with them in therapy sessions every evening instead of working overtime to make money for college as he had been doing.) My final thought was that Kip had somehow felt that as the next oldest son, he might be expected to take over Howard's place in the family. Perhaps he wondered whether *he* would have to become mother, father, son, friend, and brother to the family. This would have led him to threaten to run away or "take off" when he was feeling tough, and to mope around and act self-destructive when he was feeling his weakest. Evidence for this last thought came during the ensuing discussion, as Kip complained that his mother had already told him that he would be responsible for certain chores after Howard left. I commented that one thing Kip had been saying by his behavior in the past few weeks was that he did not feel capable of doing "Howard's work" in the family.

We spent the rest of the session exploring these ideas in their many forms. I was pleased to see the family asking each other questions and listening to each other.

> HOWARD: You know, I am not going to Mars.
> MR. MCGINN: Will you let Kip come down and visit you, or will you be too busy with friends and all?
> HOWARD: Will you *let* Kip come down and visit me, or will you treat him like he's two?

MRS. MCGINN: If Kip is responsible about his medicine, and goes to school, why shouldn't he take a train down to see Howard? What do you think, Gus?

MR. MCGINN: I think it's a fine idea. Will you take care of your new medicine and all?

KIP: Yes!!

We finished the session by completing a discharge plan that would allow Kip to leave the inpatient program after one successful overnight pass at home, which was planned for the next evening. I teased them that if Cindy did not attend the next session, there would be no discharge, and I felt that Gus and Margo sensed that I was only half joking about it.

The Fourth Family Session

Cindy joined us for the fourth family session. I greeted her happily. She resembled Margo in her face, but was taller and thinner. She had short red hair and was fashionably dressed. I asked her if the family had told her all about our earlier sessions.

CINDY: Bits and pieces.

DL: What have you found out?

CINDY: Well, I know that Kip has become a totally different person. That's about all I know. I mean he was always normal with his friends—or pretty much normal, but at home he used to act like an android. [*They all laugh.*] Some space individual.

MRS. MCGINN [*not unpleasantly*]: Cindy, don't be too hard on Kip.

CINDY [*mocking her mother's slight accent*]: "Don't be too hard on Kip."

This discussion continued a bit until Gus said proudly that Kip really had a good overnight pass. Margo added, "He really did. We all did. Except I still haven't done everything on my list." During the previous day, the parents had met with our medical staff and our school liaison specialist, and a list had been made of things they needed to do to help Kip's transition back to school: talk with the gym instructor and the principal, find him a math tutor, and so on. I asked Margo whether she planned to do all those things herself or share them with Gus.

MRS. MCGINN: I guess I didn't think. I know how he hates going to school. Hates it.

MR. MCGINN: I guess it's because I hated school when I was young. The nuns and all.

DL: But there aren't any nuns in Kip's school, are there?

MR. MCGINN: No, but—I don't know.

DL: Margo, do you want Gus's help?

MRS. MCGINN: Are you joking? I would love to split this list down the middle. Or, better yet, hand it over to him. Like, hey! It's your turn.

DL: Have you told him?

MRS. MCGINN: Hey, it's your turn.

MR. MCGINN: I know I should be doing a little more.

DL: Margo is saying "a lot more."

MR. MCGINN: Okay, okay. I guess you're right [*pleasantly*]. You're right. [*turning to Margo and affecting an Irish brogue:*] St. Margaret, will you give me half o' that list?

I was confused about the allusion to St. Margaret. It seemed half affectionate and half sardonic. Margo did not reject his acceptance of the task in order to complain about his tone, and I remained silent as well, eager to see how they would handle the list. They took their time and did it in a serious and constructive way that seemed fair to them both.

MRS. MCGINN [*to me*]: Gus really is quite wonderful, you know. I mean he does a lot more than a lot of husbands. I probably shouldn't complain so much.

CINDY: God, you guys act so nice in here. They wouldn't act so nice if they were home.

HOWARD: Cindy, that's why we're here, to get . . .

CINDY [*to me*]: As you can see, Howard is the big boss in the family.

DL: Howard is?

CINDY: Yeah.

DL: How is that?

CINDY: He likes to tell everyone what to do. He likes to act like he's the father and boss me around.

There was a pause, and I asked Cindy how she felt about Howard's going away.

CINDY: I'll miss him. But it's time for him to go on his own. And like I say, he's a big pain sometimes. Yeah, you are, Howard. Surprise, surprise.

I asked Cindy who she thought would miss him most in the family.

CINDY: Mom, probably.
DL: Why Mom?
CINDY: I guess I said Mom because she is the most weak—not weak, but hyper, one.
DL: How is that?
CINDY: Well, my dad is real calm, and she is sort of wild or real, real sensitive, like me.
HOWARD: Cindy, it's good to speak your mind, but you don't need to trash Mom. Mom is not wild.
CINDY: I'm not "trashing," Howard. I was just saying my opinion. See if you can listen for a minute, Howard. I'm nicer to Mom than you are. You're not even there half the time.
DL: Cindy, do you worry about your mom?
CINDY: Yeah, I do.
DL: What exactly do you worry about?
CINDY: I don't know. Like if anything would happen to her.
DL: Yeah, a lot of kids worry about their parents. What exactly worries you?

Cindy fidgeted with her chair and wouldn't look up. It took her a few minutes to finally say that a few years ago when her mother was really upset, she told Cindy that she had had a "mental breakdown" when Cindy was a baby. She said they had never talked about it since, and that Howard had once told her never to mention it to Kip. Kip immediately wanted to know what they were talking about, and the tension in the room felt very high. The fact that Cindy had brought up the taboo subject confirmed my suspicion that the family had indeed been "keeping her out," knowing, somehow, that she would open up the discourse about the past. I asked Margo and Gus about their feelings in the moment.

MRS. MCGINN: You said we would have to talk about this at some point.
DL: How do you feel about talking about it now?

249

MRS. MCGINN: It's not going to get any easier. And it might be good for the kids to get their feelings out. [*She starts to cry quietly.*]

MR. MCGINN: Why do we have to do this? It happened over ten years ago. You can see how upset she gets just at the thought of it. She was in a good mood when she walked in this room.

MRS. MCGINN: Gus, I'm crying and it hurts, but I do think it's better to talk.

Gus had become quite red in the face.

DL: Gus, are you afraid that something bad could come as a result of discussing the past?

MR. MCGINN: It will take her all week to get back. She'll be hysterical, and the kids have to go to school all upset.

When he said "all week," I thought he might be referring to the fact that Kip was about to be discharged and I would not be seeing them for a week. I nodded supportively all the while he was talking, and then made a comment about this being the last inpatient session. I said this might well be a week when they might want to call me to check in, or to get some extra support, especially if someone was feeling really upset—but even if no one was.

I think my offer of help by phone provided a feeling of containment for Gus, and allowed him to soften. His shoulders relaxed and he said, with much less agitation in his voice, "My motto is, 'Forgive and forget.' " I wanted him to know that the purpose of this work was not to lay blame. I said, "My motto is 'Forgive and remember.' So that history doesn't repeat itself, and the past can really be the past."

After a few more minutes of discussion, Margo began to tell the story of her hospitalization. She said that of course she loved all of her children, but that it had been very hard to have them so close together. She especially had wanted to wait a while after Kip was born, because she was tired from having two little ones and Kip had been sick as a baby.

MRS. MCGINN: Maybe it sounds selfish, but I just didn't want to take care of anybody for a while. I was worn out.

Gus had apparently understood this, and had gone to their parish priest to explain that Kip was sick, their financial situation was poor, and his wife felt overwhelmed, and asked if it were possible to use contraception. The priest gave him an emphatic "no." Margo said she knew how devout Gus was, but that nonetheless she was crushed that he would show more respect for the Church's wishes than for her own. She soon became pregnant again.

MRS. MCGINN: I felt like a nonperson. I don't know how else to say it.

DL: Can you try to tell us how that was for you?

MRS. MCGINN: A person with no rights. Like something you wind up and it cleans up everyone's mess and cooks and has babies and gets up at dawn and does it over again. Now I feel like shit saying this. You know I love them, but I really couldn't manage. And one day, when Cindy was two, I just stopped coping. Gus found me crying and I couldn't stop. I couldn't take care of the kids anymore. I couldn't even take care of myself. They put me in a mental asylum, which is probably where I belonged.

MR. MCGINN: It wasn't exactly a—

MRS. MCGINN: Yes, it was. It was exactly. Do you think it was like this place? There were shock treatments, and terrible drugs, and cloth . . . [*crying*].

HOWARD: What kind of cloth, Mom?

MRS. MCGINN: Cloth restraints.

The children were all crying, and Gus had tears in his eyes. I, myself, felt full of sadness and indignation. Margo's account sounded like a page from *Women and Madness,* Phyllis Chesler's 1972 exposé about women's treatment in the psychiatric establishment. Margo had committed the sin of being overwhelmed by the responsibilities of motherhood in a world that provides mothers little support. Instead of assistance, she was treated to drugs and confinement—the therapy of forgetting. She had been denied the right to control her sexuality by one patriarchal institution, the Church, and then been confined by another, the hospital. Gus McGinn, hardly the stereotype of the old-world patriarch, with his diffident and kind manner, had nonetheless been the implementer of the patriarchal system. The will of God the Father had come before the desires and health of his wife.

When Margo finished speaking, there was a long silence, and I asked everyone what he or she was thinking or feeling. The children asked Margo questions, Howard challenged his father about his decision to hospitalize her, and Gus talked about how different people's thinking was in those days. I intervened at this point to ask Gus to expand on this, to talk about the terrible pressures he must have been under. He said it had been very difficult for him, and he hoped everyone would understand that. I again tried to draw him out with a sympathetic comment, but he was not able to say anymore. He said that he thought all the kids, not just Cindy, still worried about Margo. I asked Gus if he himself were worried about Margo, and he said no.

DL: Kip, is it true what your dad says, that you worry about Mom?
KIP: Yeah, I guess. Not that she would go to the hospital, but that she might get mad and leave. Like when she fights with Dad.

Margo reached out for Kip and Cindy, who were sitting across from her, and said she would never, ever leave them and that they should not worry about her. Gus gave Margo some tissues; Howard left the room to get her a glass of water. Eyes were dried and hands patted, and there was a feeling of relief in the room. In the time remaining I asked Margo if she had any idea what had been going on in her own family when she was two years old, saying that that was as important to understand as what had been happening in her present family back then. Margo at first said she had no idea, but corrected herself and said she knew her mother had started drinking when Margo was a baby.

DL: How do you know that?
MRS. MCGINN: Well, her drinking was a problem as long as I can remember, and my brother, Paul, once told me she had started drinking when I was just a baby. But he didn't tell me more than that, or else I don't remember.
DL: I'm just wondering if your mother felt overwhelmed herself when you were born, or was nervous about having a daughter.
MRS. MCGINN: It could be. I just don't know. She sure seemed to get along with her son better than with her daughter. We had no closeness at all; I could do nothing right in her eyes. And as time went on, I went out of my way to get her upset.
DL: Margo, how did you feel about having a baby girl?
MRS. MCGINN: I was just upset about having a *baby,* period! And it being a girl, I don't think made it easier. I was used to boy babies, and I did wonder how we would get along.
DL: I was thinking that when Cindy was born, you maybe were afraid that an equally troubled mother-daughter relationship was in store for you. That was all you had known.
MRS. MCGINN: That's true.
DL: Maybe you were thinking, This cute little baby girl is going to grow up and act just as rotten to me as I did to my mother! Not a very cheery thought.
MRS. MCGINN [*laughing*]: No.

DL: Especially when you were stressed about other things.

MRS. MCGINN: But, you know, Cynthia and I have a good relationship. She is a wonderful daughter, and I am so proud of our relationship.

DL: That's a credit to you both. It's a shame your mother never told you what was so upsetting about having a daughter. You could have thought through all those things before you even became a mother.

MR. MCGINN: Margo's family was not one for talking. They are cold, hard people, really.

DL: I believe you.

MRS. MCGINN: It's funny to talk about it this way because it makes you feel less guilty. Like my family had a part, and the Church had a part, and the doctors, and it wasn't all my fault.

MR. MCGINN: You forgot me. Don't you blame me for it?

MRS. MCGINN: I did, because you were like a patsy for those priests. But when it was all over, it was like you really changed and became really sweet again, and you really helped me when Kip started getting sick.

Gus obviously felt some guilt about the past, which would have accounted in part for his not wanting to approach the subject in the first place. Another piece of information that emerged from Margo's comment was that Kip's asthma had provided the family with the important service of bringing Gus into the family, allowing him to assuage his guilt for not having taken better care of Margo, and allowing Margo to demand more from her husband without asking for help for herself.

Before we left, I made an appreciative comment to Cindy about bringing up the subject of Margo's hospitalization, and to the rest of the family for "hanging in" for such a difficult session. I was glad that this painful discussion had happened while the family was still feeling the extra "containment" that the inpatient experience offers. This led us to talking about their feelings about leaving the hospital, and taking care of the details about Kip's discharge.

Before we said good-bye I wanted to congratulate them again for opening up, something that is always important to emphasize in conflict-avoidant families.

DL: I want to tell you one more thing that you should feel good about. As difficult as this is for you, you should know that there are families who can never show any disagreements, or any conflict—everything has to be nice and rosy all the time, and the past can never be brought up. Those families seem to have the greatest problems of all.

MR. MCGINN: You mean there's hope for us?
DL: Of course, Gus, and I'm glad we're in this together.

When they left that night, Gus had his arm around Margo. I did indeed feel warm toward the family, and was happy to be treating them.

The Fifth Family Session

I did not hear from the family all week, and assumed that there had been no crisis. On the evening of the first outpatient session, Kip walked into my office first and picked up a small Frisbee on my toy shelf and threw it to Howard. Howard tossed it back and Kip tossed it to his dad, who threw it to Margo who threw it to Cindy. Howard said he and Kip had been throwing the Frisbee around a lot since Kip got home from the hospital. They continued to toss it around, including to me, and Howard said, "You know, this is one of the few games you can play in somebody's office." Cindy said that was why she liked it, because it was safer than baseball or football.

MRS. MCGINN: That's why I like it too.
MR. MCGINN: Watch that lamp, Howard.

A number of themes emerged during this banter. Above all, I sensed a good deal of relief. The fact that they were able to come in and be so playful suggested that they had had a good week together and that the previous session had had a good effect. I also wondered whether the family was trying to tell me that they were not up for any more "high-risk" activity—only safe topics instead. After a pause I asked whether anyone had thoughts or feelings about the last session.

MR. MCGINN [*jovially*]: Just one. I was saying to Margo, "Do you think we could be like one of those terrible anger-avoidance families just for a few days or so?"
MRS. MCGINN: Gus was wondering if we could have some of those people over for dinner and try to catch it.
DL: Are you by any chance saying that you need a rest after that heavy session last week?

The McGinns: "Irrational" Mom and a Method to Madness

MR. MCGINN: It was a bit of a workout.

DL: That's a good word. It was a workout.

After a silence, Margo smiled and said, "I was thinking about my parents this week." No one stirred or objected. I encouraged Margo to continue, and she ended up giving a good deal of information about her family of origin. She spoke of coming from an affluent family who had emigrated from France to Canada before she was born. Her paternal grandparents had remained in France, and she knew nothing about them. Her mother had been raised in an orphanage, and she knew nothing about her maternal grandparents. Margo said that her father resembled Charles de Gaulle, and that he was so stern, he could make even "good morning" sound like criticism. He was a journalist and traveled a great deal; while at home, he was always at work. Although he had had little time for her, he seemed to admire the accomplishments of her brother, Paul, who had been a brilliant student and was now a cardiologist. Her mother idolized Paul, and he was mother's companion when father was not around. Margo, who was ten years younger than Paul, felt that she was a "nuisance" in her house and, in fact, had been in convent schools throughout her adolescence.

Her mother had apparently been an extremely beautiful woman who met her husband when she was very young. Margo's mother had made it known to Margo that beauty was extremely important, and that since she, Margo, had little of it, her life was going to be difficult. Her parents did not believe in educating daughters, and Margo simply left home at a young age, and communicated with them very rarely. She had introduced them to Gus, and they thoroughly disapproved of him since he was Irish and simply not up to their standards.

This account provided one explanation for Margo's choice of Gus for a partner. He was in many ways the opposite of her family. He was affable and easygoing, without a touch of the snob. He was perhaps chosen to give her the acceptance and affection she had been denied by her parents. On the other hand, he was perhaps chosen also because she unconsciously sensed his potential for abandoning her and leaving her in the company of her oldest son—something that constituted a repetition of her family of origin while appearing to be a radical departure from it. In all marriages, as object-relations theorists have told us, there are elements of both reproducing the parents' marriage and trying to repair the past by choosing a partner different from the opposite-sex parent.

Margo's account of her family, particularly the parts about her mother being raised in an orphanage and then sending her own daughter out to boarding schools, gave me further insight into Margo's early response to our therapy. She had felt rejected by me, and angry as well, before we had even spoken to each other. Deprived of tender and attentive parents, probably from birth, she simply expected indifference or hostility from me. Because I had nurtured her on that first day, I seemed to have become the "good mother" to her, which suggested, for one thing, that I might be able to replace Howard in his role as the great sustainer of the family until more work could be done with the marriage.

The children asked more questions about their grandparents, and the more details that emerged about their interactions, the more impressed I was with how Margo had tried to reconnect with them over the years. She seemed to be fairly in touch with her complex and contradictory feelings of regret, longing, and hatred toward them and of envy toward her brother. By the end of this discussion, I felt it had been a good thing that she broke off with them for some years. Nonetheless, I hoped that she would find some way of ultimately reconnecting with them. Here the feminist viewpoint overlaps the Bowenian one in preferring to avoid "cutoffs" where possible.

Approximately halfway through the session, during a long pause, Kip said to me, "So ask me how I'm doing." I did, and learned that he had been doing very well, indeed. He had been responsible for his medications and he had been enjoying school, especially gym.

DL: Gus, it sounds like you did your part of the list.
MRS. MCGINN: Oh, he did. I am so happy about how that turned out.

Gus had balked at sharing the list at first, and in fact had "forgotten" a couple of times to do what he was supposed to but, once involved in the tasks, he became absorbed in them. He had interviewed several tutors for Kip, and talked with the principal and guidance counselors.

Without making a hero out of Gus, I expressed my sincere pleasure with how he had handled the task. I asked him in the course of this discussion whether his father would have done this sort of thing for him. He said, "Well, no, not really. He wasn't the type to get involved with kids."

DL: What kind of guy was he, Gus?
MR. MCGINN: My father was a good man. I would say he was a good man and an excellent father.

Any therapist, of course, would hear the contradiction in Gus's statement, but to the feminist ear, it had particular poignance. A man who "wasn't the type to get involved with his kids" is described as an excellent father. No mother, we can be sure, has ever been described in these terms.

According to psychoanalytic thinking, idealization is a defense mechanism that can serve as a way of protecting the ego from the fear of reprisals for one's aggressive impulses toward a loved person. (It is in fact not unusual for the more idealized parent to turn out to be the one who was an abuser of some sort.) One would assume in Gus's case that he could not face his hostile feelings toward his father and felt guilty for even having them. Since his father was no longer living, Gus idealized his father as "excellent" so as not to have to deal with his more complex feelings about him. I asked Gus specifically what he admired about his father. He said he admired his father because he was cheerful and humorous, and conveyed authority without ever being brash. He also admired his father because he had worked his way up from poverty to be successful in business. Gus's grandparents had lived in a cold water flat, and Gus's father had worked from the time he was seven years old. As an adult, the father ended up selling insurance and was considered one of the most brilliant salesmen around.

MR. MCGINN: He could sell you your own pants. They say he would sometimes meet a friend for a beer and say— this is not business, now, just a friendly beer. And before the evening was over, the man has bought insurance for himself, his family, and the pet canary.

DL: What did he want for you?

MR. MCGINN: He wanted me to take over and learn what he could teach me. My mother wanted me to be a priest! But I liked the girls too much for that. Anyway, I knew I didn't have the natural talent for business that my father had.

Gus spoke of his mother as "caring," but "excitable" and dependent. She leaned on him a lot due to his father's absence. She would cook dinner for the two of them, and he would say the rosary with her at night.

MR. MCGINN: She wouldn't talk against my father or anything, but you sort of knew. He would go out late—if you know what I mean. He was a devilish handsome man, and he had a reputation, I guess, with the ladies. But he was good to my mother, too. He would have given her anything she wanted.

Margo commented that Gus seemed to feel like he had failed his father, and she thought that was a big problem for him. My thought at that

257

moment was that Gus had had little chance to really succeed, because he had received two contradictory mandates from the family: to be successful like father, but to stay home and take care of mother. (The contemporary family *requires disloyalty* in this regard.) Gus's compromise was to go into sales and to marry a woman who was, in his eyes, like his mother. To Gus, Margo was demanding and vulnerable—a woman he could alternately take care of and then abandon, as his father had done with his mother. He could then leave Margo in the safekeeping of Howard, repeating another pattern in his early experience. I was struck with the fact that both Gus and Margo came from families in which the son became partner to the mother. Howard's current position in the family was clearly overdetermined.

I asked about Gus's father's death, and Gus said, "He died at age sixty of a heart attack when Kip was seven." This phrasing naturally made me wonder if the father's death had something to do with Kip in particular. I asked Gus how his father's death had been for him, and he said something to the effect that it hadn't hit him hard. Margo interposed here, and said she thought it *had* hit him hard and that he had been very "down" during the following year and had had a bad year in business. She recalled the one-year anniversary of Gus's father's death, when the family gathered at their house after a commemorative Mass.

MR. MCGINN: I know what you are going to say. It was that day that Kip had had the terrible asthma attack. I had mowed the grass because there were a lot of people coming over and we were going to have some lunch and whatnot outdoors, and Kip being out there in that freshly mowed grass, and being allergic, he had a terrible attack and we rushed him to the hospital. [*pause*] And it was a close call.

The rest of the family sat rapt in attention, and Gus's voice broke as he spoke.

MR. MCGINN: You can't imagine how I felt that day. It was such a mess with the family there, with my father's Mass and all. I felt I had really hurt him, forgotten him.
DL: Do you mean your father or Kip?
MR. MCGINN: I mean Kip. He was only seven. I should have known to keep him away from that freshly mowed grass.

The confusion expressed in my question was real, not feigned. Gus had said, "I felt I had really hurt him, forgotten him." From what he had said

258

earlier, I knew that in some sense this was a statement of how his father had treated Gus: he had hurt Gus by forgetting him. (The "hurt," I assumed, had been covered up by idealization.) On the anniversary of the death, the father's forgetting or abandonment of his son was simply repeated as Gus forgot about Kip's health. And instead of killing his father, as per Gus's Oedipal fantasy, it was the son who was nearly killed. In any case, there was a reproduction of violence and forgetting between fathers and sons in this incident which was highly significant. If Gus had not had to rush Kip to the hospital that day, he might have had to experience his real feelings for his father—his sadness at the loss of father, his shame at having failed him, his fear of dying at a relatively young age also, the resentment of being left to take care of his mother—and the revival of the original constellation of Oedipal desires.

As Gus talked about this subject, he showed more emotion than he had when discussing Margo's crisis, but I sensed that he was holding back tears. This made me think about the *wheezing* of the asthmatic, which psychoanalytic thinkers, following Freud's original notion of conversion reactions, have often viewed as a suppressed or distorted *cry*. Until that moment, I had not thought of linking Kip's asthma to his father's depression, but instead to Margo's. I had thought of the asthma as a replacement for her depression and a way of stabilizing the marriage. This connection is not necessarily false, but is probably incomplete. I think it reflects the tradition of associating children's symptomatology to their "inadequate" mothers. I suspect that therapists of all schools of thought have underestimated the links between children's symptoms and their *fathers'* psychopathology. In this case, the possibility that Kip was acting out something for his father seemed very compelling. Furthermore, this thought led me to wonder if Kip's recent crisis was an attempt to save Gus once again from a terrible grief, this time from grieving over Howard's departure, thereby reexperiencing his father's death. If this were the case, it would be especially important for Gus to do some grieving for his father so that he could let Howard go less ambivalently, and Kip would not be sacrificed in the process. I posed some questions to Gus about depression. He denied ever feeling suicidal, and said that when he felt "down" he worked longer, or occasionally talked to his cousin who was a priest. Sounding a little irritated, he said, "Believe me, there's not a lot of time to be depressed when you have a demanding job and three kids, one with a lot of health problems"—again making a link between Kip's poor health and his avoidance of his own emotions. I asked how Gus was feeling in the moment, and he said, "nothing in particular."

DL: You sound a little angry. Are you?

MR. MCGINN: Again, we're going on and on about something that happened ten years ago.

I nodded supportively, wanting to contain his anger, which I thought was displaced from his father onto me.

DL: Gus, if your dad were here, what would you want to tell him?

MR. MCGINN [*after a pause*]: If I could tell him something? I would want him to see how great the kids have turned out. Despite our problems. They're all bright. They're all good kids. I love 'em. [*Starts to cry for the first time in therapy.*]

DL: He would be so proud of these grandchildren of his.

There was a pause and Margo said, "He would be. It makes me sad. And, you know, mad, that he worked himself to death."

Gus was really crying now, and Margo, without hesitation, moved over to be close to him. I broke a long silence and said, "Gus, there are ways you miss your father, and admire him. Are there ways you would like to be different from him?"

MR. MCGINN: Yeah, I don't want to keel over when I'm sixty. I want to take time to smell the roses. I want to be with my family more.

It was nearing the end of the session, and I asked the kids to say or ask anything they wanted. When Gus saw their sad and intent faces, he asked me if this were really good for them—Wouldn't they just get upset? I said that they might feel upset, but that it wouldn't last. We would keep talking about it until it felt more straightened out. He sighed deeply when I said, "straightened out." I again said that they could phone me during the week. I made some appreciative comments to Gus for showing a wonderful part of himself. He had "survived another workout." Before leaving, Gus threw the Frisbee to me, smiling, but with what seemed like a lot of force. I caught it.

The Sixth Family Session

The sixth session was a couple's session. I had suggested it as something I always do, in order to fill out the history on both sides of the family and to ask about things that are not appropriately addressed in front of the younger generation.

Gus walked in the door first on this evening, and was the first to speak, admiring a painting on the wall, calling it "beautiful." He seemed to be feeling more connected to the therapy, and I felt very warm toward him for making good use of the last session. Margo and Gus said that Kip was doing very well at school, and was taking gym. After a pause, I asked them to tell me the story of their relationship from the beginning.

Margo said that she had met Gus at a dance when she was nineteen, and thought that he was the handsomest man she had ever seen. Gus returned that he thought Margo was "real sexy with her French accent." They started to date, and when she would tell him about her unhappy childhood, he would comfort her as he had his own mother.

Throughout the session, the couple recounted different aspects of their history, and I pointed out relevant repetitions from the past, as well as differences from it. Margo had felt rejected by her father, and understandably wanted to be with a man who would make her feel special. Gus had done that by bringing her gifts, cooking for her, comforting her about her childhood, and setting limits on her outbursts. In this respect, their relationship had been reparative of her early experience. However, Margo's concept of intimacy with a man, due most deeply to her experience of her parents' marriage, necessarily included the expectation that he would devalue and desert her. And indeed, Gus began spending evenings drinking at a local bar soon after they were married—although he apparently had not had affairs.

MR. MCGINN: I have never been unfaithful.

MRS. MCGINN: I honestly believe him, that he was just at McMurphy's. Any time I would go down there looking, he was there.

DL: But how was that time for you, Margo?

MRS. MCGINN: I was a new mother—nervous as could be. Guilty that I had done something that made Gus not want to be with us. It wasn't the happiest of times! After I was in the hospital, I told him if he kept going out, I would leave him. My counselor told me to do that. And

261

luckily, he really changed after that. And then the whole world seemed to change. I decided when Cindy went to first grade that I was going to work. Gus had always said "over my dead body." Imagine a person saying that because you want to work!

MR. MCGINN: Let's not forget that working mothers is a pretty new thing. It wasn't done back then unless you were dirt poor. And I didn't know if Margo would be able to handle the stress of a job, given how high-strung and irrational she can get.

My countertransferential feelings of protectiveness toward Margo were extremely strong.

DL: Margo, how does it feel when Gus calls you "irrational"?

MRS. MCGINN: Shitty. But he's right. You've seen me cry and fuss and carry on. He doesn't do that. He is very rational. It makes sense what Gus does, even if you don't agree with it.

DL: Including the things you've mentioned tonight, like his sitting in a bar while you took care of the children?

MRS. MCGINN: Well, if he does something, he doesn't make a big drama about it. He just does it.

MR. MCGINN: I haven't cried but two or three times since I was a wee boy—and you saw one of them the other evening.

What was becoming obvious was that the word *irrational* was being used as a synonym for being emotionally expressive and, especially, "angry." We spent some time that evening, and on later occasions, discussing these words. I suggested that Gus, like his father, perhaps, was actually not emotionally expressive *enough,* and that this was "simply not healthy." I went on to introduce the term "emotional literacy" to describe Margo's competence in articulating affect. I had heard her express, discriminate, and identify a range of feelings in their nuances: shame, envy, chagrin, tenderness, despair, regret—whereas Gus's emotional vocabulary seemed smaller in comparison. The deliberate legitimation of affect is an essential part of feminist therapy, for patients of both sexes. We expect, perhaps, that because women are socialized to be expressive, they are not as embarrassed by feelings as men are. Very often, however, women like Margo are ashamed of their adroitness in communicating emotion. While being socialized for competence in this area, they have also been socialized to judge the "rational"—or, more precisely, the *nonaffective*—as superior to emotion or passion.

Another subject discussed in this session was Gus's work. Margo said that one of her biggest frustrations with Gus was the fact that he stayed in the same job. He had refused a promotion several years back, which would have involved more status and a slight increase in salary. She complained that he wouldn't consider it, and wouldn't even argue it with her. Since Gus's father had been a workaholic, I asked whether this decision had anything to do with his father.

> MR. MCGINN: You bet it did! Don't think that wasn't a tough decision for me. I knew how much you wanted it, but I resent working *five* long days for those bastards. Why would you expect me to work *seven,* for an extra five dollars? You always said your father did nothing but work. And if *my* father hadn't worn himself out—
>
> MARGO [*gently*]: He'd still be here.

Margo was obviously touched by his forthrightness, and I asked what she was thinking.

> MRS. MCGINN: Thinking I'm glad I lived to see this day. That Gus would actually talk. And I would know what he was thinking. And feeling.
>
> MR. MCGINN: Tell me, Deborah, do you think this was a wrong decision on my part—irresponsible?
>
> DL: I happen to think you're right not to want to kill yourself like your father did. I admire your choice.

Margo was still smiling at Gus.

> DL: You don't mind if he gets a little irrational at times?
>
> MRS. MCGINN: It turns me on.

Margo eventually asked me why I thought she had pushed him so hard about the job. She felt selfish and stupid about it, since in fact, she already thought he worked too hard. This question took us back to Margo's family, and to my feminist interpretation of her experience. Instead of *being* a brilliant and ambitious and competent person like her brother, Margo was conditioned to marry someone brilliant and ambitious. That was to be her sign of worth in the world.

> MRS. MCGINN: That's so true.
>
> DL: You're not the only woman who feels that way.
>
> MRS. MCGINN: Meaning?

DL: I mean a lot of women feel: "If only I were a more worthwhile and attractive woman, I wouldn't be stuck with this man who doesn't want to get promoted."

Women are socialized to overvalue men's achievements, especially relative to their own. As Virginia Woolf once said, women are taught to "reflect men at twice their size." It seems to me that many women complain about their men's ambition and criticize their faults because what they *cannot* say is, "How do you expect me to idealize you and overvalue you if you are going to act like this?" I find that in therapy as women come to feel *defined by their own competence,* especially in the public sphere, they are less critical of their husbands' choices because they are *less dependent on their husbands' accomplishments for their own self-evaluation.*

I asked Margo how she felt about being promoted herself.

MRS. MCGINN: I like my job, Deborah, I told you that, but I always tell Gus this: When I get some help around the house, I'll talk about doing more on my job.

This led us into a discussion of housework. Like most mothers with outside jobs, Margo worked full-time and did all the housework. The only exception was that Gus occasionally cooked dinner.

MR. MCGINN: Let's remember this if we're keeping score. Margo had all those years off before she began to work.
DL: Gus, is there a dictionary over there?
MR. MCGINN: No, why?
DL: Because I want to know the definition of *work.*
MRS. MCGINN: Why that?
DL: Who raised the three kids and did the housework? Did you have a maid?
MRS. MCGINN: Yeah, me.
MR. MCGINN: Well, in my family, the philosophy was that men didn't go into the kitchen.

At this point we had started to laugh.

DL: Well, I want to tell you my philosophy. It's very complicated. "We all make it dirty; we all clean it up."
MRS. MCGINN: Damn it, Gus, doesn't that sound rational to you?

More bantering and teasing followed, but by the end of the session they had agreed to clean the house together on Saturday.

Before they left, Gus thanked me for understanding why he didn't want to take the promotion. Although he had never admitted it, he had always felt a little bad about not having taken it.

DL: Oh, Gus, you're not the only man who refuses to work his way to ulcers and a coronary. I really *do* respect your decision very much.

The phrase that I had used with both of them, "You're not the only woman" or "the only man" who feels a certain way, or does certain things, is a good means of introducing items that specifically pertain to gender socialization. It is a gentle way of seeding the therapy with the knowledge that behaviors have social as well as personal meaning and origins, which is sometimes opened up to discussion at later points in the therapy.

BETWEEN SESSIONS

Toward the end of the following week, Margo called asking permission to skip the next session. She said she and Gus had had a wonderful week, had cleaned together on Saturday and then gone out together on Saturday night. She said, giggling, that they had had "the best week of married life in a long time." Gus had seen an ad for a four-day getaway to Florida and they wanted to go, if I thought it was all right. Kip had been in good spirits, taking care of himself well, and Howard said he didn't mind looking after Kip and Cindy while they went away. I said it sounded fine, but that they shouldn't forget to come back.

After we hung up, I had a mixture of feelings, mostly, but not entirely, pleasant. I was pleased that they had had a lovely week, and Margo's implication was that they had enjoyed each other sexually as well. This trip could hardly be considered a "flight" in the negative sense, since they had made provisions for the kids and had called to ask for my blessing. Nonetheless, I had an odd feeling of resentment. I joked to a colleague that they must have been reading Selvini Palazolli's articles (referring to the "Tonight we are out" prescription) instead of mine. I interpret my reaction as some Oedipal jealousy about seeing the parents go off to have fun without me. This was a clue that I had truly taken over Howard's position in the family. My final thought was a question about whether Kip would have a problem with his asthma during the week in order to bring the parents back early. As it turned out, he did not. However, Cindy called during the week, saying that she had had a "terrible, *very* upsetting fight" with a teacher and needed to talk about it. I told her we could talk on the phone, or she could take the bus down to my office if she liked, after school. She jumped at the opportunity.

Seventh Session

Cindy was an excellent student, and had a great deal of respect for her teachers. During the week, the drama teacher, a woman in her fifties to whom Cindy felt very close, had criticized her for something Cindy had forgotten to do. The teacher had walked away saying something in a gruff tone. Cindy was heartbroken, although this particular teacher was known for her stern ways. Cindy was alternately angry, indignant, sad, and afraid she would be replaced in the play. She cried as we talked, and I gave her tissues. As we talked, she asked me through tears if I thought it was bad that she cried over little things.

> DL: You mean like your teacher?
> CINDY: Yeah. And all kinds of things. I had a boyfriend last year who used to say I was weird because I would cry about things one minute, and then be happy the next. Like a split personality.

I said that most teenagers felt the way she did. She talked on about the boyfriend, about teachers, about being picked on by her brothers. At length she asked, "Deborah, do you think I'm irrational like my mom?"

Again, this word! I realized that having two family members psychiatrically hospitalized might make an adolescent wonder about her own stability, but I was also aware that this particular word belonged to Gus and that Cindy was now using it against herself. I pacified myself with the thought that we had at least dealt with this in session; I had not let it slip by. Cindy, however, had not been present during that session.

> DL: Cindy, I don't think you or your mom is irrational. I'm being really straight with you. Your mom is brave and smart and loving and expressive. I think you are, too.

Cindy would probably continue to struggle with these questions all her life, and I had no illusions about permanently absolving her of her fears with this one statement. A girl who grows up with a father who views her mother as irrational or crazy (and with a mother who views herself this way) has a very good chance of believing that she shares much more with her mother than their gender. We spent the rest of the hour talking about the similarities and differences between her mother and herself, and exploring what she had thought and felt about the account of her mother's hospitalization. I realized then that her talking about the rejecting drama teacher might have been a way of talking about having felt rejected by her mother as a baby. Such feelings could have been rekindled by her mother's leaving on vacation that week.

My assurances and explanations were meant to improve the maternal introject, which father, in collusion with the psychiatric establishment, the Church, and mother herself, had helped corrupt. I wanted her to begin to change the internal representation of her mother, on which she naturally based her own sense of identity and goodness.

Before we ended I asked what she was thinking of doing about her drama teacher. She said, "I should go talk to her during lunch tomorrow. I'll finish memorizing my lines tonight and go see her tomorrow."

DL: Cindy, you are bright, articulate, beautiful, and dramatic. If the coach gave you such a big part in that play, I have the feeling she likes you a lot. How could she not?

The Eighth Family Session

Gus and Margo came in looking refreshed and lightly tanned. Cindy had told them about her talk with me, and they were pleased. Cindy told me right away that the drama coach had been nice when she went to see her the next day, and Cindy remained more animated and involved throughout this session than she had been previously. Kip was open and talkative, and spent time in the session asking the parents if he could spend the summer at the shore with his cousins. Later on, Cindy said she wanted to bring up something that had been bothering her.

CINDY: You know, Dad, I really don't like when you criticize my clothes, all right?

267

MR. MCGINN: What's all this? When did I do that?

CINDY: Always, and you said that thing about how my black skirt makes me look like a sleazebag.

MR. MCGINN: I said a *floozy* not a *sleazebag,* and that was—saints alive!—three weeks ago.

CINDY: Well, I'm not a floozy, or whatever you said. And you would never call Howard that, no matter how he dressed!

MR. MCGINN: Cindy, Howard is nineteen and a boy. You are a young girl, and spectacularly pretty, and on the—shy side. I will protect you, of course!

I commented that a shy daughter wouldn't speak up so assertively to her father, and Cindy yipped with pleasure. I interpreted this behavior of Cindy's as evidence of her feeling better about herself, and more in touch with her anger at father who had sometimes made her feel bad about herself—and about her mother. This would seem to follow logically from her session alone with me. We pursued the issue of Gus's need to keep Cindy his little girl, and several "double standard" issues in the McGinn house that defined what boys and girls were allowed to do. The fact that Cindy had used an example with sexual content (her father commenting on her sexy clothing) might have been related to the parents' going away for a romantic outing for the first time. Such a change was bound to draw some sexual tensions in the rest of the family.

Gus seemed to listen well to Cindy, although he disagreed with her on some points. Margo supported Cindy, but did not take over the father-daughter argument.

Later in the session, Howard also took his turn attacking Gus.

HOWARD: My complaint about you, Dad, is that you don't keep things together in the house. I mean, now you're taking care of Kip, and that's great, but whenever I come over there, the lawn isn't mowed, the kitchen faucet still drips.

GUS [*to me*]: Howard is a perfectionist, and I can never do anything right.

HOWARD: Maybe I am. My car is perfect. I bought a car when I was eighteen, and I keep it great. I can't understand my father. You should see his car.

Howard, I thought, was also reacting to his parents' tryst. Suddenly it was important that his machine was better than his father's.

268

DL [*laughing*]: I guess this is dump-on-Gus day. Howard, I drove a ten-year-old Volvo until it was pronounced dead on arrival by my mechanic. Maybe your father is just different from you.

I knew that Howard had always seen me as his ally, and had probably assumed that his values would always coincide with mine. I took advantage of the difference to inch the family away from making Howard the measure of all things. My alliance with father would have to push Howard on his own a bit, and would also endorse the conjugal happiness.

I suggested openly to the family that mom and dad's going away had raised a lot of feelings. Suddenly everyone was jumping on Gus. Were they afraid he was going to take mom away and leave them stranded? I asked them to discuss this.

Howard and Cindy denied such feelings, but they did express envy that their parents got to go on vacation while they were left back here "in the cold." This led to a discussion about Howard's packing up for his own journey out of the family to college. We devoted the remainder of the session to these issues. This included talking about how Howard had come to play all the parts in the family, how he was their "air supply" (my term), and how the family would carry on without him. In my view it was important that Howard separate from the family in a way that would make him really gone and yet really still connected to them. That is: *both* aspects of the transition of a family member out of the household must be highlighted in a feminist approach to therapy. The traditional family therapy motto: "Thou shalt leave home!" expresses only half of the human dilemma (albeit a very important half). The other half is finding a way to *remain at home* with one's family—to remain connected with them—for the sake of both the young person and the rest of the family. Thus we talked both about how good a time Howard would have at the university on his own, *and* about how he should remain conscientious about calls and letters home.

This turned out to be a very full and constructive discussion in which everyone participated, and yet there was a piece missing—or so I see with hindsight. One of the mistakes in this case, I now believe, was not giving Howard more time to be the "patient" and to talk about his own needs and insecurities. Here was a young man leaving home for the first time at the age of nineteen, and I had not endeavored to ask him about his fears and his sense of loss in giving up his role as the family's caretaker. It was as though I had colluded with the family myth that Howard should take care of everyone else, and did not need taking care of himself. The fact that I played a similar role in my family of origin may have blinded me to his weaknesses. As a therapist, my goal had been to move into his position and contain the family's pain. Although Howard was openly grateful to me for this, he was probably also resentful, and, unfortunately, I did not invite him to discuss his feelings about it.

The Remaining Sessions

In June, Kip received his first report card since the hospitalization, and had received Bs and Cs with an A in gym. Gus gave Kip credit in a very nice way, and Margo was eager to point out that Gus and Kip really seemed to be getting on wonderfully. She remarked that he could also be very tough with Kip, as well as supportive. (On one occasion, Gus had apparently slapped Kip across the face for calling Margo a bitch.)

During the summer, I continued to meet with the family, and at times with the couple alone or in parent-child sessions. A great deal of material was covered in these sessions, including Margo and Gus's further exploration of their families of origin. By the end of the summer, Margo had written a letter to her parents, and received a reply that was neither as warm as she might have wished nor as cold as she feared. We discussed Gus's relationship to both his parents and he especially came to see how he blamed Margo for things that were more appropriately situated with his parents. They both had come to make excellent use of the skills they had learned in the early months of treatment, and took pride in not using their children as "hostages" (Gus's word) in their fights. They both seemed more lively and energetic as the summer passed, although they said they were actually arguing *more* than they had before therapy. I told them this was good news, because so much conflict had gone underground before or had been detoured through Kip.

Margo eventually spoke of wanting a promotion in her job, but was afraid of working for a woman boss, which this would entail. We spent some time investigating her notions about what it would be like to work for a woman instead of a man. Gus was very supportive to her in this effort, saying with obvious sincerity that she could handle the promotion with no problem. With Gus I raised the subject of switching to a job he did not find so odious. He explained that at his age it was foolish to think of beginning a new career, but that he was thinking of taking some college courses. I was touched that he said one course he would like to take was psychology.

After ten months of treatment, we began to discuss termination and to schedule sessions on alternate weeks. Kip was doing well, and had not had a single asthma attack since the one that had brought him to the emergency room the previous year. He had a girlfriend and two part-time jobs. Howard was saying his good-byes around town and getting ready for school. Cindy had performed beautifully in two plays, and received a lot of attention for it.

We set a date for termination that would take them past the point of Howard's leaving. During one of the last sessions, I asked them to discuss what they had found helpful about the therapy.

Gus spoke first and said that he liked learning about how the "past ripples into the present. I liked learning that there was a method to our madness!" It was a pleasure to hear him use the pronoun *our,* instead of referring to "her" madness! Margo said, "I'll never forget the first day I barged down here. I felt so selfish, and here you were taking me in. I felt, 'Lord bless this woman,' because I could count the times someone had made extra time for me." She also said, "And cleaning! Believe me, it was worth every moment and every penny of this therapy just to get to the point we're at with housework!"

Margo's first comment reflects the benefits of creating the holding environment, particularly at the beginning of therapy. Extending the usual boundaries for a family at the very beginning can be quite reparative of early experiences with depriving parents. It is important to emphasize, then, that the point of therapy is not merely to *interpret* the present in terms of past losses, conflicts, and injuries but to work toward *healing* those injuries. The members of the family, of course, must do this for one another, but the therapist starts the process and leads the way.

I received a card from the family on the next holiday saying that Howard was enjoying school and Kip had gone down to visit him. Cindy was already thinking about colleges where she could major in theater. One year later, Margo wrote to say that she had asked for a substantial raise and been granted it. Gus was at his same job, but was taking college courses. The couple was planning a trip to Canada to see Margo's parents, a decision prompted by the fact that Margo's mother had become seriously ill.

I was curious about the visit, and phoned the family to ask about it after they returned. Margo's mother was bitter about her illness, but pleased that Margo and Gus had come. Margo managed to get her to talk a bit about the past and about her own miserable childhood, and Margo gained empathy for her mother and, predictably, was able to forgive herself a bit more.

Gus got on the phone and spoke of how well the children were doing, but he said that he and Margo were fighting a great deal, much more than before therapy. Margo said that her relationship with Gus felt more "real" than before, but that she also felt that she had missed out on a great deal in her life and that she occasionally considered leaving him! I asked if they wanted to come back for more sessions, but they both said they were very busy and they knew what they had to do.

I was disappointed not to hear a more pleasant ending, and I later debated over whether to include this case in the book. Further consideration, however, led me to include the McGinns precisely because of the ambiguity of the ending. There are few families we see in which success is monolithic. This sometimes arouses shame in the therapist, because many textbook cases end with the statement, "One year later, the family reported that the symptom had not recurred," or the inscrutable, ". . . and they were all doing fine."

Were the McGinns "fine" or not? Which of them, and in what ways? The case certainly left me with many questions. Since the marital relationship was more unsettled at the end of treatment than before, should I have kept them in therapy longer in order to work it through with them? How aggressively does a feminist therapist try to convince people to stay in therapy after they themselves have expressed the desire to terminate? Perhaps more to the painful point: How often can a therapist expect that marriage will bring happiness to wives and husbands at this point in history? If the answer is "not often," then what are the alternatives, and how do we make them known?

Other questions unrelated to the marital stability remained for me as well. What did it mean, for example, that Gus had finally hit Kip—something both parents had seen as a good thing? Is corporal punishment one of the goals of feminist therapy? To put the matter more straightforwardly, was this not an example (perhaps a small one) of the family becoming more father-present at the cost of being more patriarchal?

In general, my judgment is that the therapy with the McGinns had been more successful than not, and I believed that if they reached another crisis point, they would return to treatment.

Commentary

The McGinn family is made up of a unique group of individuals, but in many ways it is typical of American, white, middle-class families of the twentieth century. The reader may have already noted a parallel between their dilemmas and the discussion of the family as patriarchal, father-absent, and isolated from the community. One of the works mentioned in chapter 10, "The Family in History," to illustrate these important issues was Arthur Miller's *Death of a Salesman,* a play that has some relevance to our understanding of the McGinns. Like Willy Loman, Gus McGinn had worked for a decade in a sales job that he hated. For both men, their identity in the work role was, according to social dictum, their primary identity, and yet it meant nothing to them. Gus idealized his father's success in business, as Willy idealized his brother's success—and both men felt seriously diminished by the respective comparisons.

The women in both families were "housewives"; they were wives to the house and children. In both families, the strong bonds between mothers and sons were related to the absence of the fathers, both emotional and physical. Howard McGinn was a caring and protective partner to Margo, and Willy Loman's sons showed their loyalty to their mother in counterpoint to their consternation with Willy. Such "intergenerational coalitions," which family therapists think of as "aberrant" or pathological, are really anything but aberrant. The father's absenteeism from the family and/or his derogation of the mother is rife and is fostered, if not required, by a society that "milks" mothers for their labor, devalues their "relational" skills, blames them for whatever goes awry in the family, and makes it financially dangerous for them to leave it.

It is not surprising that mothers should encourage sons to be close to them and protect them, if their husbands will not do so. (As feminist Joyce Burland has said, "Women marry their children because they can't marry men!" [pers. comm. August 1987]) Fathers, feeling excluded, sense defeat and bury themselves deeper into work, affairs, or the bar. This scenario, although oversimplified, describes the "normal" (that is, the statistically average) American family to a greater degree than most therapists have been willing to admit. And this structure is reinforced by another feature of contemporary culture: the family's isolation from the world. Because of the breakdown of community in modern times, a child often comes to play all the supporting roles for the family.

This was certainly the case with the McGinns. Howard McGinn *was* the community for his family. He was "mother, father, son, friend, and brother." When it came time for him to leave, the family faced the decision of who would take on the role of sustainer. Perhaps the questions in Kip's mind at the time of his last crisis were: "Will I have to act in a similarly superhuman way to keep this family going when Howard leaves? Will I have to be their mother, father, son, friend, and brother? And if I don't will mother run away or father succumb to depression?" By ceasing his medication, Kip seemed to be going on a warning strike. He would not let them expect him to do "Howard's work," and he might not even continue to do his "own" work of detouring the marital conflict. He deplored his identity as the weird and defective one—an identity they helped impose on him—and he fantasized an escape. Whereas some more competent teenagers would have literally fled, to a friend's house, Kip's flight got him only as far as the local hospital.

What is the role of the therapist in this socioclinical analysis of the family? The therapist enters the family temporarily, to replace the community that industrialization took away. The therapist does this in a way that not merely relieves symptoms but leaves the family more able to solve future problems. I have phrased the hypostatic dilemma of the contemporary urban family as that of being patriarchal and father-absent and have suggested that feminist therapists should aim to attenuate both problems at the same time. What can we say was achieved in these areas with regard to the McGinns?

I believe that the McGinn family left treatment less patriarchal and less father-absent than they had been. Gus had become a full member of the family at last, giving Kip the opportunity to define himself in relation *to* his father, and not simply in opposition to his mother. As for patriarchy, Gus had taken up a good portion of the housework and was much more able to express feelings than before, to grieve and to be vulnerable, to face the fact that he had wounded Margo deeply, and also the fact that he himself had been wounded. Here I wish to emphasize that a family less characterized by patriarchal attributes is not simply "fairer" but also what one would have to call "healthier." For Gus to stop putting Margo down as "irrational" was not only a "better deal" for Margo, it also allowed Gus to reclaim his own "irrationality" and to rediscover the "true self." The importance of claiming one's own affect, as opposed to splitting it off and projecting it, has been most beautifully described by Alice Miller, who writes:

A person who can understand his anger as part of himself will not become violent. He has the need to strike out at others only if he is thoroughly unable to understand his rage, if he was not permitted to become familiar with this feeling as a small child, was never able to experience it as a part of himself because such a thing was totally unthinkable in his surroundings. [1983b, p. 65]

As a result of the treatment, Gus became more able to integrate his thoughts and feelings and, unlike Willy Loman who succumbs to madness, was able to change his life.

Margo left treatment feeling that a lifelong burden of shame and guilt had been lifted. She was no longer the "loony" being protected by four conflict-avoiding family members. She was not the family's servant, but a person with interests, who had a sense of deserving pleasure and who earned a living wage. She no longer felt that her ability to show anger and other emotions was irrational or bad, but that it was a strength, important and real. If Margo should decide to separate from Gus temporarily or permanently, it would certainly seem that she is in a better position to function as an independent adult in the world as a result of these changes than she would have been before. (Gus, for that matter, is too.)

The family was less isolated from the community at the end of treatment. Kip's world now included a girlfriend, two part-time jobs, a math tutor, and a gym coach he liked. Both parents had reached out to people beyond the nuclear circle to meet their work and other needs.

The nature of the therapeutic process itself I have characterized as one of *re-membering.* This word is helpful in that it requires us to see two activities that are often falsely separated in clinical discourse as in fact inseparable. Classical psychoanalytic therapists have insisted on *remembering* the past, but have turned their backs on the issue of actively fostering other kinds of change. At the other extreme are family therapists who have focused on "restructuring" or "fixing" the family without attention to insight about the past. I see these extremes as equally dangerous. The neologism *re-membering* thus guides us in the important activity of not forgetting that we are all capable of both action and reflection, and that we separate the two at our social and personal peril.

In the case of the McGinns, remembering the history of Margo's confinement and of her family of origin, and of Gus's father's death and its one-year anniversary, led to the generation of a new culture in the family in which authentic and nonstifling relationships were possible because secrecy and repression had lost their former importance. Gus's remembering and grieving his father led to the end of his idealization of the father, which allowed him to join his own family—to become a real member of it, and not merely its financial supporter. This process also led to another change in membership, that of allowing Howard to leave the family in order to go to college. Margo changed from being a present but low-status member to someone with more power and respect. In fact, the membership status of each person changed in some way as a result of the investigation of the familial history. *Re-membering* the family led to the creation of a family that was less patriarchal, less father-absent, and more connected to the community.

A Note on Social Class

My focus on *gender* in this case is intended to illuminate a dark spot in our professional literature. It is not meant to imply that *social class* is unimportant in understanding families. On the contrary, class issues in this case are rich and complex (as in all cases) and would need a companion chapter to do an analysis comparable to the one done here for gender. In such an analysis, one would investigate the fact that Gus McGinn is not just a man, but a white man with a high school education doing a very specific kind of work in a large department store chain, and that Margo McGinn is not only a woman, but a white woman, raised in an upper-middle-class household, married into a middle-class marriage, and who was out of the labor force for thirteen years. One would examine closely what Howard's dilemma (the necessity for him to leave the family and get ahead, but also to stay behind and care for them) meant in class terms. (Gus had been faced with a similar problem.) The pressure on children to "get ahead" financially simply could not have been as great in times when class mobility was more restricted.

One could not easily argue that the McGinns would necessarily have had *fewer* problems if they had been more affluent (Margo's affluent family did not sound very happy, after all), but they would have had *different* problems; of this we can be sure. A wealthier family might have hired a maid or governess long before Margo had her breakdown. A better-educated family might have challenged the overcautious orders of Kip's physicians years ago. A better-connected family might even have heard different words from the priest concerning contraception. It is no secret that the Catholic Church, at least since the medieval period of selling indulgences, has made moral concessions (on divorce, annulment, and remarriage) for the wealthy and powerful.

I sincerely hope that feminists in our field with more expertise in Marxist theory will analyze the place of families such as the McGinns in Western capitalist culture. Radical psychoanalyst Joel Kovel provided such an analysis of four individual patients in his brilliant book *The Age of Desire*. The family is not a focus of Kovel's book, but he has some invaluable insights into the family from the point of view of history and class:

> The family under capitalism is like the individual under capitalism: a creature split into greater strength and greater weakness than that which went before, and a stunted, shriveled creature compared to what it could become in a society where people can freely appropriate their own powers. [1981, p. 116]

I hope that family therapists will begin to read Kovel and to enlarge his analysis with our specific expertise.

Locating the Difference in This Treatment

It is relevant to ask how this therapy differs from any existing practice of family therapy. By what right can one call it a step toward a feminist psychotherapy with families? Let us begin by commenting on the similarities between this and traditional family treatments.

In one session, I assigned a task to the family that involved overfunctioning for Kip so that he would have to protest. This is the kind of task that strategic therapists have developed and used. I found it helpful in this case, but one would not, on the basis of this homework task, confuse my treatment with strategic treatment, since it was not primarily symptom-focused.

There are also parallels between the treatment presented here and the methods of structural family therapy. Helping the parents to collaborate better and removing Howard from the parental position were interventions reminiscent of structural therapy, but the language, methods, and definition of the problem were clearly different from what is usually meant by *structural*. Getting parents to "work together" is not a sufficient goal for a feminist therapist, for not all working together is gender-egalitarian. The best statement of this fact came from a young woman in therapy with me who said of her family of origin, "As kids, we could *never* have wedged in between my parents. My mother and father were *one*. And that 'one' was my father." Feminist therapists do indeed want fathers to be more involved, just as most structural family therapists do, but not at the expense of mothers. Another obvious difference between this treatment and structural family therapy was the work done on understanding the families of origin. This exploration of history simply does not take place within the classical structural method.

The next question is how my work differs from that of Bowen, Whitaker, Nagy, Satir, and others who do emphasize history and investigate the family of origin. Clearly, my work owes a great deal to these therapists. It differs from theirs, however, in that transference and countertransference issues were considered principal therapeutic concepts. Encouraging and interpreting these transference issues is anathema to Bowen's work in particular, and is not given a central place (if indeed any at all) in the work of the other family-of-origin therapists.

My insistence on countertransference and transference comes from the insights of object-relations theory, and, of course, my work overlaps in some ways with that of Scharff and Scharff (1987), Skynner (1981), and others. The differences between my method and theirs, however, are as salient as the similarities. The traditional object-relations family therapist is extremely nondirective, and would not have engaged in such proximity with the family as I did here—openly praising, supporting, confronting, joking and teasing, and even giving advice at times. This more direct approach, the stance of being in a personal and active relationship with the family instead of being a neutral if sympathetic observer, is more compatible with feminist principles. Feminist therapists seem to me less embarrassed by nurturance, proximity, care, service, and other qualities that have been socially devalued by virtue of their association with the maternal.

Finally, and most important, none of the therapists just mentioned would see it as important to consider the issues of patriarchy as they became apparent in the family. None would have been committed to help the family in ways that left it less patriarchal and less father-absent. Most family therapists would have dismissed all such questions as "political," and many would have devoted their therapy to helping the family be more "functional" or "adaptive," whether that left them less patriarchal or more so, whether mother felt empowered or blamed, whether the family felt they had new capacities for self-awareness or was left mystified, scratching their heads.

Finally, feminist psychotherapy with the family, as I have portrayed it, seeks not only to "do" differently; it also seeks to understand differently, more critically, more profoundly. Unlike any of the family therapists who have written to date, I have tried to describe the McGinn family not just in clinical terms but also to some degree in terms of their social-historical context. In addition, I have tried to illustrate clinically a few of the terms introduced in earlier chapters, especially the patriarchal/father-absent concept and that of the child replacing the village or community.

The skeptic may complain that a great deal of thought and energy were applied in this case to showing respect for the mother. The question may arise: Why should one need to read about such a simple idea (i.e., for example, not attacking mothers) more than once? The answer, of course, is that it shouldn't be necessary. It is absurd, but true, that even such a "small" change in one's therapy as not being disrespectful to female patients is extremely difficult for therapists of both genders. It is like "deciding" not to be racist or ethnocentric. Ideas that are deeply embedded in our cultural traditions yield but grudgingly to conscious choice. A great deal of investigating, remembering, rethinking, and overlearning is necessary to change the way one sees women and men, mothers and fathers. And if this book made no other addition except to help some therapists contribute a bit less generously to the reproduction of misogyny, it would have succeeded beyond its author's dreams.

15

The Johnsons: Dreams, Introjects, and the Black Family

LEROY JOHNSON sat on the couch in my office, resting his broken leg on the seat of a chair. His left eye was so badly bruised that it was swollen shut, and his nose was broken. After having been medically treated for these injuries, Leroy had been admitted under court order to our inpatient service for a psychological evaluation. The admitting psychologist had not been able to find out the cause of Leroy's injuries. All she knew for sure was that Leroy had been hurt while walking back from church to Judge Paxton's School for Boys, a correctional school for adolescent offenders.

Leroy had told the doctors in the emergency room that a black man had attacked him for no reason on the street as he was leaving church. The doctors found it hard to believe that Leroy, nearly six feet tall and very muscular, could be so easily victimized. More significantly, Leroy did not behave like a victim—amazed, angry, or pathetic. His demeanor suggested instead someone who was on trial for his life—bitter, guarded, and mortally fearful. He had apparently refused to tell the truth even to his mother, Julia Johnson, and her boyfriend, Stanley Gibbs, who lived with them.

Before meeting Leroy, I had pored over an enormous stack of reports about him. He had been in trouble since kindergarten, when he had ruined the completed art projects of everyone in the class during recess. In third grade he had hit a teacher. In fourth grade he was suspended five times. At age sixteen, eight months prior to our first meeting, he was arrested for breaking into a store with three other boys, and was subsequently sent by the court to Judge Paxton's—an outcome known to residents of the school as "being sent to the Judge."

According to the reports, Leroy's reputation while at the school was mixed. On the one hand, he had begun studying there more than he ever had before. At times he seemed fairly content, listening to music and playing sports. At other times he would manage to get into whatever trouble was brewing among the woolliest of his cohort. He would go through periods of violating curfew and sneaking marijuana in through visitors. He helped beat up one of the younger boys.

Leroy's mother, Julia, had approved of the judge's decision to send her son to the correctional school. According to the report, she felt she had lost control over Leroy and that the streets in their urban neighborhood held more power than her discipline could counteract. The report emphasized that the environment in which Leroy had grown up was indeed egregious. When Leroy was nine, two of his friends had fallen through the rotted floorboards of an abandoned house on the block and one boy had broken his neck. One month before Leroy had been sent away, a seven-year-old was shot to death accidentally when he wandered unknowingly into a street brawl.

I was aware of mixed countertransferential feelings toward Leroy as he sat in my office. On the one hand, it was impossible not to feel sympathetic toward him when looking at his broken nose and swollen left eye. On the other hand, he had propped his right leg up on a chair in a way that suggested arrogance, even a sexual posturing. As we talked I felt my attitude alternate between sympathy and distrust. When I saw his left side, I saw an unhappy child who had been brutalized by his conditions all his life; when I looked at his right side, I saw someone who had victimized others in the past and who might have done something to provoke the attack. At this second thought, my sympathy turned to his "victim," whoever that might be.* The part of me that sympathized with Leroy as social victim regretted that he had been caught by the legal system and that, unlike more affluent boys who had gotten into trouble, he might be under the law's eye all his life.

The patriarchal justice system, known to create as many problems as it solves, in fact required my cooperation at this point. It was my job to send Leroy back to "the Judge" if, to use the school's words, he would "shape up." The reports I had read said that Leroy wanted the opportunity to go back to Judge Paxton's. The other possibilities went through my mind as we sat together waiting for his mother and Stanley to arrive for our first session. He could not return home, because he had not yet served out his term for robbing the store. We could recommend only that he go back to

---

*These two types of transference have been labeled "concordant identification" and "complementary identification," respectively. In the former the therapist feels empathy for the patient, and in the latter the therapist's empathy is for the "object," or the person interacting with the patient (Scharff and Scharff 1987).

the same school or to another with tighter security. The next level of disciplinary school was equipped with barred windows, and the residents were strip-searched for weapons after meals. The alternative was placement in a long-term psychiatric facility. The thirty-day commitment to our inpatient facility would be used to determine which of these alternatives was most feasible, to work with the recommended placement during that time, and then to present this recommendation to the judge.

Julia Johnson arrived on time for her appointment, but alone. She was a tall, thin woman with severe features and wore her hair pulled back tightly in a rubber band. I asked about Mr. Gibbs and she said impassively that he was not able to attend. I led Leroy and his mother to a room with a one-way mirror through which my team was to observe that afternoon. When I began explaining the mirror and the team system, Ms. Johnson interrupted me somewhat curtly to say that she had been in such rooms "many times before." Leroy and Ms. Johnson sat across from each other, scarcely looking up. Leroy, appearing rigid with anger, stared at the door. His mother ruffled through some papers she had brought with her from school and repositioned them in her handbag.

I remembered reading in the report that when Leroy was assaulted on the street, his mother had stayed up all night with him in the waiting room. I asked about the frequency of their visits while Leroy had been at Judge Paxton's Ms. Johnson said she had visited him every other weekend when things were going well with him. When he would get in trouble, however, she would punish him by staying away for a month or two. Her rationale was that her absence might motivate him to try harder. She also stated, in a quiet and matter-of-fact way: "I was working two jobs, going to school, and taking care of an elderly woman down the street to pick up a few extra dollars. I had papers to write and exams, and so on. Those things have to take priority. Sometimes I would have liked to see Leroy, but I had to study."

After twenty minutes of discussion, I excused myself and went behind the mirror to talk to my team. "His mother abandons him," said one colleague. This is not a false claim, but it pulls the mother's behavior out of context. It leaves us in want of a word for what Leroy's father did when he left him at birth. According to the reports, Leroy senior had cut off all contact with Ms. Johnson and their son until Leroy was five years old. Then he returned after another relationship failed. Ms. Johnson said she had been lonely and worried and was happy to have him back. He remained with them for two years, impregnated Ms. Johnson again, and left as soon as he learned of the pregnancy. (She miscarried a few weeks after he left.)

The Johnsons: Dreams, Introjects, and the Black Family

This type of painful history is often swept away by agencies and by therapists who write reports with the bureaucratic shorthand, "No contact with father," or "Father's whereabouts unknown." Therapists who are not trained to pursue the complexities of paternal absence simply glide over it. From the point of view of some schools of family therapy, indeed, the nature of a father's absence is of no account. For a strategic therapist, the objective is to alleviate the symptom with the help of whoever is available in the family. For the structural therapist, the objective is also not to ask about past relationships, but to ask who in the current system can help perform whatever "tasks" or "functions" need to be performed.

For the psychoanalytically oriented therapist, however, it makes a great deal of difference whether a father is absent as a result of death or separation, how he behaved when he was present, and whether or not he said good-bye. This is true because, in order to understand a child, it is necessary to know about the adults whom she or he introjected. Knowing the basic information about parents, siblings, and extended kin tells the therapist whom the child has taken in and what he or she is likely to act out. The feminist point of view redoubles the importance that psychoanalytic theory gives to searching out the father, because not doing so enforces the cultural prejudice that mothers alone construct the child and are responsible for how children thrive or fail.

In this first session with Leroy, I knew that the issue of his father would be an important one. We would return to it once a therapeutic relationship was developed. For the moment, however, I doubted whether a relationship ever would develop, since it felt so difficult to engage either Leroy or Ms. Johnson in talk. When she commented that she "still didn't know what had happened in the street," I invited her to ask Leroy about it.

MS. JOHNSON: What happened, Lee?
LEROY: I told you. I got mugged.
MS. JOHNSON: What happened, Lee?
LEROY: I told you.
MS. JOHNSON [*still calm*]: You must think I'm exceptionally dumb. You want me to believe that a guy came up to you, at your size, and started beating you in broad daylight for no reason.
LEROY: That's right.
MS. JOHNSON: And what explanation do you make of that?
LEROY: I don't make no explanation of that!
MS. JOHNSON: What happened, Lee? What had you done to him?
LEROY: I hadn't done nothing to him.
MS. JOHNSON: Okay. But what are you thinking about all this, then? Or

are you going to tell us that a guy almost killed you and you're not thinking about it?

LEROY: He probably mistaked me for those other dudes!

MS. JOHNSON: What other dudes? Don't use street language in here! What other boys?

She persisted, but he would not tell her the whole story. I admired her persistence and her power with language as she talked, and wondered if she weren't beginning to feel more connected to the therapy, since she had said, "Are you going to tell *us* . . . ," putting herself and me together. I also wondered if her comment about "street language" referred to my being a white therapist. (If so, did it indicate a special deference to me, resentment of me, both, or something else?) More than anything, I felt empathic toward Ms. Johnson based on the expression on her face when she said she had been in these rooms "many times before." In the course of nine years, she had in fact been through five bouts of outpatient therapy at various mental health clinics with as many therapists. I had read their accounts; they described Leroy as a "con artist," as "oppositional," and as having "a conduct disorder"; they described his mother as "ineffectual," "depressed," "narcissistic," "dependent," "disengaged," and "overinvolved." Only one of the reports mentioned anything about Leroy's father except a passing mention of his absence. The therapists had prescribed interventions, routines, and tasks to make Ms. Johnson "tougher," "a better executive," and, of course, either to increase or to decrease the psychological distance between her and her son, depending on whether they had seen her as primarily disengaged or overinvolved.

In questioning Leroy, Ms. Johnson did manage to discover one detail that had not emerged before, something about two other guys who were being chased. I defined that as "progress," and suggested we stop that aspect of our work for the day. With Ms. Johnson's permission, I asked Leroy to return to his classroom so that his mother and I could talk alone.

When I closed the door and returned to my seat, Ms. Johnson looked at me and asked, slightly sardonic and with half a challenge, "Well?" It felt like a significant moment in the therapy, one in which we would be defining our relationship to each other. I felt that I had heard that "Well?" before, and that it meant, "Well, what are *you* going to accomplish that the other therapists have not?" That "Well?" had, in the past, triggered my self-doubts as a therapist. In the moment it evoked feelings of hopelessness in the face of the devastation Leroy had already known and seen as a child. It elicited my resentment of the court's dumping impossible problems in therapists' laps and expecting miracles in four weeks. The temptation, feeling these things, was to return the "Well?" like a tennis ball.

It was helpful to reflect for a moment on the fact that Ms. Johnson was probably "storing" some of her helplessness in me, needing me to contain it. That is, the way I was feeling in the moment reflected the way she probably felt most of the time. This realization—that what I was feeling belonged partly to her, and that I could be helpful simply by agreeing to share the pain for a while—lowered my anxiety and allowed me to respond in a very different way. My understanding provided *me* with a feeling of being contained, and I could provide containing for my patient.

MS. JOHNSON: Well, *well?*! [*laughing a little*]
DL: Ms. Johnson, I want to tell you something very important, something I don't think anyone has told you before.
MS. JOHNSON: Go ahead.
DL: Leroy's problems are not your fault.
MS. JOHNSON [*after quite a long pause*]: Well. That is news.

She had received messages for ten years like a ticker tape coming in from schools, guidance counselors, judges, and relatives saying that she had destroyed her child and that if he was on his way to prison, this too was her doing. She sat now looking thoughtful.

MS. JOHNSON: I have done a lot of things wrong.
DL: How about all the things you've done right?
MS. JOHNSON [*laughs*]: Such as what?
DL: Who has fed and clothed this child all his life?
MS. JOHNSON: I have.
DL: Who has talked to the teachers and therapists and done laundry and worked two or three other jobs?
MS. JOHNSON: Any mother does those things if she has to.
DL: Mothers need help. Who helped you?
MS. JOHNSON: No one. I am self-sufficient.
DL: Self-sufficient people need loving friends. Who has loved you?
MS. JOHNSON: Nobody.

Ms. Johnson believed, however, that this too was her fault. The counselors she had seen exhorted her to get some help in the form of a "male image" for Leroy—something she was simply not able to do for some years. She had been with her boyfriend Stanley for two years, and he was, according to her, "the best male image anyone could want." Nonetheless, she said, Leroy had not "turned around."

I strongly encouraged her to bring Mr. Gibbs to our next session and she agreed. She asked what she herself could do for Leroy while he was here. At this point it was sensible to make suggestions for change. Many non-feminist family therapists make the mistake of giving directives to mothers without first creating a sufficient holding or containing experience, and the suggestions are then either rejected out of hand or, perhaps more commonly, accepted as one more emblem of the mother's incompetence. There are also therapists, largely the classical psychoanalytic group, who don't give advice at all, or who do so very rarely. Oddly enough, many do this in the name of being "purists," although Freud himself was not loath to give advice. I think that one can err in the direction of giving either too much or too little supportive advice.

In the session with Ms. Johnson, in response to her question, I volunteered the opinion that punishing a child should never take the form of not visiting. She thanked me, and said that no one had ever told her that. I recommended that she visit Leroy for twenty minutes each day, perhaps after dinner. I recommended that she bring him an inexpensive treat like a magazine or candy bar when she could. If Leroy was in trouble on the unit that day, she should visit nonetheless. It was all right with me if she spent the twenty minutes fighting with him or setting up a punishment with our staff, but she should always show up. I told her there would certainly be days when she felt sick and tired of Leroy's attitude, and on those days she should be sure to tell me about it.

She was smiling with a look of relief as we finished, and asked me to call her by her first name. This seemed to be a sign of feeling connected with me, and I left the session feeling hopeful.

EVENING OF THE FIRST SESSION

That evening before bedtime, Leroy told Jarvis Hall, one of the counselors, that he had seen two boys steal an elderly black woman's purse on his way back from church that day, but that he had had nothing to do with it. Leroy said that his attacker was probably a relative of the woman who had simply hit the first teenager he saw walking down the street and then run off. He said he had broken his leg when he jumped off a wall, and the man beat him up before he could get to his feet. This information was written up in the night notes, and I had access to it first thing in the morning.

The Second Family Session

On the following afternoon, I was sitting in my office with Jarvis Hall and Julia Johnson, waiting for Stanley to arrive. (We were also expecting a staff member from Judge Paxton's to join us.) As we were talking, Leroy burst noisily into the office without knocking.

DL: I beg your pardon.

Jarvis winked at me and walked out to give Leroy a quick lecture about respecting boundaries and about how unwise it was to "mess with" me in particular. I wanted Leroy to respect me as his therapist and I wanted to offer his mother the encouragement to begin expecting more from him as well, while also giving him the chance to do things over, to rectify mistakes, rather than give in to a feeling of hopelessness about him. I said quietly to Julia that Leroy's having offered a partial confession the night before was no reason to "strut." She nodded. Whatever Leroy's reason was for not knocking before entering, I felt strongly that it was important for him to feel a very unequivocal boundary between us.

Leroy knocked on the door and I rose to let him in just as Stanley arrived. Stanley was taller and broader than Leroy and with a completely different demeanor. Whereas Leroy looked angry and even menacing a lot of the time, Stanley had a baby face and wore a perpetual half-smile. It had taken some work to make a connection with Julia, but Stanley and I seemed instantly comfortable with each other. He seemed to care a great deal for Julia and Leroy and said he would help in any way he could, although he felt unsure how much he should intervene. He said that, like Julia, he missed having Leroy at home, but that the school had been the best thing for him.

At that point Sandy Kline arrived from Judge Paxton's school and explained the staff's position that Leroy could be accepted back if he met certain conditions. These included participating fully in our program, being honest about what had happened in the assault, continuing outpatient therapy, and being put on a six-month probation at Judge Paxton's. Leroy agreed to these conditions. He seemed to have a comfortable relationship with Ms. Kline, as did Julia and Stanley. She agreed to remain in regular contact with me over the course of Leroy's thirty days with us.

287

The first stage of the therapy, the crisis stage, was coming to a close. Leroy had begun to let us in on what had happened, and most of the staff felt that in time he would be ready to really discuss it. He had committed himself to working his way back to school, and the school was ready to work with us. We had agreed to have three family sessions per week and frequent visits from Julia and Stanley. Leroy would continue to have his injuries treated by our medical staff.

The next stage, the remembering and reworking, was about to begin. This stage was especially poignant in the Johnson family, since there had been so much forgetting. Julia, it turned out, had had an entire life that her son did not know about, and she knew very little about Stanley's past. When the slings and arrows of even an average life remain nameless, they are impossible to sheath or to direct. Instead, they are denied, and the anger is projected into the next generation who, without understanding why, takes up battle with the world.

Since he knew little about Julia's past, and virtually nothing about his father's or Stanley's past, I guessed that Leroy was "playing out" some battle from an earlier generation. Split-off emotions from his mother and father, and possibly from Stanley too, were alive in him and kept active by their denial. One way of posing the question about Leroy's history of acting out or lawlessness was, "What is Leroy trying to remember?"

JULIA'S FAMILY OF ORIGIN

I asked Julia to tell about her family of origin. She said she had grown up in a small southern town. Her biological father had left when she was four, and Julia had just a glimmer of memory of a tall man standing in the doorway. Her mother remarried when Julia was nine, and her stepfather used to drink and beat her mother. She seemed to idealize her mother, saying she did not know how she could take so much. Her stepfather was unemployed throughout the time she was at home, and her mother worked eight hours a day in a factory and also took in people's laundry at night. Julia described her mother as tall and wide with stern features and a tight bun. This visual image of severity matched my impressions of Julia herself.

> JULIA: My mother was a very serious and intelligent person. She loved to read the Bible and she read it late at night when her work was done. She wanted me to get an education and pushed me to study. I resisted her pressure and liked to have a good time. I dated a boy my mother didn't like.

The Johnsons: Dreams, Introjects, and the Black Family

At seventeen Julia became pregnant by this boy, and her mother wanted her to have an abortion. Although abortion was illegal at the time, her mother knew midwives who would perform it. Julia said she would not have had an abortion "even if abortion were legal and enjoyable."

JULIA: I was in a very rebellious stage. I didn't want to be serious like my mother. So I got a room for myself, got a job in a diner, and worked very hard to keep up. During my last six weeks, my boyfriend left. He said he would always love the baby and me, but he wasn't ready for a family. He went up north where he had some people and I had no ideas, no way to find him.

Julia had medical complications during her delivery and her daughter, Michelle, was physically handicapped. Julia's mother constantly questioned her daughter's ability to handle the baby, and Julia eventually left Michelle with her mother.

JULIA: It was a horrible time. Like a bad dream. I had lost everything: my boyfriend, my education, my own baby. I went away. I went to the next town where I had a cousin. I started to work and decided to get my high school equivalency degree. I hoped my daughter would understand some day.

After her move, she began dating a married man. He was in love with her, but when she became pregnant by him, he stopped seeing her to preserve his marriage. She told him when the baby (Leroy) was born, but he never asked to see the child.

JULIA: In the early days, Leroy and I were really close. We went everywhere together and he really was a good little boy. He had no problems in nursery school. Michelle visited us during vacations and I felt this was the best that things could be. I was making ends meet and sending my mother some money every month.

When Leroy was five, Julia reunited with his father, who had left his marriage.

JULIA: It was trouble from the beginning. I could understand that my son would be jealous of him—but it seemed he was jealous of my son, too. There was nothing I could do without one of them getting mad at me. Lee started getting into trouble in school and they were calling me all

289

the time. His father was no help. He said, "What did I tell you? You baby him." Maybe I did, but I felt I had to balance him out, because he would just ignore Leroy and then—*wham,* pick him up and blast him when he was mad.

Julia finally asked Leroy senior to leave. It was at that point he began beating her. She took her son and moved in the middle of the night to the home of a woman friend whom Leroy senior did not know. She said that as bad as it was to be in hiding, there were no alternatives. Leroy would take Julia's side against the father and try to protect her. She stated that he got hit in that way more than once.

In our session, Leroy said he could scarcely remember the incidents his mother was describing. He said he recalled his father throwing a plate of grits at her and then twisting her arm, but that was all.

I asked Julia how she felt about her ex-partner now.

JULIA: I'm not angry at his father, if that's what you mean. I don't know where he is, but if he knocked on my door, I would let him see his son.

DL: You're not mad at him after all that? Not even a little?

JULIA: I don't get mad. I just say, if a person is ignorant, what's the point of getting upset yourself? I just don't think about him. But I know Lee is angry with him. He always says that if his father ever shows up, he would kill him.

DL: Leroy?

LEROY: He ever show up here and y'all let that jive turkey in to see me—forget it!

JULIA: That's enough street talk, please.

Julia seemed to take pride in Leroy's indignation and anger toward his father, but she could not consciously claim her own anger. It is probable that her rage toward Leroy senior seemed too great—mixed as it was with anger toward her first partner, toward her abusive stepfather, and toward the biological father who had abandoned her. She projected her anger instead onto Leroy, who had plenty of social inducements to act it out on the streets.

DL: It sounds like Leroy is angry enough for both of you.

JULIA: That's right—for both of us. The problem is sometimes he acts just like his dad.

290

The Johnsons: Dreams, Introjects, and the Black Family

DL: But that means he has to carry around your anger and his own, and that can get pretty heavy.

JULIA: I'm just not a very angry person. I'm more like Stanley. We never argue or fight—just ask him.

STANLEY: It's true. If Julia is angry at you, she'll just ignore you.

Here again we see the issue of women's anger emerge—a theme that has appeared in each of the three cases discussed in this book, despite the many differences in the families. Children, of course, have their *own* anger to act out, and sometimes they act out the rage of a father or a grandparent. However, as Teresa Bernardez (1978) has pointed out, this splitting-off of anger and storing it elsewhere is something to which women are particularly vulnerable. Thus, in the case of the Johnson family, Leroy, through the process of projective identification, became the container of his mother's denied anger at his father—and possibly of some of Stanley and Julia's anger for each other as well.

An important task in the therapy would thus be for both Julia and Stanley to take back some of their anger in order to be able to use it in more straightforward ways. This would soften the splitting that Julia showed, for example, in contrasting Stanley, the good, quiet male, to Leroy, the bad, angry male.

JULIA: Anyhow, I eventually moved north to find a job. I was still determined to make something of myself. Leroy was having some problems, so we started going to counseling. And we would start with one, and they would leave after five weeks because their training was over, or whatever.

Once again I listened to how this family had been stymied by its class position. A different school-age child whose parents could pay for private therapy would have had more continuous care—which might (or might not) have significantly changed the outcome.

In any case, Julia ended her account by stating that she now had half the credits she needed for an Associates degree in education. She said she wanted to continue and eventually to earn her teaching certificate. One year before Leroy was sent away, she had met Stanley and their relationship had developed fairly quickly. When Leroy had gotten into trouble with the courts, she said she began to feel somewhat detached from her son, since she had sacrificed everything for him and "could not force him to do what was right."

When she finished speaking, I asked Stanley what he was thinking or

291

feeling. He said hearing about everything that had happened in her life in one long story helped him realize why she didn't trust him.

> STANLEY: Julia sometimes will mention the question of marriage, and I'm a little—you know—shy about it. But as she— as you were talking, Julia, I started to think about how much you must want someone to make a commitment. How much you deserve it.
>
> JULIA: And you changed your mind right here sitting in this chair?
>
> STANLEY: Well don't go too far now. Don't quote me *yet* on this.

I encouraged them to talk to each other about their commitment to each other. The dichotomy of Julia feeling more deeply connected to him and Stanley feeling like more of a "globetrotter" (in his words) followed the traditional gender pattern, although in other ways they showed cross-gender traits. (Stanley seemed more expressive of emotions and Julia less so, in contrast to the stereotype.) Leroy always looked extremely absorbed in these conversations, as though he felt exhilarated by a dialogue whose substance essentially informed him that they could take care of each other. Some of this work has to be done with the couple privately, of course, but a feminist family therapist will want some of these discussions to go on in front of the adolescent. In this way the adolescent can learn that men and women can talk to each other and listen to each other. Both are allowed to express dependence, and both are allowed to make demands.

After the Second Session

In group therapy on the night of the third session, Leroy finished telling the story of his assault. He said that he had been with two boys who stole the old woman's purse and that they had knocked her down during the theft. Two men had seen what happened. One had stopped to take care of the woman, and the other had chased the muggers down the street. The two other boys had leapt easily over a brick wall, but Leroy had fallen trying to clear it. The attacker cleared the wall easily and punched Leroy as he lay on his back.

Hearing the story of his parents' relationship put Leroy's assault in perspective for me. Leroy had grown up in a household in which his mother and father were at war with each other. Due in part to years of loyal involvement with his mother, he was less able than other children to distance himself from their conflict; he wanted to protect her. However, he could not unambivalently take his mother's side against his father. That is, while Leroy probably did have fantasies of eliminating father and going back to his peaceful life with mother before this interloper arrived, he nonetheless wanted father to stay. Not only did he consciously enjoy his father's attention at times, but he also would suffer some guilt if he again was able to replace father next to mother.

Another part of this complex scenario is that Leroy as a child may well have felt some anger at his mother for not being able to defend herself against the father. To the extent that he had anger toward the mother, he may have identified with his father at times in father's attacks on her.

In the end, when Julia fled with him, Leroy did experience another Oedipal win, but again the victory was pyrrhic. Julia still could not keep Leroy out of poverty and its humiliations, great and small. She could not keep Leroy out of trouble in school. She could not, in her own words, prevent Leroy from being "like his father."

When Stanley arrived on the scene, the Oedipal battle was replayed. Leroy had no internal sense of how a mother could love both him and an adult partner at the same time, so he sacrificed himself by getting in trouble and ordered away to a correctional school.

These massive and conflicting passions were acted out on the street when Leroy found himself acting as both his father and his mother in a way that first allowed him to gratify his rage and then allowed him to be punished. First he attacked the woman, as his father had attacked his mother, and then he lay on the ground being beaten by the man. Only this punishment, perhaps, could lead to forgiveness. Perhaps he wanted at all costs to be pardoned for having sent his father away, and for not being able to protect his mother. His mother had, in the end, come to his aid without question in the emergency room after he had been beaten.

These were ideas I hoped to share eventually with the family so they could, in the words of Mr. McGinn from the previous chapter, find the "method to our madness." I looked forward to deepening the therapeutic connection with Leroy, but felt that at the moment his strongest connection was to his group. It is not unusual for group therapists to connect more quickly with adolescent inpatients than the individual therapist can. An adolescent who has been overstimulated in the family—as have so many children in modern families—may find it less terrifying to open up in a group than to build what may seem like yet another overstimulating one-to-one bond.

A Session with Leroy

On the following morning, Leroy knocked on my office door and waited for me to answer. He said he wanted to tell me himself what he had revealed in group therapy about the assault on the street. We spoke for two hours about his parents, about his having always been in trouble, about what he might do for the old woman he had attacked. The group had apparently given him some suggestions about sending her money or helping her in some way.

There was a pause, and then Leroy, perhaps realizing how differently we were talking together, told me he hadn't believed in therapy in the beginning but that now he did. My relationship with him began to develop significantly after this session, perhaps because he had come to feel accepted (held by) the group. In any case, it was clear that he was interested in trying to understand himself and his family. Most adolescents are interested in doing that, but Leroy seemed particularly intrigued by psychological concepts.

I told him in this session that I had a theory about him, based on my observation that kids worry about their parents and feel responsible when they can't take care of them. Leroy responded that that had been true of him in the past, but not anymore.

> LEROY: I used to worry about my mom, you know, like if anything would happen to her. But now with Stanley— shoo! I would have to say he is the best thing that ever happened to her.

What became increasingly salient was that Leroy felt he had to step out of the way for Stanley, and he had no real idea of how to do this while remaining at home. Probably the adults had no idea either, given their (or at least Julia's) early experiences. I told Leroy that part of my theory was that he got into trouble in order to leave his mother and Stanley alone to have a "honeymoon" together. He smiled. We also talked in that session about the fact that kids take out their frustrations on their moms because their dads aren't there to take the heat. This led to talk about his father, at whose name his face immediately contorted with anger. I asked Leroy what he knew about his father and he said, "Enough." It turned out that "enough" actually meant nothing at all. He knew that his father's name was Leroy, but he did not know what state he lived in, or who else was in his family. He couldn't name a single good quality of his father's or say what job or what interests he had. He had never seen a photograph of him.

DL: So you don't even know if you look like him or not.
LEROY: Don't want to know. I told you— if he ever came near me, I'd mess him up.

There was a pause, after which Leroy asked, "You mean he could just come up here and visit me and y'all would let him in?"

I was surprised to hear this idea come up for a third time. (He had raised it twice in this session and once the previous day.) Leroy knew very well that visitors to the inpatient unit were carefully screened and had to be approved by the rest of the family. There were no "surprise" visitors. Leroy seemed to be saying that he wanted to see his father, or, more precisely, that the wish/fear of encountering the father was closer to the surface than I had imagined. I brought this issue up with him, probably too hastily.

DL: Maybe a part of you would like him to visit. Maybe we should think about that.
LEROY [*jumping up and throwing his cap down*]: Did you hear me tell you that that sucker is never coming near me again unless he wants to be dead? I'm not messing with you, Deborah. I'll give him something.
DL: Leroy. Hold on. I can see how absolutely angry you are at your father. I can see it, and you are justified.

I had obviously skipped a step in my eagerness to address the father absence in the family. I had forgotten that Leroy would need to address his grievances against the father. He did so in the remainder of this session. We concluded the session by again discussing the theory that he caused trouble with mom because he couldn't get angry or cause trouble with dad.

LEROY: This is an amazing theory. I'm serious! Because I always wondered to myself, "I love my mother, and why do I make her be so miserable all the time?"

For a while, every idea Leroy and I had was a theory. "Theory" became a code word for our relationship itself. Leroy developed theories about various staff members, about art therapy, and about anorexia nervosa. He began to be taken seriously by other patients on the unit, and for the first time in his life he was considered to be a helpful person, not a menacing spoiler. Other patients called on him for "feedback" in the group. He loved encouraging the anorectic girls to eat and would sometimes buy them milkshakes from the cafeteria.

The Third Family Session

In the third family session I hazarded the theory that Mr. Leroy "the Hulk" Johnson really felt like an anorectic inside.

> DL: Leroy, I think—theoretically, that is—that you're really hungry inside for attention.
>
> LEROY: Forget about it. My theory is that we are all in this place to help each other. How do you help an anorectic? Buy 'em food. I'm serious.

Stanley laughed almost uncontrollably at this exchange, saying that he himself felt like a "starving anorectic" inside at different times in his life. I asked him to tell about his own family.

STANLEY'S FAMILY OF ORIGIN

Stanley's mother died of appendicitis when he was two years old, and his grandmother had died in a car accident before he was born. He was raised by his great-grandmother. He stated he did not know anything about his father or grandfather—not even their names or what they looked like. He spoke of his great-grandmother as a "rock of Gibraltar" who had raised eleven children as well as several grandchildren.

> STANLEY: She ran a tight ship, but by the time she was taking care of me she had mellowed out a lot and she spoiled me. Yeah, that's what they all said. When Granny died at ninety-four, whew! That was deep.
>
> DL: How did she die?
>
> STANLEY: She just died of old age. Her eyesight went. And she hated that. Sometimes the kids teased her. Once when we were having a barbecue, I had a real long fork with a brown handle on the end. Granny picked it up and put the handle in the fire, thinking it was a hot dog. We teased her a lot. But her eyesight went and she said, "Why did Jesus leave me here in the dark?"

296

Stanley began to cry. Julia looked uncomfortable, but when I motioned her to sit closer to him, she did so immediately. I asked about the last time he had gone to the cemetery and he said it had been twelve years. I recommended he go again and bring Julia with him.

Leroy looked touched by this incident, but he wouldn't comment on it. He left the session looking very reflective, and I had not anticipated that he would act out that night on the inpatient unit.

After the Third Family Session

Leroy had apparently been moody throughout dinner. After dinner, there was a meeting to plan a bake sale, and when he disrupted the meeting by ridiculing the very idea of a bake sale, he was asked to leave. He went into his room and "tore it up," making a mess and breaking a lamp. Staff members called his mother and Stanley in to talk about what had happened and to "set consequences." This was not easy for them. Stanley wanted to rush in and pay for the damages. Julia said she was so fed up with him, she didn't want to come back until he shaped up. With the staff's help, however, they were able to find some middle ground—to stay to the end of the discussion and to hold Leroy accountable without rejecting him.

We discussed the incident in the next family session. I felt confused about what had happened and somewhat responsible for it. I wondered if my comment that Leroy felt like an anorectic—i.e., a skinny girl—had infuriated him or threatened him in a way that made him want to show his machismo. I felt that I had ruined the experience of Leroy's hearing Stanley tell about his life, seeing Stanley cry and act vulnerable. I felt my interpretation about anorexia had been too flippant, as though I were strutting some interpretive skill just as Leroy had earlier strutted in front of me.

All of this may well have contributed to the blowup, but it was not the main reason for it.

The Fourth Family Session

In the family session that followed the blowup, everyone sat quietly for a while, waiting for me to take a direction. Leroy volunteered that he had had a dream the previous night. He dreamt that there was a bake sale on the unit and that his father was there, wearing a straw hat and collecting money behind one of the tables.

LEROY: Only the guy that was my father was Jarvis, the night counselor. Looked just like Jarvis. And I walk up to him and say, "Give me some ribs or barbecue chicken," I can't remember which I said. And he said, "Don't you know this is a bake sale?" And he was real mad, and then he said, "Okay, Okay, you can have some of this chocolate cake for free." And he give me this giant piece of cake. Yum.

The dream seemed to be rich with information, and I asked them if they had thoughts or feelings about it.

JULIA: You dreamed about a bake sale because of what happened last night. You see—it stayed on your mind. Only in your dream, you didn't make fun of it. You wanted something good.
STANLEY: Only he was asking for the wrong thing, because you don't get no barbecue at a bake sale. Ain't that just like you, Leroy?
DL: How did your father seem, Leroy? Was he nice or mean or what?
LEROY: I told you he looked like Jarvis. He was nice, I guess. He had a vest on like Stanley. Your silver vest.
STANLEY: The one you like to sneak.
LEROY: And there was a woman in the back. Looked real small like Aunt Lonnie.

The discussion of the dream helped me to understand some of the reasons for the blowup. Probably Leroy *had* been touched by Stanley's account of his past and had wanted to get closer to him, but that closeness would present a particular conflict for Leroy since we had also raised the issue of his father. What if Leroy should really feel love and caring for Stanley—begin to feel like a son to him—and then his father should suddenly show up on the unit, as per his fantasy? The anxiety of having to make new choices or of thinking about himself and his father differently had apparently made it necessary for him to act out on the unit to reinstate the old relationships. He again became the bad boy who needed to be punished and abandoned. It seemed very auspicious that he had remembered the dream and reported it. To me, the dream endorsed the "theory" that he was a hungry child, wanting sustenance from father as well as from mother, whom he consigned to the background of the dream in the form of his aunt.

The dream can be considered a product not only of Leroy's psyche but also of the family's unconscious processes. I prefer to think that this dream emerged from the family's process of engagement in the therapy and from their collective struggle to examine the past and to present threatening material in less threatening ways.

We spent a great deal of time on their associations to the dream. By the end of that discussion, the dream irrefutably belonged to the family, since it had been molded and elaborated and claimed by all three of them. Stanley said it had made him feel good immediately when Leroy mentioned the word *barbecue,* because it meant that Leroy had really been listening to him tell the story of his great-grandmother and had been touched by it. Julia said she liked the fact that in the dream, the father is wearing Stanley's vest. "Maybe you are wanting Stanley to be more like a father to you." Julia also added the information that Leroy's father loved anything chocolate, so for him to give Leroy a big piece of chocolate cake would have been "right on target." Leroy lit up at this news. His enthusiasm came from the idea that his dream image of the father had authenticity, and symbolized a bond between them.

What seemed to emerge from this lengthy dream discussion was a desire on the part of the entire family to come to terms with Leroy senior. I invited Leroy to ask his mother some questions about his father, but he could come up with only two: "Do I look like him?" and "Do you have a picture of him?" Leroy seemed to get anxious when I prompted him to ask more, so instead I asked his mother just to tell us some things about his father.

JULIA: Handsome. Tall like Leroy. Same blue-gray eyes and same light skin. And he had a sense of humor when he wasn't being mean. Oh, and he liked music—only not the same kind as you. He played saxophone in a jazz band for a while.

LEROY: He did!

JULIA: Yeah. He was good-looking. Only he had a big burn on his neck that he was real self-conscious about. It happened when he was little and there was a fire in his house and it was all scarred here on his throat.

Leroy was curious about the fire, about his father's family, about how poor they were. Julia answered the questions matter-of-factly, seeming neither defensive nor nostalgic.

STANLEY: Wasn't he in Vietnam, Julia? Did you tell me he had been in Nam?
JULIA: He was in Vietnam, yes. Matter of fact, his mother said that was what started the trouble, that he was never the same after that.

I asked Julia to mention some good qualities that he had, to describe a good time he had spent with Leroy and to bring in a photograph of him. She agreed. The objective here was to fill the void within Leroy. In place of a remembered father, there had been nothing but fantasies, devaluations, resentment, and a feeling of abandonment. His mother sometimes said he was like his father, which had, until this point, meant only that he was like a sadistic, odious person who had never been able to change himself. At times Leroy believed about himself that he could never be different from the way he was, that he would always be in trouble.

In a later session we discussed Leroy's getting in touch with his dad. Julia said she would be willing to track him down through friends and relatives, but Leroy said he would rather wait. "I want to get my life together first. I want to finish up with the Judge, and go back and, you know— so he could be proud of me."

The topic of Leroy senior came up at various points in the remainder of the therapy, but Leroy never budged from his position that he wanted to wait a little while before he contacted his father, and I thought that this position should be respected.

The Remainder of the Inpatient Therapy

During the inpatient sessions I felt gradually more connected with Julia. She was always cooperative, good-natured, and even openly grateful at times, but there was a level of openness and vulnerability that had remained limited. My approach to Julia was sort of a reverse weaning: I wanted her to be able to take in a little more from me as time passed. She was most able in the first few weeks to accept advice about how to deal with Leroy, and that was the form that much of my support took. I let her read the report I wrote to the court, recommending that Leroy be allowed to return to the residential school and continue outpatient treatment with me. The report was presented to the judge during the last week of Leroy's court-ordered inpatient stay. The judge made his order in accord with our recommendation. The staff members from Judge Paxton's were pleased and made several more visits that week to plan Leroy's transition back to them.

On the morning before his discharge from the inpatient department, Leroy went around saying good-bye to all the staff members and patients, and cried as he did so. His mother told him not to act like a big baby. I felt irritated with her, and was relieved when one of the male staff members said to her good-naturedly, "I always cry at times like this. What's wrong with being a baby?"

After lunch that same day, Pauline Smith, the clinic receptionist, came to my office saying that on her way back from lunch, she had noticed Leroy's mother crying all alone in the lounge. I asked her later why this had made such an impression on her, and Pauline said, "I don't know. She always walks around here so buttoned-up and cool. I thought she must be in real pain if she was crying like that."

Pauline was certainly right. I walked through the lounge and found Julia crying, in a spot where she was half hidden and half open to view. I asked if she would come back to the office and talk. She did, very embarrassed of her tears. She talked about being afraid that Leroy's progress would not be maintained when he left the hospital. This eventually led to her saying how much she was going to miss the support of inpatient therapy (three times per week) and the rest of the staff. She said it had seemed more like a family than anything she had ever known. We spent time talking about how she might send cards and visit once in a while. It was also important for her simply to mourn this loss.

> JULIA: I am so embarrassed about carrying on like this. Usually I can control myself.
> DL: That's exactly the point. It's so good that you are really letting yourself feel bad. I wish Stanley were here to see it!
> JULIA: He won't believe it, will he?

In our session that night, I asked Julia to tell about how she had felt that afternoon when she cried. I asked her to talk about why it was so important to control her feelings. I expected her to say something about her mother being stoic, but instead she mentioned her stepfather.

> JULIA: One of the few statements I ever remember hearing from him was, "No crying—or I'll give you a reason."
> DL: When did he say that? Do you remember?
> JULIA: When my mother would leave. When my mother wasn't there. And my sister, Lonnie, would put me to bed and I would cry.
> DL: You mean you would cry when your mother went to work or something?
> JULIA: No, she must have been missing or something—like she had left out.
> STANLEY: What are you talking about?

Julia remembered at around age eight discovering that her mother was not in the house, and asking for her. Sometimes her mother would come back in the morning, and sometimes not. Her stepfather never explained where her mother was; he would just tell her not to cry. I commented that it could be terrifying for a child not to know where her mother was, and to be told not to cry seemed cruel. Stanley said, "Wait a minute, y'all. This makes no sense to me. Where was your mother leaving out to? She didn't work at night. She only worked during the day, and was not one to go anywhere at night."

It did seem as though the memory was incomplete, and by the end of the session, Julia seemed interested in finding out what had happened. Stanley asked Leroy if he had a theory about it. Leroy said he didn't, but suggested that his mother call her mother and ask about it.

I complimented Leroy on the idea, but Julia responded immediately that she couldn't do that. She insisted that her mother obstinately refused to discuss any aspect of the past. Julia felt she could, however, call her sister, although even to Lonnie that would seem to come "out of the blue."

> DL: Make up an excuse if you have to.
> LEROY: Tell her she was in my dream. No lie, she was in my dream, remember?

Julia agreed to make the call. Stanley said he felt really good about how much she had shared of herself, and Leroy also said he was "proud" of her. He was on his way back to school, and thanked his mother and Stanley and me for our support. The first outpatient session was scheduled for a week from that evening.

Outpatient Therapy

Leroy had had a good week at school, according to his guidance counselor there. He was eager to know whether his mother had called his aunt. She had, and they had had a long talk. It turned out that Lonnie had some helpful information to offer her sister. Julia had been aware of the fact that her stepfather sometimes beat her mother, but she had not known that at times her mother left the house afterward. She would go to a neighbor's for physical safety and for psychological respite, and would tell her older daughter to put her younger sister to bed. No one wanted to frighten Julia with the truth. Lonnie added that their stepfather was jealous of the attention their mother paid to the girls. Julia told her that the same pattern had occurred with her son and his father. The sisters talked for over an hour, and Julia ended up telling Lonnie that she was in therapy. She felt they had begun to talk to each other in a closer way and that made her very happy. At some future point, she would be able to reconnect with her mother. Stanley said to Julia, "Imagine how your mother must have felt, leaving you in the house with him, and then coming back, knowing he could beat her again. But she came back for you and Lonnie."

This was the first time that they reached out for each other spontaneously in the session. Julia was allowing Stanley not only to remind her of the past but also to give her some of the closeness and cherishing she had missed in her youth.

The fact that Julia's mother had a good reason for leaving her daughters in the house while she got help did not mean that Julia would not have felt anger at her mother for leaving with no explanation. I realized that the anger at her mother would have to be acknowledged before she would feel ready to reconnect with her. It seemed that a good place to start feeling in touch with anger might be with Stanley since her connection to him was so strong. Julia tended to deny anger at Stanley, citing his many good qualities whenever I noted a hint of disagreement between them. Julia would say, "He is the kindest of the kind, the best of the best. Have you ever heard of a man who does more than half the housework?" Idealizing Stanley, like devaluing Leroy senior, was a way of avoiding the painful complexities of the relationship, and ultimately of not becoming really intimate with Stanley. Several months into therapy Julia was able to say that she found Stanley "too gentle" at times. She said she would like him to be more decisive in his opinions so that she didn't have to make all the decisions all the time. She also wanted him to be firmer with Leroy. Stanley said he felt nervous about that.

> STANLEY: I feel I'm too soft with Leroy because I didn't have a father of my own.
> DL: The point is not to be a father, but to be decisive and firm. Stanley, what was your Granny like? Was she ever tough on you?
> STANLEY: With the other kids, yes, but only a few times with me, since I was her favorite. She could be mean to the other kids! She would pinch them on the underside of your arm. Right there. Does that hurt! She got me once, too, when I let her dog out.
> DL: Would she have let Leroy get away with anything?
> STANLEY: Lord, no!
> DL: How would she interact with Julia?
> STANLEY: She wouldn't let her get away with anything either.
> DL: Such as?
> STANLEY: Such as when she doesn't take her blood pressure medicine.
> DL: What?!
> JULIA: I know, I know. But it's expensive. And sometimes I like to buy something frivolous.

It was clear that Stanley had, as part of his past, an internal Granny who was stubborn and strong, and I wanted him to gain access to that type of behavior by remembering her. I told him to think of her and have an argument that night with Julia over her medicine—an argument that he had to win.

He followed through. Apparently, he nagged Julia all night about getting the prescription filled, picking it up, and choosing a time of day to take it. This began a very important process for Julia. It necessitated her getting angry with him, and to some extent, at me as well for "instigating" the trouble. She eventually learned that her anger was not annihilating; she could feel it and express it and call it her own instead of denying it. As Stanley and Julia argued more with each other, Leroy acted out less and less. Stanley also became more able to set limits for Leroy's behavior, for example, when Leroy was home on passes and vacations.

The Laws of Language

Shortly after Leroy had returned to Judge Paxton's, Julia suggested that Leroy set some "goals" for himself for the year, just as he had done while he was an inpatient. Leroy seemed to find the idea agreeable. He listed some goals about grades, avoiding fights, and so on. Julia said she would like to add an item to the list if that was okay with him.

> JULIA: You've got to work on your language. Leroy's language—even when it's not full of curse words and street talk—is still full of "y'all this" and "y'all that." You don't know what a bad impression you make when you talk like that; I've said this for years to you. Dr. Luepnitz always says you're smart, but not everyone will overlook your grammar.

It has been said that patients in Freudian therapy exhibit Freudian problems, and Jungian patients exhibit Jungian problems. Perhaps it should be no surprise that patients with a therapist who is intrigued with language would come up with language problems.

This topic actually led us into a discussion of words, power, and race, which continued throughout the therapy. Julia eventually acknowledged that when she told Leroy to "talk right," she meant "use standard white English." Leroy expressed indignation at this, saying that he hated when blacks tried to talk white. Stanley's position was somewhere in between. He believed that Leroy should learn to write school assignments with correct "white" grammar, but that he should talk anyway he chose to talk. Julia assumed that I would feel the same way she did about it. I said there were college professors who accepted black or white usage, as long as it was clear and internally consistent.

> JULIA: Are you saying Leroy should use so-called "Black English" in school?
> DL: No. I don't know. I guess I agree with Stanley.
> JULIA: I can't believe it, you two. Don't you think Leroy sounds ignorant when he says, "Mom, sometimes it just *bees* that way"? Did you ever hear a news reporter or . . . or a president or somebody talk like that?

DL: It couldn't hurt.

STANLEY: I thought you sort of liked Leroy's rap, Julia. You always say he's comical and he has the gift of gab.

JULIA: It's true. He does. But I'm talking about something different.

STANLEY: Anyway, Julia, you're the one to talk about good language. You can talk real white, all right, but then again, she can curse a blue streak.

JULIA: Stanley has a thing about this. Twice a year I'll say a nasty word, and he gets all quiet and offended.

STANLEY: I'm sorry. I don't think a woman should curse.

JULIA: Now you should hear Stanley's friends. And Leroy for that matter.

STANLEY: Males, you just expect it. But I personally hate it when a woman curses. I know, I know: I'm old-fashioned. But it just seems so unfeminine. I would have to say—unnatural.

DL: Doesn't that give more freedom of speech to male children than adult women?

JULIA: Thank you. Thank you.

LEROY: Oh, no. Women's Lib.

JULIA: You're sixteen, Leroy. I think you can pronounce the whole word *liberation.*

LEROY [*laughing*]: Did you hear Deborah and Stanley agree: A person should talk however they prefer? Dag!

DL: You know, these sessions were a lot easier when Leroy was in trouble with the law.

The discussion led to an exploration of other issues related to race and gender. In a later session, Stanley said he felt that Julia sometimes seemed to want to impress their white friends, and that her studying and planning to get ahead were part of that. He admitted that he resented when her studying cut into their time together. We devoted several sessions to examining these issues, raising questions such as: To what extent was Stanley critical of Julia's ambition simply because she was a woman? To what degree was Julia's ambition her own, and to what degree was she aiming to satisfy the internal industrious mother who had always wanted her daughter to be educated?

Some therapists would be interested only in the communication and relational issues among the family members in these sessions, and would disregard the content. The communication issues and emotional transactions were, of course, very important. There was, for example, a new vitality in the relationship between Stanley and Julia. Leroy was able to disagree with them, but not in an oppositional way. (He agreed to Julia's suggestion about setting goals, whereas earlier he probably would have rejected it out of hand.)

As important as those issues are, however, I think that the content of the debates in these sessions was also important. In a sense, although we were no longer talking about the courts, we were still talking about *the law* and our relationship to it. We were talking about laws, written and unwritten, that dictate who may speak to whom in what ways and at what cost. We were dealing with the unwritten social laws that regulate who is permitted to excel. We were, at times, even talking about how one could really trust one's goals and those of others in a society that manufactures many of our felt needs and desires.

These are not the kinds of questions that find resolution in therapy, but they exist nonetheless at the foundations of all therapy, as they do at the foundation of all forms of social discourse. I find it rewarding and compatible both with feminism and with psychoanalytic theory (since both are interested in language and in desire) to make these issues an explicit part of the therapeutic discourse where possible.

The Remainder of Treatment with the Johnsons

Leroy finished his year at Judge Paxton's and did very well academically. Julia and Stanley agreed to let him spend part of the summer with his grandparents in the south. It was during his visit there that he asked to spend his last year of high school down there. It was in the context of discussing the grandparents that a new issue emerged. Leroy, it turned out, had a lot of feelings about the fact that his grandmother had raised his sister but not him. He said he had the feeling that if he had been raised with his grandmother, he would not have gotten into trouble. His resentment of the grandmother, I thought, could not be completely unrelated to the fact that he had, after all, attacked an old black woman on the street. Julia, for her part, also had some feelings about having "given up" her daughter but not her son.

The gender issues in this discussion were very salient. In some ways, she realized, she felt she would have to protect a daughter, whereas a son would perhaps be able to protect *her*. This was one of the final issues we dealt with in treatment, and as we worked on it, Julia came to feel comfortable with the idea of Leroy taking his turn living with grandmother. She no longer felt that it was a matter of "giving him up," but one of allowing him to have the chance to know his grandparents and to live in the country for a while.

Leroy finished high school, and sent frequent letters and cassette tapes home. I terminated with Julia and Stanley several months after Leroy left for his grandparents, and their relationship seemed very strong indeed. When I phoned the family two years later for an update, Leroy was in his second year of college at a small school 100 miles away. His grades were low Cs and Ds, meaning that he could not be accepted as an engineering major as he had hoped. He had enjoyed his courses, however, and had friends at school. He had been in absolutely no trouble with the law in the three years since his appearance in our facility.

One year before my call, Leroy had apparently asked Julia to track down his father. Julia did so and learned that Leroy senior had died in a car accident three years previously. Julia told me that Leroy had been grief-stricken by the news and had made a visit to his father's family in upstate New York that summer. She said he had written a paper on Vietnam veterans for a sociology course. She could not remember whether he had done so before or after learning of his father's death.

Michelle had come north to spend a summer with Julia and Stanley and had decided to look for work nearby. Both Julia and Stanley felt that the therapy had helped them tremendously.

Commentary

One year of therapy did not address all the problems in this family, but it did address the presenting problem (Leroy's acting out) in a way that left the family less father-absent and less patriarchal than it had been. Leroy started therapy with a history of antisocial behavior, and ended therapy with no further trouble with the law. He started therapy with no idea of who his father was, and ended with the ability to talk about his father, to describe him and ask questions about him, to understand how he was like his father and how he was different from him. Because of therapy, he learned of his father's death and was able to mourn the fact that he never knew him. It is reasonable to hope that this acknowledged loss of the father will contribute to the importance Leroy will one day give to taking care of his own children. This hope is strengthened by the fact that Leroy was able to accept some parental attention from Stanley (as well as from men at school and in our inpatient program). Through therapy, Stanley gained confidence in his ability to be both gentle and tough from summoning the skills of his most introjected parent, his great-grandmother. These results can be attributed to the *psychoanalytically* derived concepts of the therapy; a therapy that was dedicated to symptom removal alone would not have achieved these ends.

Because the therapy was *feminist* in addition to being psychoanalytically derived, Julia never had to hear any more "common sense" ideas about how she had caused all of Leroy's problems. On the contrary, therapy provided her with confirmation of her strengths as a parent and admiration for her stamina. I also validated her interest in finishing her education and urged Stanley to support her in this as well. The therapy was guided by the feminist maxim that men should learn to take better care of children, and women should learn to take better care of themselves. Moreover, the couple's relationship was fortified by the therapy. Julia did not leave Stanley for another abusive man, as do some women who, based on their experience, equate masculinity with abuse. Julia gained empathy for her mother who had left her alone at times because she herself was victimized by an angry husband.

There were two reasons why Julia was able to grieve these terribly sad events and to allow Stanley to take care of her: (1) Stanley had the love and generosity she needed, and (2) the therapy had provided a holding environment that permitted her to feel safe in being more vulnerable to him.

As in all therapies, the provision of the holding environment for this family was extremely important. It was not only my work as a therapist that was significant in this regard, however, but all the holding and containing that was done by the therapeutic environment in which our sessions took place. It cannot be trivial that in Leroy's dream of his father, although the father was wearing Stanley's vest, his general appearance was that of Jarvis, the male counselor who led Leroy's group therapy. Jarvis was also present in the session when Leroy burst in my office without knocking. Jarvis and I had worked together enough over the years that, without speaking, we could act as a team to set an important limit for Leroy.

Pauline, the clinic receptionist, had also contributed to the holding environment when she had made a special trip to let me know that Julia was crying. We therapists forget too easily how much information we receive from secretaries and receptionists. These employees—almost all women— also draw an enormous amount of maternal transference, probably sparing therapists much of the family's raw pain. In this particular instance, without Pauline's concern about Julia's tears, an important intervention might have been lost.

Many readers may find these comments a mere purveying of the obvious. If "everyone knows" that our support staff provides a significant aspect of the holding environment for our families, however, then why is there not a single mention of this fact in a case report in the family therapy literature? Part of the feminist contribution may be to call attention to this type of invisible and invaluable work until it routinely becomes a part of our vision.

I have mentioned several times the issue of children bearing and/or acting out the psychological conflicts of their parents. Again, I want to emphasize that this does not mean that children do not act out their *own* psychological conflicts; they certainly do. But the intergenerational acquisition and staging of parental pain and protest is something very real, and something that merits further investigation in families now and historically. I have used object-relations theory language to describe how Leroy Johnson "contained" or "stored" his mother's anger, and how Kip McGinn "stored" his father's grief, through the process that object-relations theorists call "projective identification." Other family therapists, such as Ivan Nagy, use a slightly different language and talk of "legacies" of "unfinished business" bequeathed across generations.

Intergenerational legacies have also been described by nonpsychological writers in other contexts. One very interesting example is a description of the family of Benjamin Franklin, by feminist writer Elizabeth Cady Stanton in 1875. In an essay entitled "Home Life," Stanton wrote about Dr. Franklin's mistreatment of his wife, and the effect of the wife's outrage on their children:

> Dr. Franklin . . . went to Europe, leaving his wife behind him, and never saw her face for 11 years. She had shared his poverty, practiced his poor Richard's maxims . . . bred children and nursed them . . . while Benjamin enjoyed the splendors of a court . . . and choice society. Of course, when he came back, the poor drudge was no match for the philosopher. . . . That her heart rebelled in her solitude and neglect is manifest in the headstrong acts of her children. He quarreled with his sons and disinherited one of them: thus were the mother's wrongs revenged. A just retribution for every injustice to woman is sure to come in the vice and crime of her children to the 3rd and 4th generation. [1875/1981, p. 137]

A nonfeminist reader might interpret this to mean that all crimes against society are "caused" by the repressed anger of mothers. This, of course, is untrue, and Stanton herself did not believe it. Feminists, like psychoanalytic thinkers, believe in the overdetermination of events. The point here is simply to note that women's unheard cries of anger, whether they are the cries of forgotten wives of famous men or the tranquilized fury of Margo McGinn or the desperate plea of Manolus's mother as she is bricked up in the foundations of culture, this ancient ire, cannot *not* affect the children women bear. Women's rage is passed on in some way, in some form, to their children, and sometimes children take up the mother's battle with the world. This, I think, was part of Leroy's psychology.

One of the most enjoyable aspects of discussing the Johnsons is knowing how rare it is to find a black family described in psychoanalytic terms. Structural family therapists such as Minuchin and strategic therapists such as Haley, of course, describe black families a great deal, but the more psychoanalytic authors in the field of family therapy do not. It is still not uncommon, in fact, to hear single-parent families described at psychoanalytic meetings as "pathological." There is no mention of black families *per se* in Scharff and Scharff's comprehensive *Object Relations Family Therapy*. The Scharffs, however, do make this passing comment about *poor* families: "Clients with overwhelming poverty and social problems want help that is more immediate and less abstract. It was to meet such family's needs that Minuchin and his colleagues developed structural family therapy for problem resolution. Our method alone does not help in such cases" (p. 7). The Scharffs go on to say that there are some "disadvantaged" families who, if introduced to a more reflective therapy, will "take to it," but they do not describe such families in their book.

My experience is so out of phase with the conventional wisdom about insight and the urban black family that it bears elaboration. Families do vary in their interest and skill in interpretation, their willingness to reflect on their motives, their fascination with their own history, and their openness to analyzing dreams. However, one of the best predictors of how eager and how adept a family will be at remembering and interpreting their history is the size of their families of origin. People who grow up with seven siblings and grandparents and cousins on both sides know more about families than people who grow up as only children with no extended kin. People from large families can quote more varieties of sibling rivalry and have had more opportunity to notice that certain problems repeat through generations. Since American black families tend to be larger than white families, and also because of residual African values that emphasize the importance of family, many black families (in my experience) are more adept with the psychoanalytic aspects of therapy than white families.

The Johnson family certainly had its share of "reality" problems and had "immediate" needs to be addressed. However, in a feminist object-relations approach, the task of immediate needs does not exist in opposition to the task of interpreting and reflecting with the family on their life. I have called the first stage of therapy the crisis stage—distinguishing it from the later remembering and reworking stages—but in some sense that delineation is artificial. Even in the first session of therapy with Julia, I asked her to remember that she had been the person responsible for her son, and invited her to reflect on the fact that even independent people need to depend on others. Feminist theorists in many disciplines tend to see as patriarchal the bifurcation of the world into feeling and thinking, dependent and independent, reflection and action. Whereas the goals of traditional object-relations family therapy are purely reflective and the goals of strategic therapists purely behavioral, the goals of feminist psychotherapy are both reflective and behavioral. A family who comes to the therapist in pain and leaves with insight but no symptom relief, or with relief but no new understanding, has not had the most one can have from therapy.

Another task of a feminist psychotherapy is to make some effort to understand the family in its social and historical contexts. Elaine Pinder-hughes has described the competing value systems in contemporary black culture: residual African values, mainstream white values, and the values of the "victim system" created by poverty and racism. Julia Johnson's need for achievement was consistent with the values of mainstream white culture, but it conflicted somewhat with the black values of community and family ties. Her studying conflicted with Leroy's need for her to visit him at Judge Paxton's, and was also a source of conflict with Stanley. Julia's leaving her daughter behind for her mother to raise was consistent with the norms of Afro-American families, but conflicted somewhat with the norms of the white psychiatric establishment which saw it as one more example of "instability" in her history. Julia enjoyed Leroy's style of talking and his humor, but she wanted him to present himself more in line with mainstream white standards.

The "victim system" figures greatly into the history of this family as well. As mentioned earlier, adolescent white sons of the upper class are not sent to delinquent schools like Judge Paxton's when they break the law. In countless other ways, this family suffered as families of other classes do not. Julia Johnson knew what it meant to raise a baby in a small apartment without a telephone or air conditioning, and sometimes without heat. She had been on welfare for a time, and talked about how hearing the words "welfare mother" on television made her feel angry and ashamed. She was glad to be earning a living at the present time, but she reported that she had received more money from welfare at times than she had at certain (very demanding) jobs.

Behind the one-way mirror, my team had seen a mother who repeatedly abandoned her son while he was away at school. What could not be seen through the glass was the fact that this mother had been abandoned by her own mother as a young girl because she was being physically abused by her husband. What is still less obvious to the superficial view is the fact that the husband was a black man who had been unemployed for a decade. Of him we know no more.

Leroy was also abandoned by a father who had abused his wife. Leroy senior is said to have "never been the same" after returning from Vietnam. The pain and terror that lie behind that phrase were never uncovered in our therapy; Leroy perhaps learned of it when he visited his father's family.

There are other issues here that touch on race, for example, the fact of my being a white therapist with a black family. It may be that Julia's stereotypes about whites made her distrust me in the beginning of the therapy more than she would have distrusted a black therapist. For my part, I must wonder if my stereotypes made me feel more threatened by what I saw as Leroy's sexual posturing in our first meeting. After the first or second session, I do not remember sensing any tensions around race, but we can be sure that our assumptions about race are so deeply embedded that they are never absent from any aspect of the treatment.

Two therapists who read the case of Leroy before this book was published asked me how I had come to feel so comfortable working with black families. They said that it seemed not uncommon for white therapists, in trying to overcome any trace of unconscious racism, to end up being overly deferential or cautious with families of a different race and to end up doing a pale version of treatment. I have seen therapists exhibit this problem, and it would seem that the only solution to it is simply to gain more experience with families of many racial, ethnic, and class backgrounds. My personal comfort in working with black families may also derive from my coming from a large extended family, with many values similar to those of black culture.

Students sometimes raise the question of whether or not it is best to assign a same-race therapist to a family when possible. This is a complex issue with no easy answers. People tend to assume that a white therapist will be more easily accepted by a black family than a black therapist will be accepted by a white family. This stereotype was shaken up definitively for me when I worked in a clinic with a black male team partner. Watching him do his usual outstanding work with anorectic families who came from wealthy, "lily-white" suburbs convinced me that, while certain dynamics about race will always be operative when the family and therapist are different colors, there is no reason not to refer white families to black therapists.

The overwhelmingly important issue about race in family therapy is not which therapist should treat which patient, but how to train and support nonwhite therapists to become directors, approved supervisors, and authors. To date, not a single book in family therapy has been written by a black therapist! Thus, a *re-membering* in the family of family therapists must occur, a bringing to the center of power more women therapists and therapists of color.

One other issue about race deserves mention. Several colleagues have asked if I was surprised to hear Julia Johnson, "this working-class black woman," respond comfortably to my challenging the sexist objection to women cursing, and even champion the phrase "women's *liberation"* as opposed to "women's *lib."* The answer is no, I was not surprised, and I don't think anyone who has been active in the movement could be surprised. It is true that some black women are disinterested in feminism—but so are some white women, from every social class. It is a mistake to call the women's movement in the United States a "white women's movement," and it is a great disservice to black feminists to assume that only college-educated Caucasians are committed to justice for women. I would not deny that there is vestigial reacism in the women's movment—but there is also vestigial sexism in the women's movement. None of us can stand freely above our civilization and our upbringing, for even as we are criticizing it, we are using its verbal currency to do so.

Change, while not inevitable, is plausible. As for attitudes to the feminist movement, for example, a *Newsweek* poll in 1986 found that 76 percent of nonwhite women and 70 percent of white women believed that the women's movement had "improved their lives." To the question, "Do you consider yourself a feminist?" 64 percent of nonwhite women and 56 percent of white women answered yes (p. 51). The fact that more black women than white women call themselves feminists may be because women who work outside the home use that label more than women who do not. (See also Patricia Hill Collins's *Black Feminist Thought* [1989].)

Final Thoughts on Leroy

The words of Ezekiel once again crystallize the psychological and social issues we have been discussing: "The fathers have eaten bitter fruit, and the children's teeth are set on edge." For Leroy, therapy initiated the process of discovering and identifying the bitter fruit. One would like to believe that the appetite for insight that he gained in therapy will grow to be truly subversive to the system that victimizes.

But it would be no surprise if a long-term follow-up were to uncover a much bleaker result. In college Leroy will continue to compete with young people who have enjoyed more educational privileges than he and whose lives have not been so marked by loss. He will enter a job market in which the unemployment rate is much higher for blacks than for whites, and even if he graduates college, he will earn less than his white counterpart. He will continue to face conflicts between the traditional black value system and that of mainstream society. The syntax and lexicon he will use in job interviews will not match the syntax and lexicon he is most familiar with.

Even the best therapy cannot bring about radical social change—something family interpreters must remember.

REFERENCES

Ackerman, N. 1958. *The psychodynamics of family life.* New York: Basic Books.

———. 1966. *Treating the troubled family.* New York: Basic Books.

———. 1967. The emergence of family diagnosis and treatment. A personal view. *Psychotherapy* 4: 125–29.

———, and Jahoda, M. 1950. *Anti-Semitism and emotional disorder: A psychoanalytic interpretation.* New York: Harper and Brothers.

Addams, J. 1910/1981. *Twenty years at Hull House.* New York: New American Library.

Ahern, D., and Bliss, B. 1976. *The economics of being a woman.* New York: McGraw-Hill.

Anthony, E. J. 1980. The family and the psychoanalytic process in children. In *The psychoanalytic study of the child.* New Haven: Yale University Press, vol. 35: 3–34.

Ariès, P. 1962. *Centuries of childhood.* New York: Random House.

Ault-Riché, M., ed. 1986. *Women and family therapy.* Rockville, Md.: Aspen Systems Corp.

Avis, J. M. 1985. The politics of functional family therapy: A feminist critique. *Journal of Marital and Family Therapy* 11: 127–38.

Bachofen, J. J. 1861. *Das Mutterrecht.* Published in English as *Myth, religion and mother-right.* 1967. Princeton, N.J.: Princeton University Press.

Badinter, E. 1980. *L'amour en plus.* Published in English as *Mother-love.* 1981. New York: Macmillan.

Balsdon, J. P. V. D. 1962. *Roman women: Their history and habits.* London: Bodley Head.

Barrett, M. 1980. *Women's oppression today: Problems in Marxist feminist analysis.* London: Verso Editions.

Bart, P. 1983. Review of Chodorow's *The Reproduction of Mothering.* In *Mothering: Essays in feminist theory,* ed. J. Trebilcot, pp. 147–53. Totowa, N.J.: Rowman and Allanheld.

Basow, S. 1986. *Gender stereotypes: Traditions and alternatives,* 2nd ed. New York: Brooks-Cole.

Bateson, G. 1966. From Versailles to cybernetics. In *Steps to an ecology of mind,* pp. 469–77. New York: Ballantine.

———. 1970. The roots of ecological crisis. In *Steps to an ecology of mind,* pp. 488–93. New York: Ballantine.

———. 1971. The cybernetics of "self": A theory of alcoholism. In *Steps to an ecology of mind,* pp. 309–38. New York: Ballantine.

———. 1972. *Steps to an ecology of mind.* New York: Ballantine.

———. 1979. *Mind and nature.* New York: Dutton.

Bateson, G., and Bateson, M. C. 1987. *Angels fear.* New York: Macmillan.

Bateson, G., Jackson, D., Haley, J., and Weakland, J. H. 1956. Towards a theory of schizophrenia. In *Steps to an ecology of mind,* ed. G. Bateson, pp. 201–27. New York: Ballantine.

Bateson, M. C. 1984. *With a daughter's eye.* New York: William Morrow.

Belenky, M. F., Clinchy, B. M., Goldberger, N. R., and Tarule, J. M. 1986. *Women's ways of knowing.* New York: Basic Books.

Bepko, C., and Krestan, J. 1985. *The responsibility trap.* New York: Free Press.

Bernal, G., and Ysern, E. 1986. Family therapy and ideology. *Journal of Marital and Family Therapy* 12 (2): 129–35.

Bernard, J. 1972. *The future of marriage.* New York: Bantam Books.

Bernardez, T. 1978. Women and anger: Conflicts with aggression in contemporary women. *Journal of the American Medical Women's Association* 33: 215–19.

———. 1982. The female therapist in relation to male roles. In *Men in transition,* ed. K. Solomon and N. Levy. New York: Plenum Press.

Bettelheim, B. 1982. *Freud and man's soul.* New York: Simon & Schuster.

Bion, W. R. 1961. *Experiences in groups.* London: Tavistock Publications.

Bodin, A. 1981. The interactional view: Family therapy approaches of the Mental Research Institute. In *Handbook of family therapy,* ed. A. Gurman and D. Kniskern. New York: Brunner/Mazel.

Bograd, M. 1984. Family systems approaches to wife battering: A feminist critique. *American Journal of Orthopsychiatry* 54: 558–68.

———. 1985. Does the end justify the means? The use of paradox to modify the power imbalance between spouses. Paper presented at the American Association of Marriage and Family Therapy.

Boscolo, L., Cecchin, G., Hoffman, L., and Penn, P. 1987. *Milan systemic family therapy.* New York: Basic Books.

Boss, P. 1977. A clarification of the concept of psychological father absence in families experiencing ambiguity of boundary. *Journal of Marriage and the Family* 39: 141–51.

———. 1987. The role of intuition in family research: Three issues of ethics. In Symbolic experiential journeys: A tribute to Carl Whitaker, ed. R. Garfield, A. Greenberg, and S. Sugarman. *Contemporary Family Therapy* 9 (1–2): 146–58.

Boszormenyi-Nagy, I., and Spark, G. 1973. *Invisible loyalties.* New York: Harper & Row Medical Dept.

Boszormenyi-Nagy, I., and Ulrich, D. 1981. Contextual family therapy. In *Handbook of family therapy,* ed. A. Gurman and D. Kniskern, pp. 159–86. New York: Brunner/Mazel.

Bowen, M. 1978. *Family therapy in clinical practice.* New York: Jason Aronson.

Box, S., Copley, B., Magagna, J., and Moustaki, E. 1981. *Psychotherapy with families.* London: Routledge & Kegan Paul.

Braverman, L. 1986. Social casework and strategic therapy. *Social Casework* 67 (4): 234–39.

Brendler, J. 1987. A perspective on the brief hospitalization of whole families. *Journal of Family Therapy* 9: 113–30.

Brickman, J. 1984. Feminist, nonsexist and traditional models of therapy: Implications for working with incest. *Women and Therapy* 3 (1): 49–67.

Broderick, C., and Schrader, S. 1981. The history of professional and family therapy. In *Handbook of family therapy,* ed. A. Gurman and D. Kniskern, pp. 5–31. New York: Brunner/Mazel.

Brodsky, A. M., and Hare-Mustin, R. 1980. *Women and psychotherapy.* New York: Guilford Press.

Broverman, I. K., Vogel, S. R., Broverman, D. M., Clarkson, F. E., and Rosenkrantz, P. S. 1972. Sex-role stereotypes: A current appraisal. *Journal of Social Issues* 28 (2): 59–78.

Burland, J. 1986. *Autonomy as destiny: A feminist construction of female psychology, development and self-realization.* Ph.D. diss., The Fielding Institute.

Caplan, P., and Hall-McCorquodale, I. 1985. Mother-blaming in major clinical journals. *American Journal of Orthopsychiatry* 55 (3): 345–53.

Carmen, E., Russo, N. R., and Miller, J. B. 1981. Inequality and women's mental health: An overview. *American Journal of Psychiatry* 138 (10): 1319–30.

Carter, E. A., and McGoldrick, M., eds. 1980. *The family life cycle: A framework for family therapy.* New York: Gardner Press.

References

Caust, B. L., Libow, J. A., and Raskin, P. A. 1981. Challenges and promises of training women as family systems therapists. *Family Process* 20: 439–47.

Chernin, K. 1981. *The obsession: Reflections on the tyranny of slenderness.* New York: Harper & Row.

———. 1985. *The hungry self.* New York: Times Books.

Chesler, P. 1972. *Women and madness.* Garden City, N.Y.: Doubleday.

———. 1986. *Mothers on trial.* New York: McGraw-Hill.

Chodorow, N. 1978. *The reproduction of mothering: Psychoanalysis and the sociology of gender.* Berkeley: University of California Press.

Cixous, H. 1981. The laugh of the Medusa. Trans. Keith Cohen and Paula Cohen. In *New French feminisms,* ed. E. Marks and I. de Courtivron. New York: Schocken Books.

Colapinto, J. 1985. Maturana and the ideology of conformity. *The Family Therapy Networker* 9 (3): 29–30.

Collins, P. H. 1989. *Black feminist thought.* Winchester, Mass.: Allen & Unwin.

Combrinck-Graham, L., Gursky, E., and Brendler, J. 1982. Hospitalization of single-parent families of disturbed children. *Family Process* 21: 141–52.

Cowan, R. S. 1983. *More work for mother.* New York: Basic Books.

Coyne, J. 1985. Artful, yes—but necessary? *The Family Therapy Networker* 9 (2): 59–61.

Daly, M. 1973. *Beyond God the father: Toward a philosophy of women's liberation.* Boston: Beacon Press.

———. 1978. *Gyn/Ecology.* Boston: Beacon Press.

Davis, N. Z. 1983. *The return of Martin Guerre.* Cambridge, Mass.: Harvard University Press.

de Beauvoir, S. 1952. *The second sex.* New York: Alfred A. Knopf.

———. 1956. *The Mandarins.* Paris: Gallimard.

Degler, C. 1980. *At odds: Women and the family in America from the Revolution to the present.* New York: Oxford University Press.

Dell, P. 1982. Beyond homeostasis: Toward a concept of coherence. *Family Process* 21: 21–41.

de Mause, L., ed. 1974. *The history of childhood.* New York: Psychohistory Press.

Derrida, J. 1976. *Of grammatology.* Trans. Gayatri Spivak. Baltimore: Johns Hopkins University Press.

de Saussure, F. 1907. *Course on general linguistics.* Trans. W. Baskin. New York: Fontane Books, 1974.

de Shazer, S. 1985. *Keys to solution in brief therapy.* new York: Norton.

Dewey, J. 1920. *Reconstruction in philosophy.* Boston: Beacon Press, 1948.

———. 1931. The development of American Pragmatism. In J. Dewey, *Philosophy and Civilization.* New York: Putnam.

Dicks, H. 1967. *Marital tensions.* New York: Basic Books.

Dimen, M. 1986. *Surviving sexual contradictions.* New York: Macmillan.

Dinnerstein, D. 1976. *The mermaid and the minotaur.* New York: Harper & Row.

Dobash, R., and Dobash, R. P. 1977. Love, honour and obey: Institutional ideologies and the struggle of battered women. *Contemporary Crisis* 1: 403–15.

Donzelot, J. 1979. *The policing of families.* New York: Pantheon Books. Originally published in 1977 as *La police des familles,* trans. Robert Hurley. Paris: Les Editions de Minuit.

Du Bois, E. C. 1978. *Feminism and suffrage.* Ithaca, N.Y.: Cornell University Press.

———, ed. 1981. *Elizabeth Cady Stanton and Susan B. Anthony: Correspondences, writings, speeches.* New York: Schocken Books.

Durkheim, E. 1951. *Suicide: A study in sociology.* Trans. J. A. Spaulding and G. Simpson. Glencoe, Ill.: Free Press.

Ehrenreich, B. 1983. *The hearts of men.* Garden City, N.Y.: Doubleday.

————, and English, D. 1978. *For her own good: 150 years of the experts' advice to women.* Garden City, N.Y.: Doubleday.

Ehrensaft, D. 1983. When women and men mother. In *Mothering: Essays in feminist theory,* ed. H. Trebilcot, pp. 41–61. Totowa, N.J.: Rowman & Littlefield.

Eichenbaum, L., and Orbach, S. 1983. *Understanding women: A feminist psychoanalytic view.* New York: Basic Books.

Engels, F. 1884. The origins of the family, private property and the state. In K. Marx and F. Engels, *Selected Works.* New York: International Publishers, 1968.

Erickson, G. 1984. A menu note on the cybernetic network. *Family Process* 23 (2): 200–204.

————. 1986. Prolegomena to the deconstruction of family therapy: Response to Dell and Duhl. *Journal of Marital and Family Therapy* 12 (4): 425–26.

Erikson, E. 1950. *Childhood and society.* New York: Norton.

Fanon, F. 1963. *The wretched of the earth.* New York: Grove Press.

Fast, I. 1984. *Gender identity: A differentiation model.* Hillsdale, N.J.: Lawrence Erlbaum.

Ferguson, A. 1983. On conceiving motherhood and sexuality: A feminist materialist approach. In *Mothering: Essays in feminist theory,* ed. H. Trebilcot, pp. 153–84. Totowa, N.J.: Rowman & Littlefield.

Firestone, S. 1970. *The dialectic of sex.* New York: Bantam Books.

Fisch, R., Weakland, J. H., and Segal, L. 1983. *The tactics of change: Doing therapy briefly.* San Francisco: Jossey-Bass.

Flugel, J. C. 1921. *The psychoanalytic study of the family.* London: Hogarth Press.

Framo, J. L. 1981. The integration of marital therapy sessions with family of origin. In *Handbook of family therapy,* ed. A. Gurman and D. Kniskern, pp. 133–58. New York: Brunner/Mazel.

Fraser, A. 1984. *The weaker vessel.* New York: Alfred A. Knopf.

French, M. 1985. *Beyond power: On women, men, and morals.* New York: Summit Books.

Freud, S. 1905. *Dora: An analysis of a case of Hysteria.* Collier Books edition. New York: Macmillan, 1963.

————. 1908. "Civilized" sexual morality and modern nervous illness. *Standard Edition of the Complete Psychological Works of Sigmund Freud,* vol. 9, pp. 179–204. London: Hogarth Press, 1959.

————. 1909. Notes upon a case of obsessional neurosis. In *Three case histories.* Collier Books edition. New York: Macmillan, 1963.

————. 1913. *Totem and taboo. Standard Edition,* vol. 13, pp. 1–161. London: Hogarth Press, 1955.

————. 1918. History of an infantile neurosis. In *Three case histories.* Collier Books edition. New York: Macmillan, 1963.

————. 1920. *Beyond the pleasure principle. Standard Edition,* vol. 18, pp. 3–64. London: Hogarth Press, 1959.

————. 1926. *The question of lay analysis. Standard Edition,* vol. 20, pp. 179–258. London: Hogarth Press, 1959.

————. 1930. *Civilization and its discontents.* Trans. James Strachey. New York: Norton, 1961.

————. 1935. *Letters of Sigmund Freud, 1873–1939.* Ed. Ernst Freud. London: Hogarth Press, 1961.

————. 1940. An outline of psychoanalysis. Pt. 2. "The technique of psychoanalysis." *Standard Edition,* vol. 23, pp. 172–73. London: Hogarth Press, 1964.

Friedan, B. 1963. *The feminine mystique.* New York: Norton.

References

Gallop, J. 1982. *The daughter's seduction: Feminism and psychoanalysis.* Ithaca, N.Y.: Cornell University Press.

GAP (Group for the advancement of psychiatry). 1970. The field of family therapy. (GAP Report No. 78). New York: GAP.

Gelinas, D. 1983. The persisting negative effects of incest. *Psychiatry* 46: 312–32.

Giles-Sims, J. 1983. *Wife battering: A systems theory approach.* New York: Guilford Press.

Gilligan, C. 1982. *In a different voice.* Cambridge, Mass.: Harvard University Press.

———. 1987. Oedipus and psyche: Two stories about love. Paper read at Haverford College Conference on Complex Femininity, February 1987.

Gilman, C. P. 1899. *The yellow wallpaper.* Old Westbury, N.Y.: The Feminist Press, 1973.

Glick, P. 1981. A demographic picture of black families. In *Black families,* ed. H. P. McAdoo. Beverly Hills, Cal.: Sage Publications.

Gold, A., and St. Ange, C. 1974. Development of sex-role stereotypes in black and white elementary school girls. *Developmental Psychology* 10 (3): 461.

Goldner, V. 1985. Feminism and family therapy. *Family Process* 24: 31–47.

———. 1987. Instrumentalism, feminism and the limits of family therapy. *Journal of family psychology* 1 (1): 109–16.

Gordon, L. 1977. *Woman's body, woman's right: A social history of birth control in America.* New York: Viking Penguin.

Gouldner, A. 1970. *The coming crisis in western sociology.* New York: Basic Books.

Greenberg, J. R., and Mitchell, S. A. 1983. *Object relations in psychoanalytic theory.* Cambridge, Mass.: Harvard University Press.

Greenspan, M. 1983. *A new approach to women and therapy.* New York: McGraw-Hill.

Guerin, P. 1976. *Family therapy: Theory and practice.* New York: Gardner Press.

Gurman, A., and Kniskern, D., eds. 1981. *Handbook of family therapy.* New York: Brunner/ Mazel.

Gutman, H. 1976. *The black family in slavery and freedom: 1750–1925.* New York: Pantheon.

Hafner, R. J. 1986. *Marriage and mental illness: A sex-roles perspective.* New York: Guilford Press.

Haley, J. 1963. *Strategies of psychotherapy.* New York: Grune & Stratton.

———. 1976. *Problem-solving therapy.* San Francisco: Jossey-Bass.

———. 1980. *Leaving home: The therapy of disturbed young people.* New York: McGraw-Hill.

———. 1984. *Ordeal therapy.* San Francisco: Jossey-Bass.

———, and Hoffman, L. 1967. *Techniques of family therapy.* New York: Basic Books.

Hare-Mustin, R. C. 1978. A feminist approach to family therapy. *Family Process* 17: 181–94.

———. 1987. The problem of gender in family therapy. *Family Process* 26: 15–27.

Hareven, T. 1982. American families in transition: Historical perspectives on change. In *Normal Family Processes,* ed. F. Walsh. New York: Guilford Press.

Heidegger, M. 1962. *The question of being.* Trans. W. Kluback and J. T. Wilde. New York: Twayne.

Herman, J. 1981. *Father-daughter incest.* Cambridge, Mass.: Harvard University Press.

Hines, P., and Boyd-Franklin, N. 1982. Black families. In *Ethnicity and family therapy,* ed. M. McGoldrick, J. Pearce, and J. Giordano. New York: Guilford Press.

Hoffman, L. 1981. *Foundations of family therapy.* New York: Basic Books.

Hofstadter, R. 1962. *Anti-intellectualism in American life.* New York: Vintage Books.

Horney, K. 1922. The genesis of the castration complex in women. In *Feminine psychology,* pp. 37–53. New York: Norton, 1967.

————. 1932. The dread of woman. In *Feminine psychology,* pp. 133–46. New York: Norton, 1967.

Hrdy, S. 1981. *The woman that never evolved.* Cambridge, Mass.: Harvard University Press,

Irigaray, L. 1977. *Ce sexe qui n'en est pas un.* Paris: Editions de Minuit.

Jacoby, R. 1975. *Social amnesia.* Boston: Beacon Press.

————. 1983. *The repression of psychoanalysis: Otto Fenichel and the political Freudians.* New York: Basic Books.

James, K., and McIntyre, D. 1983. The reproduction of families: The social role of family therapy? *Journal of Marital and Family Therapy* 9: 119–29.

James, W. 1906. What pragmatism means. In *Pragmatism and other essays,* pp. 22–28. New York: Washington Square Press, 1963.

Janik, A., and Toulmin, S. 1973. *Wittgenstein's Vienna.* New York: Simon & Schuster.

Joffe, C. 1985. Families, family planners and the bureaucratization of sexuality in American society. Paper presented at the American Sociological Association meetings in Washington, D.C., August 1985.

————. 1986. *The regulation of sexuality.* Philadelphia: Temple University Press.

Johnson, J. 1977. Androgyny and the maternal principle. *School Review* 86 (1): 50–69.

Johnston, H. W. 1903. *The private life of the Romans.* Chicago: Scott, Foresman.

Joshel, S. R. 1986. Nurturing the master's child: Slavery and the Roman child-nurse. *Signs* 12 (1): 3–22.

Kantor, R. M. 1977. *Men and women of the corporation.* New York: Basic Books.

Kaplan, M. 1983. A woman's view of DSM-III. *American Psychologist* (July): 786–814.

Keats, J. 1817. Letter to George and Thomas Keats. In *The Norton anthology of English literature,* vol. 2, pp. 704–5. New York: Norton, 1974.

Keeney, B. 1983. *The aesthetics of change.* New York: Guilford Press.

————, and Ross, J. 1985. The dance of duality. *The Family Therapy Networker* 9: 47–50.

Keeney, B., and Silverstein, O. 1986. *The therapeutic voice of Olga Silverstein.* New York: Guilford Press.

Keller, E. F. 1985. *Reflections on gender and science.* New Haven, Conn.: Yale University Press.

Kerber, L. 1986. Some cautionary words for historians. *Signs* 11 (2): 304–16. Special issue on *In a different voice,* by Carol Gilligan, with a reply by Gilligan.

Kirschner, D., and Kirschner, S. 1986. *Comprehensive family therapy.* New York: Brunner/ Mazel.

Klein, M. 1975. *Envy and gratitude and other works, 1946–1963.* New York: Delacorte Press.

Kovel, J. 1976. *A Complete Guide to Therapy: From Psychotherapy to Behavior Modification.* New York: Pantheon.

————. 1981. *The age of desire: Case histories of a radical psychoanalyst.* New York: Pantheon.

————. 1983. *Against the state of nuclear terror.* Boston: South End Press.

Kristeva, J. 1980. *Desire in language: A semiotic approach to literature and art.* New York: Columbia University Press.

Krüll, M. 1986. *Freud and his father.* Trans. A. Pomerans. New York: Norton. Originally published in 1979 as *Freud und sein Vater.* Munich: Oscar Beck.

Lacan, J. 1966. *Ecrits.* Paris: Editions du Seuil.

Laing, R. D., and Cooper, D. 1970. *The death of the family.* New York: Vintage Books.

Lamb, D. 1988. Inadmissible contributions of family therapy. *Feedback: The magazine of the family network of Ireland.* In press.

Lasch, C. 1977. *Haven in a heartless world.* New York: Basic Books.

Laslett, P., ed. 1972. *Household and family in past time.* Cambridge: Cambridge University Press.

References

Layton, M. 1984. Tipping the therapeutic scales—masculine, feminine, or neuter? *The Family Therapy Networker* 8 (3): 20–27.

———. 1985. Paula and Don: A marriage in search of a nag. *The Family Therapy Networker* 9 (6): 40–46.

Lederer, W., and Jackson, D. 1968. *The mirages of marriage.* New York: Norton.

Lerner, G. 1986. *The creation of patriarchy.* New York: Oxford University Press.

Lerner, H. G. 1985. *The dance of anger.* New York: Harper & Row.

———. 1986. Dianna and Lillie: Can a feminist still like Murray Bowen? *The Family Therapy Networker* 9 (6): 36–39.

———. 1987. Is family systems therapy really systemic? *Psychotherapy and the Family* 3 (4): 41–56.

———. 1988. *Women in therapy.* New York: Jason Aronson.

Levenson, E. 1983. *The ambiguity of change.* New York: Basic Books.

Levine, M., and Levine, A. 1970. *A social history of the helping services.* New York: Appleton-Century-Crofts.

Lewis, J. M., Beavers, W. R., Gossett, J. T., and Phillips, V. A. 1976. *No single thread: Psychological health in family systems.* New York: Brunner/Mazel.

Lloyd, G. 1984. *The man of reason: "Male" and "female" in western philosophy.* London: Methuen.

Luepnitz, D. A. 1982. *Child custody: A study of families after divorce.* Lexington, Mass.: Lexington Books.

———. 1984. Cybernetic baroque: The hi-tech talk of family therapy. *The Family Therapy Networker* 8 (4): 37–41.

McAdoo, H. P., ed. 1981. *Black families.* Beverly Hills, Cal.: Sage Publications.

Machotka, P., Pittman, F. S., and Flomenhaft, K. 1967. Incest as a family affair. *Family Process* 6: 98–116.

MacKinnon, L. K., and Miller, D. 1987. The new epistemology and the Milan approach: Feminist sociopolitical considerations. *Journal of Marital and Family Therapy* 13 (2): 139–55.

Mac Leod, S. 1982. *The art of starvation.* New York: Schocken Books.

Madanes, C. 1981. *Strategic family therapy.* San Francisco: Jossey-Bass.

———. 1983. With a little help from my friends. *The Family Therapy Networker* 7 (4).

———. 1984. *Behind the one-way mirror: Advances in the practice of strategic therapy.* San Francisco: Jossey-Bass.

Malcolm, J. 1978. The one-way mirror. *The New Yorker* (May 15): 39–94.

———. 1980. *Psychoanalysis: The impossible profession.* New York: Vintage Books.

———. 1984. *In the Freud archives.* New York: Alfred A. Knopf.

Mann, T. 1927. *The magic mountain.* Trans. H. T. Lowe-Porter. New York: Alfred A. Knopf.

Marcus, S. 1964. *The other Victorians.* New York: Basic Books.

Marcuse, H. 1964. *One-dimensional man.* Boston: Beacon Press.

Maruyama, M. 1968. The second cybernetics: Deviation—amplifying mutual causal process. In *Modern systems research for the behavioral scientist,* ed. W. Buckley. Chicago: Aldine.

Marx, K. 1852. *The eighteenth brumaire of Louis Bonaparte.* New York: International Publishers, 1963.

Marx, K., and Engels, F. 1848. The Manifesto of the Communist party. In *Selected Works.* New York: International Publishers, 1974.

Masson, J. 1984. *The assault on truth.* New York: Farrar, Straus & Giroux.

Maturana, H. 1980. Autopoiesis: "Reproduction, heredity and evolution." In *Autopoiesis disadaptive structures and spontaneous social orders,* ed. M. Zeleny. Boulder, Co.: Westview Press.

Melville, H. *Bartleby the scrivener.* In *The Norton anthology of American literature.* New York: Norton.

Miller, A. K. 1983a. *The drama of the gifted child.* New York: Basic Books.

———. 1983b. *For your own good.* New York: Farrar, Straus & Giroux.

———. 1984. *Thou shalt not be aware.* New York: Farrar, Straus & Giroux.

Miller, A. 1949. *Death of a salesman.* New York: Viking.

Miller, J. B. 1976. *Toward a new psychology of women.* Boston: Beacon Press.

———. 1984. The development of women's sense of self. Work in progress. Wellesley, Mass.: Stone Center for Developmental Services and Studies.

Minuchin, S. 1974. *Families and family therapy.* Cambridge, Mass.: Harvard University Press.

———. 1984. *Family kaleidoscope: Images of violence and healing.* Cambridge, Mass.: Harvard University Press.

Minuchin, S., and Fishman, H. C. 1981. *Family therapy techniques.* Cambridge, Mass.: Harvard University Press.

Minuchin, S., Montalvo, B., Guerney, B. G., Rosman, B. L., and Schumer, F. 1967. *Families of the slums: An exploration of their structure and treatment.* New York: Basic Books.

Mitchell, J. 1974. *Psychoanalysis and feminism.* New York: Random House.

Moynihan, D. P. 1965. *The negro family: The case for national action.* Washington, D.C.: U.S. Department of Labor.

Napier, A., and Whitaker, C. 1978. *The family crucible.* New York: Bantam Books.

Newsweek. How women view work, motherhood and feminism. (March 31, 1986).

Nietzsche, F. 1967. *The will to power.* Trans. W. Kaufmann and R. J. Hollindale. New York: Vintage Books.

Orbach, S. 1978. *Fat is a feminist issue.* London: Paddington Press.

Orwell, G. 1956. Politics and the English language. In *The Orwell reader,* ed. R. Rovere, pp. 355–67. New York: Harcourt Brace.

Osherson, S. 1986. *Finding our fathers.* New York: Free Press.

Papp, P. 1983. *The process of change.* New York: Guilford Press.

Parsons, T., and Bales, R. F. 1955. *Family, socialization, and interaction process.* New York: Free Press.

Peirce, C. S. 1908. A neglected argument for the reality of God. In *Charles Saunders Peirce: Selected Writings,* ed. P. Wiener, pp. 358–79. Garden City, N.Y.: Doubleday.

Peterson, S. R. 1983. Against "parenting." In *Mothering: Essays in feminist theory,* ed. H. Trebilcot, pp. 62–79. Totowa, N.J.: Rowman & Littlefield.

Pinderhughes, E. 1982. Afro-American families and the victim system. In *Ethnicity and family therapy,* ed. M. McGoldrick et al., pp. 108–22. New York: Guilford Press.

Plato, The symposium. In the Jowett translation of *Euthyphro, Apology, Crito, and Symposium.* Revised with an introduction by Moses Hadas. South Bend, Ind.: Regnery/Gateway, 1953.

Pogrebin, L. 1980. *Growing up free: Raising your child in the eighties.* New York: McGraw-Hill.

———. 1983. *Family politics.* New York: McGraw-Hill.

Pomeroy, S. 1975. *Goddesses, whores, wives and slaves: Women in classical antiquity.* New York: Schocken Books.

Poster, M. 1978. *Critical theory of the family.* New York: Seabury Press.

Radloff, L. S. 1980. Depression and the empty nest. *Sex Roles* 6: 775–81.

Rich, A. 1976. *Of woman born: Motherhood as experience and institution.* New York: Norton.

Robinson, L. 1978. *Sex, class, and culture.* Bloomington, Ind.: Indiana University Press.

References

Ross, J. B. 1974. The middle-class child in urban Italy, fourteenth to early sixteenth century. In *The history of childhood,* ed. L. De Mause, pp. 183–228. New York: Psychohistory Press.

Rubin, L. 1983. *Intimate Strangers.* New York: Harper & Row.

Russell, D. 1986. *The secret trauma.* New York: Basic Books.

Sander, F. 1978. Marriage and the family in Freud's writings. *Journal of the American Academy of Psychoanalysis* 6 (2): 157–74.

Satir, V. 1967. *Conjoint family therapy.* Palo Alto, Cal.: Science and Behavior Books.

Scharff, D., and Scharff, J. 1987. *Object relations family therapy.* Northvale, N.J.: Jason Aronson.

Scheff, T. 1966. *Being mentally ill: A sociological theory.* Chicago: Aldine.

Selvini Palazolli, M. 1974. *Self-starvation: From the intrapsychic to the transpersonal approach to anorexia nervosa.* London: Chaucer Publishing.

———, Cecchin, G., Boscolo, L., and Prata, G. 1978. *Paradox and counterparadox.* New York: Jason Aronson.

Shorter, E. 1975. *The making of the modern family.* New York: Basic Books.

Simon, R. 1984. Stranger in a strange land: An interview with Salvador Minuchin. *The Family Therapy Networker* 6 (6): 22–31.

———. 1985a. Structure is destiny: An interview with Humberto Maturana. *The Family Therapy Networker* 9 (3): 32–43.

———. 1985b. The take it or leave it therapy of Carl Whitaker. *The Family Therapy Networker* 9 (5): 26–75.

———. 1986. Behind the one-way kaleidoscope. *The Family Therapy Networker* 10 (5): 25–67.

———. 1987. Good-bye paradox, hello invariant prescription: An interview with Mara Selvini Palazolli. *The Family Therapy Networker* 11 (5): 16–33.

Skolnick, A., and Skolnick, J. 1971. *Family in transition.* Boston: Little, Brown.

Skynner, A. C. R. 1976. *Systems of family and marital psychotherapy.* New York: Brunner/Mazel.

———. 1981. An open-systems, group-analytic approach to family therapy. In *Handbook of family therapy,* ed. A. Gurman and D. Kniskern, pp. 39–84. New York: Brunner/Mazel.

Slipp, S. 1984. *Object relations: A dynamic bridge between individual and family treatment.* New York: Jason Aronson.

Smith-Rosenberg, C. 1986. *Disorderly conduct.* New York: Oxford University Press.

Speck, R., and Attneave, C. 1973. *Family networks.* New York: Vintage.

Sprenger, J., and Kramer, H. 1486. *Malleus maleficarum.* Trans. with an introduction by Montague Summers. London: Pushkin Press, 1948.

Stack, C. 1976. *All our kin: Strategies for survival in a Black community.* New York: Harper & Row.

Stanton, E. C. 1875. Home life. In *Elizabeth Cady Stanton and Susan B. Anthony: Correspondences, writings, speeches,* ed. E. C. Du Bois, pp. 131–38. New York: Schocken Books, 1981.

Statistical abstracts of the U.S. 1981, pp. 140, 388. Washington, D.C., 1981.

Stierlin, H. 1977. *Psychoanalysis and family therapy.* New York: Jason Aronson.

Stone, L. 1977. *The family, sex, and marriage in England, 1500–1800.* Abridged ed. New York: Harper & Row.

Strasser, S. 1982. *Never done: A history of American housework.* New York: Pantheon.

Streitfeld, D. 1987. For women, weight may be wrong worry. *Philadelphia Inquirer* (August 13): 1C.

Szasz, T. 1970. *The manufacture of madness.* New York: Harper & Row.

———. 1984, quoted in R. Simon, The therapeutic state: An interview with Thomas Szasz. *The Family Therapy Networker* 8 (4): 20–67.

Taggart, M. 1985. The feminist critique in epistemological perspective: Questions of context in family therapy. *Journal of Marital and Family Therapy* 11: 113–26.

Tennant, C., Bebbington, P., and Hurry, J. 1982. Female vulnerability to neurosis: The influence of social roles. *Australian and New Zealand Journal of Psychiatry* 16: 135–40.

Thomas, L. 1974. *The lives of a cell: Notes of a biology watcher.* New York: Bantam Books.

Thorne, N., and Yalom, M. 1982. *Rethinking the family: Some feminist questions.* White Plains, N.Y.: Longman.

Tomm, K. 1984. One perspective on the Milan systemic approach. Part 1. Overview of development, theory and practice. *Journal of Marital and Family Therapy* 10: 113–25.

Trebilcot, H. 1983. *Mothering: Essays in feminist theory.* Totowa, N.J.: Rowman & Little-field.

Tuchman, B. 1978. *A distant mirror: The calamitous fourteenth century.* New York: Ballantine Books.

Turkle, S. 1978. *Psychoanalytic politics: Freud's French revolution.* New York: Basic Books.

Udry, J. R. 1974. *The social context of marriage.* Philadelphia: Lippincott.

Valerius Maximus. *Factorum, dictorumque memorabilium.* Trans. C. A. F. Frémion as *Faits et paroles mémorables.* Paris: C. L. F. Panckouke, 1834.

Varela, F. 1976. Not one, but two. *Coevolution Quarterly* 11: 62–67.

———. 1979. *Principles of biological autonomy.* New York: Elsevier North Holland.

von Foerster, H. 1973a. Cybernetics of cybernetics. *The Cybernetician* 3: 30–32.

———. 1973b. On constructing a reality. In *Environmental design research II,* ed. W. Preiser. Stroudsberg, Pa.: Dowden, Hutchinson & Ross.

Wachtel, E. F., and Wachtel, P. L. 1986. *Family dynamics in individual psychotherapy.* New York: Guilford Press.

Walker, L. E. 1979. *The battered woman.* New York: Harper & Row.

Walsh, F., ed. 1982. *Normal family processes.* New York: Guilford Press.

Walters, M. 1985. Where have all the flowers gone: Family therapy in the age of the Yuppie. *The Family Therapy Networker* 9 (4): 38–41.

Watzlawick, P. 1976. *How real is real?* New York: Random House.

———, ed. 1984. *The invented reality.* New York: Norton.

———, Weakland, J. H., and Fisch, R. 1974. *Change: Principles of problem formation and problem resolution.* New York: Norton.

Weakland, J. H., Fisch, R., Watzlawick, P., and Bodin, A. 1974. Brief therapy: Focused problem resolution. *Family Process* 13: 141–68.

Weil, S. 1951. *Waiting for God.* New York: Putnam's.

Weiner, J. P., and Boss, P. 1985. Exploring gender bias against women: Ethics for marriage and family therapy. *Counseling Values* 30: 9–23.

Weitzman, L. 1985. *The divorce revolution.* New York: Free Press.

Wheeler, D., Avis, J., Miller, L. A., and Chaney, S. 1985. Rethinking family therapy education and supervision: A feminist model. *Journal of Psychotherapy and the Family* 1 (4): 53–71.

Whitaker, C., and Keith, D. 1981. Symbolic-experiential family therapy. In *Handbook of family therapy,* ed. A. Gurman and D. Kniskern, pp. 187–225. New York: Brunner/Mazel.

Winnicott, D. W. 1957. The mother's contribution to society. In *Home is where we start from,* pp. 123–27. New York: Norton, 1986.

———. 1965. *The maturational processes and the facilitating environment.* London: Hogarth Press.

References

————. 1971. *Playing and reality.* London: Tavistock.

————. 1986. *Home is where we start from.* New York: Norton.

Wollstonecraft, M. 1792. A vindication of the rights of woman. In *The feminist papers,* ed. A. Rossi, pp. 40–85. New York: Bantam Books, 1973.

Woolf, V. 1929. *A room of one's own.* New York: Harcourt, Brace & World.

Yourcenar, M. 1985. *Oriental tales.* New York: Farrar, Straus & Giroux.

INDEX

abduction, 110n, 167n
abolitionism, 130–31
abortion, 17, 130, 131n, 149, 289
Ackerman, Nathan, 28, 30–35, 38, 39, 48, 54, 58, 64, 70, 72, 76, 78, 78n, 89, 170
action vs. thought, 84–85, 100, 186
adaptation, 12, 64, 172, 186
Addams, Jane, 40, 131
adoptive parents, 12
adult, healthy, as male, 43
adultery, 114
affect, 176, 231; claiming, 274–75; legitimation of, 262; *see also* emotions
affection, 52, 122
Afro-American identity, 142–43
Age of Desire, The (Kovel), 133, 277
agoraphobia, 136
agrarian society, 129, 144
ahistoricism, 7–9, 110, 160
alcoholism, 154, 154n, 157, 192
alienation from work, 132–33
alpha error, 15–16, 78n, 156n
Ambiguity of Change, The (Levenson), 175n
ambivalence, 135
American Medical Association, 130
androgyny, 15, 78, 78n, 154n
Angels Fear (Bateson and Bateson), 155n
anger, 262, 274–75; against absent father, 295; denial of, 288, 290–91; in women, 226–27, 232, 233, 275, 290–91, 303–4, 310–11
anorexia nervosa, 86, 97, 104, 163, 191, 201–29, 296, 297
Anthony, Susan B., 131, 131n, 147
anti-interventionism, 20, 21
anti-psychiatry movement, 101
anxiety disorders, 10

apprentices, 121, 128, 147–48
Ariès, Phillipe, 111, 116–17, 118, 124, 126n, 129
aristocratic family, 112, 117–19
Assault on Truth, The (Masson), 174n
assertiveness, 77, 78
asthma, 230, 231–79
At Odds: A History of Women and the Family in America from the Revolution to the Present (Degler), 9
Ault-Riché, M., 7, 99
Austria, 123, 127
authority, 11n, 70, 88, 205; of father, 17, 32, 182; and incest, 225; of men, vs. women and children, 145; patriarchal, in father-absent family, 17–18; psychoanalysis and, 177; resistance to female, 15; of therapist, 105; vested in village, 120; and "victim system," 143
autonomy, 42, 143, 223; in Erikson, 44; women and, 180, 227; of women, and anorexia and incest problems, 223, 226

Bachofen, J. J., 111
Bacon, Francis, 156
Badinter, Elizabeth, 8, 117, 118, 121, 124, 127
Baldson, J. P. V. D., 112, 113, 115
Barrett, M., 14
Bart, Pauline, 15, 167, 175
Bartleby the Scrivener (Melville), 133
Bateson, Gregory, 6, 49, 84, 97, 110, 110n, 149, 150–67, 192
Bateson, Mary Catherine, 84, 153, 154–55, 155n

329